The Little Oxford Dictionary of Quotations

D1142739

The Little Oxford Dictionary of Quotations

Edited by Susan Ratcliffe

Oxford   New York

OXFORD UNIVERSITY PRESS

Special Edition for PAST TIMES®, Oxford, England

Oxford University Press, Great Clarendon Street, Oxford OX2 6DP

Oxford New York

Athens Auckland Bangkok Bogota Bombay Buenos Aires Calcutta
Cape Town Chennai Dar es Salaam Delhi Florence Hong Kong Istanbul
Karachi Kuala Lumpur Madrid Melbourne Mexico City Mumbai
Nairobi Paris São Paolo Singapore Taipei Tokyo Toronto Warsaw

and associated companies in Berlin Ibadan

Oxford is a registered trade mark of Oxford University Press

Published in the United States
by Oxford University Press Inc., New York

© Oxford University Press 1994

The moral rights of the author have been asserted

First published 1994

All rights reserved. No part of this publication may be reproduced,
stored in a retrieval system, or transmitted, in any form or by any means,
without the prior permission in writing of Oxford University Press.
Within the UK, exceptions are allowed in respect of any fair dealing for the
purpose of research or private study, or criticism or review, as permitted
under the Copyright, Designs and Patents Act 1988, or in the case of
reprographic reproduction in accordance with the terms of the licences
issued by the Copyright Licensing Agency. Enquiries concerning
reproduction outside these terms and in other countries should be
sent to the Rights Department, Oxford University Press,
at the address above

This book is sold subject to the condition that it shall not, by way
of trade or otherwise, be lent, re-sold, hired out or otherwise circulated
without the publisher's prior consent in any form of binding or cover
other than that in which it is published and without a similar condition
including this condition being imposed on the subsequent purchaser

ISBN 0-19-969079-0

1 3 5 7 9 10 8 6 4 2

Printed in Great Britain
on acid-free paper by
Clays Ltd.
Bungay, Suffolk

Little Oxford Dictionary of Quotations Project Team

Managing Editor	Elizabeth M. Knowles
Editor	Susan Ratcliffe
Library Research	Ralph Bates
	Marie G. Diaz
Data Capture	Sandra Vaughan
Quotation Retrieval	Helen McCurdy
	Katie Weale

Contents

Foreword   ix

List of Themes   xi

Quotations   **1**

Index of Authors   429

Foreword

The Little Oxford Dictionary of Quotations is a collection which casts a fresh light on even the most familiar sayings. It is organized by themes, such as **Action**, **Liberty**, and **Memory**, and within each theme the quotations are arranged in date order, so that the interplay of ideas down the centuries becomes apparent. It is intended for the reader who is searching for quotations on a specific subject, the reader who remembers the sense of a quotation but not the precise words, and, of course, the browser.

The themes have been chosen to reflect as wide a range of subjects as possible, concentrating on the general rather than the specific. A few themes have a slightly different character: thus **People** and **Places** cover quotations about many different individual people and places, while **Political Comment** and **Wars** include quotations relevant to specific events. The length of the sections reflects to some extent the preoccupations of people throughout history, ranging from short ones such as **Advice** to the many and varied comments on **Life** and **Love**. Where subjects overlap, the reader is directed to related themes at the head of the section; for example, at **Death**: See also **Epitaphs**, **Last Words**, **Murder**. An author index is provided to help readers wishing to trace a particular quotation or seeking quotations from specific individuals.

Within each theme, the aim is to take in a variety of viewpoints, including both the most familiar quotations and some less well-known or perhaps new material. So within **News and Journalism**, along with C. P. Scott's classic 'Comment is free, but facts are sacred', we have Tom Stoppard's gloss 'Comment is free but facts are on expenses' and more recently Lord McGregor on 'journalists dabbling their fingers in the stuff of other people's souls'. This book contains some one hundred quotations which have not previously appeared in any dictionary of quotations. These new quotations appear, for example, under the themes **Environment** ('. . . all that remains / For us will be concrete and tyres'), **Men and Women** ('Whereas nature turns girls into women, society has to make boys into men'), and **Science** ('The aim of science is not to open the door to infinite wisdom, but to set a limit to infinite error').

The chronological ordering within each theme enables the

quotations to 'talk' to one another, shedding new light on each. Thus we have Samuel Johnson telling us 'Change is not made without inconvenience, even from worse to better', followed by Voltaire: 'If we do not find anything pleasant, at least we shall find something new'. Much of the cross-referencing required by an alphabetical arrangement of authors becomes redundant: Ralegh's line written on a window-pane 'Fain would I climb, yet fear I to fall' is now immediately followed by Elizabeth I's reply 'If thy heart fails thee, climb not at all.'

The quotations have been classified by their subject rather than by keywords in the text. For example, Tom Lehrer's 'It is sobering to consider that when Mozart was my age he had already been dead for a year' is essentially about **Achievement** rather than **Music** or **Death**, and has been placed accordingly. As far as possible each quotation has been included only once, but a few, such as Pope's 'To err is human, to forgive divine' plainly had a place in two sections.

A short source reference is given for each quotation, usually including its date. Where the date is uncertain or unknown, the author's date of death has been used to determine the order within a theme. The quotations themselves have been kept as short as possible: contextual information has occasionally been added to the source note, and related but less well-known and well-expressed versions have generally been excluded. Owing to constraints of space, foreign language originals have been given only where they are well-known or where translations differ. Such information, including full finding references, can be found in *The Oxford Dictionary of Quotations*.

We are always grateful to those readers who write to us with their comments, suggestions, and discoveries, and we hope this tradition will continue. *The Little Oxford Dictionary of Quotations* draws largely on the work done for the fourth edition of *The Oxford Dictionary of Quotations*, and therefore owes a substantial debt to all those involved in the preparation of that volume. None the less, this book has its own identity, and the editor's chief pleasure as it took shape has been in listening to different voices speaking to each other across the ages: ' "What is the use of a book," thought Alice, "without pictures or conversations?" '

Susan Ratcliffe

Oxford, March 1994

List of Themes

Absence
Achievement and
  Endeavour
Acting and the
  Theatre
Action
Advertising
Advice
Alcohol
Ambition
America and
  Americans
Anger
Animals
Apology
Architecture
Argument
The Army
Art

Beauty
Beginnings and
  Endings
Behaviour
Belief and
  Unbelief
The Bible
Biography
Birds
Birth
The Body
Books
Bores and Boredom
Britain
Broadcasting
Bureaucracy

Business and
  Commerce

Careers
Cats
Censorship
Certainty and Doubt
Chance
Change
Character
Charm
Children
Choice
Christmas
The Church
The Cinema
Civilization
Class
Commerce see
  Business and
  Commerce
Conscience
Conversation
Cooperation
The Country and the
  Town
Courage
Crime and
  Punishment
Crises
Critics and
  Criticism
Cruelty
Custom and Habit
Cynicism

Dance
Day and Night
Death
Democracy
Despair see Hope and
  Despair
Determination
Diaries
Diplomacy
Discontent see
  Satisfaction and
  Discontent
Discoveries see
  Inventions and
  Discoveries
Dogs
Doubt see Certainty
  and Doubt
Drawing see
  Painting and
  Drawing
Dreams see Sleep and
  Dreams
Dress
Drink see Food and
  Drink

Economics
Education
Endeavour see
  Achievement and
  Endeavour
Endings see
  Beginnings and
  Endings
Enemies

England and the
    English
Environment
Envy and Jealousy
Epitaphs
Equality
Europe and
    Europeans
Evil *see Good and Evil*
Experience

Failure *see Success
    and Failure*
Fame
The Family
Fate
Fear
Flowers
Food and Drink
Fools and Foolishness
Forgiveness
France and the
    French
Friendship
The Future

Gardens
The Generation Gap
Genius
Gifts and Giving
God
Good and Evil
Gossip
Government
Greatness

Habit *see Custom and
    Habit*
Happiness

Hatred
Health *see Sickness
    and Health*
The Heart
Heaven and Hell
Heroes
History
The Home and
    Housework
Honour
Hope and Despair
The Human Race
Human Rights
Humour
Hypocrisy

Idealism
Ideas
Idleness
Ignorance
Imagination
Indifference
Intelligence and
    Intellectuals
Inventions and
    Discoveries
Ireland and the Irish

Jealousy *see Envy and
    Jealousy*
Journalism *see News
    and Journalism*
Justice

Knowledge

Language
Languages
Last Words

The Law and Lawyers
Leadership
Leisure
Letters and Letter-
    writing
Liberty
Libraries
Lies and Lying
Life
Life Sciences
Literature
Living
London
Love

Madness
Majorities *see
    Minorities and
    Majorities*
Management
Manners
Marriage
Mathematics
Meaning
Medicine
Meeting and Parting
Memory
Men
Men and Women
Middle Age
The Mind
Minorities and
    Majorities
Misfortune
Mistakes
Moderation
Money
Morality
Murder

Music
Musicians

Nature
News and Journalism
Night *see Day and Night*

Old Age
Opening Lines
Opinion
Optimism and Pessimism

Painting and Drawing
Parents
The Past
Patriotism
Peace
People
Perfection
Pessimism *see Optimism and Pessimism*
Philosophy
Places
Pleasure
Poetry
Poets
Political Comment
Political Parties
Politicians
Politics
Pollution
Poverty
Power
Practicality

Praise
Prayer
Prejudice
The Present
Pride
Progress
Punishment *see Crime and Punishment*

Quotations

Race
Reading
Reality
Religion
Revenge
Revolution and Rebellion
Royalty

Satisfaction and Discontent
Science
Scotland and the Scots
The Sea
The Seasons
Secrets
The Self
Self-Knowledge
Sex
Shakespeare
Sickness and Health
Silence
Singing
The Skies
Sleep and Dreams
Society

Solitude
Sorrow
Speech and Speeches
Sport
Statistics
Style
Success and Failure
Suffering
The Supernatural

Taxes
Teaching
Technology
Temptation
The Theatre *see Acting and the Theatre*
Thinking
Time
Titles
The Town *see The Country and the Town*
Transience
Transport
Travel
Trust and Treachery
Truth

Unbelief *see Belief and Unbelief*
The Universe

Vice *see Virtue and Vice*
Violence
Virtue and Vice
Voting

Wales
War
Wars
Wealth
Weather
Woman's Role
Women
Words
Work
Writers
Writing

Youth

Absence

1 The Lord watch between me and thee, when we are absent
   one from another.
   Bible: Genesis

2 Absence diminishes commonplace passions and increases
   great ones, as the wind extinguishes candles and kindles fire.
   Duc de la Rochefoucauld 1613-80: *Maximes* (1678)

3 The absent are always in the wrong.
   Philippe Néricault Destouches 1680-1754: *L'Obstacle
   imprévu* (1717)

4 With leaden foot time creeps along
   While Delia is away.
   Richard Jago 1715-81: 'Absence'

5 Presents, I often say, endear Absents.
   Charles Lamb 1775-1834: *Essays of Elia* (1823)
   'A Dissertation upon Roast Pig'

6 The heart may think it knows better: the senses know that
   absence blots people out. We have really no absent friends.
   Elizabeth Bowen 1899-1973: *Death of the Heart* (1938)

7 When I came back to Dublin, I was courtmartialled in my
   absence and sentenced to death in my absence, so I said they
   could shoot me in my absence.
   Brendan Behan 1923-64: *Hostage* (1958)

Achievement and Endeavour

See also **Ambition**

1 *Non omnia possumus omnes.*
   We can't all do everything.
   Virgil 70-19 BC: *Eclogues*

2 *Parturient montes, nascetur ridiculus mus.*
   Mountains will go into labour, and a silly little mouse will be
   born.
   Horace 65-8 BC: *Ars Poetica*

3 *Considerate la vostra semenza:*
   Fatti non foste a viver come bruti,

Ma per seguir virtute e conoscenza.
Consider your origins: you were not made to live as brutes,
but to follow virtue and knowledge.
Dante Alighieri 1265–1321: *Divina Commedia* 'Inferno'

4 There must be a beginning of any great matter, but the
continuing unto the end until it be thoroughly finished yields
the true glory.
Francis Drake *c.*1540–96: dispatch to Sir Francis
Walsingham, 17 May 1587

5 If to do were as easy as to know what were good to do,
chapels had been churches, and poor men's cottages princes'
palaces.
William Shakespeare 1564–1616: *The Merchant of Venice*
(1596–8)

6 Things won are done; joy's soul lies in the doing.
William Shakespeare 1564–1616: *Troilus and Cressida*
(1602)

7 Get place and wealth, if possible, with grace;
If not, by any means get wealth and place.
Alexander Pope 1688–1744: *Imitations of Horace* (1738)

8 I had done all that I could; and no man is well pleased to
have his all neglected, be it ever so little.
Samuel Johnson 1709–84: letter to Lord Chesterfield,
7 February 1755

9 The danger chiefly lies in acting well;
No crime's so great as daring to excel.
Charles Churchill 1731–64: *An Epistle to William Hogarth*
(1763)

10 The distance is nothing; it is only the first step that is
difficult.
Mme Du Deffand 1697–1780: commenting on the legend that
St Denis, carrying his head in his hands, walked two
leagues; letter to Jean Le Rond d'Alembert, 7 July 1763

11 Madam, if a thing is possible, consider it done; the
impossible? that will be done.
Charles Alexandre de Calonne 1734–1802: in J. Michelet
Histoire de la Révolution Française (1847); better known as
the US Armed Forces' slogan: 'The difficult we do
immediately; the impossible takes a little longer'

12 That low man seeks a little thing to do,
Sees it and does it:
This high man, with a great thing to pursue,
Dies ere he knows it.
   Robert Browning 1812–89: 'A Grammarian's Funeral' (1855)

13 Now, *here*, you see, it takes all the running *you* can do, to
keep in the same place. If you want to get somewhere else,
you must run at least twice as fast as that!
   Lewis Carroll 1832–98: *Through the Looking-Glass* (1872)

14 If a man write a better book, preach a better sermon, or
make a better mouse-trap than his neighbour, tho' he build
his house in the woods, the world will make a beaten path to
his door.
   Ralph Waldo Emerson 1803–82: attributed to Emerson in S.
   Yule *Borrowings* (1889), but claimed also by Elbert Hubbard

15 Because it's there.
   George Leigh Mallory 1886–1924: on being asked why he
   wanted to climb Mount Everest; in *New York Times*
   18 March 1923

16 Well, we knocked the bastard off!
   Edmund Hillary 1919– : on conquering Mount Everest,
   1953; in *Nothing Venture, Nothing Win* (1975)

17 That's one small step for a man, one giant leap for mankind.
   Neil Armstrong 1930– : landing on the moon, 21 July 1969
   (interference in transmission obliterated 'a')

18 It is sobering to consider that when Mozart was my age he
had already been dead for a year.
   Tom Lehrer 1928– : in N. Shapiro (ed.) *An Encyclopedia of
   Quotations about Music* (1978)

Acting and the Theatre

See also **The Cinema, Shakespeare**

1 Tragedy is thus a representation of an action that is worth
serious attention, complete in itself and of some
amplitude...by means of pity and fear bringing about the
purgation of such emotions.
   Aristotle 384–322 BC: *Poetics*

2   Can this cockpit hold
The vasty fields of France? or may we cram
Within this wooden O the very casques
That did affright the air at Agincourt?
   William Shakespeare 1564–1616: *Henry V* (1599)

3 Speak the speech, I pray you, as I pronounced it to you,
trippingly on the tongue; but if you mouth it, as many of
your players do, I had as lief the town-crier spoke my lines.
Nor do not saw the air too much with your hand, thus; but
use all gently.
   William Shakespeare 1564–1616: *Hamlet* (1601)

4 Suit the action to the word, the word to the action.
   William Shakespeare 1564–1616: *Hamlet* (1601)

5 Damn them! They will not let my play run, but they steal my
thunder!
   John Dennis 1657–1734: on hearing his new thunder effects
   used at a performance of *Macbeth*, following the
   withdrawal of one of his own plays after only a short run

6 To see him act is like reading Shakespeare by flashes of
lightning.
   Samuel Taylor Coleridge 1772–1834: on Edmund Kean;
   Table Talk (1835) 27 April 1823

7 He played the King as though under momentary
apprehension that someone else was about to play the ace.
   Eugene Field 1850–95: of Creston Clarke as King Lear;
   review attributed to Field, in *Denver Tribune* c.1880

8 How different, how very different from the home life of our
own dear Queen!
   Anonymous: a Victorian lady, overheard at a performance
   by Sarah Bernhardt in the role of Cleopatra, in I. S. Cobb
   A Laugh a Day (1924)

9 Ladies, just a little more virginity, if you don't mind.
   Herbert Beerbohm Tree 1852–1917: to the extras playing
   ladies in waiting to the queen; in A. Woollcott *Shouts and
   Murmurs* (1923)

10 She ran the whole gamut of the emotions from A to B.
   Dorothy Parker 1893–1967: of Katharine Hepburn on the
   first night of *The Lake* (1933); attributed

11 Actors are cattle.
   Alfred Hitchcock 1899–1980: in *Saturday Evening Post*
   22 May 1943

12 We never closed.
   Vivian van Damm *c.*1889–1960: of the Windmill Theatre,
   London, during the Second World War

13 Acting is merely the art of keeping a large group of people
   from coughing.
   Ralph Richardson 1902–83: in *New York Herald Tribune*
   19 May 1946

14 There's no business like show business.
   Irving Berlin 1888–1989: title of song (1946)

15 Shaw is like a train. One just speaks the words and sits in
   one's place. But Shakespeare is like bathing in the sea—one
   swims where one wants.
   Vivien Leigh 1913–67: letter from Harold Nicolson to Vita
   Sackville-West, 1 February 1956

16 Don't clap too hard—it's a very old building.
   John Osborne 1929– : *The Entertainer* (1957)

17 The weasel under the cocktail cabinet.
   Harold Pinter 1930– : on being asked what his plays were
   about, in J. Russell Taylor *Anger and After* (1962)

18 Just say the lines and don't trip over the furniture.
   Noël Coward 1899–1973: advice on acting, in D. Richards
   The Wit of Noël Coward (1968)

19 Acting is a masochistic form of exhibitionism. It is not quite
   the occupation of an adult.
   Laurence Olivier 1907–89: in *Time* 3 July 1978

Action

1 But men must know, that in this theatre of man's life it is
   reserved only for God and angels to be lookers on.
   Francis Bacon 1561–1626: *The Advancement of Learning*
   (1605)

2 If it were done when 'tis done, then 'twere well
   It were done quickly.
   William Shakespeare 1564–1616: *Macbeth* (1606)

3   Each your doing,
So singular in each particular,
Crowns what you are doing in the present deed,
That all your acts are queens.
   William Shakespeare 1564–1616: *The Winter's Tale*
   (1610–11)

4 Oh that thou hadst like others been all words,
And no performance.
   Philip Massinger 1583–1640: *The Parliament of Love* (1624)

5 They also serve who only stand and wait.
   John Milton 1608–74: 'When I consider how my light is
   spent' (1673)

6 Think nothing done while aught remains to do.
   Samuel Rogers 1763–1855: 'Human Life' (1819)

7 It is in vain to say human beings ought to be satisfied with
tranquillity: they must have action; and they will make it if
they cannot find it.
   Charlotte Brontë 1816–55: *Jane Eyre* (1847)

8 Action is consolatory. It is the enemy of thought and the
friend of flattering illusions.
   Joseph Conrad 1857–1924: *Nostromo* (1904)

9 Nothing is ever done in this world until men are prepared to
kill one another if it is not done.
   George Bernard Shaw 1856–1950: *Major Barbara* (1907)

10 A man of action forced into a state of thought is unhappy
until he can get out of it.
   John Galsworthy 1867–1933: *Maid in Waiting* (1931)

11 The world can only be grasped by action, not by
contemplation...The hand is the cutting edge of the mind.
   Jacob Bronowski 1908–74: *The Ascent of Man* (1973)

Advertising

1 Promise, large promise, is the soul of an advertisement.
   Samuel Johnson 1709–84: *The Idler* 20 January 1759

2 Advertising may be described as the science of arresting
human intelligence long enough to get money from it.
   Stephen Leacock 1869–1944: *Garden of Folly* (1924)

3 Half the money I spend on advertising is wasted, and the trouble is I don't know which half.
   Viscount Leverhulme 1851–1925: in D. Ogilvy *Confessions of an Advertising Man* (1963)

4 Those who prefer their English sloppy have only themselves to thank if the advertisement writer uses his mastery of vocabulary and syntax to mislead their weak minds.
   Dorothy L. Sayers 1893–1957: *Spectator* 19 November 1937

5 Advertising is the rattling of a stick inside a swill bucket.
   George Orwell 1903–50: attributed

6 It is not necessary to advertise food to hungry people, fuel to cold people, or houses to the homeless.
   J. K. Galbraith 1908– : *American Capitalism* (1952)

7 The consumer isn't a moron; she is your wife.
   David Ogilvy 1911– : *Confessions of an Advertising Man* (1963)

Advice

1 Advice is seldom welcome; and those who want it the most always like it the least.
   Lord Chesterfield 1694–1773: *Letters to his Son* (1774) 29 January 1748

2 It was, perhaps, one of those cases in which advice is good or bad only as the event decides.
   Jane Austen 1775–1817: *Persuasion* (1818)

3 I always pass on good advice. It is the only thing to do with it. It is never of any use to oneself.
   Oscar Wilde 1854–1900: *An Ideal Husband* (1895)

4 Well, if you knows of a better 'ole, go to it.
   Bruce Bairnsfather 1888–1959: *Fragments from France* (1915)

Alcohol

See also **Food and Drink**

1 Wine is a mocker, strong drink is raging.
   Bible: Proverbs

2 Drink no longer water, but use a little wine for thy stomach's sake.
   Bible: I Timothy

3 When the wine is in, the wit is out.
   Thomas Becon 1512–67: *Catechism* (1560)

4 Drink, sir, is a great provoker...
   Lechery, sir, it provokes, and unprovokes; it provokes the desire, but it takes away the performance.
   William Shakespeare 1564–1616: *Macbeth* (1606)

5 It would be port if it could.
   Richard Bentley 1662–1742: describing claret, in R. C. Jebb *Bentley* (1902)

6 Claret is the liquor for boys; port, for men; but he who aspires to be a hero must drink brandy.
   Samuel Johnson 1709–84: in James Boswell *Life of Johnson* (1791) 7 April 1779

7 O for a beaker full of the warm South,
   Full of the true, the blushful Hippocrene,
   With beaded bubbles winking at the brim,
   And purple-stainèd mouth.
   John Keats 1795–1821: 'Ode to a Nightingale' (1820)

8 The lips that touch liquor must never touch mine.
   George W. Young 1846–1919: title of verse (c.1870)

9 And malt does more than Milton can
   To justify God's ways to man.
   A. E. Housman 1859–1936: *A Shropshire Lad* (1896)

10 A torchlight procession marching down your throat.
   John L. O'Sullivan 1813–95: of whisky, in G. W. E. Russell *Collections and Recollections* (1898)

11 I'm only a beer teetotaller, not a champagne teetotaller.
   George Bernard Shaw 1856–1950: *Candida* (1898)

12 If merely 'feeling good' could decide, drunkenness would be the supremely valid human experience.
   William James 1842-1910: *Varieties of Religious Experience* (1902)

13 It is no time for mirth and laughter,
   The cold, grey dawn of the morning after.
   George Ade 1866-1944: *The Sultan of Sulu* (1903)

14 Alcohol is a very necessary article...It enables Parliament to do things at eleven at night that no sane person would do at eleven in the morning.
   George Bernard Shaw 1856-1950: *Major Barbara* (1907)

15 Let's get out of these wet clothes and into a dry Martini.
   Anonymous: line coined in the 1920s by Robert Benchley's press agent and adopted by Mae West in *Every Day's a Holiday* (1937 film)

16 Candy
   Is dandy
   But liquor
   Is quicker.
   Ogden Nash 1902-71: 'Reflections on Ice-breaking' (1931)

17 I'm not so think as you drunk I am.
   J. C. Squire 1884-1958: 'Ballade of Soporific Absorption' (1931)

18 It's a naïve domestic Burgundy without any breeding, but I think you'll be amused by its presumption.
   James Thurber 1894-1961: cartoon caption in *New Yorker* 27 March 1937

19 A good general rule is to state that the bouquet is better than the taste, and vice versa.
   Stephen Potter 1900-69: on wine-tasting; *One-Upmanship* (1952)

20 His mouth had been used as a latrine by some small creature of the night, and then as its mausoleum.
   Kingsley Amis 1922- : *Lucky Jim* (1953)

21 One reason why I don't drink is because I wish to know when I am having a good time.
   Nancy Astor 1879-1964: in *Christian Herald* June 1960

22 I have taken more out of alcohol than alcohol has taken out of me.
Winston Churchill 1874–1965: in Quentin Reynolds *By Quentin Reynolds* (1964)

23 You're not drunk if you can lie on the floor without holding on.
Dean Martin 1917– : in P. Dickson *Official Rules* (1978)

Ambition

See also **Achievement and Endeavour**

1 [I] had rather be first in a village than second at Rome.
Julius Caesar 100–44 BC: in Francis Bacon *Advancement of Learning*, based on Plutarch *Parallel Lives*

2 *Aut Caesar, aut nihil.*
Caesar or nothing.
Cesare Borgia 1476–1507: motto inscribed on his sword

3 Fain would I climb, yet fear I to fall.
Walter Ralegh *c.*1552–1618: line written on a window-pane, in Thomas Fuller *Worthies of England* (1662)

4 If thy heart fails thee, climb not at all.
Elizabeth I 1533–1603: line after Walter Ralegh, written on a window-pane

5 When that the poor have cried, Caesar hath wept;
Ambition should be made of sterner stuff.
William Shakespeare 1564–1616: *Julius Caesar* (1599)

6   I have no spur
To prick the sides of my intent, but only
Vaulting ambition, which o'erleaps itself,
And falls on the other.
William Shakespeare 1564–1616: *Macbeth* (1606)

7 Cromwell, I charge thee, fling away ambition:
By that sin fell the angels.
William Shakespeare 1564–1616: *Henry VIII* (with John Fletcher, 1613)

8 Well is it known that ambition can creep as well as soar.
Edmund Burke 1729–97: *Third Letter ... on the Proposals for Peace with the Regicide Directory* (1797)

9 There is always room at the top.
    Daniel Webster 1782–1852: on being advised against
    joining the overcrowded legal profession (attributed)

10 Ah, but a man's reach should exceed his grasp,
Or what's a heaven for?
    Robert Browning 1812–89: 'Andrea del Sarto' (1855)

11 Hitch your wagon to a star.
    Ralph Waldo Emerson 1803–82: *Society and Solitude* (1870)

12 If you would hit the mark, you must aim a little above it;
Every arrow that flies feels the attraction of earth.
    Henry Wadsworth Longfellow 1807–82: 'Elegiac Verse'
    (1880)

13 All ambitions are lawful except those which climb upwards
on the miseries or credulities of mankind.
    Joseph Conrad 1857–1924: *Some Reminiscences* (1912)

14 The world continues to offer glittering prizes to those who
have stout hearts and sharp swords.
    F. E. Smith 1872–1930: Rectorial Address, Glasgow
    University, 7 November 1923

15 He is loyal to his own career but only incidentally to
anything or anyone else.
    Hugh Dalton 1887–1962: of Richard Crossman; diary,
    17 September 1941

America and Americans

See also **Places**

1   Pray enter
You are learned Europeans and we worse
Than ignorant Americans.
    Philip Massinger 1583–1640: *The City Madam* (licensed
    1632)

2 A citizen, first in war, first in peace, and first in the hearts of
his countrymen.
    Henry Lee 1756–1818: *Funeral Oration on the death of
    General Washington* (1800)

3 Go West, young man, and grow up with the country.
    Horace Greeley 1811–72: *Hints toward Reforms* (1850)

4 The United States themselves are essentially the greatest poem.
>   **Walt Whitman** 1819–92: *Leaves of Grass* (1855)

5 Good Americans, when they die, go to Paris.
>   **Thomas Gold Appleton** 1812–84: in Oliver Wendell Holmes *The Autocrat of the Breakfast-Table* (1858)

6 Give me your tired, your poor,
Your huddled masses yearning to breathe free.
>   **Emma Lazarus** 1849–87: 'The New Colossus' (1883); inscribed on the Statue of Liberty, New York

7 A Boston man is the east wind made flesh.
>   **Thomas Gold Appleton** 1812–84: attributed

8 MRS ALLONBY: They say, Lady Hunstanton, that when good Americans die they go to Paris.
LADY HUNSTANTON: Indeed? And when bad Americans die, where do they go to?
LORD ILLINGWORTH: Oh, they go to America.
>   **Oscar Wilde** 1854–1900: *A Woman of No Importance* (1893)

9 America! America!
God shed His grace on thee
And crown thy good with brotherhood
From sea to shining sea!
>   **Katherine Lee Bates** 1859–1929: 'America the Beautiful' (1893)

10 It is by the goodness of God that in our country we have those three unspeakably precious things: freedom of speech, freedom of conscience, and the prudence never to practise either of them.
>   **Mark Twain** 1835–1910: *Following the Equator* (1897)

11 America is God's Crucible, the great Melting-Pot where all the races of Europe are melting and re-forming!
>   **Israel Zangwill** 1864–1926: *The Melting Pot* (1908)

12 There can be no fifty-fifty Americanism in this country. There is room here for only 100 per cent. Americanism, only for those who are Americans and nothing else.
>   **Theodore Roosevelt** 1858–1919: speech in Saratoga, 19 July 1918

13 I have fallen in love with American names,
The sharp, gaunt names that never get fat.
>   **Stephen Vincent Benét** 1898–1943: 'American Names' (1927)

14 I pledge you, I pledge myself, to a new deal for the American people.
Franklin D. Roosevelt 1882-1945: speech, 2 July 1932, accepting the presidential nomination

15 In the United States there is more space where nobody is than where anybody is. That is what makes America what it is.
Gertrude Stein 1874-1946: *The Geographical History of America* (1936)

16 God bless America,
Land that I love,
Stand beside her and guide her
Thru the night with a light from above.
Irving Berlin 1888-1989: 'God Bless America' (1939)

17 There are no second acts in American lives.
F. Scott Fitzgerald 1896-1940: Edmund Wilson (ed.) *The Last Tycoon* (1941)

18 Overpaid, overfed, oversexed, and over here.
Tommy Trinder 1909-89: of American troops in Britain during the Second World War (associated with Trinder, but probably not original)

19 California is a fine place to live—if you happen to be an orange.
Fred Allen 1894-1956: *American Magazine* December 1945

20 The most serious charge which can be brought against New England is not Puritanism but February.
Joseph Wood Krutch 1893-1970: *Twelve Seasons* (1949)

21 In America any boy may become President and I suppose it's just one of the risks he takes!
Adlai Stevenson 1900-65: speech in Indianapolis, 26 September 1952

22 This land is your land, this land is my land,
From California to the New York Island.
From the redwood forest to the Gulf Stream waters
This land was made for you and me.
Woody Guthrie 1912-67: 'This Land is Your Land' (1956 song)

23 I like to be in America!
OK by me in America!

Ev'rything free in America
For a small fee in America!
Stephen Sondheim 1930– : 'America' (1957 song)

24 Europe is the unfinished negative of which America is the
proof.
Mary McCarthy 1912–89: *On the Contrary* (1961) 'America
the Beautiful'

25 Our national flower is the concrete cloverleaf.
Lewis Mumford 1895–1982: *Quote Magazine* 8 October 1961

26 America is a vast conspiracy to make you happy.
John Updike 1932– : *Problems* (1980) 'How to love America
and Leave it at the Same Time'

Anger

1 A soft answer turneth away wrath.
Bible: Proverbs

2 *Ira furor brevis est.*
Anger is a short madness.
Horace 65–8 BC: *Epistles*

3 Be ye angry and sin not: let not the sun go down upon your
wrath.
Bible: Ephesians

4 Anger makes dull men witty, but it keeps them poor.
Francis Bacon 1561–1626: 'Baconiana' (1859), often
attributed to Queen Elizabeth I

5 Anger is one of the sinews of the soul.
Thomas Fuller 1608–61: *The Holy State and the Profane
State*

6 Beware the fury of a patient man.
John Dryden 1631–1700: *Absalom and Achitophel* (1681)

7 The tigers of wrath are wiser than the horses of instruction.
William Blake 1757–1827: *The Marriage of Heaven and Hell*
(1790–3) 'Proverbs of Hell'

8 When angry, count four; when very angry, swear.
Mark Twain 1835–1910: *Pudd'nhead Wilson* (1894)

Animals

See also **Cats, Dogs**

1 A righteous man regardeth the life of his beast: but the
tender mercies of the wicked are cruel.
  Bible: Proverbs

2 Nature's great masterpiece, an elephant,
The only harmless great thing.
  John Donne 1572–1631: 'The Progress of the Soul' (1601)

3 In so doing, use him as though you loved him.
  Izaak Walton 1593–1683: on baiting a hook with a live frog;
  The Compleat Angler (1653)

4 Wee, sleekit, cow'rin', tim'rous beastie,
O what a panic's in thy breastie!
  Robert Burns 1759–96: 'To a Mouse' (1786)

5 Tiger Tiger, burning bright,
In the forests of the night;
What immortal hand or eye,
Could frame thy fearful symmetry?
  William Blake 1757–1827: 'The Tiger' (1794)

6 Animals, whom we have made our slaves, we do not like to
consider our equal.
  Charles Darwin 1809–82: Notebook B (1837–8)

7 It ar'n't that I loves the fox less, but that I loves the 'ound
more.
  R. S. Surtees 1805–64: *Handley Cross* (1843)

8 All things bright and beautiful,
All creatures great and small,
All things wise and wonderful,
The Lord God made them all.
  Cecil Frances Alexander 1818–95: 'All Things Bright and
  Beautiful' (1848)

9 I think I could turn and live with animals, they are so placid
      and self-contained,
I stand and look at them long and long.
They do not sweat and whine about their condition,

They do not lie awake in the dark and weep for their sins,
They do not make me sick discussing their duty to God.
> **Walt Whitman** 1819–92: 'Song of Myself' (written 1855)

10 The Llama is a woolly sort of fleecy hairy goat,
With an indolent expression and an undulating throat
Like an unsuccessful literary man.
> **Hilaire Belloc** 1870–1953: 'The Llama' (1897)

11 'Twould ring the bells of Heaven
The wildest peal for years,
If Parson lost his senses
And people came to theirs,
And he and they together
Knelt down with angry prayers
For tamed and shabby tigers
And dancing dogs and bears,
And wretched, blind, pit ponies,
And little hunted hares.
> **Ralph Hodgson** 1871–1962: 'Bells of Heaven' (1917)

12 The rabbit has a charming face:
Its private life is a disgrace.
I really dare not name to you
The awful things that rabbits do.
> **Anonymous**: 'The Rabbit', in *The Week-End Book* (1925)

13 The cow is of the bovine ilk;
One end is moo, the other, milk.
> **Ogden Nash** 1902–71: 'The Cow' (1931)

14 The turtle lives 'twixt plated decks
Which practically conceal its sex.
I think it clever of the turtle
In such a fix to be so fertile.
> **Ogden Nash** 1902–71: 'Autres Bêtes, Autres Moeurs' (1931)

15 Giraffes!—a People
Who live between the earth and skies,
Each in his lone religious steeple,
Keeping a light-house with his eyes.
> **Roy Campbell** 1901–57: 'Dreaming Spires' (1946)

16 Where in this wide world can man find nobility without
pride,
Friendship without envy, or beauty without vanity?
> **Ronald Duncan** 1914–82: 'In Praise of the Horse' (1962)

17 I am fond of pigs. Dogs look up to us. Cats look down on us.
Pigs treat us as equals.
Winston Churchill 1874–1965: attributed, in M. Gilbert
Never Despair (1988)

Apology

1 Never make a defence or apology before you be accused.
Charles I 1600–49: letter to Lord Wentworth, 3 September
1636

2 Never complain and never explain.
Benjamin Disraeli 1804–81: in J. Morley *Life of Gladstone*
(1903)

3 Never explain—your friends do not need it and your enemies
will not believe you anyway.
Elbert Hubbard 1859–1915: *The Motto Book* (1907)

4 It is a good rule in life never to apologize. The right sort of
people do not want apologies, and the wrong sort take a mean
advantage of them.
P. G. Wodehouse 1881–1975: *The Man Upstairs* (1914)

5 Very sorry can't come. Lie follows by post.
Lord Charles Beresford 1846–1919: telegraphed message
to the Prince of Wales, on being summoned to dine at the
eleventh hour

6 Several excuses are always less convincing than one.
Aldous Huxley 1894–1963: *Point Counter Point* (1928)

Architecture

1 Well building hath three conditions. Commodity, firmness,
and delight.
Henry Wotton 1568–1639: *Elements of Architecture* (1624)

2 Light (God's eldest daughter) is a principal beauty in
building.
Thomas Fuller 1608–61: *The Holy State and the Profane
State* 'Of Building'

3 Architecture in general is frozen music.
   Friedrich von Schelling 1775–1854: *Philosophie der Kunst* (1809)

4 He builded better than he knew;—
   The conscious stone to beauty grew.
   Ralph Waldo Emerson 1803–82: 'The Problem' (1847)

5 Form follows function.
   Louis Henri Sullivan 1856–1924: *The Tall Office Building Artistically Considered* (1896)

6 A house is a machine for living in.
   Le Corbusier 1887–1965: *Vers une architecture* (1923)

7 Architecture, of all the arts, is the one which acts the most slowly, but the most surely, on the soul.
   Ernest Dimnet: *What We Live By* (1932)

8 The physician can bury his mistakes, but the architect can only advise his client to plant vines—so they should go as far as possible from home to build their first buildings.
   Frank Lloyd Wright 1867–1959: *New York Times* 4 October 1953

9 Architecture is the art of how to waste space.
   Philip Johnson 1906– : *New York Times* 27 December 1964

10 A monstrous carbuncle on the face of a much-loved and elegant friend.
   Charles, Prince of Wales 1948– : speech on the proposed extension to the National Gallery, London, 30 May 1984

Argument

1 It is better to dwell in a corner of the housetop, than with a brawling woman in a wide house.
   Bible: Proverbs

2 You cannot argue with someone who denies the first principles.
   Auctoritates Aristotelis: a compilation of medieval propositions

3 Your 'if' is the only peace-maker; much virtue in 'if'.
   William Shakespeare 1564–1616: *As You Like It* (1599)

4 There is no arguing with Johnson; for when his pistol misses
fire, he knocks you down with the butt end of it.
   Oliver Goldsmith 1730–74: in James Boswell *Life of Samuel
   Johnson* (1791) 26 October 1769

5 Who can refute a sneer?
   William Paley 1743–1805: *Principles of Moral and Political
   Philosophy* (1785)

6 I am not arguing with you—I am telling you.
   James McNeill Whistler 1834–1903: *The Gentle Art of
   Making Enemies* (1890)

7 It takes in reality only one to make a quarrel. It is useless for
the sheep to pass resolutions in favour of vegetarianism,
while the wolf remains of a different opinion.
   Dean Inge 1860–1954: *Outspoken Essays: First Series* (1919)

8 The argument of the broken window pane is the most
valuable argument in modern politics.
   Emmeline Pankhurst 1858–1928: in G. Dangerfield *The
   Strange Death of Liberal England* (1936)

9 The Catholic and the Communist are alike in assuming that
an opponent cannot be both honest and intelligent.
   George Orwell 1903–50: *Polemic* January 1946

10 'Yes, but not in the South', with slight adjustments, will do
for any argument about any place, if not about any person.
   Stephen Potter 1900–69: *Lifemanship* (1950)

The Army

See also **War, Wars**

1   A soldier,
Full of strange oaths, and bearded like the pard,
Jealous in honour, sudden and quick in quarrel,
Seeking the bubble reputation
Even in the cannon's mouth.
   William Shakespeare 1564–1616: *As You Like It* (1599)

2 As Lord Chesterfield said of the generals of his day, 'I only
hope that when the enemy reads the list of their names, he
trembles as I do.'
   Duke of Wellington 1769–1852: letter, 29 August 1810

(usually quoted 'I don't know what effect these men will
have upon the enemy, but, by God, they frighten me')

3 An army marches on its stomach.
　　Napoléon I 1769–1821: attributed, but probably condensed
　　from a long passage in E. A. de Las Cases *Mémorial de
　　Ste-Hélène* (1823) 14 November 1816

4 Remember that there is not one of you who does not carry in
his cartridge-pouch the marshal's baton of the duke of
Reggio; it is up to you to bring it forth.
　　Louis XVIII 1755–1824: speech to Saint-Cyr cadets, 9 August
　　1819

5 Ours [our army] is composed of the scum of the earth—the
mere scum of the earth.
　　Duke of Wellington 1769–1852: in Philip Henry Stanhope
　　Notes of Conversations with the Duke of Wellington (1888)
　　4 November 1831

6 *C'est magnifique, mais ce n'est pas la guerre.*
It is magnificent, but it is not war.
　　Pierre Bosquet 1810–61: on the charge of the Light Brigade
　　at Balaclava, 25 October 1854

7 Theirs not to make reply,
Theirs not to reason why,
Theirs but to do and die:
Into the valley of Death
Rode the six hundred.
　　Alfred, Lord Tennyson 1809–92: 'The Charge of the Light
　　Brigade' (1854)

8 They dashed on towards that thin red line tipped with steel.
　　William Howard Russell 1820–1907: of the Russians
　　charging the British, in *The British Expedition to the
　　Crimea* (1877). Russell's original dispatch to *The Times*,
　　14 November 1854, reads 'That thin red streak tipped with a
　　line of steel'

9 O it's Tommy this, an' Tommy that, an' 'Tommy, go away';
But it's 'Thank you, Mister Atkins,' when the band begins to
play.
　　Rudyard Kipling 1865–1936: 'Tommy' (1892)

10 The 'eathen in 'is blindness must end where 'e began.
But the backbone of the Army is the non-commissioned man!
　　Rudyard Kipling 1865–1936: 'The 'Eathen' (1896)

11 You can always tell an old soldier by the inside of his
holsters and cartridge boxes. The young ones carry pistols
and cartridges; the old ones, grub.
  George Bernard Shaw 1856–1950: *Arms and the Man* (1898)

12 The British soldier can stand up to anything except the
British War Office.
  George Bernard Shaw 1856–1950: *The Devil's Disciple* (1901)

13 When the military man approaches, the world locks up its
spoons and packs off its womankind.
  George Bernard Shaw 1856–1950: *Man and Superman*
(1903)

14 What passing-bells for these who die as cattle?
Only the monstrous anger of the guns.
  Wilfred Owen 1893–1918: 'Anthem for Doomed Youth'
(written 1917)

15 Soldiers are citizens of death's grey land,
Drawing no dividend from time's tomorrows.
  Siegfried Sassoon 1886–1967: 'Dreamers' (1918)

16 If I were fierce, and bald, and short of breath,
I'd live with scarlet Majors at the Base,
And speed glum heroes up the line to death.
  Siegfried Sassoon 1886–1967: 'Base Details' (1918)

17 Lions led by donkeys.
  Max Hoffmann 1869–1927: of British soldiers during the
First World War; in A. Clark *The Donkeys* (1961)

18 If it moves, salute it; if it doesn't move, pick it up; and if you
can't pick it up, paint it.
  Anonymous: 1940s saying

19 They call it easing the Spring: it is perfectly easy
If you have any strength in your thumb: like the bolt,
And the breech, and the cocking-piece, and the point of
balance,
Which in our case we have not got.
  Henry Reed 1914–86: 'Lessons of the War: 1, Naming of
Parts' (1946)

20 At the age of four with paper hats and wooden swords we're
all Generals. Only some of us never grow out of it.
  Peter Ustinov 1921– : *Romanoff and Juliet* (1956)

Art

See also **Painting and Drawing**

1 Life is short, the art long.
   Hippocrates c.460–357 BC: *Aphorisms*, often quoted as '*Ars longa, vita brevis*', after Seneca *De Brevitate Vitae*

2 In art the best is good enough.
   Johann Wolfgang von Goethe 1749–1832: *Italienische Reise* (1816–17) 3 March 1787

3 Art for art's sake, with no purpose, for any purpose perverts art. But art achieves a purpose which is not its own.
   Benjamin Constant 1767–1834: *Journal intime* 11 February 1804

4 God help the Minister that meddles with art!
   Lord Melbourne 1779–1848: in Lord David Cecil *Lord M* (1954)

5 The artist must be in his work as God is in creation, invisible and all-powerful; one must sense him everywhere but never see him.
   Gustave Flaubert 1821–80: letter to Mlle Leroyer de Chantepie, 18 March 1857

6 Art is a jealous mistress.
   Ralph Waldo Emerson 1803–82: *The Conduct of Life* (1860)

7 Human life is a sad show, undoubtedly: ugly, heavy and complex. Art has no other end, for people of feeling, than to conjure away the burden and bitterness.
   Gustave Flaubert 1821–80: letter to Amelie Bosquet, July 1864

8 All passes. Art alone
   Enduring stays to us;
   The Bust outlasts the throne,—
   The Coin, Tiberius.
   Henry Austin Dobson 1840–1921: 'Ars Victrix' (1876); translation of Théophile Gautier's 'L'Art'

9 It's clever, but is it Art?
   Rudyard Kipling 1865–1936: 'The Conundrum of the Workshops' (1892)

10 We work in the dark—we do what we can—we give what we
have. Our doubt is our passion and our passion is our task.
The rest is the madness of art.
   Henry James 1843-1916: 'The Middle Years' (1893)

11 I always said God was against art and I still believe it.
   Edward Elgar 1857-1934: letter to A. J. Jaeger, 9 October
   1900

12 The history of art is the history of revivals.
   Samuel Butler 1835-1902: *Notebooks* (1912)

13 The true artist will let his wife starve, his children go
barefoot, his mother drudge for his living at seventy, sooner
than work at anything but his art.
   George Bernard Shaw 1856-1950: *Man and Superman*
   (1903)

14 The artist, like the God of the creation, remains within or
behind or beyond or above his handiwork, invisible, refined
out of existence, indifferent, paring his fingernails.
   James Joyce 1882-1941: *A Portrait of the Artist as a Young
   Man* (1916)

15 Art is vice. You don't marry it legitimately, you rape it.
   Edgar Degas 1834-1917: in P. Lafond *Degas* (1918)

16 There is no more sombre enemy of good art than the pram in
the hall.
   Cyril Connolly 1903-74: *Enemies of Promise* (1938)

17 Art is significant deformity.
   Roger Fry 1866-1934: in Virginia Woolf *Roger Fry* (1940)

18 Art is the imposing of a pattern on experience, and our
aesthetic enjoyment is recognition of the pattern.
   Alfred North Whitehead 1861-1947: *Dialogues* (1954)
   10 June 1943

19 *L'art est un anti-destin.*
Art is a revolt against fate.
   André Malraux 1901-76: *Les Voix du silence* (1951)

20 Art is born of humiliation.
   W. H. Auden 1907-73: in Stephen Spender *World Within
   World* (1951)

21 Art is meant to disturb, science reassures.
   Georges Braque 1882-1963: *Le Jour et la nuit: Cahiers
   1917-52*

22 Art is the objectification of feeling, and the subjectification of nature.
    Suzanne K. Langer 1895–1985: *Mind* (1967)

Beauty

1 A beautiful face is a mute recommendation.
    Publilius Syrus 1st century BC: *Sententiae* tr. Thomas Tenison (1679)

2 Consider the lilies of the field, how they grow; they toil not, neither do they spin:
    And yet I say unto you, That even Solomon in all his glory was not arrayed like one of these.
    Bible: St Matthew

3 And she was fayr as is the rose in May.
    Geoffrey Chaucer *c*.1343–1400: *The Legend of Good Women* 'Cleopatra'

4 Was this the face that launched a thousand ships,
    And burnt the topless towers of Ilium?
    Sweet Helen, make me immortal with a kiss!
    Christopher Marlowe 1564–93: *Doctor Faustus* (1604)

5 O! she doth teach the torches to burn bright.
    It seems she hangs upon the cheek of night
    Like a rich jewel in an Ethiop's ear;
    Beauty too rich for use, for earth too dear.
    William Shakespeare 1564–1616: *Romeo and Juliet* (1595)

6 Shall I compare thee to a summer's day?
    Thou art more lovely and more temperate:
    Rough winds do shake the darling buds of May, .
    And summer's lease hath all too short a date.
    William Shakespeare 1564–1616: sonnet 18 (1609)

7 There is no excellent beauty that hath not some strangeness in the proportion.
    Francis Bacon 1561–1626: *Essays* (1625) 'Of Beauty'

8 The flowers anew, returning seasons bring;
    But beauty faded has no second spring.
    Ambrose Philips *c*.1675–1749: *The First Pastoral* (1708)

9 Beauty is no quality in things themselves. It exists merely in
the mind which contemplates them.
  David Hume 1711–76: 'Of the Standard of Taste' (1757)

10 She walks in beauty, like the night
Of cloudless climes and starry skies;
And all that's best of dark and bright
Meet in her aspect and her eyes.
  Lord Byron 1788–1824: 'She Walks in Beauty' (1815)

11 A thing of beauty is a joy for ever:
Its loveliness increases; it will never
Pass into nothingness.
  John Keats 1795–1821: *Endymion* (1818)

12 'Beauty is truth, truth beauty,'—that is all
Ye know on earth, and all ye need to know.
  John Keats 1795–1821: 'Ode on a Grecian Urn' (1820)

13 *I never saw an ugly thing in my life:* for let the form of an
object be what it may,—light, shade, and perspective will
always make it beautiful.
  John Constable 1776–1837: in C. R. Leslie *Memoirs of the
Life of John Constable* (1843)

14 Remember that the most beautiful things in the world are the
most useless; peacocks and lilies for instance.
  John Ruskin 1819–1900: *Stones of Venice* vol. 1 (1851)

15 If you get simple beauty and naught else,
You get about the best thing God invents.
  Robert Browning 1812–89: 'Fra Lippo Lippi' (1855)

16 The Lord prefers common-looking people. That is why he
makes so many of them.
  Abraham Lincoln 1809–65: attributed

17 All things counter, original, spare, strange;
Whatever is fickle, freckled (who knows how?)
With swift, slow; sweet, sour; adazzle, dim;
He fathers-forth whose beauty is past change:
Praise him.
  Gerard Manley Hopkins 1844–89: 'Pied Beauty' (written
1877)

18 Beauty is mysterious as well as terrible. God and devil are
fighting there, and the battlefield is the heart of man.
  Fedor Dostoevsky 1821–81: *The Brothers Karamazov*
(1879–80)

19 I have a left shoulder-blade that is a miracle of loveliness. People come miles to see it. My right elbow has a fascination that few can resist.
    W. S. Gilbert 1836–1911: *The Mikado* (1885)

20 When a woman isn't beautiful, people always say, 'You have lovely eyes, you have lovely hair.'
    Anton Chekhov 1860–1904: *Uncle Vanya* (1897)

21 Beauty is all very well at first sight; but who ever looks at it when it has been in the house three days?
    George Bernard Shaw 1856–1950: *Man and Superman* (1903)

22 I always say beauty is only sin deep.
    Saki (H. H. Munro) 1870–1916: *Reginald* (1904)

23 He was afflicted by the thought that where Beauty was, nothing ever ran quite straight, which, no doubt, was why so many people looked on it as immoral.
    John Galsworthy 1867–1933: *In Chancery* (1920)

24 Beauty is momentary in the mind—
The fitful tracing of a portal;
But in the flesh it is immortal.
The body dies; the body's beauty lives.
    Wallace Stevens 1879–1955: 'Peter Quince at the Clavier' (1923)

25 It was a blonde. A blonde to make a bishop kick a hole in a stained glass window.
    Raymond Chandler 1888–1959: *Farewell, My Lovely* (1940)

26 I'm tired of all this nonsense about beauty being only skin-deep. That's deep enough. What do you want—an adorable pancreas?
    Jean Kerr 1923– : *The Snake has all the Lines* (1958)

Beginnings and Endings

1 In the beginning God created the heaven and the earth. And the earth was without form, and void; and darkness was upon the face of the deep.
    Bible: Genesis

2 In my end is my beginning.
    Mary, Queen of Scots 1542–87: motto

3 This is the beginning of the end.
   Charles-Maurice de Talleyrand 1754–1838: on hearing the outcome of the battle at Borodino, 1812; attributed

4 Ring out the old, ring in the new,
   Ring, happy bells, across the snow:
   The year is going, let him go;
   Ring out the false, ring in the true.
   Alfred, Lord Tennyson 1809–92: *In Memoriam A. H. H.* (1850)

5 'Begin at the beginning,' the King said, gravely, 'and go on till you come to the end: then stop.'
   Lewis Carroll 1832–98: *Alice's Adventures in Wonderland* (1865)

6 Some say the world will end in fire,
   Some say in ice.
   Robert Frost 1874–1963: 'Fire and Ice' (1923)

7 This is the way the world ends
   Not with a bang but a whimper.
   T. S. Eliot 1888–1965: 'The Hollow Men' (1925)

8 In my beginning is my end.
   T. S. Eliot 1888–1965: *Four Quartets* 'East Coker' (1940)

9 What we call the beginning is often the end
   And to make an end is to make a beginning.
   The end is where we start from.
   T. S. Eliot 1888–1965: *Four Quartets* 'Little Gidding' (1942)

10 Now this is not the end. It is not even the beginning of the end. But it is, perhaps, the end of the beginning.
   Winston Churchill 1874–1965: speech at the Mansion House, London, 10 November 1942

11 Are you sitting comfortably? Then I'll begin.
   Julia Lang 1921– : *Listen with Mother* (BBC radio programme for children, 1950–82)

12 The party's over, it's time to call it a day.
   Betty Comden 1919– and **Adolph Green** 1915– : 'The Party's Over' (1956 song)

13 All this will not be finished in the first 100 days. Nor will it be finished in the first 1,000 days, nor in the life of this

Administration, nor even perhaps in our lifetime on this planet. But let us begin.
>   **John F. Kennedy** 1917–63: inaugural address, 20 January 1961

14 It ain't over till it's over.
>   **Yogi Berra** 1925– : comment on National League pennant race, 1973, quoted in many versions

15 The opera ain't over 'til the fat lady sings.
>   **Dan Cook**: in *Washington Post* 3 June 1978

Behaviour

See also **Manners**

1 *O tempora, O mores!*
Oh, the times! Oh, the manners!
>   **Cicero** 106–43 BC: *In Catilinam*

2 Caesar's wife must be above suspicion.
>   **Julius Caesar** 100–44 BC: oral tradition, based on Plutarch *Parallel Lives*

3 When I go to Rome, I fast on Saturday, but here [Milan] I do not. Do you also follow the custom of whatever church you attend, if you do not want to give or receive scandal.
>   **St Ambrose** *c*.339–97: letter to Januarius, tr. Sr W. Parsons; usually quoted 'When in Rome, do as the Romans do'

4 He was a verray, parfit gentil knyght.
>   **Geoffrey Chaucer** *c*.1343–1400: *The Canterbury Tales* 'General Prologue'

5 He does it with a better grace, but I do it more natural.
>   **William Shakespeare** 1564–1616: *Twelfth Night* (1601)

6 Never *in* the way, and never *out* of the way.
>   **Charles II** 1630–85: of Lord Godolphin, as his page

7 They [the *Letters* of Lord Chesterfield] teach the morals of a whore, and the manners of a dancing master.
>   **Samuel Johnson** 1709–84: in James Boswell *Life of Johnson* (1791) 1754

8 The courtiers who surround him [Louis XVIII] have forgotten
  nothing and learnt nothing.
    General Dumouriez 1739–1823: *Examen impartial d'un
    Écrit…de Louis XVIII* (1795)

9 *Tout comprendre rend très indulgent.*
  To be totally understanding makes one very indulgent.
    Mme de Staël 1766–1817: *Corinne* (1807)

10 In short, he was a perfect cavaliero,
   And to his very valet seemed a hero.
    Lord Byron 1788–1824: *Beppo* (1818)

11 It is almost a definition of a gentleman to say that he is one
   who never inflicts pain.
    Cardinal Newman 1801–90: *The Idea of a University* (1852)

12 The only infallible rule we know is, that the man who is
   always talking about being a gentleman never is one.
    R. S. Surtees 1805–64: *Ask Mamma* (1858)

13 Go directly—see what she's doing, and tell her she mustn't.
    Punch: 1872

14 Conduct is three-fourths of our life and its largest concern.
    Matthew Arnold 1822–88: *Literature and Dogma* (1873)

15 He combines the manners of a marquis with the morals of a
   Methodist.
    W. S. Gilbert 1836–1911: *Ruddigore* (1887)

16 Being tactful in audacity is knowing how far one can go too
   far.
    Jean Cocteau 1889–1963: *Le Rappel à l'ordre* (1926)

17 I get too hungry for dinner at eight.
   I like the theatre, but never come late.
   I never bother with people I hate.
   That's why the lady is a tramp.
    Lorenz Hart 1895–1943: 'The Lady is a Tramp' (1937 song)

Belief and Unbelief

1 Lord, I believe; help thou mine unbelief.
    Bible: St Mark

2 *Certum est quia impossibile est.*
It is certain because it is impossible.
> **Tertullian** AD *c*.160–*c*.225: *De Carne Christi*, often quoted
> '*Credo quia impossibile* [I believe because it is impossible]'

3 *Que sais-je?*
What do I know?
> **Montaigne** 1533–92: *Essais* (1580) on the position of the
> sceptic

4 A little philosophy inclineth man's mind to atheism, but
depth in philosophy bringeth men's minds about to religion.
> **Francis Bacon** 1561–1626: *Essays* (1625) 'Of Atheism'

5 By night an atheist half believes a God.
> **Edward Young** 1683–1765: *Night Thoughts* (1742–5)

6 Truth, Sir, is a cow, that will yield such people [sceptics] no
more milk, and so they are gone to milk the bull.
> **Samuel Johnson** 1709–84: in James Boswell *Life of Johnson*
> (1791) 21 July 1763

7 It is necessary to the happiness of man that he be mentally
faithful to himself. Infidelity does not consist in believing, or
in disbelieving, it consists in professing to believe what one
does not believe.
> **Thomas Paine** 1737–1809: *The Age of Reason* pt. 1 (1794)

8 *We can believe what we choose.* We are answerable for what
we choose to believe.
> **Cardinal Newman** 1801–90: letter to Mrs William Froude,
> 27 June 1848

9 There lives more faith in honest doubt,
Believe me, than in half the creeds.
> **Alfred, Lord Tennyson** 1809–92: *In Memoriam A. H. H.*
> (1850)

10 Just when we are safest, there's a sunset-touch,
A fancy from a flower-bell, some one's death,
A chorus-ending from Euripides,—
And that's enough for fifty hopes and fears
As old and new at once as Nature's self...
The grand Perhaps!
> **Robert Browning** 1812–89: 'Bishop Blougram's Apology'
> (1855)

11 The Sea of Faith
Was once, too, at the full, and round earth's shore

Lay like the folds of a bright girdle furled.
But now I only hear
Its melancholy, long, withdrawing roar.
   Matthew Arnold 1822–88: 'Dover Beach' (1867)

12 Why, sometimes I've believed as many as six impossible
   things before breakfast.
      Lewis Carroll 1832–98: *Through the Looking-Glass* (1872)

13 When suave politeness, tempering bigot zeal,
   Corrected *I believe* to *One does feel*.
      Monsignor Ronald Knox 1888–1957: 'Absolute and
      Abitofhell' (1913)

14 I do not consider it an insult, but rather a compliment to be
   called an agnostic. I do not pretend to know where many
   ignorant men are sure—that is all that agnosticism means.
      Clarence Darrow 1857–1938: speech at trial of John
      Thomas Scopes, 15 July 1925

15 Every time a child says 'I don't believe in fairies' there is
   a little fairy somewhere that falls down dead.
      J. M. Barrie 1860–1937: *Peter Pan* (1928)

16 Of course not, but I am told it works even if you don't believe
   in it.
      Niels Bohr 1885–1962: when asked whether he really
      believed a horseshoe hanging over his door would bring
      him luck, c.1930; in A. Pais *Inward Bound* (1986)

17 The dust of exploded beliefs may make a fine sunset.
      Geoffrey Madan 1895–1947: *Livre sans nom: Twelve
      Reflections* (1934)

18 An atheist is a man who has no invisible means of support.
      John Buchan 1875–1940: in H. E. Fosdick *On Being a Real
      Person* (1943)

19 Man is a credulous animal, and must believe *something*; in
   the absence of good grounds for belief, he will be satisfied
   with bad ones.
      Bertrand Russell 1872–1970: *Unpopular Essays* (1950)

20 I confused things with their names: that is belief.
      Jean-Paul Sartre 1905–80: *Les Mots* (1964)

21 She [my grandmother] believed in nothing; only her
   scepticism kept her from being an atheist.
      Jean-Paul Sartre 1905–1980: *Les Mots* (1964)

22 There is a lot to be said in the Decade of Evangelism for
　believing more and more in less and less.
　　Bishop John Yates 1925– : *Gloucester Diocesan Gazette*
　　August 1991

The Bible

1 The devil can cite Scripture for his purpose.
　　William Shakespeare 1564–1616: *The Merchant of Venice*
　　(1596–8)

2 *Scrutamini scripturas* [Let us look at the scriptures]. These
　two words have undone the world.
　　John Selden 1584–1654: *Table Talk* (1689) 'Bible Scripture'

3 Here is wisdom; this is the royal Law; these are the lively
　Oracles of God.
　　Coronation Service 1689: The Presenting of the Holy Bible

4 The English Bible, a book which, if everything else in our
　language should perish, would alone suffice to show the
　whole extent of its beauty and power.
　　Lord Macaulay 1800–59: 'John Dryden' (1828)

5 There's a great text in Galatians,
　Once you trip on it, entails
　Twenty-nine distinct damnations,
　One sure, if another fails.
　　Robert Browning 1812–89: 'Soliloquy of the Spanish
　　Cloister' (1842)

6 We have used the Bible as if it was a constable's
　handbook—an opium-dose for keeping beasts of burden
　patient while they are being overloaded.
　　Charles Kingsley 1819–75: *Letters to the Chartists*

7 LORD ILLINGWORTH: The Book of Life begins with a man and a
　woman in a garden.
　MRS ALLONBY: It ends with Revelations.
　　Oscar Wilde 1854–1900: *A Woman of No Importance* (1893)

8 An apology for the Devil: It must be remembered that we
　have only heard one side of the case. God has written all the
　books.
　　Samuel Butler 1835–1902: *Notebooks* (1912)

Biography

1 Read no history: nothing but biography, for that is life without theory.
   Benjamin Disraeli 1804–81: *Contarini Fleming* (1832)

2 Lives of great men all remind us
   We can make our lives sublime,
   And, departing, leave behind us
   Footprints on the sands of time.
   Henry Wadsworth Longfellow 1807–82: 'A Psalm of Life' (1838)

3 A well-written Life is almost as rare as a well-spent one.
   Thomas Carlyle 1795–1881: *Critical and Miscellaneous Essays* (1838)

4 Then there is my noble and biographical friend who has added a new terror to death.
   Charles Wetherell 1770–1846: on Lord Campbell's *Lives of the Lord Chancellors* being written without the consent of heirs or executors; also attributed to Lord Lyndhurst (1772–1863)

5 No quailing, Mrs Gaskell! no drawing back!
   Patrick Brontë 1777–1861: apropos her undertaking to write the life of Charlotte Brontë; letter from Mrs Gaskell to Ellen Nussey, 24 July 1855

6 It is not a Life at all. It is a Reticence, in three volumes.
   W. E. Gladstone 1809–98: on J. W. Cross's *Life of George Eliot*; in E. F. Benson *As We Were* (1930)

7 The Art of Biography
   Is different from Geography.
   Geography is about Maps,
   But Biography is about Chaps.
   Edmund Clerihew Bentley 1875–1956: *Biography for Beginners* (1905)

8 Discretion is not the better part of biography.
   Lytton Strachey 1880–1932: in M. Holroyd *Lytton Strachey* vol. 1 (1967)

9 To write one's memoirs is to speak ill of everybody except oneself.
   Marshal Pétain 1856–1951: in *Observer* 26 May 1946

10 An autobiography is an obituary in serial form with the last
instalment missing.
> **Quentin Crisp** 1908– : *The Naked Civil Servant* (1968)

Birds

1 *Vox et praeterea nihil.*
A voice and nothing more.
> **Anonymous**: describing a nightingale. See Plutarch *Moralia*

2 The bisy larke, messager of day.
> **Geoffrey Chaucer** *c.*1343–1400: *The Canterbury Tales* 'The
> Knight's Tale'

3 O blithe new-comer! I have heard,
I hear thee and rejoice:
O Cuckoo! Shall I call thee bird,
Or but a wandering voice?
> **William Wordsworth** 1770–1850: 'To the Cuckoo' (1807)

4 Hail to thee, blithe Spirit!
Bird thou never wert,
That from Heaven, or near it,
Pourest thy full heart
In profuse strains of unpremeditated art.
> **Percy Bysshe Shelley** 1792–1822: 'To a Skylark' (1819)

5 Alone and warming his five wits,
The white owl in the belfry sits.
> **Alfred, Lord Tennyson** 1809–92: 'Song—The Owl' (1830)

6 That's the wise thrush; he sings each song twice over,
Lest you should think he never could recapture
The first fine careless rapture!
> **Robert Browning** 1812–89: 'Home-Thoughts, from Abroad'
> (1845)

7 He clasps the crag with crookèd hands;
Close to the sun in lonely lands,
Ringed with the azure world, he stands.
> **Alfred, Lord Tennyson** 1809–92: 'The Eagle' (1851)

8 I caught this morning morning's minion, kingdom of
daylight's dauphin, dapple-dawn-drawn Falcon.
> **Gerard Manley Hopkins** 1844–89: 'The Windhover' (written
> 1877)

9 An aged thrush, frail, gaunt, and small,
In blast-beruffled plume.
> **Thomas Hardy** 1840–1928: 'The Darkling Thrush' (1902)

10 It was the Rainbow gave thee birth,
And left thee all her lovely hues.
> **W. H. Davies** 1871–1940: 'Kingfisher' (1910)

11 Oh, a wondrous bird is the pelican!
His beak holds more than his belican.
He takes in his beak
Food enough for a week.
But I'll be darned if I know how the helican.
> **Dixon Lanier Merritt** 1879–1972: in *Nashville Banner*
> 22 April 1913

12 And hear the pleasant cuckoo, loud and long—
The simple bird that thinks two notes a song.
> **W. H. Davies** 1871–1940: 'April's Charms' (1916)

13 From troubles of the world
I turn to ducks
Beautiful comical things.
> **F. W. Harvey** b. 1888: 'Ducks' (1919)

14 I do not know which to prefer,
The beauty of inflections
Or the beauty of innuendoes,
The blackbird whistling
Or just after.
> **Wallace Stevens** 1879–1955: 'Thirteen Ways of Looking at
> a Blackbird' (1923)

15 It took the whole of Creation
To produce my foot, my each feather:
Now I hold Creation in my foot.
> **Ted Hughes** 1930– : 'Hawk Roosting' (1960)

16 Blackbirds are the cellos of the deep farms.
> **Anne Stevenson** 1933– : 'Green Mountain, Black Mountain'
> (1982)

Birth

1 In sorrow thou shalt bring forth children.
> **Bible**: Genesis

2 *Maior erat natu; non omnia possumus omnes.*
He was born first; we cannot all do everything.
    Lucilius *c.*180-102 BC: in Macrobius *Saturnalia*

3 The queen of Scots is this day leichter of a fair son, and I am
but a barren stock.
    Elizabeth I 1533-1603: to her ladies, 1566

4 Men should be bewailed at their birth, and not at their death.
    Montesquieu 1689-1755: *Lettres Persanes* (1721), tr. J. Ozell,
1722

5 So for the mother's sake the child was dear,
And dearer was the mother for the child.
    Samuel Taylor Coleridge 1772-1834: 'Sonnet to a Friend
Who Asked How I Felt When the Nurse First Presented My
Infant to Me' (1797)

6 Our birth is but a sleep and a forgetting...
Not in entire forgetfulness,
And not in utter nakedness,
But trailing clouds of glory do we come.
    William Wordsworth 1770-1850: 'Ode. Intimations of
Immortality' (1807)

7   I had seen birth and death
But had thought they were different.
    T. S. Eliot 1888-1965: 'Journey of the Magi' (1927)

8 Good work, Mary. We all knew you had it in you.
    Dorothy Parker 1893-1967: telegram to Mrs Sherwood on
the arrival of her baby; in A. Woollcott *While Rome Burns*
(1934)

9 Death and taxes and childbirth! There's never any
convenient time for any of them.
    Margaret Mitchell 1900-49: *Gone with the Wind* (1936)

10 I am not yet born; O fill me
With strength against those who would freeze my
humanity.
    Louis MacNeice 1907-63: 'Prayer Before Birth' (1944)

11 Let them not make me a stone and let them not spill me,
Otherwise kill me.
    Louis MacNeice 1907-63: 'Prayer Before Birth' (1944)

12 It's all any reasonable child can expect if the dad is present
at the conception.
    Joe Orton 1923-67: *Entertaining Mr Sloane* (1964)

13 If men had to have babies, they would only ever have one
each.
    Diana, Princess of Wales 1961– : *Observer* 29 July 1984
    'Sayings of the Week'

The Body

1 I will give thanks unto thee, for I am fearfully and
wonderfully made.
    Bible: Psalm 139

2 Doth not even nature itself teach you, that if a man have long
hair, it is a shame unto him?
    But if a woman have long hair, it is a glory to her.
    Bible: I Corinthians

3   Falstaff sweats to death
And lards the lean earth as he walks along.
    William Shakespeare 1564–1616: *Henry IV, Part 1* (1597)

4 Thou seest I have more flesh than another man, and
therefore more frailty.
    William Shakespeare 1564–1616: *Henry IV, Part 1* (1597)

5   There's no art
To find the mind's construction in the face.
    William Shakespeare 1564–1616: *Macbeth* (1606)

6 Fain would I kiss my Julia's dainty leg,
Which is as white and hairless as an egg.
    Robert Herrick 1591–1674: 'On Julia's Legs' (1648)

7 Had Cleopatra's nose been shorter, the whole face of the
world would have changed.
    Blaise Pascal 1623–62: *Pensées* (1670)

8 Our body is a machine for living. It is organized for that, it is
its nature. Let life go on in it unhindered and let it defend
itself.
    Leo Tolstoy 1828–1910: *War and Peace* (1865–9), tr. A. and
L. Maude

9 I am the family face;
Flesh perishes, I live on.
    Thomas Hardy 1840–1928: 'Heredity' (1917)

10 Anatomy is destiny.
  Sigmund Freud 1856-1939: *Collected Writings* (1924)

11 i like my body when it is with your
  body. It is so quite new a thing.
  Muscles better and nerves more.
  e. e. cummings 1894-1962: 'Sonnets-Actualities' no. 8 (1925)

12 I'm fat, but I'm thin inside. Has it ever struck you that
  there's a thin man inside every fat man, just as they say
  there's a statue inside every block of stone?
  George Orwell 1903-50: *Coming up For Air* (1939)

13 At 50, everyone has the face he deserves.
  George Orwell 1903-50: last words in his notebook,
  17 April 1949

14 I'd the upbringing a nun would envy...Until I was fifteen
  I was more familiar with Africa than my own body.
  Joe Orton 1933-67: *Entertaining Mr Sloane* (1964)

15 Your cameraman might enjoy himself because my face looks
  like a wedding-cake left out in the rain.
  W. H. Auden 1907-1973: in H. Carpenter *W. H. Auden* (1963)

Books

See also **Libraries, Reading, Writing**

1 Of making many books there is no end; and much study is a
  weariness of the flesh.
  Bible: Ecclesiastes

2 A great book is like great evil.
  Callimachus *c.*305-*c.*240 BC: proverbially 'Great book, great
  evil'

3 Books will speak plain when counsellors blanch.
  Francis Bacon 1561-1626: *Essays* (1625) 'Of Counsel'

4 Some books are to be tasted, others to be swallowed, and
  some few to be chewed and digested.
  Francis Bacon 1561-1626: *Essays* (1625) 'Of Studies'

5 A good book is the precious life-blood of a master spirit.
  John Milton 1608-74: *Areopagitica* (1644)

6 Deep-versed in books and shallow in himself.
  John Milton 1608–74: *Paradise Regained* (1671)

7 Never literary attempt was more unfortunate than my
  Treatise of Human Nature. It fell *dead-born from the press.*
  David Hume 1711–76: *My Own Life* (1777)

8 You shall see them on a beautiful quarto page where a neat
  rivulet of text shall meander through a meadow of margin.
  Richard Brinsley Sheridan 1751–1816: *The School for
  Scandal* (1777)

9 Dictionaries are like watches, the worst is better than none,
  and the best cannot be expected to go quite true.
  Samuel Johnson 1709–84: letter to Francesco Sastres,
  21 August 1784

10 Publish and be damned.
  Duke of Wellington 1769–1852: replying to Harriette
  Wilson's blackmail threat, *c.*1825; attributed

11 Though an angel should write, still 'tis *devils* must print.
  Thomas Moore 1779–1852: *The Fudges in England* (1835)

12 A good book is the best of friends, the same to-day and for
  ever.
  Martin Tupper 1810–89: *Proverbial Philosophy* Series I
  (1838) 'Of Reading'

13 Now Barabbas was a publisher.
  Thomas Campbell 1777–1844: attributed, in Samuel Smiles
  A Publisher and his Friends (1891); also attributed,
  wrongly, to Byron

14 No furniture so charming as books.
  Sydney Smith 1771–1845: in Lady Holland *Memoir* (1855)

15 Books are made not like children but like pyramids...and
  they're just as useless! and they stay in the desert!...Jackals
  piss at their foot and the bourgeois climb up on them.
  Gustave Flaubert 1821–80: letter to Ernest Feydeau,
  November/December 1857

16 'What is the use of a book', thought Alice, 'without pictures
  or conversations?'
  Lewis Carroll 1832–98: *Alice's Adventures in Wonderland*
  (1865)

17 All books are divisible into two classes, the books of the
  hour, and the books of all time.
  John Ruskin 1819–1900: *Sesame and Lilies* (1865)

18 There is no such thing as a moral or an immoral book. Books
are well written, or badly written.
   Oscar Wilde 1854–1900: *The Picture of Dorian Gray* (1891)

19 Child! do not throw this book about;
Refrain from the unholy pleasure
Of cutting all the pictures out!
   Hilaire Belloc 1870–1953: *A Bad Child's Book of Beasts*
   (1896)

20 'Classic.' A book which people praise and don't read.
   Mark Twain 1835–1910: *Following the Equator* (1897)

21 To my daughter Leonora without whose never-failing
sympathy and encouragement this book would have been
finished in half the time.
   P. G. Wodehouse 1881–1975: *The Heart of a Goof* (1926)
   dedication

22 From the moment I picked up your book until I laid it down,
I was convulsed with laughter. Some day I intend reading it.
   Groucho Marx 1895–1977: blurb written for S. J. Perelman
   Dawn Ginsberg's Revenge (1928)

23 This is an important book, the critic assumes, because it
deals with war. This is an insignificant book because it deals
with the feelings of women in a drawing-room.
   Virginia Woolf 1882–1941: *A Room of One's Own* (1929)

24 A best-seller is the gilded tomb of a mediocre talent.
   Logan Pearsall Smith 1865–1946: *Afterthoughts* (1931) 'Art
   and Letters'

25 I would sooner read a time-table or a catalogue than nothing
at all...They are much more entertaining than half the
novels that are written.
   W. Somerset Maugham 1874–1965: *Summing Up* (1938)

26 The principle of procrastinated rape is said to be the ruling
one in all the great best-sellers.
   V. S. Pritchett 1900– : *The Living Novel* (1946)

27 I have known her pass the whole evening without
mentioning a single book, or *in fact anything unpleasant*,
at all.
   Henry Reed 1914–86: *A Very Great Man Indeed* (1953 radio
   play)

28 Some books are undeservedly forgotten; none are
undeservedly remembered.
W. H. Auden 1907–73: *The Dyer's Hand* (1963) 'Reading'

29 Books do furnish a room.
Anthony Powell 1905– : title of novel (1971)

30 Far too many relied on the classic formula of a beginning,
a muddle, and an end.
Philip Larkin 1922–85: of the books entered for the 1977
Booker Prize; *New Fiction* January 1978

31 Books say: she did this because. Life says: she did this. Books
are where things are explained to you; life is where things
aren't.
Julian Barnes 1946– : *Flaubert's Parrot* (1984)

··

Bores and Boredom
··

1 The secret of being a bore...is to tell everything.
Voltaire 1694–1778: *Discours en vers sur l'homme* (1737)

2 Gentle Dullness ever loves a joke.
Alexander Pope 1688–1744: *The Dunciad* (1742)

3 He is not only dull in himself, but the cause of dullness in
others.
Samuel Foote 1720–77: of a dull law lord, in James Boswell
Life of Samuel Johnson

4 Society is now one polished horde,
Formed of two mighty tribes, the *Bores* and *Bored*.
Lord Byron 1788–1824: *Don Juan* (1819–24)

5 BORE, *n.* A person who talks when you wish him to listen.
Ambrose Bierce 1842–?1914: *Cynic's Word Book* (1906)

6 He is an old bore. Even the grave yawns for him.
Herbert Beerbohm Tree 1852–1917: of Israel Zangwill, in
Max Beerbohm *Herbert Beerbohm Tree* (1920)

7 Boredom is...a vital problem for the moralist, since half the
sins of mankind are caused by the fear of it.
Bertrand Russell 1872–1970: *The Conquest of Happiness*
(1930)

8 Millions long for immortality who don't know what to do
with themselves on a rainy Sunday afternoon.
  Susan Ertz 1894–1985: *Anger in the Sky* (1943)

9 The effect of boredom on a large scale in history is
underestimated. It is a main cause of revolutions, and would
soon bring to an end all the static Utopias and the farmyard
civilization of the Fabians.
  Dean Inge 1860–1954: *End of an Age* (1948)

10 Nothing happens, nobody comes, nobody goes, it's awful!
  Samuel Beckett 1906–89: *Waiting for Godot* (1955)

11 Nothing, like something, happens anywhere.
  Philip Larkin 1922–1985: 'I Remember, I Remember' (1955)

12 Punctuality is the virtue of the bored.
  Evelyn Waugh 1903–66: diary, 26 March 1962

13 Life, friends, is boring. We must not say so...
And moreover my mother taught me as a boy
(repeatingly) 'Ever to confess you're bored
means you have no
Inner Resources.'
  John Berryman 1914–72: *77 Dream Songs* (1964)

14 A healthy male adult bore consumes *each year* one and a half
times his own weight in other people's patience.
  John Updike 1932– : *Assorted Prose* (1965)

15 Everyone is a bore to someone. That is unimportant. The
thing to avoid is being a bore to oneself.
  Gerald Brenan 1894–1987: *Thoughts in a Dry Season* (1978)

Britain

See also **England**

1 Rule, Britannia, rule the waves;
Britons never will be slaves.
  James Thomson 1700–48: *Alfred: a Masque* (1740)

2 It must be owned, that the Graces do not seem to be natives
of Great Britain; and I doubt, the best of us here have more
of rough than polished diamond.
  Lord Chesterfield 1694–1773: *Letters to his Son* (1774)
18 November 1748

3 What is our task? To make Britain a fit country for heroes to live in.
   David Lloyd George 1863–1945: speech at Wolverhampton, 23 November 1918

4 Other nations use 'force'; we Britons alone use 'Might'.
   Evelyn Waugh 1903–66: *Scoop* (1938)

5 The British nation is unique in this respect. They are the only people who like to be told how bad things are, who like to be told the worst.
   Winston Churchill 1874–1965: speech, House of Commons, 10 June 1941

6 Britain will be honoured by historians more for the way she disposed of an empire than for the way in which she acquired it.
   Lord Harlech 1918–85: in *New York Times* 28 October 1962

7 Great Britain has lost an empire and has not yet found a role.
   Dean Acheson 1893–1971: speech at the Military Academy, West Point, 5 December 1962

8 The land of embarrassment and breakfast.
   Julian Barnes 1946– : *Flaubert's Parrot* (1984)

Broadcasting

1 Nation shall speak peace unto nation.
   Montague John Rendall 1862–1950: motto of the BBC (1927)

2 The whole Fleet's lit up. When I say 'lit up', I mean lit up by fairy lamps.
   Thomas Woodroofe 1899–1978: first live outside broadcast, Spithead Review, 20 May 1937

3 TV—a clever contraction derived from the words Terrible Vaudeville. However, it is our latest medium—we call it a medium because nothing's well done.
   Goodman Ace 1899–1982: letter to Groucho Marx, *c.*1953

4 So much chewing gum for the eyes.
   Anonymous: small boy's definition of certain television programmes, in J. B. Simpson *Best Quotes* (1957)

5 Today, thanks to technical progress, the radio and television, to which we devote so many of the leisure hours once spent listening to parlour chatter and parlour music, have succeeded in lifting the manufacture of banality out of the sphere of handicraft and placed it in that of a major industry.
   Nathalie Sarraute 1902- : *Times Literary Supplement* 10 June 1960

6 Like having your own licence to print money.
   Roy Thomson 1894–1976: on the profitability of commercial television in Britain; in R. Braddon *Roy Thomson* (1965)

7 Television has brought back murder into the home—where it belongs.
   Alfred Hitchcock 1899–1980: in *Observer* 19 December 1965

8 Television contracts the imagination and radio expands it.
   Terry Wogan 1938- : *Observer* 30 December 1984 'Sayings of the Year'

9 They [men] are happier with women who make their coffee than make their programmes.
   Denise O'Donoghue: in G. Kinnock and F. Miller *By Faith and Daring* (1993)

Bureaucracy

See also **Management**

1 Whatever was required to be done, the Circumlocution Office was beforehand with all the public departments in the art of perceiving—HOW NOT TO DO IT.
   Charles Dickens 1812–70: *Little Dorrit* (1857)

2 Where there is officialism every human relationship suffers.
   E. M. Forster 1879–1970: *A Passage to India* (1924)

3 Here lies a civil servant. He was civil
   To everyone, and servant to the devil.
   C. H. Sisson 1914- : in *The London Zoo* (1961)

4 The Civil Service is profoundly deferential—'Yes, Minister! No, Minister! If you wish it, Minister!'
   Richard Crossman 1907–74: diary, 22 October 1964

5 Guidelines for bureaucrats: (1) When in charge, ponder.
(2) When in trouble, delegate. (3) When in doubt, mumble.
   James H. Boren 1925- : in *New York Times* 8 November
   1970

6 A memorandum is written not to inform the reader but to
protect the writer.
   Dean Acheson 1893–1971: in *Wall Street Journal*
   8 September 1977

Business and Commerce

1 A merchant shall hardly keep himself from doing wrong.
   Bible (Apocrypha): Ecclesiasticus

2 Neither a borrower, nor a lender be.
   William Shakespeare 1564–1616: *Hamlet* (1601)

3 They [corporations] cannot commit treason, nor be outlawed,
nor excommunicate, for they have no souls.
   Edward Coke 1552–1634: *Reports of Sir Edward Coke* (1658)
   'The case of Sutton's Hospital'

4 A Company for carrying on an undertaking of Great
Advantage, but no one to know what it is.
   Anonymous: The South Sea Company Prospectus (1711)

5 There is nothing more requisite in business than dispatch.
   Joseph Addison 1672–1719: *The Drummer* (1716)

6 I have heard of a man who had a mind to sell his house, and
therefore carried a piece of brick in his pocket, which he
showed as a pattern to encourage purchasers.
   Jonathan Swift 1667–1745: *The Drapier's Letters* (1724)

7 Necessity never made a good bargain.
   Benjamin Franklin 1706–90: *Poor Richard's Almanac*
   (1735)

8 Remember that time is money.
   Benjamin Franklin 1706–90: *Advice to a Young Tradesman*
   (1748)

9 It is the nature of all greatness not to be exact; and great
trade will always be attended with considerable abuses.
   Edmund Burke 1729–97: *On American Taxation* (1775)

10 A nation of shop-keepers are very seldom so disinterested.
Samuel Adams 1722–1803: *Oration in Philadelphia* 1 August
1776 (of doubtful authenticity)

11 People of the same trade seldom meet together, even for
merriment and diversion, but the conversation ends in a
conspiracy against the public, or in some contrivance to raise
prices.
Adam Smith 1723–90: *Wealth of Nations* (1776)

12 To found a great empire for the sole purpose of raising up a
people of customers, may at first sight appear a project fit
only for a nation of shopkeepers. It is, however, a project
altogether unfit for a nation of shopkeepers; but extremely fit
for a nation whose government is influenced by shopkeepers.
Adam Smith 1723–90: *Wealth of Nations* (1776)

13 Here's the rule for bargains: 'Do other men, for they would
do you.' That's the true business precept.
Charles Dickens 1812–70: *Martin Chuzzlewit* (1844) Jonas
Chuzzlewit

14 It is because we put up with bad things that hotel-keepers
continue to give them to us.
Anthony Trollope 1815–82: *Orley Farm* (1862)

15 Earned a precarious living by taking in one another's
washing.
Anonymous: attributed to Mark Twain by William Morris,
in *The Commonweal* 6 August 1887

16 The growth of a large business is merely a survival of the
fittest…The American beauty rose can be produced in the
splendour and fragrance which bring cheer to its beholder
only by sacrificing the early buds which grow up around it.
John D. Rockefeller 1839–1937: in W. J. Ghent *Our
Benevolent Feudalism* (1902); 'American Beauty Rose'
became the title of a 1950 song by Hal David and others

17 The customer is never wrong.
César Ritz 1850–1918: in R. Nevill and C. E. Jerningham
Piccadilly to Pall Mall (1908)

18 The best of all monopoly profits is a quiet life.
J. R. Hicks 1904– : *Econometrica* (1935)

19 He's a man way out there in the blue, riding on a smile and
a shoeshine. And when they start not smiling back—that's an

earthquake...A salesman is got to dream, boy. It comes with
the territory.
  Arthur Miller 1915- : *Death of a Salesman* (1949)

20 For years I thought what was good for our country was good
for General Motors and vice versa.
  Charles E. Wilson 1890-1961: testimony to the Senate
  Armed Services Committee, 15 January 1953

21 Few have heard of Fra Luca Pacioli, the inventor of
double-entry book-keeping; but he has probably had much
more influence on human life than has Dante or
Michelangelo.
  Herbert J. Muller 1905- : *Uses of the Past* (1957)

22 Accountants are the witch-doctors of the modern world and
willing to turn their hands to any kind of magic.
  Lord Justice Harman 1894-1970: speech, February 1964, in
  A. Sampson *The New Anatomy of Britain* (1971)

23 [Commercialism is] doing well that which should not be done
at all.
  Gore Vidal 1925- : in *Listener* 7 August 1975

24 We even sell a pair of earrings for under £1, which is cheaper
than a prawn sandwich from Marks & Spencers. But I have
to say the earrings probably won't last as long.
  Gerald Ratner 1949- : speech to the Institute of Directors,
  Albert Hall, 23 April 1991

25 The green shoots of economic spring are appearing once
again.
  Norman Lamont 1942- : speech at Conservative Party
  Conference, 9 October 1991; often quoted 'the green shoots
  of recovery'

Careers

See also **Work**

1 For promotion cometh neither from the east, nor from the
west: nor yet from the south.
  Bible: Psalm 75

2 I hold every man a debtor to his profession.
Francis Bacon 1561-1626: *The Elements of the Common Law* (1596)

3 Thou art not for the fashion of these times,
Where none will sweat but for promotion.
William Shakespeare 1564-1616: *As You Like It* (1599)

4 It is wonderful, when a calculation is made, how little the mind is actually employed in the discharge of any profession.
Samuel Johnson 1709-84: in James Boswell *Life of Johnson* (1791) 6 April 1775

5 All professions are conspiracies against the laity.
George Bernard Shaw 1856-1950: *The Doctor's Dilemma* (1911)

6 The test of a vocation is the love of the drudgery it involves.
Logan Pearsall Smith 1865-1946: *Afterthoughts* (1931)

7 Professional men, they have no cares;
Whatever happens, they get theirs.
Ogden Nash 1902-71: 'I Yield to My Learned Brother' (1935)

8 I will undoubtedly have to seek what is happily known as gainful employment, which I am glad to say does not describe holding public office.
Dean Acheson 1893-1971: in *Time* 22 December 1952

Cats

See also **Animals**

1 When I play with my cat, who knows whether she isn't amusing herself with me more than I am with her?
Montaigne 1533-92: *Essais* (1580)

2 For I will consider my Cat Jeoffry...
For he counteracts the powers of darkness by his electrical skin and glaring eyes.
For he counteracts the Devil, who is death, by brisking about the life.
Christopher Smart 1722-71: *Jubilate Agno* (c.1758-63)

3 Cruel, but composed and bland,
Dumb, inscrutable and grand,

So Tiberius might have sat,
Had Tiberius been a cat.
  Matthew Arnold 1822–88: 'Poor Matthias' (1885)

4 He walked by himself, and all places were alike to him.
  Rudyard Kipling 1865–1936: *Just So Stories* (1902) 'The Cat
  that Walked by Himself'

5 Cats, no less liquid than their shadows,
Offer no angles to the wind.
  A. S. J. Tessimond 1902–62: *Cats* (1934)

6 The trouble with a kitten is
THAT
Eventually it becomes a
CAT.
  Ogden Nash 1902–71: 'The Kitten' (1940)

7 Cats seem to go on the principle that it never does any harm
to ask for what you want.
  Joseph Wood Krutch 1893–1970: *Twelve Seasons* (1949)

Censorship

1 As good almost kill a man as kill a good book: who kills a
man kills a reasonable creature, God's image; but he who
destroys a good book, kills reason itself, kills the image of
God, as it were in the eye.
  John Milton 1608–74: *Areopagitica* (1644)

2 I disapprove of what you say, but I will defend to the death
your right to say it.
  Voltaire 1694–1778: attributed to Voltaire, but actually
  S. G. Tallentyre's summary of Voltaire's attitude towards
  Helvétius following the burning of the latter's *De l'esprit* in
  1759; in *The Friends of Voltaire* (1907)

3 What a fuss about an omelette!
  Voltaire 1694–1778: what Voltaire *apparently* said on the
  burning of *De l'esprit*; in J. Parton *Life of Voltaire* (1881)

4 Wherever books will be burned, men also, in the end, are
burned.
  Heinrich Heine 1797–1856: *Almansor* (1823)

5 Assassination is the extreme form of censorship.
   George Bernard Shaw 1856–1950: *The Showing-Up of
   Blanco Posnet* (1911)

6 The power of the press is very great, but not so great as the
   power of suppress.
   Lord Northcliffe 1865–1922: office message, *Daily Mail*
   1918

7 It is obvious that 'obscenity' is not a term capable of exact
   legal definition; in the practice of the Courts, it means
   'anything that shocks the magistrate'.
   Bertrand Russell 1872–1970: *Sceptical Essays* (1928) 'The
   Recrudescence of Puritanism'

8 [This film] is so cryptic as to be almost meaningless. If there
   is a meaning, it is doubtless objectionable.
   British Board of Film Censors: banning Jean Cocteau's
   film *The Seashell and the Clergyman* (1929)

9 We all know that books burn—yet we have the greater
   knowledge that books can not be killed by fire. People die,
   but books never die. No man and no force can abolish
   memory. No man and no force can put thought in
   a concentration camp forever.
   Franklin D. Roosevelt 1882–1945: 'Message to the
   Booksellers of America' 6 May 1942

10 Is it a book you would even wish your wife or your servants
   to read?
   Mervyn Griffith-Jones 1909–79: of D. H. Lawrence's *Lady
   Chatterley's Lover*, while appearing for the prosecution at
   the Old Bailey; in *The Times* 21 October 1960

11 One has to multiply thoughts to the point where there aren't
   enough policemen to control them.
   Stanislaw Lec 1909–66: *Unkempt Thoughts* (1962),
   tr. J. Galazka

Certainty and Doubt

1 How long halt ye between two opinions?
   Bible: I Kings

2 Probable impossibilities are to be preferred to improbable
possibilities.
  Aristotle 384–322 BC: *Poetics*

3 Now, the melancholy god protect thee, and the tailor make
thy doublet of changeable taffeta, for thy mind is a very opal.
  William Shakespeare 1564–1616: *Twelfth Night* (1601)

4 If a man will begin with certainties, he shall end in doubts;
but if he will be content to begin with doubts, he shall end in
certainties.
  Francis Bacon 1561–1626: *The Advancement of Learning*
  (1605)

5 I wish I was as cocksure of anything as Tom Macaulay is of
everything.
  Lord Melbourne 1779–1848: in Lord Cowper's preface to
  Lord Melbourne's Papers (1889)

6 Ah, what a dusty answer gets the soul
When hot for certainties in this our life!
  George Meredith 1828–1909: *Modern Love* (1862)

7 Ten thousand difficulties do not make one doubt.
  Cardinal Newman 1801–90: *Apologia pro Vita Sua* (1864)

8 I must have a prodigious quantity of mind; it takes me as
much as a week, sometimes, to make it up.
  Mark Twain 1835–1910: *The Innocents Abroad* (1869)

9 I am too much of a sceptic to deny the possibility of
anything.
  T. H. Huxley 1825–95: letter to H. Spencer, 22 March 1886

10 There is no more miserable human being than one in whom
nothing is habitual but indecision.
  William James 1842–1910: *Principles of Psychology* (1890)

11 Oh! let us never, never doubt
What nobody is sure about!
  Hilaire Belloc 1870–1953: 'The Microbe' (1897)

12 Life is doubt,
And faith without doubt is nothing but death.
  Miguel de Unamuno 1864–1937: 'Salmo II' (1907)

13 Like all weak men he laid an exaggerated stress on not
changing one's mind.
  W. Somerset Maugham 1874–1965: *Of Human Bondage*
  (1915)

14 [The Government] go on in strange paradox, decided only to be undecided, resolved to be irresolute, adamant for drift, solid for fluidity.
   Winston Churchill 1874–1965: speech, House of Commons, 12 November 1936

15 My mind is not a bed to be made and re-made.
   James Agate 1877–1947: diary, 9 June 1943

16 I'll give you a definite maybe.
   Sam Goldwyn 1882–1974: attributed

17 The archbishop is usually to be found nailing his colours to the fence.
   Frank Field 1942– : of Archbishop Runcie; attributed in *Crockfords 1987/88* (1987)

Chance

1 Cast thy bread upon the waters: for thou shalt find it after many days.
   Bible: Ecclesiastes

2 And a certain man drew a bow at a venture, and smote the king of Israel between the joints of the harness.
   Bible: I Kings

3 But for the grace of God there goes John Bradford.
   John Bradford *c.*1510–55: on seeing a group of criminals being led to their execution; in *Dictionary of National Biography* (1917–), usually quoted 'There but for the grace of God go I'

4 There is a tide in the affairs of men,
   Which, taken at the flood, leads on to fortune;
   Omitted, all the voyage of their life
   Is bound in shallows and in miseries.
   William Shakespeare 1564–1616: *Julius Caesar* (1599)

5 The chapter of knowledge is a very short, but the chapter of accidents is a very long one.
   Lord Chesterfield 1694–1773: letter to Solomon Dayrolles, 16 February 1753

6 The best laid schemes o' mice an' men
   Gang aft a-gley.
   Robert Burns 1759–96: 'To a Mouse' (1786)

7 O! many a shaft, at random sent,
Finds mark the archer little meant!
And many a word, at random spoken,
May soothe or wound a heart that's broken.
    Sir Walter Scott 1771–1832: *The Lord of the Isles* (1813)

8 At this moment he was unfortunately called out by a person
on business from Porlock.
    Samuel Taylor Coleridge 1772–1834: 'Kubla Khan' (1816)
preliminary note, explaining why the poem remained
unfinished

9 Accidents will occur in the best-regulated families.
    Charles Dickens 1812–70: *David Copperfield* (1850) Mr
Micawber

10 I am convinced that *He* [God] does not play dice.
    Albert Einstein 1879–1955: letter to Max Born, 4 December
1926

11 Predictability: Does the flap of a butterfly's wings in Brazil
set off a tornado in Texas?
    Edward N. Lorenz: title of paper given to the American
Association for the Advancement of Science, Washington,
29 December 1979

....

Change

....

See also **Beginnings and Endings**

1 Can the Ethiopian change his skin, or the leopard his spots?
    Bible: Jeremiah

2 You can't step twice into the same river.
    Heraclitus *c.*540–*c.*480 BC: in Plato *Cratylus*

3 *Tempora mutantur, et nos mutamur in illis.*
Times change, and we change with them.
    Anonymous: in William Harrison *Description of Britain*
(1577)

4 O! swear not by the moon, the inconstant moon,
That monthly changes in her circled orb,
Lest that thy love prove likewise variable.
    William Shakespeare 1564–1616: *Romeo and Juliet* (1595)

5 He that will not apply new remedies must expect new evils;
for time is the greatest innovator.
  Francis Bacon 1561-1626: *Essays* (1625) 'Of Innovations'

6 Tomorrow to fresh woods, and pastures new.
  John Milton 1608-74: 'Lycidas' (1638)

7 When it is not necessary to change, it is necessary not to
change.
  Lucius Cary, Viscount Falkland 1610-43: 'A Speech
  concerning Episcopacy' (1641)

8 Change is not made without inconvenience, even from worse
to better.
  Samuel Johnson 1709-84: *Dictionary of the English
  Language* (1755) preface

9 If we do not find anything pleasant, at least we shall find
something new.
  Voltaire 1694-1778: *Candide* (1759)

10 Variety's the very spice of life,
That gives it all its flavour.
  William Cowper 1731-1800: *The Task* (1785) 'The
  Timepiece'

11 There is nothing stable in the world—uproar's your only
music.
  John Keats 1795-1821: letter to George and Thomas Keats,
  13 January 1818

12 There is a certain relief in change, even though it be from
bad to worse...it is often a comfort to shift one's position and
be bruised in a new place.
  Washington Irving 1783-1859: *Tales of a Traveller* (1824)

13 Let the great world spin for ever down the ringing grooves of
change.
  Alfred, Lord Tennyson 1809-92: 'Locksley Hall' (1842)

14 Change and decay in all around I see;
O Thou, who changest not, abide with me.
  Henry Francis Lyte 1793-1847: 'Abide with Me' (c.1847)

15 *Plus ça change, plus c'est la même chose.*
The more things change, the more they are the same.
  Alphonse Karr 1808-90: *Les Guêpes* January 1849

16 Wandering between two worlds, one dead,
The other powerless to be born.
    Matthew Arnold 1822–88: 'Stanzas from the Grande
Chartreuse' (1855)

17 It is best not to swap horses when crossing streams.
    Abraham Lincoln 1809–65: reply to National Union League,
9 June 1864

18 There is in all change something at once sordid and
agreeable, which smacks of infidelity and household
removals. This is sufficient to explain the French Revolution.
    Charles Baudelaire 1821–67: *Journaux intimes* (1887), tr.
Christopher Isherwood

19 The old order changeth, yielding place to new,
And God fulfils himself in many ways,
Lest one good custom should corrupt the world.
    Alfred, Lord Tennyson 1809–92: *Idylls of the King* 'The
Passing of Arthur' (1869)

20 Most of the change we think we see in life
Is due to truths being in and out of favour.
    Robert Frost 1874–1963: 'The Black Cottage' (1914)

21 All changed, changed utterly:
A terrible beauty is born.
    W. B. Yeats 1865–1939: 'Easter, 1916' (1921)

22 The whole worl's in a state o' chassis!
    Sean O'Casey 1880–1964: *Juno and the Paycock* (1925)

23 Consistency is contrary to nature, contrary to life. The only
completely consistent people are the dead.
    Aldous Huxley 1894–1963: *Do What You Will* (1929)

24 In olden days a glimpse of stocking
Was looked on as something shocking
Now, heaven knows,
Anything goes.
    Cole Porter 1891–1964: 'Anything Goes' (1934 song)

25 God, give us the serenity to accept what cannot be changed;
Give us the courage to change what should be changed;
Give us the wisdom to distinguish one from the other.
    Reinhold Niebuhr 1892–1971: prayer said to have been first
published in 1951; in R. W. Fox *Reinhold Niebuhr* (1985)

26 If we want things to stay as they are, things will have to change.
  Giuseppe di Lampedusa 1896–1957: *The Leopard* (1957)

Character

1 A man's character is his fate.
  Heraclitus *c.*540–*c.*480 BC: *On the Universe*, tr. W. H. S. Jones; see also Novalis (1772–1801) *Heinrich von Ofterdingen* (1802)

2 I see the better things, and approve; I follow the worse.
  Ovid 43 BC–AD *c.*17: *Metamorphoses*

3   Give me that man
That is not passion's slave, and I will wear him
In my heart's core, ay, in my heart of heart,
As I do thee.
  William Shakespeare 1564–1616: *Hamlet* (1601)

4   My nature is subdued
To what it works in, like the dyer's hand.
  William Shakespeare 1564–1616: sonnet 111 (1609)

5 Youth, what man's age is like to be doth show;
We may our ends by our beginnings know.
  John Denham 1615–69: 'Of Prudence' (1668)

6 A fiery soul, which working out its way,
Fretted the pigmy body to decay:
And o'er informed the tenement of clay.
  John Dryden 1631–1700: *Absalom and Achitophel* (1681)

7 She's as headstrong as an allegory on the banks of the Nile.
  Richard Brinsley Sheridan 1751–1816: *The Rivals* (1775)

8 It is not in the still calm of life, or the repose of a pacific station, that great characters are formed…Great necessities call out great virtues.
  Abigail Adams 1744–1818: letter to John Quincy Adams, 19 January 1780

9 Talent develops in quiet places, character in the full current of human life.
  Johann Wolfgang von Goethe 1749–1832: *Torquato Tasso* (1790)

10 What is character but the determination of incident? What is incident but the illustration of character?
   Henry James 1843–1916: *Partial Portraits* (1888) 'The Art of Fiction'

11 If you can fill the unforgiving minute
   With sixty seconds' worth of distance run,
   Yours is the Earth and everything that's in it,
   And—which is more—you'll be a Man, my son!
   Rudyard Kipling 1865–1936: 'If—' (1910)

12 A very weak-minded fellow I am afraid, and, like the feather pillow, bears the marks of the last person who has sat on him!
   Earl Haig 1861–1928: describing the 17th Earl of Derby in a letter to Lady Haig, 14 January 1918

13 The true index of a man's character is the health of his wife.
   Cyril Connolly 1903–74: *The Unquiet Grave* (1944)

14 It is the nature, and the advantage, of strong people that they can bring out the crucial questions and form a clear opinion about them. The weak always have to decide between alternatives that are not their own.
   Dietrich Bonhoeffer 1906–45: *Widerstand und Ergebung* (1951), tr. R. Fuller

15 He's so wet you could shoot snipe off him.
   Anthony Powell 1905– : *A Question of Upbringing* (1951)

16 If you can't stand the heat, get out of the kitchen.
   Harry Vaughan: in *Time* 28 April 1952 (associated with Harry S. Truman, but attributed by him to Vaughan, his 'military jester')

17 A thick skin is a gift from God.
   Konrad Adenauer 1876–1967: in *New York Times* 30 December 1959

18 Those who stand for nothing fall for anything.
   Alex Hamilton 1936– : 'Born Old' (radio broadcast), in *Listener* 9 November 1978

19 You can tell a lot about a fellow's character by his way of eating jellybeans.
   Ronald Reagan 1911– : in *New York Times* 15 January 1981

Charm

1 Charm...it's a sort of bloom on a woman. If you have it, you don't need to have anything else; and if you don't have it, it doesn't much matter what else you have.
J. M. Barrie 1860–1937: *What Every Woman Knows* (1908)

2 All charming people have something to conceal, usually their total dependence on the appreciation of others.
Cyril Connolly 1903–1974: *Enemies of Promise* (1938)

3 Charm is the great English blight. It does not exist outside these damp islands. It spots and kills anything it touches. It kills love, it kills art.
Evelyn Waugh 1903–66: *Brideshead Revisited* (1945)

4 Oozing charm from every pore,
He oiled his way around the floor.
Alan Jay Lerner 1918–86: 'You Did It' (1956 song)

5 You know what charm is: a way of getting the answer yes without having asked any clear question.
Albert Camus 1913–60: *The Fall* (1957)

6 What is charm then?...something extra, superfluous, unnecessary, essentially a power thrown away.
Doris Lessing 1919– : *Particularly Cats* (1967)

Children

See also **The Family, Parents, Youth**

1 Like as the arrows in the hand of the giant: even so are the young children.
Happy is the man that hath his quiver full of them.
Bible: Psalm 127

2 Train up a child in the way he should go: and when he is old, he will not depart from it.
Bible: Proverbs

3 Suffer the little children to come unto me, and forbid them not: for of such is the kingdom of God.
Bible: St Mark

4 When I was a child, I spake as a child, I understood as a child, I thought as a child: but when I became a man, I put away childish things.
Bible: I Corinthians

5 A child is owed the greatest respect; if you ever have something disgraceful in mind, don't ignore your son's tender years.
Juvenal AD c.60–c.130: *Satires*

6 It should be noted that children at play are not playing about; their games should be seen as their most serious-minded activity.
Montaigne 1533–92: *Essais* (1580)

7 My son—and what's a son? A thing begot
Within a pair of minutes, thereabout,
A lump bred up in darkness.
Thomas Kyd 1558–94: *The Spanish Tragedy* The Third Addition (1602 ed.)

8   At first the infant,
Mewling and puking in the nurse's arms.
And then the whining schoolboy, with his satchel,
And shining morning face, creeping like snail
Unwillingly to school.
William Shakespeare 1564–1616: *As You Like It* (1599)

9 How sharper than a serpent's tooth it is
To have a thankless child!
William Shakespeare 1564–1616: *King Lear* (1605–6)

10 Children sweeten labours, but they make misfortunes more bitter.
Francis Bacon 1561–1626: *Essays* (1625) 'Of Parents and Children'

11 Men are generally more careful of the breed of their horses and dogs than of their children.
William Penn 1644–1718: *Some Fruits of Solitude* (1693)

12 Behold the child, by Nature's kindly law
Pleased with a rattle, tickled with a straw.
Alexander Pope 1688–1744: *An Essay on Man* Epistle 2 (1733)

13 Alas, regardless of their doom,
The little victims play!

No sense have they of ills to come,
Nor care beyond to-day.
>   **Thomas Gray** 1716–71: *Ode on a Distant Prospect of Eton College* (1747)

14 The Child is father of the Man.
>   **William Wordsworth** 1770–1850: 'My heart leaps up when I behold' (1807)

15 A child's a plaything for an hour.
>   **Charles Lamb** 1775–1834: 'Parental Recollections' (1809); often attributed to Lamb's sister Mary

16 The place is very well and quiet and the children only scream in a low voice.
>   **Lord Byron** 1788–1824: letter to Lady Melbourne, 21 September 1813

17 In the little world in which children have their existence, whosoever brings them up, there is nothing so finely perceived and so finely felt, as injustice.
>   **Charles Dickens** 1812–70: *Great Expectations* (1861)

18 Go practise if you please
With men and women: leave a child alone
For Christ's particular love's sake!
>   **Robert Browning** 1812–89: *The Ring and the Book* (1868–9)

19 Oh, for an hour of Herod!
>   **Anthony Hope** 1863–1933: at the first night of *Peter Pan* (1904); in D. Mackail *Story of JMB* (1941)

20 Children with Hyacinth's temperament don't know better as they grow older; they merely know more.
>   **Saki (H. H. Munro)** 1870–1916: *Toys of Peace and Other Papers* (1919)

21 Childhood is the kingdom where nobody dies.
Nobody that matters, that is.
>   **Edna St Vincent Millay** 1892–1950: 'Childhood is the Kingdom where Nobody dies' (1934)

22 There is no end to the violations committed by children on children, quietly talking alone.
>   **Elizabeth Bowen** 1899–1973: *The House in Paris* (1935)

23 There is no more sombre enemy of good art than the pram in the hall.
>   **Cyril Connolly** 1903–74: *Enemies of Promise* (1938)

24 Any man who hates dogs and babies can't be all bad.
   Leo Rosten 1908- : of W. C. Fields, and often attributed to
   him, in speech at Masquers' Club dinner, 16 February 1939

25 There is always one moment in childhood when the door
   opens and lets the future in.
   Graham Greene 1904-91: *The Power and the Glory* (1940)

26 Grown-ups never understand anything for themselves, and it
   is tiresome for children to be always and forever explaining
   things to them.
   Antoine de Saint-Exupéry 1900-44: *Le Petit Prince* (1943)

27 A loud noise at one end and no sense of responsibility at the
   other.
   Monsignor Ronald Knox 1888-1957: definition of a baby
   (attributed)

28 Literature is mostly about having sex and not much about
   having children. Life is the other way round.
   David Lodge 1935- : *The British Museum is Falling Down*
   (1965)

29 One of the most obvious facts about grown-ups, to a child, is
   that they have forgotten what it is like to be a child.
   Randall Jarrell 1914-65: introduction to Christina Stead
   The Man Who Loved Children (1965)

30 A child becomes an adult when he realizes that he has
   a right not only to be right but also to be wrong.
   Thomas Szasz 1920- : *The Second Sin* (1973)

31 With the birth of each child, you lose two novels.
   Candia McWilliam 1955- : *Guardian* 5 May 1993

Choice

1 The die is cast.
   Julius Caesar 100-44 BC: at the crossing of the Rubicon, in
   Suetonius *Lives of the Caesars*

2 To be, or not to be: that is the question:
   Whether 'tis nobler in the mind to suffer
   The slings and arrows of outrageous fortune,
   Or to take arms against a sea of troubles,
   And by opposing end them?
   William Shakespeare 1564-1616: *Hamlet* (1601)

3 How happy could I be with either,
Were t'other dear charmer away!
   John Gay 1685–1732: *The Beggar's Opera* (1728)

4 You pays your money and you takes your choice.
   Punch: 1846

5 White shall not neutralize the black, nor good
Compensate bad in man, absolve him so:
Life's business being just the terrible choice.
   Robert Browning 1812–89: *The Ring and the Book* (1868–9)

6 Take care to get what you like or you will be forced to like
what you get.
   George Bernard Shaw 1856–1950: *Man and Superman*
   (1903)

7 Two roads diverged in a wood, and I—
I took the one less travelled by,
And that has made all the difference.
   Robert Frost 1874–1963: 'The Road Not Taken' (1916)

8 Between two evils, I always pick the one I never tried before.
   Mae West 1892–1980: *Klondike Annie* (1936)

9 Any colour—so long as it's black.
   Henry Ford 1863–1947: on the choice of colour for the
   Model T Ford, in A. Nevins *Ford* (1957)

10 Was there ever in anyone's life span a point free in time,
devoid of memory, a night when choice was any more than
the sum of all the choices gone before?
   Joan Didion 1934– : *Run River* (1963)

Christmas

1 She brought forth her firstborn son, and wrapped him in
swaddling clothes, and laid him in a manger; because there
was no room for them in the inn.
   Bible: St Luke

2 Welcome, all wonders in one sight!
Eternity shut in a span.
   Richard Crashaw *c.*1612–49: 'Hymn of the Nativity' (1652)

3 'Bah,' said Scrooge. 'Humbug!'
   Charles Dickens 1812–70: *A Christmas Carol* (1843)

4 I'm dreaming of a white Christmas,
Just like the ones I used to know.
   Irving Berlin 1888-1989: 'White Christmas' (1942)

5 And girls in slacks remember Dad,
And oafish louts remember Mum,
And sleepless children's hearts are glad,
And Christmas-morning bells say 'Come!'
   John Betjeman 1906-84: 'Christmas' (1954)

6 Still xmas is a good time with all those presents and good
food and i hope it will never die out or at any rate not until i
am grown up and hav to pay for it all.
   Geoffrey Willans 1911-1958 and **Ronald Searle** 1920- :
How To Be Topp (1954)

The Church

See also **Religion**

1 As often as we are mown down by you, the more we grow in
numbers; the blood of Christians is the seed.
   Tertullian AD *c.*160–*c.*225: *Apologeticus*, traditionally 'The
blood of the martyrs is the seed of the Church'

2 He cannot have God for his father who has not the church for
his mother.
   St Cyprian AD *c.*200-258: *De Ecclesiae Catholicae Unitate*

3 In old time we had treen chalices and golden priests, but now
we have treen priests and golden chalices.
   Bishop John Jewel 1522-71: *Certain Sermons Preached
Before the Queen's Majesty* (1609)

4 The nearer the Church the further from God.
   Bishop Lancelot Andrewes 1555-1626: *Of the Nativity* (1622)
Sermon 15

5 And of all plagues with which mankind are curst,
Ecclesiastic tyranny's the worst.
   Daniel Defoe 1660-1731: *The True-Born Englishman* (1701)

6 I look upon all the world as my parish.
   John Wesley 1703-91: diary, 11 June 1739

7 I never saw, heard, nor read, that the clergy were beloved in
any nation where Christianity was the religion of the

country. Nothing can render them popular, but some degree
of persecution.
> **Jonathan Swift** 1667-1745: *Thoughts on Religion* (1765)

8 What bishops like best in their clergy is a
dropping-down-deadness of manner.
> **Sydney Smith** 1771-1845: 'First Letter to Archdeacon
> Singleton, 1837'

9 She [the Roman Catholic Church] may still exist in
undiminished vigour when some traveller from New Zealand
shall, in the midst of a vast solitude, take his stand on a
broken arch of London Bridge to sketch the ruins of St
Paul's.
> **Lord Macaulay** 1800-59: *Essays* (1843) 'Von Ranke'

10 As the French say, there are three sexes—men, women, and
clergymen.
> **Sydney Smith** 1771-1845: in Lady Holland *Memoir* (1855)

11 But the churchmen fain would kill their church,
As the churches have killed their Christ.
> **Alfred, Lord Tennyson** 1809-92: *Maud* (1855)

12 'The Church is an anvil which has worn out many hammers',
and the story of the first collision is, in essentials, the story
of all.
> **Alexander Maclaren** 1826-1910: *Expositions of Holy
> Scripture: Acts of the Apostles* (1907)

13 The Church [of England] should go forward along the path of
progress and be no longer satisfied only to represent the
Conservative Party at prayer.
> **Maude Royden** 1876-1956: in *The Times* 17 July 1917

14 The two dangers which beset the Church of England are good
music and bad preaching.
> **Lord Hugh Cecil** 1869-1956: in K. Rose *The Later Cecils*
> (1975)

The Cinema

See also **Acting and the Theatre**

1 The lunatics have taken charge of the asylum.
> **Richard Rowland** c.1881-1947: on the take-over of United

Artists by Charles Chaplin and others, in T. Ramsaye
A Million and One Nights (1926)

2 There is only one thing that can kill the Movies, and that is
education.
  Will Rogers 1879–1935: *Autobiography of Will Rogers* (1949)

3 Bring on the empty horses!
  Michael Curtiz 1888–1962: while directing *The Charge of
  the Light Brigade* (1936 film); in David Niven *Bring on the
  Empty Horses* (1975)

4 The trouble, Mr Goldwyn, is that you are only interested in
art and I am only interested in money.
  George Bernard Shaw 1856–1950: telegraphed version of
  the outcome of a conversation between Shaw and Sam
  Goldwyn; in A. Johnson *The Great Goldwyn* (1937)

5 If my books had been any worse, I should not have been
invited to Hollywood, and if they had been any better, I
should not have come.
  Raymond Chandler 1888–1959: letter to Charles W. Morton,
  12 December 1945

6 JOE GILLIS: You used to be in pictures. You used to be big.
NORMA DESMOND: I am big. It's the pictures that got small.
  Charles Brackett 1892–1969 and **Billy Wilder** 1906– :
  Sunset Boulevard (1950 film, with D. M. Marshman Jr.)

7 This is the biggest electric train set any boy ever had!
  Orson Welles 1915–85: of the RKO studios, in P. Noble *The
  Fabulous Orson Welles* (1956)

8 Why should people go out and pay to see bad movies when
they can stay at home and see bad television for nothing?
  Sam Goldwyn 1882–1974: in *Observer* 9 September 1956

9 Hollywood money isn't money. It's congealed snow, melts in
your hand, and there you are.
  Dorothy Parker 1893–1967: in Malcolm Cowley *Writers at
  Work* 1st Series (1958)

10 It's like kissing Hitler.
  Tony Curtis 1925– : when asked what it was like to kiss
  Marilyn Monroe; in A. Hunter *Tony Curtis* (1985)

11 Photography is truth. The cinema is truth 24 times per
second.
  Jean-Luc Godard 1930– : *Le Petit Soldat* (1960 film)

12 I seldom go to films. They are too exciting,
said the Honourable Possum.
   John Berryman 1914–72: *77 Dream Songs* (1964)

13 All I need to make a comedy is a park, a policeman and a
pretty girl.
   Charlie Chaplin 1889–1977: *My Autobiography* (1964)

14 Pictures are for entertainment, messages should be delivered
by Western Union.
   Sam Goldwyn 1882–1974: in A. Marx *Goldwyn* (1976)

15 I wouldn't say when you've seen one Western you've seen the
lot; but when you've seen the lot you get the feeling you've
seen one.
   Katharine Whitehorn 1926– : *Sunday Best* (1976) 'Decoding
the West'

16 Words are cheap. The biggest thing you can say is 'elephant'.
   Charlie Chaplin 1889–1977: on the universality of silent
films; in B. Norman *The Movie Greats* (1981)

17 'Movies should have a beginning, a middle and an end,'
harrumphed French film maker Georges Franju…'Certainly,'
replied Jean-Luc Godard. 'But not necessarily in that order.'
   Jean-Luc Godard 1930– : *Time* 14 September 1981

Civilization

1 The three great elements of modern civilization, Gunpowder,
Printing, and the Protestant Religion.
   Thomas Carlyle 1795–1881: *Critical and Miscellaneous
Essays* (1838)

2 Civilization advances by extending the number of important
operations which we can perform without thinking about
them.
   Alfred North Whitehead 1861–1947: *Introduction to
Mathematics* (1911)

3 The lamps are going out all over Europe; we shall not see
them lit again in our lifetime.
   Lord Grey of Fallodon 1862–1933: on the eve of the First
World War; *25 Years* (1925)

4 Civilization and profits go hand in hand.
  Calvin Coolidge 1872–1933: speech in New York,
  27 November 1920

5 You can't say civilization don't advance, however, for in
  every war they kill you in a new way.
  Will Rogers 1879–1935: *New York Times* 23 December 1929

6 [A journalist] asked, 'Mr Gandhi, what do you think of
  modern civilization?' And Mr Gandhi said, 'That would be
  a good idea.'
  Mahatma Gandhi 1869–1948: on arriving in England in
  1930; in E . F. Schumacher *Good Work* (1979)

7 Civilization has made the peasantry its pack animal. The
  bourgeoisie in the long run only changed the form of the
  pack.
  Leon Trotsky 1879–1940: *History of the Russian Revolution*
  (1933)

8 Whenever I hear the word culture...I release the safety-catch
  of my Browning!
  Hanns Johst 1890–1978: *Schlageter* (1933) often attributed to
  Hermann Goering, and quoted 'Whenever I hear the word
  culture, I reach for my pistol!'

9 Disinterested intellectual curiosity is the life-blood of real
  civilization.
  G. M. Trevelyan 1876–1962: *English Social History* (1942)

10 In Italy for thirty years under the Borgias they had warfare,
  terror, murder, bloodshed—they produced Michelangelo,
  Leonardo da Vinci and the Renaissance. In Switzerland they
  had brotherly love, five hundred years of democracy and
  peace and what did that produce...? The cuckoo clock.
  Orson Welles 1915–85: *The Third Man* (1949 film); words
  added by Welles to Graham Greene's screenplay

Class

1 When Adam dalfe and Eve spane...
  Where was than the pride of man?
  Richard Rolle de Hampole *c.*1290–1349: in G. G. Perry
  Religious Pieces (1914). Taken in the form 'When Adam
  delved and Eve span, who was then the gentleman?' by

John Ball as the text of his revolutionary sermon on the
outbreak of the Peasants' Revolt, 1381

2 Take but degree away, untune that string,
And, hark! what discord follows.
   William Shakespeare 1564–1616: *Troilus and Cressida*
   (1602)

3 That in the captain's but a choleric word,
Which in the soldier is flat blasphemy.
   William Shakespeare 1564–1616: *Measure for Measure*
   (1604)

4 He told me…that mine was the middle state, or what might
be called the upper station of low life, which he had found by
long experience was the best state in the world, the most
suited to human happiness.
   Daniel Defoe 1660–1731: *Robinson Crusoe* (1719)

5 O let us love our occupations,
Bless the squire and his relations,
Live upon our daily rations,
And always know our proper stations.
   Charles Dickens 1812–70: *The Chimes* (1844)

6 The history of all hitherto existing society is the history of
class struggles.
   Karl Marx 1818–83 and **Friedrich Engels** 1820–95: *The
   Communist Manifesto* (1848)

7 The proletarians have nothing to lose but their chains. They
have a world to win. WORKING MEN OF ALL COUNTRIES, UNITE!
   Karl Marx 1818–83 and **Friedrich Engels** 1820–95: *The
   Communist Manifesto* (1848); tr. S. Moore, 1888, commonly
   rendered 'Workers of the world, unite!'

8 The rich man in his castle,
The poor man at his gate,
God made them, high or lowly,
And ordered their estate.
   Cecil Frances Alexander 1818–95: 'All Things Bright and
   Beautiful' (1848)

9 *Il faut épater le bourgeois.*
One must astonish the bourgeois.
   Charles Baudelaire 1821–67: attributed

10 The State is an instrument in the hands of the ruling class,
used to break the resistance of the adversaries of that class.
    Joseph Stalin 1879–1953: *Foundations of Leninism* (1924)

11 The bourgeois prefers comfort to pleasure, convenience to
liberty, and a pleasant temperature to the deathly inner
consuming fire.
    Hermann Hesse 1877–1962: *Der Steppenwolf* (1927)

12 Like many of the Upper Class
He liked the Sound of Broken Glass.
    Hilaire Belloc 1870–1953: 'About John' (1930)

13 We of the sinking middle class…may sink without further
struggles into the working class where we belong, and
probably when we get there it will not be so dreadful as we
feared, for, after all, we have nothing to lose but our aitches.
    George Orwell 1903–50: *The Road to Wigan Pier* (1937)

14 The Stately Homes of England,
How beautiful they stand,
To prove the upper classes
Have still the upper hand.
    Noël Coward 1899–1973: 'The Stately Homes of England'
(1938 song).

15 You can be in the Horseguards and still be common, dear.
    Terence Rattigan 1911–77: *Separate Tables* (1954)

16 Impotence and sodomy are socially O.K. but birth control is
flagrantly middle-class.
    Evelyn Waugh 1903–66: 'An Open Letter' in Nancy Mitford
(ed.) *Noblesse Oblige* (1956)

17 First you take their faces from 'em by calling 'em the masses
and then you accuse 'em of not having any faces.
    J. B. Priestley 1894–1984: *Saturn Over the Water* (1961)

Commerce see Business and Commerce

Conscience

1 Every subject's duty is the king's; but every subject's soul is
his own.
    William Shakespeare 1564–1616: *Henry V* (1599)

2 Thus conscience doth make cowards of us all.
   William Shakespeare 1564-1616: *Hamlet* (1601)

3 We have erred, and strayed from thy ways like lost sheep. We
   have followed too much the devices and desires of our own
   hearts.
   Book of Common Prayer 1662: *Morning Prayer*

4 Corporations have neither bodies to be punished, nor souls to
   be condemned, they therefore do as they like.
   Edward, 1st Baron Thurlow 1731-1806: in J. Poynder
   Literary Extracts (1844), usually quoted 'Did you ever
   expect a corporation to have a conscience, when it has no
   soul to be damned, and no body to be kicked?'

5 Conscience is thoroughly well-bred and soon leaves off
   talking to those who do not wish to hear it.
   Samuel Butler 1835-1902: *Further Extracts from Notebooks*
   (1934)

6 Conscience: the inner voice which warns us that someone
   may be looking.
   H. L. Mencken 1880-1956: *A Little Book in C major* (1916)

7 Most people sell their souls, and live with a good conscience
   on the proceeds.
   Logan Pearsall Smith 1865-1946: *Afterthoughts* (1931)
   'Other People'

8 I cannot and will not cut my conscience to fit this year's
   fashions.
   Lillian Hellman 1905-84: letter to John S. Wood, 19 May
   1952

Conversation

See also **Speech and Speeches**

1 Religion is by no means a proper subject of conversation in a
   mixed company.
   Lord Chesterfield 1694-1773: *Letters... to his Godson and
   Successor* (1890)

2 John Wesley's conversation is good, but he is never at
   leisure. He is always obliged to go at a certain hour. This is

very disagreeable to a man who loves to fold his legs and
have out his talk, as I do.
  Samuel Johnson 1709–84: in James Boswell *Life of Johnson*
  (1791) 31 March 1778

3 On every formal visit a child ought to be of the party, by way
of provision for discourse.
  Jane Austen 1775–1817: *Sense and Sensibility* (1811)

4 From politics, it was an easy step to silence.
  Jane Austen 1775–1817: *Northanger Abbey* (1818)

5 He talked on for ever; and you wished him to talk on for
ever.
  William Hazlitt 1778–1830: of Coleridge; *Lectures on the
  English Poets* (1818)

6 He has occasional flashes of silence, that make his
conversation perfectly delightful.
  Sydney Smith 1771–1845: of Macaulay; in Lady Holland
  Memoir (1855)

7 'The time has come,' the Walrus said,
'To talk of many things:
Of shoes—and ships—and sealing wax—
Of cabbages—and kings.
  Lewis Carroll 1832–98: *Through the Looking-Glass* (1872)

8 He speaks to Me as if I was a public meeting.
  Queen Victoria 1819–1901: of Gladstone, in G. W. E. Russell
  Collections and Recollections (1898)

9 Most English talk is a quadrille in a sentry-box.
  Henry James 1843–1916: *The Awkward Age* (1899)

Cooperation

1 Is not a Patron, my Lord, one who looks with unconcern on a
man struggling for life in the water, and, when he has
reached ground, encumbers him with help?
  Samuel Johnson 1709–84: letter to Lord Chesterfield,
  7 February 1755

2 When bad men combine, the good must associate; else they
  will fall, one by one, an unpitied sacrifice in a contemptible
  struggle.
    Edmund Burke 1729–97: *Thoughts on the Cause of the
    Present Discontents* (1770)

3 We must indeed all hang together, or, most assuredly, we
  shall all hang separately.
    Benjamin Franklin 1706–90: at the Signing of the
    Declaration of Independence, 4 July 1776 (possibly not
    original)

4 All for one, one for all.
    Alexandre Dumas 1802–70: *Les Trois Mousquetaires* (1844)

5 You may call it combination, you may call it the accidental
  and fortuitous concurrence of atoms.
    Lord Palmerston 1784–1865: on a projected
    Palmerston–Disraeli coalition, House of Commons, 5 March
    1857

6 My apple trees will never get across
  And eat the cones under his pines, I tell him.
  He only says, 'Good fences make good neighbours.'
    Robert Frost 1874–1963: 'Mending Wall' (1914)

7 We must learn to live together as brothers or perish together
  as fools.
    Martin Luther King 1929–68: speech at St Louis, 22 March
    1964

8 When Hitler attacked the Jews I was not a Jew, therefore,
  I was not concerned. And when Hitler attacked the Catholics,
  I was not a Catholic, and therefore, I was not concerned. And
  when Hitler attacked the unions and the industrialists, I was
  not a member of the unions and I was not concerned. Then,
  Hitler attacked me and the Protestant church—and there was
  nobody left to be concerned.
    Martin Niemöller 1892–1984: in *Congressional Record*
    14 October 1968

The Country and the Town

See also **Environment**

1 God made the country, and man made the town.
   William Cowper 1731–1800: *The Task* (1785) 'The Sofa'

2 'Tis distance lends enchantment to the view,
   And robes the mountain in its azure hue.
   Thomas Campbell 1777–1844: *Pleasures of Hope* (1799)

3 There is nothing good to be had in the country, or if there is,
   they will not let you have it.
   William Hazlitt 1778–1830: *The Round Table* (1817)
   'Observations on…*The Excursion*'

4 If you would be known, and not know, vegetate in a village;
   if you would know, and not be known, live in a city.
   Charles Caleb Colton *c.*1780–1832: *Lacon* (1820)

5 I have no relish for the country; it is a kind of healthy grave.
   Sydney Smith 1771–1845: letter to Miss G. Harcourt, 1838

6 But a house is much more to my mind than a tree,
   And for groves, O! a good grove of chimneys for me.
   Charles Morris 1745–1838: 'Country and Town' (1840)

7 It is my belief, Watson, founded upon my experience, that the
   lowest and vilest alleys in London do not present a more
   dreadful record of sin than does the smiling and beautiful
   countryside.
   Arthur Conan Doyle 1859–1930: *Adventures of Sherlock
   Holmes* (1892)

8 The Farmer will never be happy again;
   He carries his heart in his boots;
   For either the rain is destroying his grain
   Or the drought is destroying his roots.
   A. P. Herbert 1890–1971: 'The Farmer' (1922)

9 So *that's* what hay looks like.
   Queen Mary 1867–1953: at Badminton House, where she
   was evacuated during the Second World War; in James
   Pope-Hennessy *Life of Queen Mary* (1959)

10 An industrial worker would sooner have a £5 note but
   a countryman must have praise.
   Ronald Blythe 1922– : *Akenfield* (1969)

Courage

1 *Audentis Fortuna iuvat.*
Fortune assists the bold.
> **Virgil** 70–19 BC: *Aeneid* (often quoted 'Fortune favours the brave')

2 Cowards die many times before their deaths;
The valiant never taste of death but once.
> **William Shakespeare** 1564–1616: *Julius Caesar* (1599)

3   Boldness be my friend!
Arm me, audacity.
> **William Shakespeare** 1564–1616: *Cymbeline* (1609–10)

4 All men would be cowards if they durst.
> **John Wilmot, Earl of Rochester** 1647–80: 'A Satire against Mankind' (1679)

5 Tender-handed stroke a nettle,
And it stings you for your pains;
Grasp it like a man of mettle,
And it soft as silk remains.
> **Aaron Hill** 1685–1750: 'Verses Written on a Window in Scotland'

6 *De l'audace, et encore de l'audace, et toujours de l'audace!*
Boldness, and again boldness, and always boldness!
> **Georges Jacques Danton** 1759–94: speech to the Legislative Committee of General Defence, 2 September 1792

7 As to moral courage, I have very rarely met with two o'clock in the morning courage: I mean instantaneous courage.
> **Napoléon I** 1769–1821: in E. A. de Las Cases *Mémorial de Ste-Hélène* (1823) 4–5 December 1815

8 No coward soul is mine,
No trembler in the world's storm-troubled sphere:
I see Heaven's glories shine,
And faith shines equal, arming me from fear.
> **Emily Brontë** 1818–48: 'No coward soul is mine' (1846)

9 Better be killed than frightened to death.
> **R. S. Surtees** 1805–64: *Mr Facey Romford's Hounds* (1865)

10 Grace under pressure.
> **Ernest Hemingway** 1899–1961: when asked what he meant

by 'guts' in an interview with Dorothy Parker; in *New Yorker* 30 November 1929

11 Cowardice, as distinguished from panic, is almost always simply a lack of ability to suspend the functioning of the imagination.
Ernest Hemingway 1899–1961: *Men at War* (1942)

12 Courage is not simply *one* of the virtues but the form of every virtue at the testing point.
C. S. Lewis 1898–1963: in Cyril Connolly *The Unquiet Grave* (1944)

Crime and Punishment

See also **Justice, The Law and Lawyers, Murder**

1 I the Lord thy God am a jealous God, visiting the iniquity of the fathers upon the children unto the third and fourth generation of them that hate me.
Bible: Exodus

2 My father hath chastised you with whips, but I will chastise you with scorpions.
Bible: I Kings

3 He that spareth his rod hateth his son.
Bible: Proverbs

4 This is the first of punishments, that no guilty man is acquitted if judged by himself.
Juvenal AD *c*.60–*c*.130: *Satires*

5 I went out to Charing Cross, to see Major-general Harrison hanged, drawn, and quartered; which was done there, he looking as cheerful as any man could do in that condition.
Samuel Pepys 1633–1703: diary, 13 October 1660

6 Men are not hanged for stealing horses, but that horses may not be stolen.
George Savile, Marquess of Halifax 1633–95: *Political, Moral, and Miscellaneous Thoughts* (1750) 'Of Punishment'

7 Stolen sweets are best.
Colley Cibber 1671–1757: *The Rival Fools* (1709)

8 All punishment is mischief: all punishment in itself is evil.
Jeremy Bentham 1748–1832: *Principles of Morals and Legislation* (1789)

9 As for rioting, the old Roman way of dealing with that is always the right one; flog the rank and file, and fling the ringleaders from the Tarpeian rock.
Thomas Arnold 1795–1842: from a letter written before 1828

10 Prisoner, God has given you good abilities, instead of which you go about the country stealing ducks.
William Arabin 1773–1841: also attributed to a Revd Mr Alderson

11 They will steal the very teeth out of your mouth as you walk through the streets. *I know it from experience.*
William Arabin 1773–1841: on the citizens of Uxbridge

12 Deserves to be preached to death by wild curates.
Sydney Smith 1771–1845: in Lady Holland *Memoir* (1855)

13 In that case, if we are to abolish the death penalty, let the murderers take the first step.
Alphonse Karr 1808–90: *Les Guêpes* January 1849

14 Better build schoolrooms for 'the boy',
Than cells and gibbets for 'the man'.
Eliza Cook 1818–89: 'A Song for the Ragged Schools' (1853)

15 Thou shalt not steal; an empty feat,
When it's so lucrative to cheat.
Arthur Hugh Clough 1819–61: 'The Latest Decalogue' (1862)

16 When constabulary duty's to be done,
A policeman's lot is not a happy one.
W. S. Gilbert 1836–1911: *The Pirates of Penzance* (1879)

17 Awaiting the sensation of a short, sharp shock,
From a cheap and chippy chopper on a big black block.
W. S. Gilbert 1836–1911: *The Mikado* (1885)

18 My object all sublime
I shall achieve in time—
To let the punishment fit the crime—
The punishment fit the crime.
W. S. Gilbert 1836–1911: *The Mikado* (1885)

19 What hangs people...is the unfortunate circumstance of guilt.
  Robert Louis Stevenson 1850–94: *The Wrong Box* (with Lloyd Osbourne, 1889)

20 Singularity is almost invariably a clue. The more featureless and commonplace a crime is, the more difficult is it to bring it home.
  Arthur Conan Doyle 1859–1930: *Adventures of Sherlock Holmes* (1892)

21 Thieves respect property. They merely wish the property to become their property that they may more perfectly respect it.
  G. K. Chesterton 1874–1936: *The Man who was Thursday* (1908)

22 Anarchism is a game at which the police can beat you.
  George Bernard Shaw 1856–1950: *Misalliance* (1914)

23 For de little stealin' dey gits you in jail soon or late. For de big stealin' dey makes you Emperor and puts you in de Hall o' Fame when you croaks.
  Eugene O'Neill 1888–1953: *The Emperor Jones* (1921)

24 Any one who has been to an English public school will always feel comparatively at home in prison. It is the people brought up in the gay intimacy of the slums, Paul learned, who find prison so soul-destroying.
  Evelyn Waugh 1903–66: *Decline and Fall* (1928)

25 He always has an alibi, and one or two to spare:
At whatever time the deed took place—MACAVITY WASN'T THERE!
  T. S. Eliot 1888–1965: *Old Possum's Book of Practical Cats* (1939) 'Macavity: the Mystery Cat'

26 Even the most hardened criminal a few years ago would help an old lady across the road and give her a few quid if she was skint.
  Charlie Kray c.1930– : *Observer* 28 December 1986 'Sayings of the Year'

27 Society needs to condemn a little more and understand a little less.
  John Major 1943– : interview with *Mail on Sunday* 21 February 1993

Crises

1 For it is your business, when the wall next door catches fire.
   Horace 65–8 BC: *Epistles*

2 If you can keep your head when all about you
   Are losing theirs and blaming it on you.
   Rudyard Kipling 1865–1936: 'If—' (1910)

3 Business carried on as usual during alterations on the map of Europe.
   Winston Churchill 1874–1965: speech at Guildhall, 9 November 1914

4 Comin' in on a wing and a pray'r.
   Harold Adamson 1906–80: title of song (1943)

5 We're eyeball to eyeball, and I think the other fellow just blinked.
   Dean Rusk 1909–94 : on the Cuban missile crisis, 24 October 1962

6 Crisis? What Crisis?
   Anonymous: *Sun* headline, 11 January 1979, summarizing James Callaghan: 'I don't think other people in the world would share the view [that] there is mounting chaos'

Critics and Criticism

1 Critics are like brushers of noblemen's clothes.
   Henry Wotton 1568–1639: in Francis Bacon *Apophthegms New and Old* (1625)

2 How science dwindles, and how volumes swell,
   How commentators each dark passage shun,
   And hold their farthing candle to the sun.
   Edward Young 1683–1765: *The Love of Fame* (1725–8)

3 As learned commentators view
   In Homer more than Homer knew.
   Jonathan Swift 1667–1745: 'On Poetry' (1733)

4 You *may* abuse a tragedy, though you cannot write one. You may scold a carpenter who has made you a bad table, though you cannot make a table. It is not your trade to make tables.
   Samuel Johnson 1709-84: on literary criticism; in James Boswell *Life of Johnson* (1791) 25 June 1763

5 I have always suspected that the reading is right, which requires many words to prove it wrong; and the emendation wrong, that cannot without so much labour appear to be right.
   Samuel Johnson 1709-84: *Plays of William Shakespeare...* (1765) preface

6 A man must serve his time to every trade
   Save censure—critics all are ready made.
   Lord Byron 1788-1824: *English Bards and Scotch Reviewers* (1809)

7 This will never do.
   Francis, Lord Jeffrey 1773-1850: on Wordsworth's *The Excursion* (1814) in *Edinburgh Review* November 1814

8 I never read a book before reviewing it; it prejudices a man so.
   Sydney Smith 1771-1845: in H. Pearson *The Smith of Smiths* (1934)

9 People who like this sort of thing will find this the sort of thing they like.
   Abraham Lincoln 1809-65: judgement of a book, in G. W. E. Russell *Collections and Recollections* (1898)

10 I maintain that two and two would continue to make four, in spite of the whine of the amateur for three, or the cry of the critic for five.
   James McNeill Whistler 1834-1903: *Whistler v. Ruskin. Art and Art Critics* (1878)

11 I don't care anything about reasons, but I know what I like.
   Henry James 1843-1916: *Portrait of a Lady* (1881)

12 The good critic is he who relates the adventures of his soul in the midst of masterpieces.
   Anatole France 1844-1924: *La Vie littéraire* (1888)

13 I am sitting in the smallest room of my house. I have your review before me. In a moment it will be behind me.
   Max Reger 1873-1916: responding to a savage review by

Rudolph Louis in *Münchener Neueste Nachrichten*,
7 February 1906

14 Everything must be like something, so what is this like?
E. M. Forster 1879–1970: *Abinger Harvest* (1936)

15 Remember, a statue has never been set up in honour of
a critic!
Jean Sibelius 1865–1957: in B. de Törne *Sibelius: A Close-Up*
(1937)

16 I cry all the way to the bank.
Liberace 1919–87: on bad reviews, from the mid-1950s;
Autobiography (1973)

17 A critic is a bundle of biases held loosely together by a sense
of taste.
Whitney Balliett 1926– : *Dinosaurs in the Morning* (1962)

18 Interpretation is the revenge of the intellect upon art.
Susan Sontag 1933– : *Evergreen Review* December 1964

19 A critic is a man who knows the way but can't drive the car.
Kenneth Tynan 1927–80: in *New York Times Magazine*
9 January 1966

20 It is nice, but in one of the chapters the author made a
mistake. He describes the sun as rising twice on the same
day.
Paul Dirac 1902–84: comment on the novel *Crime and
Punishment*; in G. Gamow *Thirty Years that Shook Physics*
(1966)

Cruelty

1 This was the most unkindest cut of all.
William Shakespeare 1564–1616: *Julius Caesar* (1599)

2 I must be cruel only to be kind.
William Shakespeare 1564–1616: *Hamlet* (1601)

3 Man's inhumanity to man
Makes countless thousands mourn!
Robert Burns 1759–96: 'Man was made to Mourn' (1786)

4 A robin red breast in a cage
Puts all Heaven in a rage.
William Blake 1757–1827: 'Auguries of Innocence' (c.1803)

5 The infliction of cruelty with a good conscience is a delight
   to moralists. That is why they invented Hell.
     Bertrand Russell 1872–1970: *Sceptical Essays* (1928)

6 The wish to hurt, the momentary intoxication with pain, is
   the loophole through which the pervert climbs into the minds
   of ordinary men.
     Jacob Bronowski 1908–74: *The Face of Violence* (1954)

Custom and Habit

1 But to my mind,—though I am native here,
   And to the manner born,—it is a custom
   More honoured in the breach than the observance.
     William Shakespeare 1564–1616: *Hamlet* (1601)

2 Actions receive their tincture from the times,
   And as they change are virtues made or crimes.
     Daniel Defoe 1660–1731: *A Hymn to the Pillory* (1703)

3 Custom, then, is the great guide of human life.
     David Hume 1711–76: *An Enquiry Concerning Human
     Understanding* (1748)

4 Custom reconciles us to everything.
     Edmund Burke 1729–97: *On the Sublime and Beautiful* (1757)

5 Habit with him was all the test of truth,
   'It must be right: I've done it from my youth.'
     George Crabbe 1754–1832: *The Borough* (1810)

6 The tradition of all the dead generations weighs like a
   nightmare on the brain of the living.
     Karl Marx 1818–83: *The Eighteenth Brumaire of Louis
     Bonaparte* (1852)

7 Sow an act, and you reap a habit. Sow a habit and you reap a
   character. Sow a character, and you reap a destiny.
     Charles Reade 1814–84: attributed

8 Tradition means giving votes to the most obscure of all
   classes, our ancestors. It is the democracy of the dead.
     G. K. Chesterton 1874–1936: *Orthodoxy* (1908)

9 Every public action, which is not customary, either is wrong, or, if it is right, is a dangerous precedent. It follows that nothing should ever be done for the first time.
Francis M. Cornford 1874–1943: *Microcosmographia Academica* (1908)

10 One can't carry one's father's corpse about everywhere.
Guillaume Apollinaire 1880–1918: on tradition, in *Les peintres cubistes* (1965)

11 Habit is a great deadener.
Samuel Beckett 1906–89: *Waiting for Godot* (1955)

Cynicism

1 Paris is well worth a mass.
Henri IV 1553–1610: attributed to Henri IV; alternatively to his minister Sully, in conversation with him

2 What makes all doctrines plain and clear?
About two hundred pounds a year.
And that which was proved true before,
Prove false again? Two hundred more.
Samuel Butler 1612–80: *Hudibras* pt. 3 (1680)

3 Never glad confident morning again!
Robert Browning 1812–89: 'The Lost Leader' (1845)

4 Cynicism is intellectual dandyism without the coxcomb's feathers.
George Meredith 1828–1909: *The Egoist* (1879)

5 A man who knows the price of everything and the value of nothing.
Oscar Wilde 1854–1900: definition of a cynic; *Lady Windermere's Fan* (1892)

6 Pathos, piety, courage—they exist, but are identical, and so is filth. Everything exists, nothing has value.
E. M. Forster 1879–1970: *A Passage to India* (1924)

7 Cynicism is an unpleasant way of saying the truth.
Lillian Hellman 1905–1984: *The Little Foxes* (1939)

Dance

1 This wondrous miracle did Love devise,
  For dancing is love's proper exercise.
  > **Sir John Davies** 1569-1626: 'Orchestra, or a Poem of
  > Dancing' (1596)

2 A dance is a measured pace, as a verse is a measured speech.
  > **Francis Bacon** 1561-1626: *The Advancement of Learning*
  > (1605)

3 Sport that wrinkled Care derides,
  And Laughter holding both his sides.
  Come, and trip it as ye go
  On the light fantastic toe.
  > **John Milton** 1608-74: 'L'Allegro' (1645)

4 On with the dance! let joy be unconfined;
  No sleep till morn, when Youth and Pleasure meet
  To chase the glowing Hours with flying feet.
  > **Lord Byron** 1788-1824: *Childe Harold's Pilgrimage* (1812-18)

5 Everyone knows that the real business of a ball is either to
  look out for a wife, to look after a wife, or to look after
  somebody else's wife.
  > **R. S. Surtees** 1805-64: *Mr Facey Romford's Hounds* (1865)

6 O body swayed to music, O brightening glance
  How can we know the dancer from the dance?
  > **W. B. Yeats** 1865-1939: 'Among School Children' (1928)

7 Can't act. Slightly bald. Also dances.
  > **Anonymous**: studio official's comment on Fred Astaire, in
  > B. Thomas *Astaire* (1985)

8 There may be trouble ahead,
  But while there's moonlight and music and love and
    romance,
  Let's face the music and dance.
  > **Irving Berlin** 1888-1989: 'Let's Face the Music and Dance'
  > (1936)

9 [Dancing is] a perpendicular expression of a horizontal
  desire.
  > **George Bernard Shaw** 1856-1950: in *New Statesman*
  > 23 March 1962 (attributed)

10 But the zest goes out of a beautiful waltz
When you dance it bust to bust.
   Joyce Grenfell 1910–79: 'Stately as a Galleon' (1978 song)

Day and Night

1 The gaudy, blabbing, and remorseful day
Is crept into the bosom of the sea.
   William Shakespeare 1564–1616: *Henry VI, Part 2* (1592)

2 Night's candles are burnt out, and jocund day
Stands tiptoe on the misty mountain tops.
   William Shakespeare 1564–1616: *Romeo and Juliet* (1595)

3 But, look, the morn, in russet mantle clad,
Walks o'er the dew of yon high eastern hill.
   William Shakespeare 1564–1616: *Hamlet* (1601)

4 Dear Night! this world's defeat;
The stop to busy fools; care's check and curb.
   Henry Vaughan 1622–95: *Silex Scintillans* (1650–5)

5 Lighten our darkness, we beseech thee, O Lord; and by thy
great mercy defend us from all perils and dangers of this
night.
   Book of Common Prayer 1662: *Evening Prayer*

6 The curfew tolls the knell of parting day,
The lowing herd wind slowly o'er the lea,
The ploughman homeward plods his weary way,
And leaves the world to darkness and to me.
   Thomas Gray 1716–71: *Elegy Written in a Country
   Churchyard* (1751)

7 The Sun's rim dips; the stars rush out;
At one stride comes the dark.
   Samuel Taylor Coleridge 1772–1834: 'The Rime of the
   Ancient Mariner' (1798)

8 When I behold, upon the night's starred face
Huge cloudy symbols of a high romance.
   John Keats 1795–1821: 'When I have fears that I may cease
   to be' (written 1818)

9 The cares that infest the day
Shall fold their tents, like the Arabs,
And as silently steal away.
   Henry Wadsworth Longfellow 1807–82: 'The Day is Done'
   (1844)

10 The splendour falls on castle walls
And snowy summits old in story:
The long light shakes across the lakes,
And the wild cataract leaps in glory.
   Alfred, Lord Tennyson 1809–92: *The Princess* (1847) song
   (added 1850)

11 There midnight's all a glimmer, and noon a purple glow,
And evening full of the linnet's wings.
   W. B. Yeats 1865–1939: 'The Lake Isle of Innisfree' (1892)

12 Summer afternoon—summer afternoon…the two most
beautiful words in the English language.
   Henry James 1843–1916: in Edith Wharton *A Backward
   Glance* (1934)

13 Let us go then, you and I,
When the evening is spread out against the sky
Like a patient etherized upon a table.
   T. S. Eliot 1888–1965: 'Love Song of J. Alfred Prufrock'
   (1917)

14 The winter evening settles down
With smell of steaks in passageways.
Six o'clock.
The burnt-out ends of smoky days.
   T. S. Eliot 1888–1965: 'Preludes' (1917)

15 I have a horror of sunsets, they're so romantic, so operatic.
   Marcel Proust 1871–1922: *Cities of the Plain* (1922)

16 What are days for?
Days are where we live.
   Philip Larkin 1922–85: 'Days' (1964)

Death

See also **Epitaphs, Last Words, Murder**

1 I would rather be tied to the soil as another man's serf, even
a poor man's, who hadn't much to live on himself, than be
King of all these the dead and destroyed.
   Homer 8th century BC: *The Odyssey*

2 For dust thou art, and unto dust shalt thou return.
   Bible: Genesis

3 He died in a good old age, full of days, riches, and honour.
   Bible: I Chronicles

4 *Non omnis moriar.*
I shall not altogether die.
   Horace 65–8 BC: *Odes*

5 O death, where is thy sting? O grave, where is thy victory?
   Bible: I Corinthians

6 And I looked, and behold a pale horse: and his name that sat
on him was Death.
   Bible: Revelation

7 *Abiit ad plures.*
He's gone to join the majority [the dead].
   Petronius d. AD 65: *Satyricon*

8 Anyone can stop a man's life, but no one his death; a
thousand doors open on to it.
   Seneca ('the Younger') c.4 BC–AD 65: *Phoenissae*

9 With thanks to God we know the way to heaven, to be as
ready by water as by land, and therefore we care not which
way we go.
   Friar Elstow: when threatened with drowning by Henry
   VIII; in John Stow *Annals of England* (1615)

10 Let's talk of graves, of worms, and epitaphs;
Make dust our paper, and with rainy eyes
Write sorrow on the bosom of the earth.
Let's choose executors, and talk of wills.
   William Shakespeare 1564–1616: *Richard II* (1595)

11 I care not; a man can die but once; we owe God a death.
   William Shakespeare 1564–1616: *Henry IV, Part 2* (1597)

12 Brightness falls from the air;
Queens have died young and fair;
Dust hath closed Helen's eye.
I am sick, I must die.
   Lord have mercy on us.
   Thomas Nashe 1567–1601: *Summer's Last Will and
   Testament* (1600)

13   To die, to sleep;
To sleep: perchance to dream: ay, there's the rub;
For in that sleep of death what dreams may come
When we have shuffled off this mortal coil,
Must give us pause.
   William Shakespeare 1564–1616: *Hamlet* (1601)

14   Nothing in his life
Became him like the leaving it.
   William Shakespeare 1564–1616: *Macbeth* (1606)

15 Death be not proud, though some have called thee
Mighty and dreadful, for thou art not so.
   John Donne 1572–1631: 'Death, be not proud' (1609)

16 One short sleep past, we wake eternally,
And death shall be no more; Death thou shalt die.
   John Donne 1572–1631: 'Death, be not proud' (1609)

17 He that dies pays all debts.
   William Shakespeare 1564–1616: *The Tempest* (1611)

18 O eloquent, just, and mighty Death!…thou hast drawn
together all the farstretched greatness, all the pride, cruelty,
and ambition of man, and covered it all over with these two
narrow words, *Hic jacet* [Here lies].
   Walter Ralegh *c.*1552–1618: *The History of the World* (1614)

19 'Tis a sharp remedy, but a sure one for all ills.
   Walter Ralegh *c.*1552–1618: on feeling the edge of the axe
   prior to his execution

20 I know death hath ten thousand several doors
For men to take their exits.
   John Webster *c.*1580–*c.*1625: *The Duchess of Malfi* (1623)

21 Any man's death diminishes me, because I am involved in
Mankind; And therefore never send to know for whom the
bell tolls; it tolls for thee.
   John Donne 1572–1631: *Devotions upon Emergent Occasions*
   (1624)

22 Revenge triumphs over death; love slights it; honour aspireth to it; grief flieth to it.
Francis Bacon 1561–1626: *Essays* (1625) 'Of Death'

23   How little room
Do we take up in death, that, living know
No bounds?
James Shirley 1596–1666: *The Wedding* (1629)

24 One dies only once, and it's for such a long time!
Molière 1622–73: *Le Dépit amoureux* (performed 1656)

25 The long habit of living indisposeth us for dying.
Sir Thomas Browne 1605–82: *Hydriotaphia* (Urn Burial, 1658)

26 Forasmuch as it hath pleased Almighty God of his great mercy to take unto himself the soul of our dear brother here departed, we therefore commit his body to the ground; earth to earth, ashes to ashes, dust to dust; in sure and certain hope of the Resurrection to eternal life.
Book of Common Prayer 1662: *The Burial of the Dead*

27 In the midst of life we are in death.
Book of Common Prayer 1662: *The Burial of the Dead*

28 We shall die alone.
Blaise Pascal 1623–62: *Pensées* (1670)

29 Death never takes the wise man by surprise; he is always ready to go.
Jean de la Fontaine 1621–95: *Fables* (1678–9) 'La Mort et le Mourant'

30 They that die by famine die by inches.
Matthew Henry 1662–1714: *Exposition on the Old and New Testament* (1710)

31 Can storied urn or animated bust
Back to its mansion call the fleeting breath?
Thomas Gray 1716–71: *Elegy Written in a Country Churchyard* (1751)

32 The bodies of those that made such a noise and tumult when alive, when dead, lie as quietly among the graves of their neighbours as any others.
Jonathan Edwards 1703–58: sermon on procrastination, *Miscellaneous Discourses*

33 Depend upon it, Sir, when a man knows he is to be hanged in a fortnight, it concentrates his mind wonderfully.
   Samuel Johnson 1709–84: in James Boswell *Life of Johnson* (1791) 19 September 1777

34   The good die first,
And they whose hearts are dry as summer dust
Burn to the socket.
   William Wordsworth 1770–1850: *The Excursion* (1814)

35 Now more than ever seems it rich to die,
To cease upon the midnight with no pain.
   John Keats 1795–1821: 'Ode to a Nightingale' (1820)

36 The cemetery is an open space among the ruins, covered in winter with violets and daisies. It might make one in love with death, to think that one should be buried in so sweet a place.
   Percy Bysshe Shelley 1792–1822: *Adonais* (1821) preface

37 From the contagion of the world's slow stain
He is secure, and now can never mourn
A heart grown cold, a head grown grey in vain.
   Percy Bysshe Shelley 1792–1822: *Adonais* (1821)

38 Death must be distinguished from dying, with which it is often confused.
   Sydney Smith 1771–1845: in H. Pearson *The Smith of Smiths* (1934)

39 And all our calm is in that balm—
Not lost but gone before.
   Caroline Norton 1808–77: 'Not Lost but Gone Before'.

40 For though from out our bourne of time and place
The flood may bear me far,
I hope to see my pilot face to face
When I have crossed the bar.
   Alfred, Lord Tennyson 1809–92: 'Crossing the Bar' (1889)

41 Death is nothing at all; it does not count. I have only slipped away into the next room.
   Henry Scott Holland 1847–1918: sermon preached on Whitsunday, 1910

42 If I should die, think only this of me:
That there's some corner of a foreign field
That is for ever England.
   Rupert Brooke 1887–1915: 'The Soldier' (1914)

43 Blow out, you bugles, over the rich Dead!
There's none of these so lonely and poor of old,
But, dying, has made us rarer gifts than gold.
  Rupert Brooke 1887–1915: 'The Dead' (1914)

44 The pallor of girls' brows shall be their pall;
Their flowers the tenderness of patient minds,
And each slow dusk a drawing-down of blinds.
  Wilfred Owen 1893–1918: 'Anthem for Doomed Youth'
  (written 1917)

45 Webster was much possessed by death
And saw the skull beneath the skin.
  T. S. Eliot 1888–1965: 'Whispers of Immortality' (1919)

46 The dead don't die. They look on and help.
  D. H. Lawrence 1885–1930: letter to J. Middleton Murry,
  2 February 1923

47 A man's dying is more the survivors' affair than his own.
  Thomas Mann 1875–1955: *The Magic Mountain* (1924), tr. H.
  T. Lowe-Porter

48 To die will be an awfully big adventure.
  J. M. Barrie 1860–1937: *Peter Pan* (1928)

49 Nor dread nor hope attend
A dying animal;
A man awaits his end
Dreading and hoping all.
  W. B. Yeats 1865–1939: 'Death' (1933)

50 He knows death to the bone—
Man has created death.
  W. B. Yeats 1865–1939: 'Death' (1933)

51 Though lovers be lost love shall not;
And death shall have no dominion.
  Dylan Thomas 1914–53: 'And death shall have no dominion'
  (1936)

52 Guns aren't lawful;
Nooses give;
Gas smells awful;
You might as well live.
  Dorothy Parker 1893–1967: 'Résumé' (1937)

53 Kill a man, and you are an assassin. Kill millions of men,
and you are a conqueror. Kill everyone, and you are a god.
  Jean Rostand 1894–1977: *Pensées d'un biologiste* (1939)

54 For here the lover and killer are mingled
who had one body and one heart.
And death, who had the soldier singled
has done the lover mortal hurt.
　　Keith Douglas 1920–44: 'Vergissmeinnicht, 1943'

55 [Death is] nature's way of telling you to slow down.
　　Anonymous: life insurance proverb; in *Newsweek* 25 April
　　1960

56 A suicide kills two people, Maggie, that's what it's for!
　　Arthur Miller 1915– : *After the Fall* (1964)

57 Let me die a youngman's death
Not a clean & in-between-
The-sheets, holy-water death.
　　Roger McGough 1937– : 'Let Me Die a Youngman's Death'
　　(1967)

58 This parrot is no more! It has ceased to be! It's expired and
gone to meet its maker! This is a late parrot! It's a stiff!
Bereft of life it rests in peace—if you hadn't nailed it to the
perch it would be pushing up the daisies! It's rung down the
curtain and joined the choir invisible! THIS IS AN EX-PARROT!
　　Graham Chapman 1941–89 et al.: *Monty Python's Flying
　　Circus* (BBC TV programme,1969)

59 If there wasn't death, I think you couldn't go on.
　　Stevie Smith 1902–71: in *Observer* 9 November 1969

60 I don't want to achieve immortality through my work…
I want to achieve it through not dying.
　　Woody Allen 1935– : epigraph to Eric Lax *Woody Allen
　　and his Comedy* (1975)

61 It's not that I'm afraid to die. I just don't want to be there
when it happens.
　　Woody Allen 1935– : *Death* (1975)

62 Death has got something to be said for it:
There's no need to get out of bed for it.
　　Kingsley Amis 1922– : 'Delivery Guaranteed' (1979)

63 However many ways there may be of being alive, it is certain
that there are vastly more ways of being dead.
　　Richard Dawkins 1941– : *The Blind Watchmaker* (1986)

Democracy

See also **Minorities and Majorities, Politics, Voting**

1 I never could believe that Providence had sent a few men into the world, ready booted and spurred to ride, and millions ready saddled and bridled to be ridden.
   Richard Rumbold c.1622–85: on the scaffold, in T. B. Macaulay *History of England* vol. 1 (1849)

2 One man shall have one vote.
   John Cartwright 1740–1824: *The People's Barrier Against Undue Influence* (1780)

3 Fourscore and seven years ago our fathers brought forth upon this continent a new nation, conceived in liberty, and dedicated to the proposition that all men are created equal...We here highly resolve that the dead shall not have died in vain, that this nation, under God, shall have a new birth of freedom; and that government of the people, by the people, and for the people, shall not perish from the earth.
   Abraham Lincoln 1809–65: address at the Dedication of the National Cemetery at Gettysburg, 19 November 1863; the Lincoln Memorial inscription reads 'by the people, for the people'

4 All the world over, I will back the masses against the classes.
   W. E. Gladstone 1809–98: speech in Liverpool, 28 June 1886

5 Democracy substitutes election by the incompetent many for appointment by the corrupt few.
   George Bernard Shaw 1856–1950: *Man and Superman* (1903)

6 The world must be made safe for democracy.
   Woodrow Wilson 1856–1924: speech to Congress, 2 April 1917

7 All the ills of democracy can be cured by more democracy.
   Alfred Emanuel Smith 1873–1944: speech, 27 June 1933

8 Democracy is the recurrent suspicion that more than half of the people are right more than half of the time.
   E. B. White 1899–1985: *New Yorker* 3 July 1944

9 Man's capacity for justice makes democracy possible, but man's inclination to injustice makes democracy necessary.
   Reinhold Niebuhr 1892–1971: *Children of Light and Children of Darkness* (1944)

10 Democracy is the worst form of Government except all those other forms that have been tried from time to time.
   Winston Churchill 1874–1965: speech, House of Commons, 11 November 1947

11 After each war there is a little less democracy to save.
   Brooks Atkinson 1894–1984: *Once Around the Sun* (1951)

12 So Two cheers for Democracy: one because it admits variety and two because it permits criticism. Two cheers are quite enough: there is no occasion to give three. Only Love the Beloved Republic deserves that.
   E. M. Forster 1879–1970: *Two Cheers for Democracy* (1951)
   'Love, the beloved republic' borrowed from Swinburne's poem 'Hertha'

13 Democracy means government by discussion, but it is only effective if you can stop people talking.
   Clement Attlee 1883–1967: speech at Oxford, 14 June 1957

14 For many Chinese, the Russian lesson appears to be that only after a nation achieves a relatively high level of economic prosperity can it afford the fruit and peril of democracy.
   Xiao-Huang Yin: in *Independent* 8 October 1993

Despair see Hope and Despair

Determination

1 Thought shall be the harder, heart the keener, courage the greater, as our might lessens.
   Anonymous: *The Battle of Maldon* (*c.*1000), tr. R. K. Gordon

2 The drop of rain maketh a hole in the stone, not by violence, but by oft falling.
   Hugh Latimer *c.*1485–1555: *Second Sermon preached before the King's Majesty* (19 April 1549)

3   Perseverance, dear my lord,
Keeps honour bright.
> **William Shakespeare** 1564–1616: *Troilus and Cressida*
> (1602)

4 'Tis known by the name of perseverance in a good
cause,—and of obstinacy in a bad one.
> **Laurence Sterne** 1713–68: *Tristram Shandy* (1759–67)

5   That which we are, we are;
One equal temper of heroic hearts,
Made weak by time and fate, but strong in will
To strive, to seek, to find, and not to yield.
> **Alfred, Lord Tennyson** 1809–92: 'Ulysses' (1842)

6 Say not the struggle naught availeth,
The labour and the wounds are vain,
The enemy faints not, nor faileth,
And as things have been, things remain.
> **Arthur Hugh Clough** 1819–61: 'Say not the struggle naught
> availeth' (1855)

7 I am the master of my fate:
I am the captain of my soul.
> **W. E. Henley** 1849–1903: 'Invictus. In Memoriam R.T.H.B.'
> (1888)

8 Under the bludgeonings of chance
My head is bloody, but unbowed.
> **W. E. Henley** 1849–1903: 'Invictus. In Memoriam R.T.H.B.'
> (1888)

9 One who never turned his back but marched breast forward,
Never doubted clouds would break,
Never dreamed, though right were worsted, wrong would
    triumph,
Held we fall to rise, are baffled to fight better,
Sleep to wake.
> **Robert Browning** 1812–89: *Asolando* (1889)

10 Fanaticism consists in redoubling your effort when you have
forgotten your aim.
> **George Santayana** 1863–1952: *The Life of Reason* (1905)

11 The best way out is always through.
> **Robert Frost** 1874–1963: 'A Servant to Servants' (1914)

12 Pick yourself up,
Dust yourself off,
Start all over again.
Dorothy Fields 1905–74: 'Pick Yourself Up' (1936 song)

13 *Nil carborundum illegitimi.*
Anonymous: cod Latin for 'Don't let the bastards grind you
down', in circulation during the Second World War, though
possibly of earlier origin

14 When the going gets tough, the tough get going.
Joseph P. Kennedy 1888–1969: in J. H. Cutler *Honey Fitz*
(1962); also attributed to Knute Rockne

Diaries

1 And so I betake myself to that course, which is almost as
much as to see myself go into my grave—for which, and all
the discomforts that will accompany my being blind, the good
God prepare me!
Samuel Pepys 1633–1703: diary, 31 May 1669, closing words

2 A page of my Journal is like a cake of portable soup. A little
may be diffused into a considerable portion.
James Boswell 1740–95: *Journal of a Tour to the Hebrides*
(1785)

3 I never travel without my diary. One should always have
something sensational to read in the train.
Oscar Wilde 1854–1900: *The Importance of Being Earnest*
(1895)

4 What sort of diary should I like mine to be?…I should like it
to resemble some deep old desk, or capacious hold-all, in
which one flings a mass of odds and ends without looking
them through.
Virginia Woolf 1882–1941: diary, 20 April 1919

5 What is more dull than a discreet diary? One might just as
well have a discreet soul.
Henry 'Chips' Channon 1897–1958: diary, 26 July 1935

6 I always say, keep a diary and some day it'll keep you.
Mae West 1892–1980: *Every Day's a Holiday* (1937 film)

Diplomacy

1 By indirections find directions out.
   William Shakespeare 1564-1616: *Hamlet* (1601)

2 An ambassador is an honest man sent to lie abroad for the good of his country.
   Henry Wotton 1568-1639: written in the album of Christopher Fleckmore in 1604

3 In things that are tender and unpleasing, it is good to break the ice by some whose words are of less weight, and to reserve the more weighty voice to come in as by chance.
   Francis Bacon 1561-1626: *Essays* (1625) 'Of Cunning'

4 We are prepared to go to the gates of Hell—but no further.
   Pope Pius VII 1742-1823: attempting to reach an agreement with Napoleon, *c.*1800-1

5 *Le congrès ne marche pas, il danse.*
   The Congress makes no progress; it dances.
   Charles-Joseph, Prince de Ligne 1735-1814: in A. de la Garde-Chambonas *Souvenirs du Congrès de Vienne* (1820)

6 I'm afraid you've got a bad egg, Mr Jones.
   Oh no, my Lord, I assure you! Parts of it are excellent!
   Punch: 1895

7 Speak softly and carry a big stick; you will go far.
   Theodore Roosevelt 1858-1919: speech, 3 April 1903 (quoting an 'old adage')

8 Negotiating with de Valera...is like trying to pick up mercury with a fork.
   David Lloyd George 1863-1945: to which de Valera replied, 'Why doesn't he use a spoon?'; in M. J. MacManus *Eamon de Valera* (1944)

9 I feel happier now that we have no allies to be polite to and to pamper.
   George VI 1895-1952: to Queen Mary, 27 June 1940

10 To jaw-jaw is always better than to war-war.
   Winston Churchill 1874-1965: speech at White House, 26 June 1954

11 A diplomat these days is nothing but a head-waiter who's allowed to sit down occasionally.
   Peter Ustinov 1921- : *Romanoff and Juliet* (1956)

12 A diplomat...is a person who can tell you to go to hell in
such a way that you actually look forward to the trip.
   Caskie Stinnett 1911- : *Out of the Red* (1960)

13 Let us never negotiate out of fear. But let us never fear to
negotiate.
   John F. Kennedy 1917-63: inaugural address, 20 January
   1961

14 Treaties, you see, are like girls and roses: they last while
they last.
   Charles de Gaulle 1890-1970: speech at Elysée Palace,
   2 July 1963

Discontent see Satisfaction and Discontent

Discoveries see Inventions and Discoveries

Dogs

See also **Animals**

1 I am his Highness' dog at Kew;
Pray, tell me sir, whose dog are you?
   Alexander Pope 1688-1744: 'Epigram Engraved on the
   Collar of a Dog which I gave to his Royal Highness' (1738)

2 The more one gets to know of men, the more one values dogs.
   A. Toussenel 1803-85: *L'Esprit des bêtes* (1847), attributed to
   Mme Roland in the form 'The more I see of men, the more I
   like dogs'

3 The great pleasure of a dog is that you may make a fool of
yourself with him and not only will he not scold you, but he
will make a fool of himself too.
   Samuel Butler 1835-1902: *Notebooks* (1912)

4 Brothers and Sisters, I bid you beware
Of giving your heart to a dog to tear.
   Rudyard Kipling 1865-1936: 'The Power of the Dog' (1909)

5 My hand will miss the insinuated nose,
Mine eyes the tail that wagged contempt at Fate.
   William Watson 1858-1936: 'An Epitaph' (for his dog)

6 Any man who hates dogs and babies can't be all bad.
   Leo Rosten 1908- : of W. C. Fields, and often attributed to
   him, in speech at Masquers' Club dinner, 16 February 1939

7 A door is what a dog is perpetually on the wrong side of.
   Ogden Nash 1902-71: 'A Dog's Best Friend is his Illiteracy'
   (1953)

8 That indefatigable and unsavoury engine of pollution, the
   dog.
   John Sparrow 1906-92: letter to *The Times* 30 September
   1975

Doubt see Certainty and Doubt

Drawing see Painting and Drawing

Dreams see Sleep and Dreams

Dress

1 The apparel oft proclaims the man.
   William Shakespeare 1564-1616: *Hamlet* (1601)

2 A sweet disorder in the dress
   Kindles in clothes a wantonness.
   Robert Herrick 1591-1674: 'Delight in Disorder' (1648)

3 Whenas in silks my Julia goes,
   Then, then (methinks) how sweetly flows
   That liquefaction of her clothes.
   Robert Herrick 1591-1674: 'Upon Julia's Clothes' (1648)

4 No perfumes, but very fine linen, plenty of it, and country
   washing.
   Beau Brummell 1778-1840: in *Memoirs of Harriette Wilson*
   (1825)

5 She just wore
   Enough for modesty—no more.
   Robert Buchanan 1841-1901: 'White Rose and Red' (1873)

6 The sense of being well-dressed gives a feeling of inward
tranquillity which religion is powerless to bestow.
   Miss C. F. Forbes 1817–1911: in R. W. Emerson *Letters and
   Social Aims* (1876)

7 You should never have your best trousers on when you go
out to fight for freedom and truth.
   Henrik Ibsen 1828–1906: *An Enemy of the People* (1882)

8 His socks compelled one's attention without losing one's
respect.
   Saki (H. H. Munro) 1870–1916: *Chronicles of Clovis* (1911)

9 From the cradle to the grave, underwear first, last and all the
time.
   Bertolt Brecht 1898–1956: *The Threepenny Opera* (1928)

10 Men seldom make passes
At girls who wear glasses.
   Dorothy Parker 1893–1967: 'News Item' (1937)

11 Where's the man could ease a heart like a satin gown?
   Dorothy Parker 1893–1967: 'The Satin Dress' (1937)

12 Haute Couture should be fun, foolish and almost unwearable.
   Christian Lacroix 1951– : *Observer* 27 December 1987
   'Sayings of the Year'

Drink see Food and Drink

Economics

1 We are just statistics, born to consume resources.
   Horace 65–8 BC: *Epistles*

2 It is not that pearls fetch a high price *because* men have
dived for them; but on the contrary, men dive for them
because they fetch a high price.
   Richard Whately 1787–1863: *Introductory Lectures on
   Political Economy* (1832)

3 Finance is, as it were, the stomach of the country, from
which all the other organs take their tone.
   W. E. Gladstone 1809–98: article on finance, 1858

4 Economy is going without something you do want in case
you should, some day, want something you probably won't
want.
   Anthony Hope 1863–1933: *The Dolly Dialogues* (1894)

5 The National Debt is a very Good Thing and it would be
dangerous to pay it off, for fear of Political Economy.
   W. C. Sellar 1898–1951 and **R. J. Yeatman** 1898–1968: *1066
   and All That* (1930)

6 The cold metal of economic theory is in Marx's pages
immersed in such a wealth of steaming phrases as to acquire
a temperature not naturally its own.
   J. A. Schumpeter 1883–1950: *Capitalism, Socialism and
   Democracy* (1942)

7 What a country calls its vital economic interests are not the
things which enable its citizens to live, but the things which
enable it to make war.
   Simone Weil 1909–43: in W. H. Auden *A Certain World*
   (1971)

8 There is enough in the world for everyone's need, but not
enough for everyone's greed.
   Frank Buchman 1878–1961: *Remaking the World* (1947)

9 In a community where public services have failed to keep
abreast of private consumption things are very different.
Here, in an atmosphere of private opulence and public
squalor, the private goods have full sway.
   J. K. Galbraith 1908– : *The Affluent Society* (1958)

10 It's a recession when your neighbour loses his job; it's
a depression when you lose yours.
   Harry S. Truman 1884–1972: in *Observer* 13 April 1958

11 There's no such thing as a free lunch.
   Anonymous: colloquial axiom in US economics from the
   1960s, much associated with Milton Friedman; first found
   in printed form in Robert Heinlein *The Moon is a Harsh
   Mistress* (1966)

12 Call a thing immoral or ugly, soul-destroying or
a degradation of man, a peril to the peace of the world or to
the well-being of future generations: as long as you have not
shown it to be 'uneconomic' you have not really questioned
its right to exist, grow, and prosper.
   E. F. Schumacher 1911–77: *Small is Beautiful* (1973)

13 Greed—for lack of a better word—is good. Greed is right.
  Greed works.
> **Stanley Weiser** and **Oliver Stone** 1946- : *Wall Street* (1987
> film)

14 If the policy isn't hurting, it isn't working.
> **John Major** 1943- : on controlling inflation; speech in
> Northampton, 27 October 1989

15 Rising unemployment and the recession have been the price
  that we've had to pay to get inflation down. [Labour shouts]
  That is a price well worth paying.
> **Norman Lamont** 1942- : speech in House of Commons,
> 16 May 1991

16 Trickle-down theory—the less than elegant metaphor that if
  one feeds the horse enough oats, some will pass through to
  the road for the sparrows.
> **J. K. Galbraith** 1908- : *The Culture of Contentment* (1992)

Education

See also **Teaching**

1 And gladly wolde he lerne and gladly teche.
> **Geoffrey Chaucer** *c*.1343-1400: *The Canterbury Tales*
> 'General Prologue'

2 That lyf so short, the craft so long to lerne.
> **Geoffrey Chaucer** *c*.1343-1400: *The Parliament of Fowls*

3 I said…how, and why, young children, were sooner allured
  by love, than driven by beating, to attain good learning.
> **Roger Ascham** 1515-68: *The Schoolmaster* (1570)

4 I would I had bestowed that time in the tongues that I have
  in fencing, dancing, and bear-baiting. O! had I but followed
  the arts!
> **William Shakespeare** 1564-1616: *Twelfth Night* (1601)

5 I have been at my book, and am now past the craggy paths of
  study, and come to the flowery plains of honour and
  reputation.
> **Ben Jonson** *c*.1573-1637: *Volpone* (1606)

6 And let a scholar all Earth's volumes carry,
He will be but a walking dictionary.
   George Chapman c.1559–1634: *The Tears of Peace* (1609)

7 Histories make men wise; poets, witty; the mathematics,
subtle; natural philosophy, deep; moral, grave; logic and
rhetoric, able to contend.
   Francis Bacon 1561–1626: *Essays* (1625) 'Of Studies'

8 Studies serve for delight, for ornament, and for ability.
   Francis Bacon 1561–1626: *Essays* (1625) 'Of Studies'

9 Know then thyself, presume not God to scan;
The proper study of mankind is man.
   Alexander Pope 1688–1744: *An Essay on Man* Epistle 2
   (1733)

10 Public schools are the nurseries of all vice and immorality.
   Henry Fielding 1707–54: *Joseph Andrews* (1742)

11 There mark what ills the scholar's life assail,
Toil, envy, want, the patron, and the jail.
   Samuel Johnson 1709–84: *The Vanity of Human Wishes*
   (1749)

12 Examinations are formidable even to the best prepared, for
the greatest fool may ask more than the wisest man can
answer.
   Charles Caleb Colton c.1780–1832: *Lacon* (1820)

13 My object will be, if possible, to form Christian men, for
Christian boys I can scarcely hope to make.
   Thomas Arnold 1795–1842: letter to Revd John Tucker,
   2 March 1828, on his appointment to the Headmastership of
   Rugby School

14 C-l-e-a-n, clean, verb active, to make bright, to scour. W-i-n,
win, d-e-r, der, winder, a casement. When the boy knows this
out of the book, he goes and does it.
   Charles Dickens 1812–70: *Nicholas Nickleby* (1839) Mr
   Squeers

15 'That's the reason they're called lessons,' the Gryphon
remarked: 'because they lessen from day to day.'
   Lewis Carroll 1832–98: *Alice's Adventures in Wonderland*
   (1865)

16 Soap and education are not as sudden as a massacre, but they
are more deadly in the long run.
   Mark Twain 1835–1910: *A Curious Dream* (1872)

17 Cauliflower is nothing but cabbage with a college education.
   Mark Twain 1835–1910: *Pudd'nhead Wilson* (1894)

18 Give me a child for the first seven years, and you may do
   what you like with him afterwards.
   Anonymous: attributed as a Jesuit maxim, in *Lean's
   Collectanea* (1903)

19 Nothing in education is so astonishing as the amount of
   ignorance it accumulates in the form of inert facts.
   Henry Brooks Adams 1838–1918: *The Education of Henry
   Adams* (1907)

20 What one knows is, in youth, of little moment; they know
   enough who know how to learn.
   Henry Brooks Adams 1838–1918: *The Education of Henry
   Adams* (1907)

21 What poor education I have received has been gained in the
   University of Life.
   Horatio Bottomley 1860–1933: speech at the Oxford Union,
   2 December 1920

22 The proper study of mankind is books.
   Aldous Huxley 1894–1963: *Crome Yellow* (1921)

23 In examinations those who do not wish to know ask
   questions of those who cannot tell.
   Walter Raleigh 1861–1922: *Laughter from a Cloud* (1923)

24 My spelling is Wobbly. It's good spelling but it Wobbles, and
   the letters get in the wrong places.
   A. A. Milne 1882–1956: *Winnie-the-Pooh* (1926)

25 Do not on any account attempt to write on both sides of the
   paper at once.
   W. C. Sellar 1898–1951 and **R. J. Yeatman** 1898–1968: *1066
   and All That* (1930) 'Test Paper 5'

26 [Education] has produced a vast population able to read but
   unable to distinguish what is worth reading, an easy prey to
   sensations and cheap appeals.
   G. M. Trevelyan 1876–1962: *English Social History* (1942)

27 No more Latin, no more French,
   No more sitting on a hard board bench.
   Anonymous: children's rhyme for the end of school term,
   in Iona and Peter Opie *Lore and Language of
   Schoolchildren* (1959)

28 The dread of beatings! Dread of being late!
And, greatest dread of all, the dread of games!
  John Betjeman 1906-84: *Summoned by Bells* (1960)

29 The delusion that there are thousands of young people about
who are capable of benefiting from university training, but
have somehow failed to find their way there, is...a necessary
component of the expansionist case...More will mean worse.
  Kingsley Amis 1922- : *Encounter* July 1960

30 Education is what survives when what has been learned has
been forgotten.
  B. F. Skinner 1904-90: *New Scientist* 21 May 1964

Endeavour see **Achievement and Endeavour**

Endings see **Beginnings and Endings**

Enemies

1 If thine enemy be hungry, give him bread to eat; and if he be
thirsty, give him water to drink.
For thou shalt heap coals of fire upon his head, and the
Lord shall reward thee.
  Bible: Proverbs

2 Love your enemies, do good to them which hate you.
  Bible: St Luke

3 I wish my deadly foe, no worse
Than want of friends, and empty purse.
  Nicholas Breton c.1545-1626: 'A Farewell to Town' (1577)

4 An open foe may prove a curse,
But a pretended friend is worse.
  John Gay 1685-1732: *Fables* (1727) 'The Shepherd's Dog and
the Wolf'

5 People wish their enemies dead—but I do not; I say give them
the gout, give them the stone!
  Lady Mary Wortley Montagu 1689-1762: quoted in letter
from Horace Walpole to Earl of Harcourt, 17 September
1778

6 An injury is much sooner forgotten than an insult.
   Lord Chesterfield 1694–1773: *Letters to his Son* (1774)
   9 October 1746

7 You can calculate the worth of a man by the number of his
   enemies, and the importance of a work of art by the harm
   that is spoken of it.
   Gustave Flaubert 1821–80: letter to Louise Colet, 14 June
   1853

8 Not while I'm alive 'e ain't!
   Ernest Bevin 1881–1951: reply to the observation that Nye
   Bevan was sometimes his own worst enemy; in R. Barclay
   Ernest Bevin and the Foreign Office (1975)

9 Better to have him inside the tent pissing out, than outside
   pissing in.
   Lyndon Baines Johnson 1908–73: of J. Edgar Hoover, in
   D. Halberstam *The Best and the Brightest* (1972)

England and the English

See also **Britain, London, Places**

1 England is the paradise of women, the purgatory of men, and
   the hell of horses.
   John Florio *c.*1553–1625: *Second Frutes* (1591)

2 This royal throne of kings, this sceptred isle,
   This earth of majesty, this seat of Mars,
   This other Eden, demi-paradise,
   This fortress built by Nature for herself
   Against infection and the hand of war,
   This happy breed of men, this little world,
   This precious stone set in the silver sea…
   This blessèd plot, this earth, this realm, this England.
   William Shakespeare 1564–1616: *Richard II* (1595)

3 Come the three corners of the world in arms,
   And we shall shock them: nought shall make us rue,
   If England to itself do rest but true.
   William Shakespeare 1564–1616: *King John* (1591–8)

4   An Englishman,
Being flattered, is a lamb; threatened, a lion.
> **George Chapman** c.1559–1634: *Alphonsus, Emperor of Germany* (1654)

5 The English take their pleasures sadly after the fashion of their country.
> **Maximilien de Béthune, Duc de Sully** 1559–1641: attributed

6 Let not England forget her precedence of teaching nations how to live.
> **John Milton** 1608–74: *The Doctrine and Discipline of Divorce* (1643) 'To the Parliament of England'

7 In England there are sixty different religions, and only one sauce.
> **Francesco Caracciolo** 1752–99: attributed

8 England expects that every man will do his duty.
> **Horatio, Lord Nelson** 1758–1805: at the battle of Trafalgar, in R. Southey *Life of Nelson* (1813)

9 And did those feet in ancient time
Walk upon England's mountains green?
And was the holy Lamb of God
On England's pleasant pastures seen?...

I will not cease from mental fight,
Nor shall my sword sleep in my hand,
Till we have built Jerusalem,
In England's green and pleasant land.
> **William Blake** 1757–1827: *Milton* (1804–10)

10 England is a nation of shopkeepers.
> **Napoléon I** 1769–1821: in B. O'Meara *Napoleon in Exile* (1822)

11 The French want no-one to be their *superior*. The English want *inferiors*. The Frenchman constantly raises his eyes above him with anxiety. The Englishman lowers his beneath him with satisfaction.
> **Alexis de Tocqueville** 1805–59: *Voyage en Angleterre et en Irlande de 1835* 8 May 1835

12 Oh, to be in England
Now that April's there.
> **Robert Browning** 1812–89: 'Home-Thoughts, from Abroad' (1845)

13 What a pity it is that we have no amusements in England but vice and religion!
   Sydney Smith 1771–1845: in H. Pearson *The Smith of Smiths* (1934)

14 For he might have been a Roosian,
   A French, or Turk, or Proosian,
   Or perhaps Ital-ian!
   But in spite of all temptations
   To belong to other nations,
   He remains an Englishman!
   W. S. Gilbert 1836–1911: *HMS Pinafore* (1878)

15 What should they know of England who only England know?
   Rudyard Kipling 1865–1936: 'The English Flag' (1892)

16 The English country gentleman galloping after a fox—the unspeakable in full pursuit of the uneatable.
   Oscar Wilde 1854–1900: *A Woman of No Importance* (1893)

17 Ask any man what nationality he would prefer to be, and ninety-nine out of a hundred will tell you that they would prefer to be Englishmen.
   Cecil Rhodes 1853–1902: in G. Le Sueur *Cecil Rhodes* (1913)

18 Englishmen never will be slaves: they are free to do whatever the Government and public opinion allow them to do.
   George Bernard Shaw 1856–1950: *Man and Superman* (1903)

19 An Englishman thinks he is moral when he is only uncomfortable.
   George Bernard Shaw 1856–1950: *Man and Superman* (1903)

20 Smile at us, pay us, pass us; but do not quite forget.
   For we are the people of England, that never have spoken yet.
   G. K. Chesterton 1874–1936: 'The Secret People' (1915)

21 God! I will pack, and take a train,
   And get me to England once again!
   For England's the one land, I know,
   Where men with Splendid Hearts may go.
   Rupert Brooke 1887–1915: 'The Old Vicarage, Grantchester' (1915)

22 England is the paradise of individuality, eccentricity, heresy, anomalies, hobbies, and humours.
   George Santayana 1863–1952: *Soliloquies in England* (1922)

23 Mad dogs and Englishmen
   Go out in the midday sun.
   Noël Coward 1899–1973: 'Mad Dogs and Englishmen' (1931 song)

24 In England we have come to rely upon a comfortable time-lag of fifty years or a century intervening between the perception that something ought to be done and a serious attempt to do it.
   H. G. Wells 1866–1946: *The Work, Wealth and Happiness of Mankind* (1931)

25 They go forth into it [the world] with well-developed bodies, fairly developed minds, and undeveloped hearts.
   E. M. Forster 1879–1970: *Abinger Harvest* (1936) 'Notes on English Character' of public-school men

26 This Englishwoman is so refined
   She has no bosom and no behind.
   Stevie Smith 1902–71: 'This Englishwoman' (1937)

27 Down here it was still the England I had known in my childhood: the railway cuttings smothered in wild flowers...the red buses, the blue policemen—all sleeping the deep, deep sleep of England, from which I sometimes fear that we shall never wake till we are jerked out of it by the roar of bombs.
   George Orwell 1903–50: *Homage to Catalonia* (1938)

28 I am American bred,
   I have seen much to hate here—much to forgive,
   But in a world where England is finished and dead,
   I do not wish to live.
   Alice Duer Miller 1874–1942: *The White Cliffs* (1940)

29 Think of what our Nation stands for,
   Books from Boots' and country lanes,
   Free speech, free passes, class distinction,
   Democracy and proper drains.
   John Betjeman 1906–84: 'In Westminster Abbey' (1940)

30 It resembles a family, a rather stuffy Victorian family, with not many black sheep in it but with all its cupboards bursting with skeletons...A family with the wrong members

in control—that, perhaps, is as near as one can come to describing England in a phrase.
   George Orwell 1903–50: *The Lion and the Unicorn* (1941)

31 The Thames is liquid history.
   John Burns 1858–1943: to an American, who had compared the Thames disparagingly with the Mississippi; in *Daily Mail* 25 January 1943

32 An Englishman, even if he is alone, forms an orderly queue of one.
   George Mikes 1912– : *How to be an Alien* (1946)

33 You never find an Englishman among the under-dogs—except in England, of course.
   Evelyn Waugh 1903–66: *The Loved One* (1948)

34 A soggy little island huffing and puffing to keep up with Western Europe.
   John Updike 1932– : of England, in *Picked Up Pieces* (1976) 'London Life' (written 1969)

35 England's not a bad country…It's just a mean, cold, ugly, divided, tired, clapped-out, post-imperial, post-industrial slag-heap covered in polystyrene hamburger cartons.
   Margaret Drabble 1939– : *A Natural Curiosity* (1989)

Environment

See also **The Country and the Town, Pollution**

1 Woe unto them that join house to house, that lay field to field, till there be no place.
   Bible: Isaiah

2 The desert shall rejoice, and blossom as the rose.
   Bible: Isaiah

3 O all ye Green Things upon the Earth, bless ye the Lord.
   Book of Common Prayer 1662: *Morning Prayer*

4 Consult the genius of the place in all.
   Alexander Pope 1688–1744: *Epistles to Several Persons* 'To Lord Burlington' (1731)

5 The parks are the lungs of London.
> **William Pitt, Earl of Chatham** 1708–78: quoted by
> William Windham in the House of Commons, 30 June 1808

6 The poplars are felled, farewell to the shade
And the whispering sound of the cool colonnade.
> **William Cowper** 1731–1800: 'The Poplar-Field' (written
> 1784)

7 O leave this barren spot to me!
Spare, woodman, spare the beechen tree.
> **Thomas Campbell** 1777–1844: 'The Beech-Tree's Petition'
> (1800)

8 And was Jerusalem builded here
Among these dark Satanic mills?
> **William Blake** 1757–1827: *Milton* (1804–10)

9 What would the world be, once bereft
Of wet and wildness? Let them be left,
O let them be left, wildness and wet;
Long live the weeds and the wilderness yet.
> **Gerard Manley Hopkins** 1844–89: 'Inversnaid' (written
> 1881)

10 The forest laments in order that Mr Gladstone may perspire.
> **Lord Randolph Churchill** 1849–94: on Gladstone's
> fondness for felling trees; speech in Blackpool, 24 January
> 1884

11 Wiv a ladder and some glasses,
You could see to 'Ackney Marshes,
If it wasn't for the 'ouses in between.
> **Edgar Bateman** and **George Le Brunn**: 'If it wasn't for the
> 'Ouses in between' (1894 song)

12 I am I plus my surroundings and if I do not preserve the
latter, I do not preserve myself.
> **José Ortega y Gasset** 1883–1955: *Meditaciones del Quijote*
> (1914)

13 Praise the green earth. Chance has appointed her
home, workshop, larder, middenpit.
Her lousy skin scabbed here and there by
cities provides us with name and nation.
> **Basil Bunting** 1900–85: 'Attis: or, Something Missing' (1931)

14 It will be said of this generation that it found England a land
of beauty and left it a land of 'beauty spots'.
   C. E. M. Joad 1891–1953: *The Horrors of the Countryside*
   (1931)

15 I think that I shall never see
A billboard lovely as a tree.
Perhaps, unless the billboards fall,
I'll never see a tree at all.
   Ogden Nash 1902–71: 'Song of the Open Road' (1933)

16 Come, friendly bombs, and fall on Slough!
It isn't fit for humans now,
There isn't grass to graze a cow.
Swarm over, Death!
   John Betjeman 1906–84: 'Slough' (1937)

17 Little boxes on the hillside...
And they're all made out of ticky-tacky
And they all look just the same.
   Malvina Reynolds 1900–78: 'Little Boxes' (1962 song); on
   the tract houses in the hills to the south of San Francisco

18 Over increasingly large areas of the United States, spring
now comes unheralded by the return of the birds, and the
early mornings are strangely silent where once they were
filled with the beauty of bird song.
   Rachel Carson 1907–64: *The Silent Spring* (1962)

19 Now there is one outstandingly important fact regarding
Spaceship Earth, and that is that no instruction book came
with it.
   R. Buckminster Fuller 1895–1983: *Operating Manual for
   Spaceship Earth* (1969)

20 Small is beautiful.
   E. F. Schumacher 1911–77: title of book (1973)

21 And that will be England gone,
The shadows, the meadows, the lanes,
The guildhalls, the carved choirs.
There'll be books; it will linger on
In galleries; but all that remains
For us will be concrete and tyres.
   Philip Larkin 1922–85: 'Going, Going' (1974)

22 It is not what they built. It is what they knocked down.
It is not the houses. It is the spaces between the houses.

It is not the streets that exist. It is the streets that no longer exist.
James Fenton 1949- : *German Requiem* (1981)

23 How inappropriate to call this planet Earth when it is clearly Ocean.
Arthur C. Clarke 1917- : attributed in *Nature* 1990

Envy and Jealousy

1 Thou shalt not covet thy neighbour's house, thou shalt not covet thy neighbour's wife.
Bible: Exodus

2   Trifles light as air
Are to the jealous confirmations strong
As proofs of holy writ.
William Shakespeare 1564-1616: *Othello* (1602-4)

3   O! beware, my lord, of jealousy;
It is the green-eyed monster which doth mock
The meat it feeds on.
William Shakespeare 1564-1616: *Othello* (1602-4)

4 Some folks rail against other folks, because other folks have what some folks would be glad of.
Henry Fielding 1707-54: *Joseph Andrews* (1742)

5 Thou shalt not covet; but tradition
Approves all forms of competition.
Arthur Hugh Clough 1819-61: 'The Latest Decalogue' (1862)

6 Jealousy is no more than feeling alone against smiling enemies.
Elizabeth Bowen 1899-1973: *The House in Paris* (1935)

7 To jealousy, nothing is more frightful than laughter.
Françoise Sagan 1935- : *La Chamade* (1965)

Epitaphs

See also **Death**

1 Go, tell the Spartans, thou who passest by,
That here obedient to their laws we lie.
   Simonides *c.*556–468 BC: in Herodotus *Histories* (attributed)

2 Saul and Jonathan were lovely and pleasant in their lives,
and in their death they were not divided.
   Bible: II Samuel

3 And some there be, which have no memorial...and are
become as though they had never been born...
   But these were merciful men, whose righteousness hath
not been forgotten...
   Their bodies are buried in peace; but their name liveth for
evermore.
   Bible (Apocrypha): Ecclesiasticus

4 *Et in Arcadia ego.*
And I too in Arcadia.
   Anonymous: tomb inscription, of disputed meaning, often
   depicted in classical paintings

5 Betwixt the stirrup and the ground
Mercy I asked, mercy I found.
   William Camden 1551–1623: *Remains Concerning Britain*
   (1605) 'Epitaphs' (for a man who fell from his horse)

6 Rest in soft peace, and, asked, say here doth lie
Ben Jonson his best piece of poetry.
   Ben Jonson *c.*1573–1637: 'On My First Son' (1616)

7 Good friend, for Jesu's sake forbear
To dig the dust enclosed here.
Blest be the man that spares these stones,
And curst be he that moves my bones.
   William Shakespeare 1564–1616: epitaph on his tomb,
   probably composed by himself

8 Here lies a great and mighty king
Whose promise none relies on;
He never said a foolish thing,
Nor ever did a wise one.
   John Wilmot, Earl of Rochester 1647–80: 'The King's
   Epitaph' (alternatively 'Here lies our sovereign lord the

King'), to which Charles II replied 'This is very true: for
my words are my own, and my actions are my ministers'';
in C. E. Doble et al. *Thomas Hearne: Remarks and
Collections* (1885–1921) 17 November 1706

9 Life is a jest; and all things show it.
I thought so once; but now I know it.
   John Gay 1685–1732: 'My Own Epitaph' (1720)

10 *Si monumentum requiris, circumspice.*
If you seek a monument, gaze around.
   Anonymous: inscription in St Paul's Cathedral, London,
   attributed to the son of Sir Christopher Wren 1632–1723, its
   architect

11 Under this stone, Reader, survey
Dead Sir John Vanbrugh's house of clay.
Lie heavy on him, Earth! for he
Laid many heavy loads on thee!
   Abel Evans 1679–1737: 'Epitaph on Sir John Vanbrugh,
   Architect of Blenheim Palace'

12 Where fierce indignation can no longer tear his heart.
   Jonathan Swift 1667–1745: Swift's epitaph. See S. Leslie
   The Skull of Swift (1928)

13 Here lies one whose name was writ in water.
   John Keats 1795–1821: epitaph for himself, in R. Monckton
   Milnes *Life, Letters and Literary Remains of John Keats*
   (1848)

14 Here he lies where he longed to be;
Home is the sailor, home from sea,
And the hunter home from the hill.
   Robert Louis Stevenson 1850–94: 'Requiem' (1887)

15 Hereabouts died a very gallant gentleman, Captain
L. E. G. Oates of the Inniskilling Dragoons. In March 1912,
returning from the Pole, he walked willingly to his death in a
blizzard to try and save his comrades, beset by hardships.
   E. L. Atkinson 1882–1929 and **Apsley Cherry-Garrard**
   1882–1959: epitaph on cairn erected in the Antarctic,
   15 November 1912

16 They shall grow not old, as we that are left grow old.
Age shall not weary them, nor the years condemn.

At the going down of the sun and in the morning
We will remember them.
  Laurence Binyon 1869–1943: 'For the Fallen' (1914)

17 His foe was folly and his weapon wit.
  Anthony Hope 1863–1933: inscription for W. S. Gilbert's
  memorial on the Victoria Embankment, London (1915)

18 When you go home, tell them of us and say,
  'For your tomorrows these gave their today.'
    John Maxwell Edmonds 1875–1958: *Inscriptions Suggested
    for War Memorials* (1919). Particularly associated with the
    Burma campaign of the Second World War, in the form
    'For your tomorrow, we gave our today'

19 Here lies W. C. Fields. I would rather be living in
  Philadelphia.
    W. C. Fields 1880–1946: suggested epitaph for himself, in
    Vanity Fair June 1925

Equality

See also **Human Rights**

1 He maketh his sun to rise on the evil and on the good, and
  sendeth rain on the just and on the unjust.
    Bible: St Matthew

2 Hath not a Jew eyes? hath not a Jew hands, organs,
  dimensions, senses, affections, passions?
    William Shakespeare 1564–1616: *The Merchant of Venice*
    (1596–8)

3 If you prick us, do we not bleed? if you tickle us, do we not
  laugh? if you poison us, do we not die? and if you wrong us,
  shall we not revenge?
    William Shakespeare 1564–1616: *The Merchant of Venice*
    (1596–8)

4 Your levellers wish to level *down* as far as themselves; but
  they cannot bear levelling *up* to themselves.
    Samuel Johnson 1709–84: in James Boswell *Life of Johnson*
    (1791) 21 July 1763

5 Sir, there is no settling the point of precedency between a
   louse and a flea.
      Samuel Johnson 1709–84: on the relative merits of two
      minor poets, 1783; in James Boswell *Life of Johnson* (1791)

6 A man's a man for a' that.
      Robert Burns 1759–96: 'For a' that and a' that' (1790)

7 When every one is somebodee,
   Then no one's anybody.
      W. S. Gilbert 1836–1911: *The Gondoliers* (1889)

8 The terrorist and the policeman both come from the same
   basket.
      Joseph Conrad 1857–1924: *The Secret Agent* (1907)

9 All animals are equal but some animals are more equal than
   others.
      George Orwell 1903–50: *Animal Farm* (1945)

10 I have a dream that one day on the red hills of Georgia the
   sons of former slaves and the sons of former slave owners
   will be able to sit down together at the table of brotherhood.
      Martin Luther King 1929–68: speech at Civil Rights March
      in Washington, 28 August 1963

Europe and Europeans

See also **Places**

1 The age of chivalry is gone.—That of sophisters, economists,
   and calculators, has succeeded; and the glory of Europe is
   extinguished for ever.
      Edmund Burke 1729–97: *Reflections on the Revolution in
   France* (1790)

2 Roll up that map; it will not be wanted these ten years.
      William Pitt 1759–1806: of a map of Europe, on hearing of
      Napoleon's victory at Austerlitz, December 1805

3 Better fifty years of Europe than a cycle of Cathay.
      Alfred, Lord Tennyson 1809–92: 'Locksley Hall' (1842)

4 *Qui parle Europe a tort, notion géographique.*
  Whoever speaks of Europe is wrong, [it is] a geographical
  concept.
    Otto von Bismarck 1815-98: marginal note on a letter from
    the Russian Chancellor Gorchakov, November 1876

5 *Je regrette l'Europe aux anciens parapets!*
  I pine for Europe of the ancient parapets!
    Arthur Rimbaud 1854-91: 'Le Bâteau ivre' (1883)

6 We are part of the community of Europe and we must do our
  duty as such.
    Lord Salisbury 1830-1903: speech at Caernarvon, 10 April
    1888

7 Europe is a continent of energetic mongrels.
    H. A. L. Fisher 1856-1940: *A History of Europe* (1935)

8 From Stettin in the Baltic to Trieste in the Adriatic an iron
  curtain has descended across the Continent.
    Winston Churchill 1874-1965: speech at Westminster
    College, Fulton, Missouri, 5 March 1946. 'Iron curtain'
    previously had been applied by others to the Soviet Union
    or her sphere of influence

9 If you open that Pandora's Box, you never know what Trojan
  'orses will jump out.
    Ernest Bevin 1881-1951: on the Council of Europe, in R.
    Barclay *Ernest Bevin and the Foreign Office* (1975)

10 When an American heiress wants to buy a man, she at once
  crosses the Atlantic. The only really materialistic people
  I have ever met have been Europeans.
    Mary McCarthy 1912-89: *On the Contrary* (1961)

11 It means the end of a thousand years of history.
    Hugh Gaitskell 1906-63: on a European federation; speech
    at Labour Party Conference, 3 October 1962

12 You ask if they were happy. This is not a characteristic of a
  European. To be contented—that's for the cows.
    Coco Chanel 1883-1971: in A. Madsen *Coco Chanel* (1990)

Evil see **Good and Evil**

Experience

1 *Experto credite.*
Trust one who has gone through it.
Virgil 70–19 BC: *Aeneid*

2 No man's knowledge here can go beyond his experience.
John Locke 1632–1704: *Essay concerning Human Understanding* (1690)

3 Experience is the child of Thought, and Thought is the child of Action. We cannot learn men from books.
Benjamin Disraeli 1804–81: *Vivian Grey* (1826)

4 Experience is the name everyone gives to their mistakes.
Oscar Wilde 1854–1900: *Lady Windermere's Fan* (1892)

5 All experience is an arch to build upon.
Henry Brooks Adams 1838–1918: *The Education of Henry Adams* (1907)

6 Experience is not what happens to a man; it is what a man does with what happens to him.
Aldous Huxley 1894–1963: *Texts and Pretexts* (1932)

7 Experience isn't interesting till it begins to repeat itself—in fact, till it does that, it hardly *is* experience.
Elizabeth Bowen 1899–1973: *Death of the Heart* (1938)

8 We had the experience but missed the meaning.
T. S. Eliot 1888–1965: *Four Quartets* 'The Dry Salvages' (1941)

9 You should make a point of trying every experience once, excepting incest and folk-dancing.
Anonymous: Arnold Bax (1883–1953), quoting 'a sympathetic Scot' in *Farewell My Youth* (1943)

Failure see Success and Failure

Fame

1 Famous men have the whole earth as their memorial.
Pericles *c.*495–429 BC: in Thucydides *History of the Peloponnesian War* (tr. R. Warner)

2 *Exegi monumentum aere perennius.*
I have erected a monument more lasting than bronze.
  Horace 65–8 BC: *Odes*

3 A prophet is not without honour, save in his own country,
and in his own house.
  Bible: St Matthew

4 Fame is like a river, that beareth up things light and swollen,
and drowns things weighty and solid.
  Francis Bacon 1561–1626: *Essays* (1625) 'Of Praise'

5 Fame is the spur that the clear spirit doth raise
(That last infirmity of noble mind)
To scorn delights, and live laborious days.
  John Milton 1608–74: 'Lycidas' (1638)

6 Seven wealthy towns contend for HOMER dead
Through which the living HOMER begged his bread.
  Anonymous: epilogue to *Aesop at Tunbridge* By No Person
of Quality (1698)

7 Content thyself to be obscurely good.
When vice prevails, and impious men bear sway,
The post of honour is a private station.
  Joseph Addison 1672–1719: *Cato* (1713)

8 Far from the madding crowd's ignoble strife,
Their sober wishes never learned to stray;
Along the cool sequestered vale of life
They kept the noiseless tenor of their way.
  Thomas Gray 1716–71: *Elegy Written in a Country
Churchyard* (1751)

9 Full many a flower is born to blush unseen,
And waste its sweetness on the desert air.

Some village-Hampden, that with dauntless breast
The little tyrant of his fields withstood;
Some mute inglorious Milton here may rest,
Some Cromwell guiltless of his country's blood.
  Thomas Gray 1716–71: *Elegy Written in a Country
Churchyard* (1751)

10 Every man has a lurking wish to appear considerable in his
native place.
  Samuel Johnson 1709–84: in James Boswell *Life of Johnson*
(1791) 17 July 1771

11 Oh, talk not to me of a name great in story;
The days of our youth are the days of our glory;
And the myrtle and ivy of sweet two-and-twenty
Are worth all your laurels, though ever so plenty.
   Lord Byron 1788–1824: 'Stanzas Written on the Road
   between Florence and Pisa, November 1821'

12 I awoke one morning and found myself famous.
   Lord Byron 1788–1824: on the instantaneous success of
   Childe Harold, in Thomas Moore *Letters and Journals of
   Lord Byron* (1830)

13 The deed is all, the glory nothing.
   Johann Wolfgang von Goethe 1749–1832: *Faust* pt. 2
   (1832)

14 Martyrdom...the only way in which a man can become
famous without ability.
   George Bernard Shaw 1856–1950: *The Devil's Disciple* (1901)

15 Fame is a food that dead men eat,—
I have no stomach for such meat.
   Henry Austin Dobson 1840–1921: 'Fame is a Food' (1906)

16 I don't care what you say about me, as long as you say
something about me, and as long as you spell my name right.
   George M. Cohan 1878–1942: said to a newspaperman in
   1912

17 He's always backing into the limelight.
   Lord Berners 1883–1950: of T. E. Lawrence; oral tradition

18 Whom the gods wish to destroy they first call promising.
   Cyril Connolly 1903–74: *Enemies of Promise* (1938)

19 The celebrity is a person who is known for his
well-knownness.
   Daniel J. Boorstin 1914– : *The Image* (1961)

20 There's no such thing as bad publicity except your own
obituary.
   Brendan Behan 1923–64: in Dominic Behan *My Brother
   Brendan* (1965)

21 We're more popular than Jesus now; I don't know which will
go first—rock 'n' roll or Christianity.
   John Lennon 1940–80: of The Beatles; interview in *Evening
   Standard* 4 March 1966

22 In the future everybody will be world famous for fifteen
minutes.
   Andy Warhol 1927–87: in *Andy Warhol* (1968)

23 The best fame is a writer's fame: it's enough to get a table at
a good restaurant, but not enough that you get interrupted
when you eat.
   Fran Lebowitz 1946– : in *Observer* 30 May 1993 'Sayings of
   the Week'

The Family

See also **Children, Parents**

1 Thy wife shall be as the fruitful vine: upon the walls of thine
house.
   Thy children like the olive-branches: round about thy
table.
   Bible: Psalm 128

2 A little more than kin, and less than kind.
   William Shakespeare 1564–1616: *Hamlet* (1601)

3 He that hath wife and children hath given hostages to
fortune; for they are impediments to great enterprises, either
of virtue or mischief.
   Francis Bacon 1561–1626: *Essays* (1625) 'Of Marriage and
   the Single Life'

4 We begin our public affections in our families. No cold
relation is a zealous citizen.
   Edmund Burke 1729–97: *Reflections on the Revolution in
   France* (1790)

5 A poor relation—is the most irrelevant thing in nature.
   Charles Lamb 1775–1834: *Last Essays of Elia* (1833) 'Poor
   Relations'

6 If a man's character is to be abused, say what you will,
there's nobody like a relation to do the business.
   William Makepeace Thackeray 1811–63: *Vanity Fair*
   (1847–8)

7 All happy families resemble one another, but each unhappy family is unhappy in its own way.
Leo Tolstoy 1828-1910: *Anna Karenina* (1875-7), tr. A. and L. Maude

8 One would be in less danger
From the wiles of the stranger
If one's own kin and kith
Were more fun to be with.
Ogden Nash 1902-71: 'Family Court' (1931)

9 It is no use telling me that there are bad aunts and good aunts. At the core, they are all alike. Sooner or later, out pops the cloven hoof.
P. G. Wodehouse 1881-1975: *The Code of the Woosters* (1938)

10 The family—that dear octopus from whose tentacles we never quite escape.
Dodie Smith 1896-1990: *Dear Octopus* (1938)

11 The Princesses would never leave without me and I couldn't leave without the King, and the King will never leave.
Queen Elizabeth, the Queen Mother 1900- : on the suggestion that the royal family be evacuated during the Blitz

12 Far from being the basis of the good society, the family, with its narrow privacy and tawdry secrets, is the source of all our discontents.
Edmund Leach 1910- : BBC Reith Lectures, 1967

13 I have never understood this liking for war. It panders to instincts already catered for within the scope of any respectable domestic establishment.
Alan Bennett 1934- : *Forty Years On* (1969)

Fate

1 Canst thou bind the sweet influences of Pleiades, or loose the bands of Orion?
Bible: Job

2 There's a divinity that shapes our ends,
Rough-hew them how we will.
William Shakespeare 1564-1616: *Hamlet* (1601)

3 Not a whit, we defy augury; there's a special providence in
the fall of a sparrow. If it be now, 'tis not to come; if it be not
to come, it will be now; if it be not now, yet it will come: the
readiness is all.
William Shakespeare 1564–1616: *Hamlet* (1601)

4 Our remedies oft in ourselves do lie
Which we ascribe to heaven.
William Shakespeare 1564–1616: *All's Well that Ends Well*
(1603–4)

5 We are merely the stars' tennis-balls, struck and bandied
Which way please them.
John Webster *c.*1580–*c.*1625: *The Duchess of Malfi* (1623)

6 Every bullet has its billet.
William III 1650–1702: in John Wesley's diary, 6 June 1765

7 Must it be? It must be.
Ludwig van Beethoven 1770–1827: *String Quartet in F
Major* (1827) epigraph

8 Out flew the web and floated wide;
The mirror cracked from side to side;
'The curse is come upon me,' cried
The Lady of Shalott.
Alfred, Lord Tennyson 1809–92: 'The Lady of Shalott'
(1832)

9 There once was an old man who said, 'Damn!
It is borne in upon me I am
An engine that moves
In determinate grooves,
I'm not even a bus, I'm a tram.'
Maurice Evan Hare 1886–1967: 'Limerick' (1905)

10 Fate is not an eagle, it creeps like a rat.
Elizabeth Bowen 1899–1973: *The House in Paris* (1935)

11 The spring is wound up tight. It will uncoil of itself. That is
what is so convenient in tragedy. The least little turn of the
wrist will do the job. Anything will set it going.
Jean Anouilh 1910–87: *Antigone* (1944), tr. L. Galantiere

Fear

1   Present fears
Are less than horrible imaginings.
   William Shakespeare 1564–1616: *Macbeth* (1606)

2 Letting 'I dare not' wait upon 'I would,'
Like the poor cat i' the adage.
   William Shakespeare 1564–1616: *Macbeth* (1606)

3 In time we hate that which we often fear.
   William Shakespeare 1564–1616: *Antony and Cleopatra* (1606–7)

4 Every drop of ink in my pen ran cold.
   Horace Walpole 1717–97: letter to George Montagu, 30 July 1752

5 No passion so effectually robs the mind of all its powers of acting and reasoning as fear.
   Edmund Burke 1729–97: *On the Sublime and Beautiful* (1757)

6 If hopes were dupes, fears may be liars.
   Arthur Hugh Clough 1819–61: 'Say not the struggle naught availeth' (1855)

7 I have seen the moment of my greatness flicker,
And I have seen the eternal Footman hold my coat, and snicker,
And in short, I was afraid.
   T. S. Eliot 1888–1965: 'Love Song of J. Alfred Prufrock' (1917)

8 I will show you fear in a handful of dust.
   T. S. Eliot 1888–1965: *The Waste Land* (1922)

9 The only thing we have to fear is fear itself.
   Franklin D. Roosevelt 1882–1945: inaugural address, 4 March 1933

10 We must travel in the direction of our fear.
   John Berryman 1914–72: 'A Point of Age' (1942)

Flowers

1 That wel by reson men it calle may
The 'dayesye,' or elles the 'ye of day,'
The emperice and flour of floures alle.
   Geoffrey Chaucer *c.*1343–1400: *The Legend of Good Women*

2 I know a bank whereon the wild thyme blows,
Where oxlips and the nodding violet grows
Quite over-canopied with luscious woodbine,
With sweet musk-roses, and with eglantine.
   William Shakespeare 1564–1616: *A Midsummer Night's Dream* (1595–6)

3   Daffodils,
That come before the swallow dares, and take
The winds of March with beauty.
   William Shakespeare 1564–1616: *The Winter's Tale* (1610–11)

4   Pale prime-roses,
That die unmarried, ere they can behold
Bright Phoebus in his strength,—a malady
Most incident to maids.
   William Shakespeare 1564–1616: *The Winter's Tale* (1610–11)

5 For you there's rosemary and rue; these keep
Seeming and savour all the winter long.
   William Shakespeare 1564–1616: *The Winter's Tale* (1610–11)

6 The marigold, that goes to bed wi' the sun,
And with him rises weeping.
   William Shakespeare 1564–1616: *The Winter's Tale* (1610–11)

7 I wandered lonely as a cloud
That floats on high o'er vales and hills,
When all at once I saw a crowd,
A host, of golden daffodils;
Beside the lake, beneath the trees,
Fluttering and dancing in the breeze.
   William Wordsworth 1770–1850: 'I wandered lonely as a cloud' (1815 ed.)

8 Daisies, those pearled Arcturi of the earth,
The constellated flower that never sets.
Percy Bysshe Shelley 1792–1822: 'The Question' (1822)

9 I sometimes think that never blows so red
The rose as where some buried Caesar bled.
Edward Fitzgerald 1809–83: *The Rubáiyát of Omar
Khayyám* (1859)

10 Oh, no man knows
Through what wild centuries
Roves back the rose.
Walter de la Mare 1873–1956: 'All That's Past' (1912)

11 Unkempt about those hedges blows
An English unofficial rose.
Rupert Brooke 1887–1915: 'The Old Vicarage, Grantchester'
(1915)

Food and Drink

See also **Alcohol**

1 She brought forth butter in a lordly dish.
Bible: Judges

2 The appetite grows by eating.
François Rabelais c.1494–c.1553: *Gargantua* (1534)

3 I am a great eater of beef, and I believe that does harm to my
wit.
William Shakespeare 1564–1616: *Twelfth Night* (1601)

4 Hunger is the best sauce in the world.
Cervantes 1547–1616: *Don Quixote* (1605)

5 Now good digestion wait on appetite,
And health on both!
William Shakespeare 1564–1616: *Macbeth* (1606)

6 A good, honest, wholesome, hungry breakfast.
Izaak Walton 1593–1683: *The Compleat Angler* (1653)

7 One should eat to live, and not live to eat.
Molière 1622–73: *L'Avare* (1669)

8 Coffee, (which makes the politician wise,
And see thro' all things with his half-shut eyes).
    Alexander Pope 1688-1744: *The Rape of the Lock* (1714)

9 [Tar water] is of a nature so mild and benign and
proportioned to the human constitution, as to warm without
heating, to cheer but not inebriate.
    Bishop George Berkeley 1685-1753: *Siris* (1744)

10 Take your hare when it is cased.
    Hannah Glasse fl. 1747: *The Art of Cookery Made Plain and
Easy* (1747) (*cased* skinned); the proverbial 'First catch your
hare' dates from *c.*1300

11 A cucumber should be well sliced, and dressed with pepper
and vinegar, and then thrown out, as good for nothing.
    Samuel Johnson 1709-84: in James Boswell *Journal of a
Tour to the Hebrides* (1785) 5 October 1773

12 Heaven sends us good meat, but the Devil sends cooks.
    David Garrick 1717-79: 'On Doctor Goldsmith's
Characteristical Cookery' (1777)

13 For my part now, I consider supper as a turnpike through
which one must pass, in order to get to bed.
    Oliver Edwards 1711-91: in James Boswell *Life of Samuel
Johnson*

14 Some have meat and cannot eat,
Some cannot eat that want it:
But we have meat and we can eat,
Sae let the Lord be thankit.
    Robert Burns 1759-96: 'The Kirkudbright Grace' (1790),
also known as 'The Selkirk Grace'

15 That all-softening, overpowering knell,
The tocsin of the soul—the dinner bell.
    Lord Byron 1788-1824: *Don Juan* (1819-24)

16 Tell me what you eat and I will tell you what you are.
    Anthelme Brillat-Savarin 1755-1826: *Physiologie du Goût*
(1825)

17 Please, sir, I want some more.
    Charles Dickens 1812-70: *Oliver Twist* (1838)

18 Serenely full, the epicure would say,
Fate cannot harm me, I have dined to-day.
    Sydney Smith 1771-1845: in Lady Holland *Memoir* (1855)

19 Madam, I have been looking for a person who disliked gravy all my life; let us swear eternal friendship.
Sydney Smith 1771–1845: in Lady Holland *Memoir* (1855)

20 Kissing don't last: cookery do!
George Meredith 1828–1909: *The Ordeal of Richard Feverel* (1859)

21 We each day dig our graves with our teeth.
Samuel Smiles 1812–1904: *Duty* (1880)

22 The cook was a good cook, as cooks go; and as good cooks go, she went.
Saki (H. H. Munro) 1870–1916: *Reginald* (1904) 'Reginald on Besetting Sins'

23 Is there no Latin word for Tea? Upon my soul, if I had known that I would have let the vulgar stuff alone.
Hilaire Belloc 1870–1953: *On Nothing* (1908)

24 Tea, although an Oriental,
Is a gentleman at least;
Cocoa is a cad and coward,
Cocoa is a vulgar beast.
G. K. Chesterton 1874–1936: 'Song of Right and Wrong' (1914)

25 Time for a little something.
A. A. Milne 1882–1956: *Winnie-the-Pooh* (1926)

26 Last night we went to a Chinese dinner at six and a French dinner at nine, and I can feel the sharks' fins navigating unhappily in the Burgundy.
Peter Fleming 1907–71: letter from Yunnanfu, 20 March 1938

27 And now with some pleasure I find that it's seven; and must cook dinner. Haddock and sausage meat. I think it is true that one gains a certain hold on sausage and haddock by writing them down.
Virginia Woolf 1882–1941: diary, 8 March 1941

28 Milk's leap toward immortality.
Clifton Fadiman 1904– : of cheese; *Any Number Can Play* (1957)

29 I never see any home cooking. All I get is fancy stuff.
Prince Philip, Duke of Edinburgh 1921– : in *Observer* 28 October 1962

30 If I had the choice between smoked salmon and tinned
salmon, I'd have it tinned. With vinegar.
   Harold Wilson 1916- : in *Observer* 11 November 1962

31 Take away that pudding—it has no theme.
   Winston Churchill 1874-1965: in Lord Home *The Way the
   Wind Blows* (1976)

....

Fools and Foolishness
....

1 Answer not a fool according to his folly, lest thou also be like
unto him.
   Answer a fool according to his folly, lest he be wise in his
own conceit.
   Bible: Proverbs

2 As the crackling of thorns under a pot, so is the laughter of a
fool.
   Bible: Ecclesiastes

3 *Misce stultitiam consiliis brevem:*
   Dulce est desipere in loco.
   Mix a little foolishness with your prudence: it's good to be
silly at the right moment.
   Horace 65-8 BC: *Odes*

4 For ye suffer fools gladly, seeing ye yourselves are wise.
   Bible: II Corinthians

5 I am two fools, I know,
   For loving, and for saying so
   In whining poetry.
   John Donne 1572-1631: 'The Triple Fool'

6 A knowledgeable fool is a greater fool than an ignorant fool.
   Molière 1622-73: *Les Femmes savantes* (1672)

7 The rest to some faint meaning make pretence,
   But Shadwell never deviates into sense.
   John Dryden 1631-1700: *MacFlecknoe* (1682)

8 The world is full of fools, and he who would not see it should
live alone and smash his mirror.
   Anonymous: adaptation of an original form attributed to
   Claude Le Petit (1640-65) in *Discours satiriques* (1686)

9 Fools rush in where angels fear to tread.
   Alexander Pope 1688–1744: *An Essay on Criticism* (1711)

10   Be wise with speed;
   A fool at forty is a fool indeed.
   Edward Young 1683–1765: *The Love of Fame* (1725–8)

11 Sir, I admit your gen'ral rule
   That every poet is a fool:
   But you yourself may serve to show it,
   That every fool is not a poet.
   Alexander Pope 1688–1744: 'Epigram from the French'
   (1732)

12 The picture, placed the busts between,
   Adds to the thought much strength:
   Wisdom and Wit are little seen,
   But Folly's at full length.
   Jane Brereton 1685–1740: 'On Mr Nash's Picture at Full
   Length, between the Busts of Sir Isaac Newton and Mr
   Pope' (1744)

13 If the fool would persist in his folly he would become wise.
   William Blake 1757–1827: *The Marriage of Heaven and Hell*
   (1790–3) 'Proverbs of Hell'

14 A fool sees not the same tree that a wise man sees.
   William Blake 1757–1827: *The Marriage of Heaven and Hell*
   (1790–3) 'Proverbs of Hell'

15 You may fool all the people some of the time; you can even
   fool some of the people all the time; but you can't fool all of
   the people all the time.
   Abraham Lincoln 1809–65: in A. McClure *Lincoln's Yarns
   and Stories* (1904); also attributed to Phineas Barnum

16 Hain't we got all the fools in town on our side? and ain't that
   a big enough majority in any town?
   Mark Twain 1835–1910: *The Adventures of Huckleberry Finn*
   (1884)

17 There's a sucker born every minute.
   Phineas T. Barnum 1810–91: attributed

18 Let us be thankful for the fools. But for them the rest of us
   could not succeed.
   Mark Twain 1835–1910: *Following the Equator* (1897)

19 The follies which a man regrets most, in his life, are those
which he didn't commit when he had the opportunity.
   Helen Rowland 1875–1950: *A Guide to Men* (1922)

20 Never give a sucker an even break.
   W. C. Fields 1880–1946: title of a W. C. Fields film (1941); the
   catch-phrase is said to have originated in the musical
   comedy *Poppy* (1923)

Forgiveness

1 Her sins, which are many, are forgiven; for she loved much.
   Bible: St Luke

2 God may pardon you, but I never can.
   Elizabeth I 1533–1603: to the dying Countess of Nottingham

3 To err is human; to forgive, divine.
   Alexander Pope 1688–1744: *An Essay on Criticism* (1711)

4 I shall be an autocrat: that's my trade. And the good Lord
will forgive me: that's his.
   Empress Catherine the Great 1729–96: attributed

5 And blessings on the falling out
That all the more endears,
When we fall out with those we love
And kiss again with tears!
   Alfred, Lord Tennyson 1809–92: *The Princess* (1847) song
   (added 1850)

6 Youth, which is forgiven everything, forgives itself nothing:
age, which forgives itself everything, is forgiven nothing.
   George Bernard Shaw 1856–1950: *Man and Superman*
   (1903)

7 After such knowledge, what forgiveness?
   T. S. Eliot 1888–1965: 'Gerontion' (1920)

8 The stupid neither forgive nor forget; the naïve forgive and
forget; the wise forgive but do not forget.
   Thomas Szasz 1920– : *The Second Sin* (1973)

France and the French

See also **Places**

1 *France, mère des arts, des armes et des lois.*
France, mother of arts, of warfare, and of laws.
    Joachim Du Bellay 1522-60: *Les Regrets* (1558)

2 That sweet enemy, France.
    Philip Sidney 1554-86: *Astrophil and Stella* (1591)

3 Tilling and grazing are the two breasts by which France is
fed.
    Maximilien de Béthune, Duc de Sully 1559-1641: *Mémoires*
    (1638)

4 They order, said I, this matter better in France.
    Laurence Sterne 1713-68: *A Sentimental Journey* (1768)

5 *Ce qui n'est pas clair n'est pas français.*
What is not clear is not French.
    Antoine de Rivarol 1753-1801: *Discours sur l'Universalité
    de la Langue Française* (1784)

6 The French want no-one to be their *superior*. The English
want *inferiors*. The Frenchman constantly raises his eyes
above him with anxiety. The Englishman lowers his beneath
him with satisfaction.
    Alexis de Tocqueville 1805-59: *Voyage en Angleterre et en
    Irlande de 1835* 8 May 1835

7 France was long a despotism tempered by epigrams.
    Thomas Carlyle 1795-1881: *History of the French Revolution*
    (1837)

8 France, famed in all great arts, in none supreme.
    Matthew Arnold 1822-88: 'To a Republican
    Friend—Continued' (1849)

9 The best thing I know between France and England is—the
sea.
    Douglas Jerrold 1803-57: *Wit and Opinions* (1859) 'The
    Anglo-French Alliance'

10 If the French noblesse had been capable of playing cricket
with their peasants, their chateaux would never have been
burnt.
    G. M. Trevelyan 1876-1962: *English Social History* (1942)

11 How can you govern a country which has 246 varieties of cheese?
   Charles de Gaulle 1890-1970: in E. Mignon *Les Mots du Général* (1962)

Friendship

1 Intreat me not to leave thee, or to return from following after thee: for whither thou goest, I will go; and where thou lodgest, I will lodge: thy people shall be my people, and thy God my God.
   Bible: Ruth

2 One soul inhabiting two bodies.
   Aristotle 384-322 BC: definition of a friend, in Diogenes Laertius *Lives of Philosophers*

3 Friendship is constant in all other things
Save in the office and affairs of love.
   William Shakespeare 1564-1616: *Much Ado About Nothing* (1598-9)

4 A crowd is not company, and faces are but a gallery of pictures, and talk but a tinkling cymbal, where there is no love.
   Francis Bacon 1561-1626: *Essays* (1625) 'Of Friendship'

5 It redoubleth joys, and cutteth griefs in halves.
   Francis Bacon 1561-1626: *Essays* (1625) 'Of Friendship'

6 If a man does not make new acquaintance as he advances through life, he will soon find himself left alone. A man, Sir, should keep his friendship in constant repair.
   Samuel Johnson 1709-84: in James Boswell *Life of Johnson* (1791) 1755

7 If it is abuse,—why one is always sure to hear of it from one damned goodnatured friend or another!
   Richard Brinsley Sheridan 1751-1816: *The Critic* (1779)

8 Should auld acquaintance be forgot
And never brought to mind?
   Robert Burns 1759-96: 'Auld Lang Syne' (1796)

9 Give me the avowed, erect and manly foe;
Firm I can meet, perhaps return the blow;

But of all plagues, good Heaven, thy wrath can send,
Save me, oh, save me, from the candid friend.
    George Canning 1770–1827: 'New Morality' (1821)

10 Of two close friends, one is always the slave of the other.
    Mikhail Lermontov 1814–41: *A Hero of our Time* (1840) tr.
    P. Longworth

11 The only reward of virtue is virtue; the only way to have a
    friend is to be one.
    Ralph Waldo Emerson 1803–82: *Essays* (1841) 'Friendship'

12 There is no man so friendless but what he can find a friend
    sincere enough to tell him disagreeable truths.
    Edward Bulwer-Lytton 1803–73: *What will he do with it?*
    (1857)

13 A woman can become a man's friend only in the following
    stages—first an acquaintance, next a mistress, and only then
    a friend.
    Anton Chekhov 1860–1904: *Uncle Vanya* (1897)

14 I have lost friends, some by death…others through sheer
    inability to cross the street.
    Virginia Woolf 1882–1941: *The Waves* (1931)

15 Oh I get by with a little help from my friends,
    Mm, I get high with a little help from my friends.
    John Lennon 1940–80 and **Paul McCartney** 1942– : 'With
    a Little Help From My Friends' (1967 song)

16 I do not believe that friends are necessarily the people you
    like best, they are merely the people who got there first.
    Peter Ustinov 1921– : *Dear Me* (1977)

The Future

1 Lord! we know what we are, but know not what we may be.
    William Shakespeare 1564–1616: *Hamlet* (1601)

2 If you can look into the seeds of time,
    And say which grain will grow and which will not.
    William Shakespeare 1564–1616: *Macbeth* (1606)

3 'We are always doing', says he, 'something for Posterity, but I
    would fain see Posterity do something for us.'
    Joseph Addison 1672–1719: *The Spectator* 20 August 1714

4 People will not look forward to posterity, who never look
backward to their ancestors.
Edmund Burke 1729–97: *Reflections on the Revolution in
France* (1790)

5 You can never plan the future by the past.
Edmund Burke 1729–97: *Letter to a Member of the National
Assembly* (1791)

6 You cannot fight against the future. Time is on our side.
W. E. Gladstone 1809–98: speech on the Reform Bill, House
of Commons, 27 April 1866

7 Such is: what is to be?
The pulp so bitter, how shall taste the rind?
Francis Thompson 1859–1907: 'The Hound of Heaven' (1913)

8 I never think of the future. It comes soon enough.
Albert Einstein 1879–1955: in an interview given on the
Belgenland, December 1930

9 We have trained them [men] to think of the Future as
a promised land which favoured heroes attain—not as
something which everyone reaches at the rate of sixty
minutes an hour, whatever he does, whoever he is.
C. S. Lewis 1898–1963: *The Screwtape Letters* (1942)

10 The empires of the future are the empires of the mind.
Winston Churchill 1874–1965: speech at Harvard,
6 September 1943

11 If you want a picture of the future, imagine a boot stamping
on a human face—for ever.
George Orwell 1903–50: *Nineteen Eighty-Four* (1949)

12 The future ain't what it used to be.
Yogi Berra 1925– : attributed

Gardens

1 And the Lord God planted a garden eastward in Eden.
Bible: Genesis

2 Sowe Carrets in your Gardens, and humbly praise God for
them, as for a singular and great blessing.
Richard Gardiner b. *c*.1533: *Profitable Instructions for the
Manuring, Sowing and Planting of Kitchen Gardens* (1599)

3 God Almighty first planted a garden; and, indeed, it is the purest of human pleasures.
Francis Bacon 1561-1626: *Essays* (1625) 'Of Gardens'

4 Annihilating all that's made
To a green thought in a green shade.
Andrew Marvell 1621-78: 'The Garden' (1681)

5 I value my garden more for being full of blackbirds than of cherries, and very frankly give them fruit for their songs.
Joseph Addison 1672-1719: *The Spectator* 6 September 1712

6 A garden was the primitive prison till man with Promethean felicity and boldness luckily sinned himself out of it.
Charles Lamb 1775-1834: letter to William Wordsworth, 22 January 1830

7 Come into the garden, Maud,
For the black bat, night, has flown,
Come into the garden, Maud,
I am here at the gate alone;
And the woodbine spices are wafted abroad,
And the musk of the rose is blown.
Alfred, Lord Tennyson 1809-92: *Maud* (1855)

8 What is a weed? A plant whose virtues have not been discovered.
Ralph Waldo Emerson 1803-82: *Fortune of the Republic* (1878)

9 A garden is a lovesome thing, God wot!
T. E. Brown 1830-97: 'My Garden' (1893)

10 Our England is a garden, and such gardens are not made
By singing:—'Oh, how beautiful!' and sitting in the shade,
While better men than we go out and start their working lives
At grubbing weeds from gravel paths with broken dinner-knives.
Rudyard Kipling 1865-1936: 'The Glory of the Garden' (1911)

11 The kiss of the sun for pardon,
The song of the birds for mirth,
One is nearer God's Heart in a garden
Than anywhere else on earth.
Dorothy Frances Gurney 1858-1932: 'God's Garden' (1913)

12 I will keep returning to the virtues of sharp and swift drainage, whether a plant prefers to be wet or dry...I would have called this book Better Drains, but you would never have bought it or borrowed it for bedtime.
  Robin Lane Fox 1946– : *Better Gardening* (1982)

....

The Generation Gap

....

See also **Youth**

1 *Si jeunesse savait; si vieillesse pouvait.*
  If youth knew; if age could.
  Henri Estienne 1531–98: *Les Prémices* (1594)

2 Age is deformed, youth unkind,
  We scorn their bodies, they our mind.
  Thomas Bastard 1566–1618: *Chrestoleros* (1598)

3 Crabbed age and youth cannot live together:
  Youth is full of pleasance, age is full of care.
  William Shakespeare 1564–1616: *The Passionate Pilgrim* (1599)

4 When I was a boy of 14, my father was so ignorant I could hardly stand to have the old man around. But when I got to be 21, I was astonished at how much the old man had learned in seven years.
  Mark Twain 1835–1910: attributed in *Reader's Digest* September 1939, but not traced in his works

5 Where, where but here have Pride and Truth,
  That long to give themselves for wage,
  To shake their wicked sides at youth
  Restraining reckless middle age?
  W. B. Yeats 1865–1939: 'On hearing that the Students of our New University have joined the Agitation against Immoral Literature' (1912)

6 It's all that the young can do for the old, to shock them and keep them up to date.
  George Bernard Shaw 1856–1950: *Fanny's First Play* (1914)

7 Every generation revolts against its fathers and makes friends with its grandfathers.
  Lewis Mumford 1895–1982: *The Brown Decades* (1931)

8 Come mothers and fathers,
Throughout the land
And don't criticize
What you can't understand.
   Bob Dylan 1941- : 'The Times They Are A-Changing' (1964 song)

9 Hope I die before I get old.
   Pete Townshend 1945- : 'My Generation' (1965 song)

10 Each year brings new problems of Form and Content,
new foes to tug with: at Twenty I tried to
vex my elders, past Sixty it's the young whom
I hope to bother.
   W. H. Auden 1907-73: 'Shorts I' (1969)

Genius

1 Great wits are sure to madness near allied,
And thin partitions do their bounds divide.
   John Dryden 1631-1700: *Absalom and Achitophel* (1681)

2 When a true genius appears in the world, you may know him
by this sign, that the dunces are all in confederacy against
him.
   Jonathan Swift 1667-1745: *Thoughts on Various Subjects* (1711)

3 The true genius is a mind of large general powers,
accidentally determined to some particular direction.
   Samuel Johnson 1709-84: *Lives of the English Poets* (1779-81)

4 Genius is only a greater aptitude for patience.
   Comte de Buffon 1707-88: in H. de Séchelles *Voyage à Montbar* (1803)

5 Rules and models destroy genius and art.
   William Hazlitt 1778-1830: *Sketches and Essays* (1839) 'On Taste'

6 'Genius' (which means transcendent capacity of taking
trouble, first of all).
   Thomas Carlyle 1795-1881: *History of Frederick the Great* (1858-65)

7 Genius does what it must, and Talent does what it can.
    Owen Meredith 1831–91: 'Last Words of a Sensitive
    Second-Rate Poet' (1868)

8 I have nothing to declare except my genius.
    Oscar Wilde 1854–1900: at the New York Custom House; in
    Frank Harris *Oscar Wilde* (1918)

9 Genius is one per cent inspiration, ninety-nine per cent
perspiration.
    Thomas Alva Edison 1847–1931: said *c*.1903, in *Harper's
    Monthly Magazine* September 1932

10 Little minds are interested in the extraordinary; great minds
in the commonplace.
    Elbert Hubbard 1859–1915: *Thousand and One Epigrams*
    (1911)

11 Mediocrity knows nothing higher than itself, but talent
instantly recognizes genius.
    Arthur Conan Doyle 1859–1930: *The Valley of Fear* (1915)

12 Every positive value has its price in negative terms…The
genius of Einstein leads to Hiroshima.
    Pablo Picasso 1881–1973: in F. Gilot and C. Lake *Life With
    Picasso* (1964)

Gifts and Giving

1 *Inopi beneficium bis dat qui dat celeriter.*
He gives the poor man twice as much good who gives
quickly.
    Publilius Syrus 1st century BC: *Sententiae* (proverbially
    '*Bis dat qui cito dat* [He gives twice who gives soon]')

2 When thou doest alms, let not thy left hand know what thy
right hand doeth.
    Bible: St Matthew

3 Give, and it shall be given unto you; good measure, pressed
down, and shaken together, and running over.
    Bible: St Luke

4 It is more blessed to give than to receive.
    Bible: Acts of the Apostles

5 God loveth a cheerful giver.
  Bible: II Corinthians

6 Thy necessity is yet greater than mine.
  Philip Sidney 1554–86: on giving his water-bottle to a dying
  soldier on the battle-field of Zutphen, 1586; in Fulke
  Greville *Life of Sir Philip Sidney* (1652). Commonly quoted
  'thy need is greater than mine'

7 When they will not give a doit to relieve a lame beggar, they
  will lay out ten to see a dead Indian.
  William Shakespeare 1564–1616: *The Tempest* (1611)

8 Item, I give unto my wife my second best bed, with the
  furniture.
  William Shakespeare 1564–1616: Will, 1616

9 Surprises are foolish things. The pleasure is not enhanced,
  and the inconvenience is often considerable.
  Jane Austen 1775–1817: *Emma* (1816)

10 Behold, I do not give lectures or a little charity,
   When I give I give myself.
   Walt Whitman 1819–92: 'Song of Myself' (written 1855)

11 Why is it no one ever sent me yet
   One perfect limousine, do you suppose?
   Ah no, it's always just my luck to get
   One perfect rose.
   Dorothy Parker 1893–1967: 'One Perfect Rose' (1937)

12 No one would remember the Good Samaritan if he'd only had
   good intentions. He had money as well.
   Margaret Thatcher 1925– : television interview,
   6 January 1986

God

See also **The Bible, Religion**

1 In the beginning was the Word, and the Word was with God,
  and the Word was God.
  Bible: St John

2 He that loveth not knoweth not God; for God is love.
  Bible: I John

3 The nature of God is a circle of which the centre is
everywhere and the circumference is nowhere.
  Anonymous: said to have been traced to a lost treatise of
  Empedocles; quoted in the *Roman de la Rose*, and by
  St Bonaventura

4 For man proposes, but God disposes.
  Thomas à Kempis *c.*1380-1471: *De Imitatione Christi*

5 O Lord, to what a state dost Thou bring those who love Thee!
  St Teresa of Ávila 1512-82: *Interior Castle* (tr.
  Benedictines of Stanbrook, 1921)

6 Our God, our help in ages past
Our hope for years to come,
Our shelter from the stormy blast,
And our eternal home.
  Isaac Watts 1674-1748: *Psalms of David Imitated* (1719)
  'Our God' altered to 'O God' by John Wesley, 1738

7 If the triangles were to make a God they would give him
three sides.
  Montesquieu 1689-1755: *Lettres Persanes* (1721), tr. J. Ozell,
  1722

8 God is on the side not of the heavy battalions, but of the best
shots.
  Voltaire 1694-1778: 'The Piccini Notebooks' (*c.*1735-50)

9 If God did not exist, it would be necessary to invent him.
  Voltaire 1694-1778: *Épîtres* (1769)

10 God moves in a mysterious way
His wonders to perform;
He plants his footsteps in the sea,
And rides upon the storm.
  William Cowper 1731-1800: 'Light Shining out of Darkness'
  (1779)

11 All service ranks the same with God—
With God, whose puppets, best and worst,
Are we: there is no last nor first.
  Robert Browning 1812-89: *Pippa Passes* (1841)

12 The word is the Verb, and the Verb is God.
  Victor Hugo 1802-85: *Contemplations* (1856)

13 And almost every one when age,
Disease, or sorrows strike him,

Inclines to think there is a God,
Or something very like Him.
Arthur Hugh Clough 1819–61: *Dipsychus* (1865)

14 Unresting, unhasting, and silent as light,
Nor wanting, nor wasting, thou rulest in might.
Walter Chalmers Smith 1824–1908: 'Immortal, invisible,
God only wise' (1867 hymn)

15 Though the mills of God grind slowly, yet they grind
exceeding small;
Though with patience He stands waiting, with exactness
grinds He all.
Henry Wadsworth Longfellow 1807–82: 'Retribution'
(1870); translation of Friedrich von Logau *Sinngedichte*
(1654), being itself a translation of an anonymous line in
Sextus Empiricus *Adversus Mathematicos*

16 An honest God is the noblest work of man.
Robert G. Ingersoll 1833–99: *The Gods* (1876)

17 Too high a price is asked for harmony; it's beyond our means
to pay so much to enter. And so I hasten to give back my
entrance ticket…It's not God that I don't accept, Alyosha,
only I most respectfully return Him the ticket.
Fedor Dostoevsky 1821–81: *The Brothers Karamazov*
(1879–80)

18 God is subtle but he is not malicious.
Albert Einstein 1879–1955: remark made at Princeton
University, May 1921

19 There once was a man who said, 'God
Must think it exceedingly odd
If he finds that this tree
Continues to be
When there's no one about in the Quad.'
Monsignor Ronald Knox 1888–1957: in L. Reed *Complete
Limerick Book* (1924), to which came the anonymous reply:
'Dear Sir, / Your astonishment's odd: / I am always about
in the Quad. / And that's why the tree / Will continue to
be, / Since observed by / Yours faithfully, / God'

20 God is on everyone's side…And, in the last analysis, he is on
the side of those with plenty of money and large armies.
Jean Anouilh 1910–87: *L'Alouette* (1953)

21 Operationally, God is beginning to resemble not a ruler but
the last fading smile of a cosmic Cheshire cat.
   Julian Huxley 1887–1975: *Religion without Revelation*
   (1957 ed.)

22 God is really only another artist. He invented the giraffe, the
elephant, and the cat. He has no real style. He just goes on
trying other things.
   Pablo Picasso 1881–1973: in F. Gilot and C. Lake *Life With
   Picasso* (1964)

23 God seems to have left the receiver off the hook, and time is
running out.
   Arthur Koestler 1905–83: *The Ghost in the Machine* (1967)

24 I am not clear that God manoeuvres physical things...After
all, a conjuring trick with bones only proves that it is as
clever as a conjuring trick with bones.
   David Jenkins, Bishop of Durham 1925– : on the
   Resurrection; radio interview, 4 October 1984

Good and Evil

See also **Virtue and Vice**

1 There is no peace, saith the Lord, unto the wicked.
   Bible: Isaiah

2 Every art and every investigation, and likewise every
practical pursuit or undertaking, seems to aim at some good:
hence it has been well said that the Good is That at which all
things aim.
   Aristotle 384–322 BC: *Nicomachean Ethics*

3 All things work together for good to them that love God.
   Bible: Romans

4 With love for mankind and hatred of sins.
   St Augustine of Hippo AD 354–430: letter 211 in J.-P. Migne
   (ed.) *Patrologiae Latinae* (1845), often quoted 'Love the
   sinner but hate the sin'

5 For, where God built a church, there the devil would also
build a chapel...In such sort is the devil always God's ape.
   Martin Luther 1483–1546: *Colloquia Mensalia* (1566) tr. H.
   Bell, 1652

6 I come to bury Caesar, not to praise him.
The evil that men do lives after them,
The good is oft interrèd with their bones.
   William Shakespeare 1564–1616: *Julius Caesar* (1599)

7 Something is rotten in the state of Denmark.
   William Shakespeare 1564–1616: *Hamlet* (1601)

8 There is nothing either good or bad, but thinking makes it
so.
   William Shakespeare 1564–1616: *Hamlet* (1601)

9   By the pricking of my thumbs,
Something wicked this way comes.
   William Shakespeare 1564–1616: *Macbeth* (1606)

10 For sweetest things turn sourest by their deeds;
Lilies that fester smell far worse than weeds.
   William Shakespeare 1564–1616: sonnet 94 (1609)

11 And out of good still to find means of evil.
   John Milton 1608–74: *Paradise Lost* (1667)

12 Farewell remorse! All good to me is lost;
Evil, be thou my good.
   John Milton 1608–74: *Paradise Lost* (1667)

13 BELINDA: Ay, but you know we must return good for evil.
LADY BRUTE: That may be a mistake in the translation.
   John Vanbrugh 1664–1726: *The Provoked Wife* (1697)

14 Let humble Allen, with an awkward shame,
Do good by stealth, and blush to find it fame.
   Alexander Pope 1688–1744: *Imitations of Horace* (1738)

15 It is necessary only for the good man to do nothing for evil to
triumph.
   Edmund Burke 1729–97: attributed (in a number of forms)
   to Burke, but not found in his writings

16 That best portion of a good man's life,
His little, nameless, unremembered, acts
Of kindness and of love.
   William Wordsworth 1770–1850: 'Lines composed a few
   miles above Tintern Abbey' (1798)

17 He who would do good to another, must do it in minute
particulars.
   William Blake 1757–1827: *Jerusalem* (1815)

18 I expect to pass through this world but once; any good thing
  therefore that I can do, or any kindness that I can show to
  any fellow-creature, let me do it now; let me not defer or
  neglect it, for I shall not pass this way again.
  Stephen Grellet 1773–1855: attributed. See John o' London
  Treasure Trove (1925) for some of the many other claimants
  to authorship

19 No people do so much harm as those who go about doing
  good.
  Bishop Mandell Creighton 1843–1901: in *Life and Letters of
  Mandell Creighton* by his wife (1904)

20 What we call evil is simply ignorance bumping its head in
  the dark.
  Henry Ford 1863–1947: in *Observer* 16 March 1930

21 'Goodness, what beautiful diamonds!'
  'Goodness had nothing to do with it.'
  Mae West 1892–1980: *Night After Night* (1932 film)

22 I and the public know
  What all schoolchildren learn,
  Those to whom evil is done
  Do evil in return.
  W. H. Auden 1907–73: 'September 1, 1939' (1940)

23 There is no evil in the atom; only in men's souls.
  Adlai Stevenson 1900–65: speech at Hartford, Connecticut,
  18 September 1952

24 Innocence always calls mutely for protection, when we would
  be so much wiser to guard ourselves against it: innocence is
  like a dumb leper who has lost his bell, wandering the world
  meaning no harm.
  Graham Greene 1904–91: *The Quiet American* (1955)

25 The face of 'evil' is always the face of total need.
  William S. Burroughs 1914– : *The Naked Lunch* (1959)

26 The fearsome, word-and-thought-defying *banality of evil*.
  Hannah Arendt 1906–75: *Eichmann in Jerusalem* (1963)

Gossip

1 Be thou as chaste as ice, as pure as snow, thou shalt not
escape calumny.
   William Shakespeare 1564-1616: *Hamlet* (1601)

2 How these curiosities would be quite forgot, did not such idle
fellows as I am put them down.
   John Aubrey 1626-97: *Brief Lives*

3 They come together like the Coroner's Inquest, to sit upon
the murdered reputations of the week.
   William Congreve 1670-1729: *The Way of the World* (1700)

4 Love and scandal are the best sweeteners of tea.
   Henry Fielding 1707-54: *Love in Several Masques* (1728)

5 The Town small-talk flows from lip to lip;
Intrigues half-gathered, conversation-scraps,
Kitchen-cabals, and nursery-mishaps.
   George Crabbe 1754-1832: *The Borough* (1810)

6 Every man is surrounded by a neighbourhood of voluntary
spies.
   Jane Austen 1775-1817: *Northanger Abbey* (1818)

7 Gossip is a sort of smoke that comes from the dirty
tobacco-pipes of those who diffuse it: it proves nothing but
the bad taste of the smoker.
   George Eliot 1819-80: *Daniel Deronda* (1876)

8 There is only one thing in the world worse than being talked
about, and that is not being talked about.
   Oscar Wilde 1854-1900: *The Picture of Dorian Gray* (1891)

9 It takes your enemy and your friend, working together, to
hurt you to the heart: the one to slander you and the other to
get the news to you.
   Mark Twain 1835-1910: *Following the Equator* (1897)

10 There is so much good in the worst of us,
And so much bad in the best of us,
That it hardly becomes any of us
To talk about the rest of us.
   Anonymous: attributed, among others, to E. W. Hoch
   (1849-1945), but disclaimed by him

11 Like all gossip—it's merely one of those half-alive things that try to crowd out real life.
E. M. Forster 1879–1970: *A Passage to India* (1924)

12 Careless talk costs lives.
Anonymous: Second World War security slogan

Government

See also **Politics**

1 Let them hate, so long as they fear.
Accius 170–*c*.86 BC: from *Atreus*

2 It is much safer for a prince to be feared than loved, if he is to fail in one of the two.
Niccolò Machiavelli 1469–1527: *The Prince* (1513) tr. A. Gilbert

3 A parliament can do any thing but make a man a woman, and a woman a man.
2nd Earl of Pembroke *c*.1534–1601: quoted by his son, the 4th Earl

4 Though God hath raised me high, yet this I count the glory of my crown: that I have reigned with your loves.
Elizabeth I 1533–1603: The Golden Speech, 1601

5 Dost thou not know, my son, with how little wisdom the world is governed?
Count Oxenstierna 1583–1654: letter to his son, 1648. In *Table Talk* (1689), John Selden quotes 'a certain Pope': 'Thou little thinkest what *a little foolery governs the whole world!*'

6 All empire is no more than power in trust.
John Dryden 1631–1700: *Absalom and Achitophel* (1681)

7 For forms of government let fools contest;
Whate'er is best administered is best.
Alexander Pope 1688–1744: *An Essay on Man* Epistle 3 (1733)

8 The use of force alone is but *temporary*. It may subdue for a moment; but it does not remove the necessity of subduing

again; and a nation is not governed, which is perpetually to
be conquered.
  Edmund Burke 1729–97: *On Conciliation with America* (1775)

9 Government, even in its best state, is but a necessary evil; in
  its worst state, an intolerable one. Government, like dress, is
  the badge of lost innocence; the palaces of kings are built
  upon the ruins of the bowers of paradise.
  Thomas Paine 1737–1809: *Common Sense* (1776)

10 Fear is the foundation of most governments.
  John Adams 1735–1826: *Thoughts on Government* (1776)

11 The happiness of society is the end of government.
  John Adams 1735–1826: *Thoughts on Government* (1776)

12 My people and I have come to an agreement which satisfies
  us both. They are to say what they please, and I am to do
  what I please.
  Frederick the Great 1712–86: his interpretation of
  benevolent despotism (attributed)

13 A state without the means of some change is without the
  means of its conservation.
  Edmund Burke 1729–97: *Reflections on the Revolution in
  France* (1790)

14 When, in countries that are called civilized, we see age going
  to the workhouse and youth to the gallows, something must
  be wrong in the system of government.
  Thomas Paine 1737–1809: *The Rights of Man* pt. 2 (1792)

15 A monarchy is a merchantman which sails well, but will
  sometimes strike on a rock, and go to the bottom; whilst a
  republic is a raft which would never sink, but then your feet
  are always in the water.
  Fisher Ames 1758–1808: speech in the House of
  Representatives, 1795; attributed by R. W. Emerson in
  Essays (1844)

16 *Gouverner, c'est choisir.*
  To govern is to choose.
  Duc de Lévis 1764–1830: *Maximes et Réflexions* (1812 ed.)

17 The best government is that which governs least.
  John L. O'Sullivan 1813–95: *United States Magazine and
  Democratic Review* (1837)

18 The reluctant obedience of distant provinces generally costs more than it is worth.
　　Lord Macaulay 1800–59: *Essays* (1843) 'The War of Succession in Spain'

19 No Government can be long secure without a formidable Opposition.
　　Benjamin Disraeli 1804–81: *Coningsby* (1844)

20 Now, is it to lower the price of corn, or isn't it? It is not much matter which we say, but mind, we must all say *the same*.
　　Lord Melbourne 1779–1848: on cabinet government; attributed, in Walter Bagehot *The English Constitution* (1867)

21 Your business is not to govern the country but it is, if you think fit, to call to account those who do govern it.
　　W. E. Gladstone 1809–98: speech to the House of Commons, 29 January 1855

22 Every country has its own constitution; ours is absolutism moderated by assassination.
　　Anonymous: 'An intelligent Russian', in *Political Sketches of the State of Europe, 1814–1867* (1868)

23 England is the mother of Parliaments.
　　John Bright 1811–89: speech at Birmingham, 18 January 1865

24 The Crown is, according to the saying, the 'fountain of honour'; but the Treasury is the spring of business.
　　Walter Bagehot 1826–77: *The English Constitution* (1867)

25 I work for a Government I despise for ends I think criminal.
　　John Maynard Keynes 1883–1946: letter to Duncan Grant, 15 December 1917

26 The important thing for Government is not to do things which individuals are doing already, and to do them a little better or a little worse; but to do those things which at present are not done at all.
　　John Maynard Keynes 1883–1946: *End of Laissez-Faire* (1926)

27 Democracy means government by the uneducated, while aristocracy means government by the badly educated.
　　G. K. Chesterton 1874–1936: *New York Times* 1 February 1931

28 BIG BROTHER IS WATCHING YOU.
  George Orwell 1903-50: *Nineteen Eighty-Four* (1949)

29 Wherever you have an efficient government you have
  a dictatorship.
  Harry S. Truman 1884-1972: lecture at Columbia
  University, 28 April 1959

30 If the Government is big enough to give you everything you
  want, it is big enough to take away everything you have.
  Gerald Ford 1909- : in J. F. Parker *If Elected* (1960)

31 Government of the busy by the bossy for the bully.
  Arthur Seldon 1916- : *Capitalism* (1990), subheading on
  over-government

32 We give the impression of being in office but not in power.
  Norman Lamont 1942- : speech, House of Commons, 9
  June 1993

Greatness

1 The beauty of Israel is slain upon thy high places: how are
  the mighty fallen!
  Bible: II Samuel

2   Rightly to be great
  Is not to stir without great argument,
  But greatly to find quarrel in a straw
  When honour's at the stake.
  William Shakespeare 1564-1616: *Hamlet* (1601)

3 But be not afraid of greatness: some men are born great,
  some achieve greatness, and some have greatness thrust
  upon them.
  William Shakespeare 1564-1616: *Twelfth Night* (1601)

4 Farewell! a long farewell, to all my greatness!
  William Shakespeare 1564-1616: *Henry VIII* (with John
  Fletcher, 1613)

5 To be great is to be misunderstood.
  Ralph Waldo Emerson 1803-82: *Essays* (1841) 'Self-Reliance'

Habit see Custom and Habit

Happiness

1 Call no man happy before he dies, he is at best but fortunate.
  Solon c.640–after 556 BC: in Herodotus *Histories*

2 *Nil admirari prope res est una, Numici,*
  Solaque quae possit facere et servare beatum.
  To marvel at nothing is just about the one and only thing,
  Numicius, that can make a man happy and keep him that
  way.
  Horace 65–8 BC: *Epistles*

3 For all the happiness mankind can gain
  Is not in pleasure, but in rest from pain.
  John Dryden 1631–1700: *The Indian Emperor* (1665)

4 Mirth is like a flash of lightning that breaks through a gloom
  of clouds, and glitters for a moment: cheerfulness keeps up a
  kind of day-light in the mind.
  Joseph Addison 1672–1719: *The Spectator* 17 May 1712

5 Not to admire, is all the art I know,
  To make men happy, and to keep them so.
  Alexander Pope 1688–1744: *Imitations of Horace* (1738)

6 A little miss, dressed in a new gown for a dancing-school
  ball, receives as complete enjoyment as the greatest orator,
  who...governs the passions and resolutions of a numerous
  assembly.
  David Hume 1711–76: *Essays: Moral and Political* (1741–2)

7 *Freude, schöner Götterfunken,*
  Tochter aus Elysium.
  Joy, beautiful radiance of the gods, daughter of Elysium.
  Friedrich von Schiller 1759–1805: 'An die Freude' (1785)

8 Happiness is not an ideal of reason but of imagination.
  Immanuel Kant 1724–1804: *Fundamental Principles of the
  Metaphysics of Ethics* (1785), tr. T. K. Abbott

9 A large income is the best recipe for happiness I ever heard
  of. It certainly may secure all the myrtle and turkey part
  of it.
  Jane Austen 1775–1817: *Mansfield Park* (1814)

10 Ask yourself whether you are happy, and you cease to be so.
  John Stuart Mill 1806–73: *Autobiography* (1873)

11 We have no more right to consume happiness without
producing it than to consume wealth without producing it.
   George Bernard Shaw 1856–1950: *Candida* (1898)

12 But a lifetime of happiness! No man alive could bear it: it
would be hell on earth.
   George Bernard Shaw 1856–1950: *Man and Superman*
(1903)

13 I can sympathize with people's pains, but not with their
pleasures. There is something curiously boring about
somebody else's happiness.
   Aldous Huxley 1894–1963: *Limbo* (1920)

14 Happiness is a wine of the rarest vintage, and seems insipid
to a vulgar taste.
   Logan Pearsall Smith 1865–1946: *Afterthoughts* (1931)

15 Happiness makes up in height for what it lacks in length.
   Robert Frost 1874–1963: title of poem (1942)

16 Happiness is an imaginary condition, formerly often
attributed by the living to the dead, now usually attributed
by adults to children, and by children to adults.
   Thomas Szasz 1920– : *The Second Sin* (1973) 'Emotions'

17 I always say I don't think everyone has the right to
happiness or to be loved. Even the Americans have written
into their constitution that you have the right to the 'pursuit
of happiness'. You have the right to try but that is all.
   Claire Rayner 1931– : in G. Kinnock and F. Miller *By
Faith and Daring* (1993)

Hatred

1 Better is a dinner of herbs where love is, than a stalled ox
and hatred therewith.
   Bible: Proverbs

2 *Non amo te, Sabidi, nec possum dicere quare:*
  Hoc tantum possum dicere, non amo te.
I don't love you, Sabidius, and I can't tell you why; all I can
tell you is this, that I don't love you.
   Martial AD *c.*40–*c.*104: *Epigrammata*

3 I do not love thee, Dr Fell.
  The reason why I cannot tell;

But this I know, and know full well,
I do not love thee, Dr Fell.
> **Thomas Brown** 1663-1704: written while an undergraduate
> at Christ Church, Oxford, of which Dr Fell was Dean

4 We can scarcely hate any one that we know.
> **William Hazlitt** 1778-1830: *Table Talk* (1822)

5 Now hatred is by far the longest pleasure;
Men love in haste, but they detest at leisure.
> **Lord Byron** 1788-1824: *Don Juan* (1819-24)

6 Gr-r-r—there go, my heart's abhorrence!
Water your damned flower-pots, do!
If hate killed men, Brother Lawrence,
God's blood, would not mine kill you!
> **Robert Browning** 1812-89: 'Soliloquy of the Spanish
> Cloister' (1842)

7 If you hate a person, you hate something in him that is part
of yourself. What isn't part of ourselves doesn't disturb us.
> **Hermann Hesse** 1877-1962: *Demian* (1919)

8 I never hated a man enough to give him diamonds back.
> **Zsa Zsa Gabor** 1919- : in *Observer* 25 August 1957

Health see Sickness and Health

The Heart

1   A man whose blood
Is very snow-broth; one who never feels
The wanton stings and motions of the sense.
> **William Shakespeare** 1564-1616: *Measure for Measure*
> (1604)

2 The heart has its reasons which reason knows nothing of.
> **Blaise Pascal** 1623-62: *Pensées* (1670)

3 Calm of mind, all passion spent.
> **John Milton** 1608-74: *Samson Agonistes* (1671)

4 The ruling passion, be it what it will,
The ruling passion conquers reason still.
> **Alexander Pope** 1688-1744: 'To Lord Bathurst' (1733)

5 Unlearn'd, he knew no schoolman's subtle art,
No language, but the language of the heart.
Alexander Pope 1688–1744: 'An Epistle to Dr Arbuthnot'
(1735)

6 The desires of the heart are as crooked as corkscrews
Not to be born is the best for man.
W. H. Auden 1907–73: 'Death's Echo' (1937)

7 Now that my ladder's gone
I must lie down where all ladders start
In the foul rag and bone shop of the heart.
W. B. Yeats 1865–1939: 'The Circus Animals' Desertion'
(1939)

8 They had been corrupted by money, and he had been
corrupted by sentiment. Sentiment was the more dangerous,
because you couldn't name its price. A man open to bribes
was to be relied upon below a certain figure, but sentiment
might uncoil in the heart at a name, a photograph, even a
smell remembered.
Graham Greene 1904–91: *The Heart of the Matter* (1948)

9 A man who has not passed through the inferno of his
passions has never overcome them.
Carl Gustav Jung 1875–1961: *Memories, Dreams, Reflections*
(1962)

Heaven and Hell

1 And I saw a new heaven and a new earth: for the first heaven
and the first earth were passed away; and there was no more
sea.
Bible: Revelation

2 LASCIATE OGNI SPERANZA VOI CH'ENTRATE!
Abandon all hope, you who enter!
Dante Alighieri 1265–1321: inscription at the entrance to
Hell; *Divina Commedia* 'Inferno'

3 Better to reign in hell, than serve in heaven.
John Milton 1608–74: *Paradise Lost* (1667)

4 Me miserable! which way shall I fly
Infinite wrath, and infinite despair?
Which way I fly is hell; myself am hell.
   John Milton 1608–74: *Paradise Lost* (1667)

5 Hell is a city much like London.
   Percy Bysshe Shelley 1792–1822: 'Peter Bell the Third'
   (1819)

6 My idea of heaven is, eating *pâté de foie gras* to the sound of
trumpets.
   Sydney Smith 1771–1845: in H. Pearson *The Smith of Smiths*
   (1934)

7 A perpetual holiday is a good working definition of hell.
   George Bernard Shaw 1856–1950: *Parents and Children*
   (1914)

8 The true paradises are the paradises that we have lost.
   Marcel Proust 1871–1922: *Time Regained* (1926)

9 Hell, madam, is to love no more.
   Georges Bernanos 1888–1948: *Journal d'un curé de
   campagne* (1936)

10 Whose love is given over-well
Shall look on Helen's face in hell
Whilst they whose love is thin and wise
Shall see John Knox in Paradise.
   Dorothy Parker 1893–1967: 'Partial Comfort' (1937)

11 Hell is other people.
   Jean-Paul Sartre 1905–80: *Huis Clos* (1944)

12 What is hell?
Hell is oneself,
Hell is alone, the other figures in it
Merely projections.
   T. S. Eliot 1888–1965: *The Cocktail Party* (1950)

Heroes

1 No man is a hero to his valet.
   Mme Cornuel 1605–94: in *Lettres de Mlle Aïssé à Madame C*
   (1787) Letter 13 'De Paris, 1728'

2 Every hero becomes a bore at last.
   Ralph Waldo Emerson 1803–82: *Representative Men* (1850)

3 Heroing is one of the shortest-lived professions there is.
   Will Rogers 1879–1935: newspaper article, 15 February 1925

4 ANDREA: Unhappy the land that has no heroes!...
   GALILEO: No. Unhappy the land that needs heroes.
   Bertolt Brecht 1898–1956: *Life of Galileo* (1939)

5 Faster than a speeding bullet!...Look! Up in the sky! It's a
   bird! It's a plane! It's Superman! Yes, it's
   Superman!...who—disguised as Clark Kent, mild-mannered
   reporter for a great metropolitan newspaper—fights a never
   ending battle for truth, justice and the American way!
   Anonymous: *Superman* (US radio show, 1940 onwards)
   preamble

History

1 History is philosophy from examples.
   Dionysius of Halicarnassus fl. 30–7 BC: *Ars Rhetorica*

2 Happy the people whose annals are blank in history-books!
   Montesquieu 1689–1755: attributed by Thomas Carlyle

3 History...is, indeed, little more than the register of the
   crimes, follies, and misfortunes of mankind.
   Edward Gibbon 1737–94: *Decline and Fall of the Roman
   Empire* (1776–88)

4 This province of literature [history] is a debatable line. It lies
   on the confines of two distinct territories...It is sometimes
   fiction. It is sometimes theory.
   Lord Macaulay 1800–59: 'History' (1828)

5 What experience and history teach is this—that nations and
   governments have never learned anything from history, or
   acted upon any lessons they might have drawn from it.
   G. W. F. Hegel 1770–1831: *Lectures on the Philosophy of
   World History: Introduction* (1830), tr. H. B. Nisbet

6 History [is] a distillation of rumour.
   Thomas Carlyle 1795–1881: *History of the French Revolution*
   (1837)

7 History is the essence of innumerable biographies.
   Thomas Carlyle 1795–1881: *Critical and Miscellaneous Essays* (1838) 'On History'

8 There is properly no history; only biography.
   Ralph Waldo Emerson 1803–82: *Essays* (1841) 'History'

9 Hegel says somewhere that all great events and personalities in world history reappear in one fashion or another. He forgot to add: the first time as tragedy, the second as farce.
   Karl Marx 1818–83: *Eighteenth Brumaire of Louis Bonaparte* (1852)

10 History is a gallery of pictures in which there are few originals and many copies.
   Alexis de Tocqueville 1805–59: *L'Ancien régime* (1856), tr. M. W. Patterson

11 That great dust-heap called 'history'.
   Augustine Birrell 1850–1933: *Obiter Dicta* (1884)

12 History is past politics, and politics is present history.
   E. A. Freeman 1823–92: *Methods of Historical Study* (1886)

13 War makes rattling good history; but Peace is poor reading.
   Thomas Hardy 1840–1928: *The Dynasts* (1904)

14 HISTORY, *n.* An account, mostly false, of events, mostly unimportant, which are brought about by rulers, mostly knaves, and soldiers, mostly fools.
   Ambrose Bierce 1842–c.1914: *The Cynic's Word Book* (1906)

15 History is more or less bunk.
   Henry Ford 1863–1947: in *Chicago Tribune* 25 May 1916

16 Human history becomes more and more a race between education and catastrophe.
   H. G. Wells 1866–1946: *The Outline of History* (1920)

17 History is not what you thought. *It is what you can remember*.
   W. C. Sellar 1898–1951 and **R. J. Yeatman** 1898–1968: *1066 and All That* (1930) 'Compulsory Preface'

18 History gets thicker as it approaches recent times.
   A. J. P. Taylor 1906–90: *English History 1914–45* (1965) bibliography

19 Does history repeat itself, the first time as tragedy, the second time as farce? No, that's too grand, too considered a

process. History just burps, and we taste again that
raw-onion sandwich it swallowed centuries ago.
   Julian Barnes 1946- : *A History of the World in 10 ½
   Chapters* (1989)

The Home and Housework

1 There is scarcely any less bother in the running of a family
than in that of an entire state. And domestic business is no
less importunate for being less important.
   Montaigne 1533-92: *Essais* (1580)

2 For a man's house is his castle, *et domus sua cuique est
tutissimum refugium* [and each man's home is his safest
refuge].
   Edward Coke 1552-1634: *Third Part of the Institutes of the
   Laws of England* (1628)

3 Home is home, though it be never so homely.
   John Clarke d. 1658: *Paraemiologia Anglo-Latina* (1639)

4 The accent of one's birthplace lingers in the mind and in the
heart as it does in one's speech.
   Duc de la Rochefoucauld 1613-80: *Maximes* (1678)

5 Mid pleasures and palaces though we may roam,
Be it ever so humble, there's no place like home.
   J. H. Payne 1791-1852: 'Home, Sweet Home' (1823)

6 Have nothing in your houses that you do not know to be
useful, or believe to be beautiful.
   William Morris 1834-96: *Hopes and Fears for Art* (1882)

7 What's the good of a home if you are never in it?
   George Grossmith 1847-1912 and **Weedon Grossmith**
   1854-1919: *Diary of a Nobody* (1894)

8 Dirt is only matter out of place.
   John Chipman Gray 1839-1915: *Restraints on the Alienation
   of Property* (2nd ed., 1895)

9 Some dish more sharply spiced than this
Milk-soup men call domestic bliss.
   Coventry Patmore 1823-96: 'Olympus'

10 Home is the girl's prison and the woman's workhouse.
    George Bernard Shaw 1856–1950: *Man and Superman*
    (1903)

11 'Home is the place where, when you have to go there,
    They have to take you in.'
    'I should have called it
    Something you somehow haven't to deserve.'
    Robert Frost 1874–1963: 'The Death of the Hired Man'
    (1914)

12   The best
    Thing we can do is to make wherever we're lost in
    Look as much like home as we can.
    Christopher Fry 1907– : *The Lady's not for Burning* (1949)

13 MR PRITCHARD: I must dust the blinds and then I must raise
    them.
    MRS OGMORE-PRITCHARD: And before you let the sun in, mind it
    wipes its shoes.
    Dylan Thomas 1914–1953: *Under Milk Wood* (1954)

14 There was no need to do any housework at all. After the first
    four years the dirt doesn't get any worse.
    Quentin Crisp 1908– : *The Naked Civil Servant* (1968)

15 Conran's Law of Housework—it expands to fill the time
    available plus half an hour.
    Shirley Conran 1932– : *Superwoman 2* (1977)

....

Honour

....

1 The purest treasure mortal times afford
    Is spotless reputation; that away,
    Men are but gilded loam or painted clay.
    William Shakespeare 1564–1616: *Richard II* (1595)

2 What is honour? A word. What is that word, honour? Air. A
    trim reckoning! Who hath it? He that died o' Wednesday.
    William Shakespeare 1564–1616: *Henry IV, Part 1* (1597)

3 Who steals my purse steals trash; 'tis something, nothing;
    'Twas mine, 'tis his, and has been slave to thousands;
    But he that filches from me my good name

Robs me of that which not enriches him,
And makes me poor indeed.
   William Shakespeare 1564–1616: *Othello* (1602–4)

4 O! I have lost my reputation. I have lost the immortal part of myself, and what remains is bestial.
   William Shakespeare 1564–1616: *Othello* (1602–4)

5 I could not love thee, Dear, so much,
Loved I not honour more.
   Richard Lovelace 1618–58: 'To Lucasta, Going to the Wars' (1649)

6 His honour rooted in dishonour stood,
And faith unfaithful kept him falsely true.
   Alfred, Lord Tennyson 1809–92: *Idylls of the King* 'Lancelot and Elaine' (1859)

7 The louder he talked of his honour, the faster we counted our spoons.
   Ralph Waldo Emerson 1803–82: *The Conduct of Life* (1860)

8 Remember, you're fighting for this woman's honour...which is probably more than she ever did.
   Bert Kalmar 1884–1947 et al.: *Duck Soup* (1933 film);
   spoken by Groucho Marx

Hope and Despair

See also **Optimism and Pessimism**

1 Hope deferred maketh the heart sick: but when the desire cometh, it is a tree of life.
   Bible: Proverbs

2 *Nil desperandum.*
Never despair.
   Horace 65–8 BC: *Odes*

3 He that lives in hope danceth without music.
   George Herbert 1593–1633: *Outlandish Proverbs* (1640)

4 Magnanimous Despair alone
Could show me so divine a thing,
Where feeble Hope could ne'er have flown
But vainly flapped its tinsel wing.
   Andrew Marvell 1621–78: 'The Definition of Love' (1681)

5 I can endure my own despair,
But not another's hope.
   William Walsh 1663–1708: 'Song: Of All the Torments'

6 'Blessed is the man who expects nothing, for he shall never
be disappointed' was the ninth beatitude.
   Alexander Pope 1688–1744: letter to Fortescue,
   23 September 1725

7 Hope springs eternal in the human breast:
Man never Is, but always To be blest.
   Alexander Pope 1688–1744: *An Essay on Man* Epistle 1
   (1733)

8 He that lives upon hope will die fasting.
   Benjamin Franklin 1706–90: *Poor Richard's Almanac* (1758)

9 What is hope? nothing but the paint on the face of Existence;
the least touch of truth rubs it off, and then we see what a
hollow-cheeked harlot we have got hold of.
   Lord Byron 1788–1824: letter to Thomas Moore, 28 October
   1815

10   O, Wind,
If Winter comes, can Spring be far behind?
   Percy Bysshe Shelley 1792–1822: 'Ode to the West Wind'
   (1819)

11 Work without hope draws nectar in a sieve,
And hope without an object cannot live.
   Samuel Taylor Coleridge 1772–1834: 'Work without Hope'
   (1828)

12 Hopeless hope hopes on and meets no end,
Wastes without springs and homes without a friend.
   John Clare 1793–1864: 'Child Harold' (written 1841)

13 No worst, there is none. Pitched past pitch of grief,
More pangs will, schooled at forepangs, wilder wring.
Comforter, where, where is your comforting?
   Gerard Manley Hopkins 1844–89: 'No worst, there is none'
   (written 1885)

14 Not, I'll not, carrion comfort, Despair, not feast on thee;
Not untwist—slack they may be—these last strands of man
In me or, most weary, cry *I can no more.* I can;
Can something, hope, wish day come, not choose not to be.
   Gerard Manley Hopkins 1844–89: 'Carrion Comfort'
   (written 1885)

15 He who has never hoped can never despair.
    George Bernard Shaw 1856–1950: *Caesar and Cleopatra* (1901)

16 If way to the Better there be, it exacts a full look at the worst.
    Thomas Hardy 1840–1928: 'De Profundis' (1902)

17 After all, tomorrow is another day.
    Margaret Mitchell 1900–49: *Gone with the Wind* (1936)

18 In a real dark night of the soul it is always three o'clock in the morning.
    F. Scott Fitzgerald 1896–1940: 'Handle with Care' in *Esquire* March 1936

19 Human life begins on the far side of despair.
    Jean-Paul Sartre 1905–80: *Les Mouches* (1943)

20 Anything that consoles is fake.
    Iris Murdoch 1919– : in R. Harries *Prayer and the Pursuit of Happiness* (1985)

The Human Race

1 Man is the measure of all things.
    Protagoras b. *c.*485 BC: in Plato *Theaetetus*

2 There are many wonderful things, and nothing is more wonderful than man.
    Sophocles *c.*496–406 BC: *Antigone*

3 I am a man, I count nothing human foreign to me.
    Terence *c.*190–159 BC: *Heauton Timorumenos*

4 Lord, what fools these mortals be!
    William Shakespeare 1564–1616: *A Midsummer Night's Dream* (1595–6)

5 What a piece of work is a man! How noble in reason! how infinite in faculty! in form, in moving, how express and admirable! in action how like an angel! in apprehension how like a god! the beauty of the world! the paragon of animals!
    William Shakespeare 1564–1616: *Hamlet* (1601)

6 One touch of nature makes the whole world kin.
    William Shakespeare 1564–1616: *Troilus and Cressida* (1602)

7 Man is a torch borne in the wind; a dream
But of a shadow, summed with all his substance.
   George Chapman *c.*1559-1634: *Bussy D'Ambois* (1607-8)

8   We are such stuff
As dreams are made on, and our little life
Is rounded with a sleep.
   William Shakespeare 1564-1616: *The Tempest* (1611)

9 How beauteous mankind is! O brave new world,
That has such people in't.
   William Shakespeare 1564-1616: *The Tempest* (1611)

10 Man is man's A.B.C. There is none that can
Read God aright, unless he first spell Man.
   Francis Quarles 1592-1644: *Hieroglyphics of the Life of Man*
   (1638)

11 We carry within us the wonders we seek without us: there is
all Africa and her prodigies in us.
   Sir Thomas Browne 1605-82: *Religio Medici* (1643)

12 Man is only a reed, the weakest thing in nature; but he is a
thinking reed.
   Blaise Pascal 1623-62: *Pensées* (1670)

13 An honest man's the noblest work of God.
   Alexander Pope 1688-1744: *An Essay on Man* Epistle 4
   (1734)

14 Man is a tool-making animal.
   Benjamin Franklin 1706-90: in James Boswell *Life of
Samuel Johnson* (1791) 7 April 1778

15 Out of the crooked timber of humanity no straight thing can
ever be made.
   Immanuel Kant 1724-1804: *Idee zu einer allgemeinen
Geschichte in weltbürgerlicher Absicht* (1784)

16 Drinking when we are not thirsty and making love all year
round, madam; that is all there is to distinguish us from
other animals.
   Pierre-Augustin Caron de Beaumarchais 1732-99: *The
Marriage of Figaro* (1785)

17 For Mercy has a human heart
Pity a human face:

And Love, the human form divine,
And Peace, the human dress.
    William Blake 1757-1827: *Songs of Innocence* (1789) 'The Divine Image'

18 Cruelty has a human heart,
And Jealousy a human face;
Terror the human form divine,
And Secrecy the human dress.
    William Blake 1757-1827: 'A Divine Image'; etched but not included in *Songs of Experience* (1794)

19 Is man an ape or an angel? Now I am on the side of the angels.
    Benjamin Disraeli 1804-81: speech at Oxford, 25 November 1864

20 I teach you the superman. Man is something to be surpassed.
    Friedrich Nietzsche 1844-1900: *Also Sprach Zarathustra* (1883)

21 Man is the Only Animal that Blushes. Or needs to.
    Mark Twain 1835-1910: *Following the Equator* (1897)

22 I wish I loved the Human Race;
I wish I loved its silly face;
I wish I liked the way it walks;
I wish I liked the way it talks;
And when I'm introduced to one
I wish I thought *What Jolly Fun!*
    Walter Raleigh 1861-1922: 'Wishes of an Elderly Man' (1923)

23 Many people believe that they are attracted by God, or by Nature, when they are only repelled by man.
    Dean Inge 1860-1954: *More Lay Thoughts of a Dean* (1931)

24 What is man, when you come to think upon him, but a minutely set, ingenious machine for turning, with infinite artfulness, the red wine of Shiraz into urine?
    Isak Dinesen 1885-1962: *Seven Gothic Tales* (1934)

25 Man, unlike any other thing organic or inorganic in the universe, grows beyond his work, walks up the stairs of his concepts, emerges ahead of his accomplishments.
    John Steinbeck 1902-68: *Grapes of Wrath* (1939)

26 I hate 'Humanity' and all such abstracts: but I love *people*.
Lovers of 'Humanity' generally hate *people and children*, and
keep parrots or puppy dogs.
   Roy Campbell 1901–57: *Light on a Dark Horse* (1951)

27 We're all of us guinea pigs in the laboratory of God.
Humanity is just a work in progress.
   Tennessee Williams 1911–83: *Camino Real* (1953)

Human Rights

1 To no man will we sell, or deny, or delay, right or justice.
   Magna Carta 1215: clause 40

2 The poorest he that is in England hath a life to live as the
greatest he.
   Thomas Rainborowe d. 1648: during the Army debates at
   Putney, 29 October 1647

3 We hold these truths to be self-evident, that all men are
created equal, that they are endowed by their Creator with
certain unalienable rights, that among these are life, liberty
and the pursuit of happiness.
   American Declaration of Independence 1776: from a draft
   by Thomas Jefferson (1743–1826)

4 *Liberté! Égalité! Fraternité!*
Freedom! Equality! Brotherhood!
   Anonymous: motto of the French Revolution, but of earlier
   origin

5 Whatever each man can separately do, without trespassing
upon others, he has a right to do for himself; and he has a
right to a fair portion of all which society, with all its
combinations of skill and force, can do in his favour.
   Edmund Burke 1729–97: *Reflections on the Revolution in
   France* (1790)

6 Any law which violates the inalienable rights of man is
essentially unjust and tyrannical; it is not a law at all.
   Maximilien Robespierre 1758–94: *Déclaration des droits de
   l'homme* 24 April 1793

7 Natural rights is simple nonsense: natural and
imprescriptible rights, rhetorical nonsense—nonsense upon
stilts.
   Jeremy Bentham 1748–1832: *Anarchical Fallacies*

8 The first duty of a State is to see that every child born
therein shall be well housed, clothed, fed and educated, till it
attain years of discretion.
   John Ruskin 1819–1900: *Time and Tide* (1867)

9 We look forward to a world founded upon four essential
human freedoms. The first is freedom of speech and
expression—everywhere in the world. The second is freedom
of every person to worship God in his own way—everywhere
in the world. The third is freedom from want…The fourth is
freedom from fear.
   Franklin D. Roosevelt 1882–1945: message to Congress,
   6 January 1941

10 All human beings are born free and equal in dignity and
rights.
   Universal Declaration of Human Rights 1948: article 1

Humour

1 Delight hath a joy in it either permanent or present.
Laughter hath only a scornful tickling.
   Philip Sidney 1554–86: *The Defence of Poetry* (1595)

2 A jest's prosperity lies in the ear
Of him that hears it, never in the tongue
Of him that makes it.
   William Shakespeare 1564–1616: *Love's Labour's Lost* (1595)

3 I am not only witty in myself, but the cause that wit is in
other men.
   William Shakespeare 1564–1616: *Henry IV, Part 2* (1597)

4 He uses his folly like a stalking-horse, and under the
presentation of that he shoots his wit.
   William Shakespeare 1564–1616: *As You Like It* (1599)

5 Brevity is the soul of wit.
   William Shakespeare 1564–1616: *Hamlet* (1601)

6 A thing well said will be wit in all languages.
   John Dryden 1631–1700: *Essay of Dramatic Poesy* (1668)

7 If we may believe our logicians, man is distinguished from
all other creatures by the faculty of laughter.
   Joseph Addison 1672–1719: *The Spectator* 26 September 1712

8 I make myself laugh at everything, for fear of having to weep
at it.
   Pierre-Augustin Caron de Beaumarchais 1732–99: *Le
Barbier de Séville* (1755)

9 What is an Epigram? a dwarfish whole,
Its body brevity, and wit its soul.
   Samuel Taylor Coleridge 1772–1834: 'Epigram' (1809)

10 For what do we live, but to make sport for our neighbours,
and laugh at them in our turn?
   Jane Austen 1775–1817: *Pride and Prejudice* (1813)

11 Laughter is pleasant, but the exertion is too much for me.
   Thomas Love Peacock 1785–1866: *Nightmare Abbey* (1818)

12 [A pun] is a pistol let off at the ear; not a feather to tickle the
intellect.
   Charles Lamb 1775–1834: *Last Essays of Elia* (1833) 'Popular
Fallacies'

13 A difference of taste in jokes is a great strain on the
affections.
   George Eliot 1819–80: *Daniel Deronda* (1876)

14 Wit is the epitaph of an emotion.
   Friedrich Nietzsche 1844–1900: *Menschliches,
Allzumenschliches* (1867–80)

15 We are not amused.
   Queen Victoria 1819–1901: attributed, in Caroline Holland
Notebooks of a Spinster Lady (1919) 2 January 1900

16 Everything is funny as long as it is happening to Somebody
Else.
   Will Rogers 1879–1935: *The Illiterate Digest* (1924)

17 People must not do things for fun. We are not here for fun.
There is no reference to fun in any Act of Parliament.
   A. P. Herbert 1890–1971: *Uncommon Law* (1935)

18 What do you mean, funny? Funny-peculiar or funny ha-ha?
   Ian Hay 1876–1952: *The Housemaster* (1938)

19 The funniest thing about comedy is that you never know why
people laugh. I know *what* makes them laugh but trying to

get your hands on the *why* of it is like trying to pick an eel
out of a tub of water.

> **W. C. Fields** 1880–1946: in R. J. Anobile *A Flask of Fields*
> (1972)

20 Humour is emotional chaos remembered in tranquillity.

> **James Thurber** 1894–1961: in *New York Post* 29 February
> 1960

21 Forgive, O Lord, my little jokes on Thee
And I'll forgive Thy great big one on me.

> **Robert Frost** 1874–1963: 'Cluster of Faith' (1962)

22 Among those whom I like or admire, I can find no common
denominator, but among those whom I love, I can: all of them
make me laugh.

> **W. H. Auden** 1907–73: *The Dyer's Hand* (1963) 'Notes on the
> Comic'

23 The trouble with Freud is that he never had to play the old
Glasgow Empire on a Saturday night after Rangers and Celtic
had both lost.

> **Ken Dodd** 1931– : *Guardian* 30 April 1991; quoted in many
> forms since the mid-1960s

Hypocrisy

1 My tongue swore, but my mind's unsworn.

> **Euripides** *c*.485–*c*.406 BC: *Hippolytus* (lamenting the
> breaking of an oath)

2 Woe unto them that call evil good, and good evil.

> **Bible**: Isaiah

3 Ye are like unto whited sepulchres.

> **Bible**: St Matthew

4 The smylere with the knyf under the cloke.

> **Geoffrey Chaucer** *c*.1343–1400: *The Canterbury Tales* 'The
> Knight's Tale'

5 Do not, as some ungracious pastors do,
Show me the steep and thorny way to heaven,
Whiles, like a puffed and reckless libertine,
Himself the primrose path of dalliance treads,
And recks not his own rede.

> **William Shakespeare** 1564–1616: *Hamlet* (1601)

6   I want that glib and oily art
To speak and purpose not.
   William Shakespeare 1564–1616: *King Lear* (1605–6)

7 Compound for sins, they are inclined to,
By damning those they have no mind to.
   Samuel Butler 1612–80: *Hudibras* pt. 1 (1663)

8 Hypocrisy, the only evil that walks
Invisible, except to God alone.
   John Milton 1608–74: *Paradise Lost* (1667)

9 Hypocrisy is a tribute which vice pays to virtue.
   Duc de la Rochefoucauld 1613–80: *Maximes* (1678)

10 Keep up appearances; there lies the test;
The world will give thee credit for the rest.
Outward be fair, however foul within;
Sin if thou wilt, but then in secret sin.
   Charles Churchill 1731–64: *Night* (1761)

11 I sit on a man's back, choking him and making him carry
me, and yet assure myself and others that I am very sorry for
him and wish to ease his lot by all possible means—except by
getting off his back.
   Leo Tolstoy 1828–1910: *What Then Must We Do?* (1886), tr.
   A. Maude

12 Talk about the pews and steeples
And the cash that goes therewith!
But the souls of Christian peoples…
Chuck it, Smith!
   G. K. Chesterton 1874–1936: 'Antichrist' (1915)

13 All Reformers, however strict their social conscience, live in
houses just as big as they can pay for.
   Logan Pearsall Smith 1865–1946: *Afterthoughts* (1931)

Idealism

1 We are all in the gutter, but some of us are looking at the
stars.
   Oscar Wilde 1854–1900: *Lady Windermere's Fan* (1892)

2 I have spread my dreams under your feet;
  Tread softly because you tread on my dreams.
    W. B. Yeats 1865–1939: 'He Wishes for the Cloths of Heaven'
    (1899)

3 A cause may be inconvenient, but it's magnificent. It's like
  champagne or high heels, and one must be prepared to suffer
  for it.
    Arnold Bennett 1867–1931: *The Title* (1918)

4 If a man hasn't discovered something he will die for, he isn't
  fit to live.
    Martin Luther King 1929–68: speech in Detroit, 23 June
    1963

Ideas

See also **Thinking**

1 It could be said of me that in this book I have only made up a
  bunch of other men's flowers, providing of my own only the
  string that ties them together.
    Montaigne 1533–92: *Essais* (1580)

2 It is the nature of an hypothesis, when once a man has
  conceived it, that it assimilates every thing to itself, as
  proper nourishment; and, from the first moment of your
  begetting it, it generally grows the stronger by every thing
  you see, hear, read, or understand.
    Laurence Sterne 1713–68: *Tristram Shandy* (1759–67)

3 A stand can be made against invasion by an army; no stand
  can be made against invasion by an idea.
    Victor Hugo 1802–85: *Histoire d'un Crime* (written 1851–2,
    published 1877)

4 When you are a Bear of Very Little Brain, and you Think of
  Things, you find sometimes that a Thing which seemed very
  Thingish inside you is quite different when it gets out into
  the open and has other people looking at it.
    A. A. Milne 1882–1956: *The House at Pooh Corner* (1928)

5 It isn't that they can't see the solution. It is that they can't see the problem.
  G. K. Chesterton 1874–1936: *The Scandal of Father Brown* (1935)

6 Nothing is more dangerous than an idea, when you have only one idea.
  Alain 1868–1951: *Propos sur la religion* (1938)

7 There is one thing stronger than all the armies in the world; and that is an idea whose time has come.
  Anonymous: *Nation* 15 April 1943

8 It is better to entertain an idea than to take it home to live with you for the rest of your life.
  Randall Jarrell 1914–65: *Pictures from an Institution* (1954)

Idleness

1 Go to the ant thou sluggard; consider her ways, and be wise.
  Bible: Proverbs

2 Bankrupt of life, yet prodigal of ease.
  John Dryden 1631–1700: *Absalom and Achitophel* (1681)

3 For Satan finds some mischief still
  For idle hands to do.
  Isaac Watts 1674–1748: *Divine Songs for Children* (1715) 'Against Idleness and Mischief'

4 It is better to wear out than to rust out.
  Bishop Richard Cumberland 1631–1718: in G. Horne *The Duty of Contending for the Faith* (1786)

5 Procrastination is the thief of time.
  Edward Young 1683–1765: *Night Thoughts* (1742–5)

6 Idleness is only the refuge of weak minds.
  Lord Chesterfield 1694–1773: *Letters to his Son* (1774) 20 July 1749

7 The foul sluggard's comfort: 'It will last my time.'
  Thomas Carlyle 1795–1881: *Critical and Miscellaneous Essays* (1838)

8 How dull it is to pause, to make an end,
   To rust unburnished, not to shine in use!
   As though to breathe were life.
   Alfred, Lord Tennyson 1809–92: 'Ulysses' (1842)

9 It is impossible to enjoy idling thoroughly unless one has
   plenty of work to do.
   Jerome K. Jerome 1859–1927: *Idle Thoughts of an Idle
   Fellow* (1886)

10 procrastination is the
   art of keeping
   up with yesterday.
   Don Marquis 1878–1937: *archy and mehitabel* (1927)

11 I do nothing, granted. But I see the hours pass—which is
   better than trying to fill them.
   E.M. Cioran 1911– : *Guardian* 11 May 1993

Ignorance

1 If one does not know to which port one is sailing, no wind is
   favourable.
   Seneca ('the Younger') *c*.4 BC–AD 65: *Epistulae Morales*

2 Lo! the poor Indian, whose untutored mind
   Sees God in clouds, or hears him in the wind.
   Alexander Pope 1688–1744: *An Essay on Man* Epistle 1
   (1733)

3   Where ignorance is bliss,
   'Tis folly to be wise.
   Thomas Gray 1716–71: *Ode on a Distant Prospect of Eton
   College* (1747)

4 Ignorance, madam, pure ignorance.
   Samuel Johnson 1709–84: on being asked why he had
   defined *pastern* as the 'knee' of a horse, 1755; in James
   Boswell *Life of Johnson* (1791)

5 Where people wish to attach, they should always be ignorant.
   To come with a well-informed mind, is to come with an
   inability of administering to the vanity of others, which a
   sensible person would always wish to avoid. A woman

especially, if she have the misfortune of knowing any thing,
should conceal it as well as she can.
   Jane Austen 1775–1817: *Northanger Abbey* (1818)

6 Ignorance is not innocence but sin.
   Robert Browning 1812–89: *The Inn Album* (1875)

7 You know everybody is ignorant, only on different subjects.
   Will Rogers 1879–1935: in *New York Times* 31 August 1924

8 It was absolutely marvellous working for Pauli. You could
ask him anything. There was no worry that he would think a
particular question was stupid, since he thought *all* questions
were stupid.
   Victor Weisskopf 1908– : in *American Journal of Physics*
   1977

Imagination

1 The lunatic, the lover, and the poet,
   Are of imagination all compact.
   William Shakespeare 1564–1616: *A Midsummer Night's
   Dream* (1595–6)

2 Tell me where is fancy bred.
   Or in the heart or in the head?
   William Shakespeare 1564–1616: *The Merchant of Venice*
   (1596–8)

3 Go, and catch a falling star,
   Get with child a mandrake root,
   Tell me, where all past years are,
   Or who cleft the Devil's foot.
   John Donne 1572–1631: 'Song: Go and catch a falling star'

4 Were it not for imagination, Sir, a man would be as happy in
the arms of a chambermaid as of a Duchess.
   Samuel Johnson 1709–84: in James Boswell *Life of Johnson*
   (1791) 9 May 1778

5 To see a world in a grain of sand
   And a heaven in a wild flower
   Hold infinity in the palm of your hand
   And eternity in an hour.
   William Blake 1757–1827: 'Auguries of Innocence' (*c.*1803)

6 Whither is fled the visionary gleam?
  Where is it now, the glory and the dream?
    William Wordsworth 1770–1850: 'Ode. Intimations of
    Immortality' (1807)

7 Heard melodies are sweet, but those unheard
  Are sweeter.
    John Keats 1795–1821: 'Ode on a Grecian Urn' (1820)

8 His imagination resembled the wings of an ostrich. It enabled
  him to run, though not to soar.
    Lord Macaulay 1800–59: 'John Dryden' (1828)

9 Where there is no imagination there is no horror.
    Arthur Conan Doyle 1859–1930: *A Study in Scarlet* (1888)

10 An adventure is only an inconvenience rightly considered.
   An inconvenience is only an adventure wrongly considered.
     G. K. Chesterton 1874–1936: *All Things Considered* (1908)
     'On Running after one's Hat'

11 I never saw a Purple Cow,
   I never hope to see one;
   But I can tell you, anyhow,
   I'd rather see than be one!
     Gelett Burgess 1866–1951: 'The Purple Cow' (1914)

12 When I was but thirteen or so
   I went into a golden land,
   Chimborazo, Cotopaxi
   Took me by the hand.
     Walter James Redfern Turner 1889–1946: 'Romance' (1916)

13 Must then a Christ perish in torment in every age to save
   those that have no imagination?
     George Bernard Shaw 1856–1950: *Saint Joan* (1924)
     epilogue

Indifference

1 It is the disease of not listening, the malady of not marking,
  that I am troubled withal.
    William Shakespeare 1564–1616: *Henry IV, Part 2* (1597)

2 All colours will agree in the dark.
    Francis Bacon 1561–1626: *Essays* (1625) 'Of Unity in
    Religion'

3 *Qu'ils mangent de la brioche.*
Let them eat cake.
> **Marie-Antoinette** 1755-93: on being told that her people
> had no bread. In *Confessions* (1740) Rousseau refers to
> a similar remark being a well-known saying; in *Relation*
> *d'un Voyage à Bruxelles et à Coblentz en 1791* (1823), Louis
> XVIII attributes 'Why don't they eat pastry?' to
> Marie-Thérèse (1638-83), wife of Louis XIV

4 Vacant heart and hand, and eye,—
Easy live and quiet die.
> **Sir Walter Scott** 1771-1832: *The Bride of Lammermoor*
> (1819)

5 If Jesus Christ were to come to-day, people would not even
crucify him. They would ask him to dinner, and hear what
he had to say, and make fun of it.
> **Thomas Carlyle** 1795-1881: in D. A. Wilson *Carlyle at his*
> *Zenith* (1927)

6 The worst sin towards our fellow creatures is not to hate
them, but to be indifferent to them: that's the essence of
inhumanity.
> **George Bernard Shaw** 1856-1950: *The Devil's Disciple* (1901)

7 When Jesus came to Birmingham they simply passed Him
   by,
They never hurt a hair of Him, they only let Him die.
> **G. A. Studdert Kennedy** 1883-1929: 'Indifference' (1921)

8 Science may have found a cure for most evils; but it has
found no remedy for the worst of them all — the apathy of
human beings.
> **Helen Keller** 1880-1968: *My Religion* (1927)

9 I wish I could care what you do or where you go but
I can't…My dear, I don't give a damn.
> **Margaret Mitchell** 1900-49: *Gone with the Wind* (1936).
> 'Frankly, my dear, I don't give a damn!' in Sidney
> Howard's 1939 screenplay

10 Cast a cold eye
On life, on death.
Horseman pass by!
> **W. B. Yeats** 1865-1939: 'Under Ben Bulben' (1939)

11 I was much further out than you thought
And not waving but drowning.
   Stevie Smith 1902–71: 'Not Waving but Drowning' (1957)

12 Catholics and Communists have committed great crimes, but
at least they have not stood aside, like an established society,
and been indifferent. I would rather have blood on my hands
than water like Pilate.
   Graham Greene 1904–91: *The Comedians* (1966)

Intelligence and Intellectuals

1 You beat your pate, and fancy wit will come:
Knock as you please, there's nobody at home.
   Alexander Pope 1688–1744: 'Epigram: You beat your pate'
   (1732)

2 Sir, I have found you an argument; but I am not obliged to
find you an understanding.
   Samuel Johnson 1709–84: in James Boswell *Life of Johnson*
   (1791) June 1784

3 With stupidity the gods themselves struggle in vain.
   Friedrich von Schiller 1759–1805: *Die Jungfrau von
   Orleans* (1801)

4 Not body enough to cover his mind decently with; his
intellect is improperly exposed.
   Sydney Smith 1771–1845: in Lady Holland *Memoir* (1855)

5 'Excellent,' I cried. 'Elementary,' said he.
   Arthur Conan Doyle 1859–1930: *Memoirs of Sherlock
   Holmes* (1894). 'Elementary, my dear Watson' is not found
   in any book by Conan Doyle, although a review of the film
   The Return of Sherlock Holmes in *New York Times*
   19 October 1929, states: 'In the final scene Dr Watson is
   there with his "Amazing, Holmes", and Holmes comes forth
   with his "Elementary, my dear Watson, elementary" '

6 No one in this world, so far as I know—and I have searched
the records for years, and employed agents to help me—has
ever lost money by underestimating the intelligence of the
great masses of the plain people.
   H. L. Mencken 1880–1956: *Chicago Tribune* 19 September
   1926

7 'Hullo! friend,' I call out, 'Won't you lend us a hand?' 'I am an
intellectual and don't drag wood about,' came the answer.
'You're lucky,' I reply. 'I too wanted to become an
intellectual, but I didn't succeed.'
   Albert Schweitzer 1875–1965: *More from the Primeval
   Forest* (1928), tr. by C. T. Campion

8 See the happy moron,
He doesn't give a damn,
I wish I were a moron,
My God! perhaps I am!
   Anonymous: *Eugenics Review* July 1929

9 As a human being, one has been endowed with just enough
intelligence to be able to see clearly how utterly inadequate
that intelligence is when confronted with what exists.
   Albert Einstein 1879–1955: letter to Queen Elizabeth of
   Belgium, 19 September 1932

10 The test of a first-rate intelligence is the ability to hold two
opposed ideas in the mind at the same time, and still retain
the ability to function.
   F. Scott Fitzgerald 1896–1940: *Esquire* February 1936

11 Intelligence is quickness to apprehend as distinct from
ability, which is capacity to act wisely on the thing
apprehended.
   Alfred North Whitehead 1861–1947: *Dialogues* (1954)
   15 December 1939

12 To the man-in-the-street, who, I'm sorry to say,
Is a keen observer of life,
The word 'Intellectual' suggests straight away
A man who's untrue to his wife.
   W. H. Auden 1907–73: *New Year Letter* (1941)

13 An intellectual is someone whose mind watches itself.
   Albert Camus 1913–60: *Notebooks 1935–42* (1963)

14 It takes little talent to see clearly what lies under one's nose,
a good deal of it to know in which direction to point that
organ.
   W. H. Auden 1907–73: *The Dyer's Hand* (1963)

15 So dumb he can't fart and chew gum at the same time.
   Lyndon Baines Johnson 1908–73: of Gerald Ford, in R.
   Reeves *A Ford, not a Lincoln* (1975)

Inventions and Discoveries

See also **Science**

1 Thus were they stained with their own works: and went
a whoring with their own inventions.
   Bible: Psalm 106

2 *Eureka!*
I've got it!
   Archimedes *c*.287–212 BC: in Vitruvius Pollio *De
   Architectura*

3 *Semper aliquid novi Africam adferre.*
Africa always brings [us] something new.
   Pliny the Elder AD 23–79: *Historia Naturalis* (often quoted
   'Ex Africa semper aliquid novi [Always something new out
   of Africa]')

4 Printing, gunpowder, and the magnet [Mariner's
Needle]...these three have changed the whole face and state
of things throughout the world.
   Francis Bacon 1561–1626: *Novum Organum* (1620)

5 I don't know what I may seem to the world, but as to myself,
I seem to have been only like a boy playing on the sea-shore
and diverting myself in now and then finding a smoother
pebble or a prettier shell than ordinary, whilst the great
ocean of truth lay all undiscovered before me.
   Isaac Newton 1642–1727: in Joseph Spence *Anecdotes*
   (ed. J. Osborn, 1966)

6 What is the use of a new-born child?
   Benjamin Franklin 1706–90: when asked what was the use
   of a new invention

7 Then felt I like some watcher of the skies
When a new planet swims into his ken;
Or like stout Cortez when with eagle eyes
He stared at the Pacific—and all his men
Looked at each other with a wild surmise—
Silent, upon a peak in Darien.
   John Keats 1795–1821: 'On First Looking into Chapman's
   Homer' (1817)

8 The discovery of a new dish does more for human happiness
than the discovery of a star.
   Anthelme Brillat-Savarin 1755–1826: *Physiologie du Goût*
   (1826)

9 *Au fond de l'Inconnu pour trouver du nouveau!*
Through the unknown, we'll find the new.
   Charles Baudelaire 1821–67: *Les fleurs du mal* (1857),
   tr. Robert Lowell

10 Why sir, there is every possibility that you will soon be able
to tax it!
   Michael Faraday 1791–1867: to Gladstone, when asked
   about the usefulness of electricity; in W. E. H. Lecky
   Democracy and Liberty (1899 ed.)

11 What one man can invent another can discover.
   Arthur Conan Doyle 1859–1930: *The Return of Sherlock
   Holmes* (1905)

12 When man wanted to make a machine that would walk he
created the wheel, which does not resemble a leg.
   Guillaume Apollinaire 1880–1918: *Les Mamelles de Tirésias*
   (1918)

13 Discovery consists of seeing what everybody has seen and
thinking what nobody has thought.
   Albert von Szent-Györgyi 1893–1986: in I. Good (ed.) *The
   Scientist Speculates* (1962)

Ireland and the Irish

1 Icham of Irlaunde
Ant of the holy londe of irlonde
Gode sir pray ich ye
for of saynte charite,
come ant daunce wyt me,
in irlaunde.
   Anonymous: fourteenth century

2 I met wid Napper Tandy, and he took me by the hand,
And he said, 'How's poor ould Ireland, and how does she
   stand?'

She's the most disthressful country that iver yet was
  seen,
For they're hangin' men an' women for the wearin' o' the
  Green.
  Anonymous: 'The Wearin' o' the Green' (c.1795 ballad)

3 The moment the very name of Ireland is mentioned, the
English seem to bid adieu to common feeling, common
prudence, and common sense, and to act with the barbarity
of tyrants, and the fatuity of idiots.
  Sydney Smith 1771–1845: *Letters of Peter Plymley* (1807)

4 Thus you have a starving population, an absentee
aristocracy, and an alien Church, and in addition the
weakest executive in the world. That is the Irish
Question.
  Benjamin Disraeli 1804–81: speech, House of Commons,
16 February 1844

5 Ulster will fight; Ulster will be right.
  Lord Randolph Churchill 1849–94: public letter, 7 May
1886

6 For the great Gaels of Ireland
Are the men that God made mad,
For all their wars are merry,
And all their songs are sad.
  G. K. Chesterton 1874–1936: *The Ballad of the White Horse*
(1911)

7 Romantic Ireland's dead and gone,
It's with O'Leary in the grave.
  W. B. Yeats 1865–1939: 'September, 1913' (1914)

8 Ireland is the old sow that eats her farrow.
  James Joyce 1882–1941: *A Portrait of the Artist as a Young
Man* (1916)

9 In Ireland the inevitable never happens and the unexpected
constantly occurs.
  John Pentland Mahaffy 1839–1919: in W. B. Stanford and
R. B. McDowell *Mahaffy* (1971)

10   The famous
Northern reticence, the tight gag of place
And times.
> **Seamus Heaney** 1939- : 'Whatever You Say Say Nothing'
> (1975)

Jealousy see Envy and Jealousy

Journalism see News and Journalism

Justice

See also **The Law and Lawyers**

1 Life for life,
Eye for eye, tooth for tooth.
> **Bible**: Exodus

2 They have sown the wind, and they shall reap the whirlwind.
> **Bible**: Hosea

3 What I say is that 'just' or 'right' means nothing but what is
in the interest of the stronger party.
> **Plato** 429-347 BC: spoken by Thrasymachus in *The
> Republic* (tr. F. M. Cornford)

4 *Audi partem alteram.*
Hear the other side.
> **St Augustine of Hippo** AD 354-430: *De Duabus Animabus
> contra Manicheos*

5 *Fiat justitia et pereat mundus.*
Let justice be done, though the world perish.
> **Emperor Ferdinand I** 1503-64: motto

6 Thrice is he armed that hath his quarrel just.
> **William Shakespeare** 1564-1616: *Henry VI, Part 2* (1592)

7 The quality of mercy is not strained,
It droppeth as the gentle rain from heaven
Upon the place beneath: it is twice blessed;
It blesseth him that gives and him that takes.
> **William Shakespeare** 1564-1616: *The Merchant of Venice*
> (1596-8)

8 Though justice be thy plea, consider this,
That in the course of justice none of us
Should see salvation.
    William Shakespeare 1564–1616: *The Merchant of Venice*
(1596–8)

9 Use every man after his desert, and who should 'scape
whipping?
    William Shakespeare 1564–1616: *Hamlet* (1601)

10 I'm armed with more than complete steel—The justice of my
quarrel.
    Anonymous: *Lust's Dominion* (1657) attributed to Marlowe,
though of doubtful authorship

11 Here they hang a man first, and try him afterwards.
    Molière 1622–73: *Monsieur de Pourceaugnac* (1670)

12 It is better that ten guilty persons escape than one innocent
suffer.
    William Blackstone 1723–80: *Commentaries on the Laws of
England* (1765)

13 A lawyer has no business with the justice or injustice of the
cause which he undertakes, unless his client asks his
opinion, and then he is bound to give it honestly. The justice
or injustice of the cause is to be decided by the judge.
    Samuel Johnson 1709–84: in James Boswell *Journal of a
Tour to the Hebrides* (1785) 15 August 1773

14 Justice is truth in action.
    Benjamin Disraeli 1804–81: speech, House of Commons,
11 February 1851

15 All sensible people are selfish, and nature is tugging at every
contract to make the terms of it fair.
    Ralph Waldo Emerson 1803–82: *The Conduct of Life* (1860)

16 No! No! Sentence first—verdict afterwards.
    Lewis Carroll 1832–98: *Alice's Adventures in Wonderland*
(1865)

17 If, of all words of tongue and pen,
The saddest are, 'It might have been,'
More sad are these we daily see:
'It is, but hadn't ought to be!'
    Bret Harte 1836–1902: 'Mrs Judge Jenkins' (1867)

18 When I hear of an 'equity' in a case like this, I am reminded
of a blind man in a dark room—looking for a black
hat—which isn't there.
   Lord Bowen 1835-94: in J. A. Foote *Pie-Powder* (1911)

19 In England, justice is open to all—like the Ritz Hotel.
   James Mathew 1830-1908: in R. E. Megarry
   Miscellany-at-Law (1955).

20 It's the same the whole world over,
It's the poor wot gets the blame,
It's the rich wot gets the gravy.
Ain't it all a bleedin' shame?
   Anonymous: 'She was Poor but she was Honest' (sung by
   British soldiers in the First World War)

21 Justice should not only be done, but should manifestly and
undoubtedly be seen to be done.
   Lord Hewart 1870-1943: Rex v Sussex Justices, 9 November
   1923

22 The price of justice is eternal publicity.
   Arnold Bennett 1867-1931: *Things that have Interested Me*
   (1923) 'Secret Trials'

23 Injustice anywhere is a threat to justice everywhere.
   Martin Luther King 1929-68: letter from Birmingham Jail,
   Alabama, 16 April 1963

24 Two wrongs don't make a right, but they make a good
excuse.
   Thomas Szasz 1920- : *The Second Sin* (1973)

25 If this is justice, I am a banana.
   Ian Hislop 1940- : on the Sutcliffe libel damages, 24 May
   1989

Knowledge

1 The fox knows many things—the hedgehog one *big* one.
   Archilochus 7th century BC

2 I know nothing except the fact of my ignorance.
   Socrates 469-399 BC: in Diogenes Laertius *Lives of the
   Philosophers*

3 The price of wisdom is above rubies.
   Bible: Job

4 He that increaseth knowledge increaseth sorrow.
   Bible: Ecclesiastes

5 For now we see through a glass, darkly; but then face to face:
   now I know in part; but then shall I know even as also I am
   known.
   Bible: I Corinthians

6 Everyman, I will go with thee, and be thy guide,
   In thy most need to go by thy side.
   Anonymous: *Everyman* (*c.*1509-19) spoken by Knowledge

7 For also knowledge itself is power.
   Francis Bacon 1561-1626: *Meditationes Sacrae* (1597)

8 [The true end of knowledge] is the discovery of all operations
   and possibilities of operations from immortality (if it were
   possible) to the meanest mechanical practice.
   Francis Bacon 1561-1626: *Valerius Terminus*

9 We have first raised a dust and then complain we cannot see.
   Bishop George Berkeley 1685-1753: *A Treatise Concerning
   the Principles of Human Knowledge* (1710)

10 A little learning is a dangerous thing;
   Drink deep, or taste not the Pierian spring.
   Alexander Pope 1688-1744: *An Essay on Criticism* (1711)

11 And still they gazed, and still the wonder grew,
   That one small head could carry all he knew.
   Oliver Goldsmith 1730-74: *The Deserted Village* (1770)

12 Knowledge may give weight, but accomplishments give
   lustre, and many more people see than weigh.
   Lord Chesterfield 1694-1773: *Maxims* (1774)

13 Knowledge is of two kinds. We know a subject ourselves, or
   we know where we can find information upon it.
   Samuel Johnson 1709-84: in James Boswell *Life of Johnson*
   (1791) 18 April 1775

14 Does the eagle know what is in the pit?
   Or wilt thou go ask the mole:
   Can wisdom be put in a silver rod?
   Or love in a golden bowl?
   William Blake 1757-1827: *The Book of Thel* (1789)

15 If the doors of perception were cleansed everything would
appear to man as it is, infinite.
William Blake 1757-1827: *The Marriage of Heaven and Hell*
(1790-3)

16 Our meddling intellect
Mis-shapes the beauteous forms of things:—
We murder to dissect.
William Wordsworth 1770-1850: 'The Tables Turned' (1798)

17 Knowledge enormous makes a god of me.
John Keats 1795-1821: 'Hyperion: A Fragment' (1820)

18 Grace is given of God, but knowledge is bought in the
market.
Arthur Hugh Clough 1819-61: *The Bothie of
Tober-na-Vuolich* (1848)

19 Now, what I want is, Facts...Facts alone are wanted in life.
Charles Dickens 1812-70: *Hard Times* (1854) Mr Gradgrind

20 You will find it a very good practice always to verify your
references, sir!
Martin Joseph Routh 1755-1854: in J. W. Burgon *Lives of
Twelve Good Men* (1888 ed.)

21 If a little knowledge is dangerous, where is the man who has
so much as to be out of danger?
T. H. Huxley 1825-95: 'On Elementary Instruction in
Physiology' (written 1877)

22 There is no such thing on earth as an uninteresting subject;
the only thing that can exist is an uninterested person.
G. K. Chesterton 1874-1936: *Heretics* (1905)

23 For lust of knowing what should not be known,
We take the Golden Road to Samarkand.
James Elroy Flecker 1884-1915: *The Golden Journey to
Samarkand* (1913)

24 Pedantry is the dotage of knowledge.
Holbrook Jackson 1874-1948: *Anatomy of Bibliomania*
(1930)

25 Where is the wisdom we have lost in knowledge?
Where is the knowledge we have lost in information?
T. S. Eliot 1888-1965: *The Rock* (1934)

26 An expert is one who knows more and more about less and less.
   Nicholas Murray Butler 1862–1947: Commencement address at Columbia University (attributed)

Language

See also **Meaning, Words**

1 A word fitly spoken is like apples of gold in pictures of silver.
   Bible: Proverbs

2 You taught me language; and my profit on't
   Is, I know how to curse.
   William Shakespeare 1564–1616: *The Tempest* (1611)

3 All that is not prose is verse; and all that is not verse is prose.
   Molière 1622–73: *Le Bourgeois Gentilhomme* (1671)

4 Good heavens! For more than forty years I have been speaking prose without knowing it.
   Molière 1622–73: *Le Bourgeois Gentilhomme* (1671)

5 Language is the dress of thought.
   Samuel Johnson 1709–84: *Lives of the English Poets* (1779–81)

6 In language, the ignorant have prescribed laws to the learned.
   Richard Duppa 1770–1831: *Maxims* (1830)

7 Language is fossil poetry.
   Ralph Waldo Emerson 1803–82: *Essays* (1844) 'The Poet'

8 Take care of the sense, and the sounds will take care of themselves.
   Lewis Carroll 1832–98: *Alice's Adventures in Wonderland* (1865)

9 I will not go down to posterity talking bad grammar.
   Benjamin Disraeli 1804–81: correcting proofs of his last Parliamentary speech, 31 March 1881

10 Merely corroborative detail, intended to give artistic
verisimilitude to an otherwise bald and unconvincing
narrative.
  W. S. Gilbert 1836–1911: *The Mikado* (1885)

11 A definition is the enclosing a wilderness of idea within
a wall of words.
  Samuel Butler 1835–1902: *Notebooks* (1912)

12 The limits of my language mean the limits of my world.
  Ludwig Wittgenstein 1889–1951: *Tractatus
Logico-Philosophicus* (1922)

13 There's a cool web of language winds us in,
Retreat from too much joy or too much fear.
  Robert Graves 1895–1985: 'The Cool Web' (1927)

14 One picture is worth ten thousand words.
  Frederick R. Barnard: *Printers' Ink* 10 March 1927

15 When I split an infinitive, God damn it, I split it so it will
stay split.
  Raymond Chandler 1888–1959: on a proof-reader's
corrections to his work; letter to Edward Weeks,
18 January 1947

16 This is the sort of English up with which I will not put.
  Winston Churchill 1874–1965: in Ernest Gowers *Plain
Words* (1948) 'Troubles with Prepositions'

17 Where in this small-talking world can I find
A longitude with no platitude?
  Christopher Fry 1907– : *The Lady's not for Burning* (1949)

18 Colourless green ideas sleep furiously.
  Noam Chomsky 1928– : *Syntactic Structures* (1957)
illustrating that grammatical structure is independent of
meaning

19 Slang is a language that rolls up its sleeves, spits on its
hands and goes to work.
  Carl Sandburg 1878–1967: in *New York Times* 13 February
1959

20 Language tethers us to the world; without it we spin like
atoms.
  Penelope Lively 1933– : *Moon Tiger* (1987)

Languages

1 To God I speak Spanish, to women Italian, to men French,
and to my horse—German.
   Emperor Charles V 1500–58: attributed

2 It is a thing plainly repugnant to the Word of God, and the
custom of the Primitive Church, to have publick Prayer in
the Church, or to minister the Sacraments in a tongue not
understanded of the people.
   Book of Common Prayer 1662: *Articles of Religion* (1562)

3 So now they have made our English tongue a gallimaufry or
hodgepodge of all other speeches.
   Edmund Spenser c.1552–99: *The Shepherd's Calendar* (1579)

4 Some hold translations not unlike to be
The wrong side of a Turkey tapestry.
   James Howell c.1593–1666: *Familiar Letters* (1645–55)

5 I am always sorry when any language is lost, because
languages are the pedigree of nations.
   Samuel Johnson 1709–84: in James Boswell *Journal of a
tour to the Hebrides* (1785)

6 My English text is chaste, and all licentious passages are left
in the obscurity of a learned language.
   Edward Gibbon 1737–94: *Memoirs of My Life* (1796) parodied
as 'decent obscurity' in the *Anti-Jacobin*, 1797–8

7 The original is unfaithful to the translation.
   Jorge Luis Borges 1899–1986: of Henley's translation, in
Sobre el 'Vathek' de William Beckford (1943)

8 England and America are two countries divided by a
common language.
   George Bernard Shaw 1856–1950: attributed in this and
other forms, but not found in Shaw's published writings

9 We are walking lexicons. In a single sentence of idle chatter
we preserve Latin, Anglo-Saxon, Norse; we carry a museum
inside our heads, each day we commemorate peoples of
whom we have never heard.
   Penelope Lively 1933– : *Moon Tiger* (1987)

Last Words

1 Crito, we owe a cock to Aesculapius; please pay it and don't forget it.
   Socrates 469–399 BC: in Plato *Phaedo*

2 Had I but served God as diligently as I have served the King, he would not have given me over in my grey hairs.
   Cardinal Wolsey c.1475–1530: in George Cavendish *Negotiations of Thomas Wolsey* (1641)

3 I pray you, master Lieutenant, see me safe up, and my coming down let me shift for my self.
   Sir Thomas More 1478–1535: on mounting the scaffold; in William Roper *Life of Sir Thomas More*

4 After his head was upon the block, [he] lift it up again, and gently drew his beard aside, and said, *This hath not offended the king*.
   Sir Thomas More 1478–1535: Francis Bacon *Apophthegms New and Old* (1625)

5 I am going to seek a great perhaps…Bring down the curtain, the farce is played out.
   François Rabelais c.1494–c.1553: attributed

6 All my possessions for a moment of time.
   Elizabeth I 1533–1603: attributed, probably apocryphal

7 So the heart be right, it is no matter which way the head lies.
   Walter Ralegh c.1552–1618: at his execution, on being asked which way he preferred to lay his head

8 My design is to make what haste I can to be gone.
   Oliver Cromwell 1599–1658: in J. Morley *Oliver Cromwell* (1900)

9 I am about to take my last voyage, a great leap in the dark.
   Thomas Hobbes 1588–1679: last words

10 He had been, he said, an unconscionable time dying; but he hoped that they would excuse it.
   Charles II 1630–85: Lord Macaulay *History of England* (1849)

11 This is no time for making new enemies.
   Voltaire 1694–1778: on being asked to renounce the Devil, on his deathbed (attributed)

12 We are all going to Heaven, and Vandyke is of the company.
Thomas Gainsborough 1727–88: attributed in W. B. Boulton
Thomas Gainsborough

13 Kiss me, Hardy.
Horatio, Lord Nelson 1758–1805: at the battle of Trafalgar,
in R. Southey *Life of Nelson* (1813)

14 Thank God, I have done my duty.
Horatio, Lord Nelson 1758–1805: at the battle of Trafalgar,
in R. Southey *Life of Nelson* (1813)

15 Oh, my country! how I leave my country!
William Pitt 1759–1806: in Earl Stanhope *Life of the Rt.
Hon. William Pitt* vol. 3 (1879). Also variously reported as
'How I love my country'; 'My country! oh, my country!';
'I think I could eat one of Bellamy's veal pies'

16 Well, I've had a happy life.
William Hazlitt 1778–1830: in W. C. Hazlitt *Memoirs of
William Hazlitt* (1867)

17 More light!
Johann Wolfgang von Goethe 1749–1832: attributed;
actually 'Open the second shutter, so that more light can
come in'

18 *Dieu me pardonnera, c'est son métier.*
God will pardon me, it is His trade.
Heinrich Heine 1797–1856: on his deathbed, in A. Meissner
Heinrich Heine. Erinnerungen (1856)

19 It is a far, far better thing that I do, than I have ever done; it
is a far, far better rest that I go to, than I have ever known.
Charles Dickens 1812–70: *A Tale of Two Cities* (1859)
Sydney Carton

20 Die, my dear Doctor, that's the last thing I shall do!
Lord Palmerston 1784–1865: in E. Latham *Famous Sayings
and their Authors* (1904)

21 So little done, so much to do.
Cecil Rhodes 1853–1902: on the day of his death, in
L. Michell *Life of Rhodes* (1910).

22 I am just going outside and may be some time.
Captain Lawrence Oates 1880–1912: in Robert Falcon
Scott's diary, 16–17 March 1912

23 For God's sake look after our people.
Robert Falcon Scott 1868–1912: last diary entry, 29 March 1912

24 Why fear death? It is the most beautiful adventure in life.
Charles Frohman 1860–1915: before drowning in the *Lusitania*, 7 May 1915

25 If this is dying, then I don't think much of it.
Lytton Strachey 1880–1932: on his deathbed; in M. Holroyd *Lytton Strachey* vol. 2 (1968)

26 How's the Empire?
George V 1865–1936: to his private secretary on the morning of his death; in K. Rose *King George V* (1983)

27 Bugger Bognor.
George V 1865–1936: attributed; possibly on his deathbed. See K. Rose *King George V* (1983)

28 Just before she [Stein] died she asked, 'What *is* the answer?' No answer came. She laughed and said, 'In that case what is the question?' Then she died.
Gertrude Stein 1874–1946: in D. Sutherland *Gertrude Stein* (1951)

....

The Law and Lawyers

....

See also **Crime and Punishment, Justice**

---

1 Written laws are like spider's webs; they will catch, it is true, the weak and poor, but would be torn in pieces by the rich and powerful.
Anacharsis 6th century BC: in Plutarch *Parallel Lives*

2 *Cui bono?*
To whose profit?
Cicero 106–43 BC: *Pro Roscio Amerino* and *Pro Milone* (quoting L. Cassius Longinus Ravilla)

3 *Salus populi suprema est lex.*
The good of the people is the chief law.
Cicero 106–43 BC: *De Legibus*

4 The sabbath was made for man, and not man for the sabbath.
Bible: St Mark

5 The first thing we do, let's kill all the lawyers.
  William Shakespeare 1564–1616: *Henry VI, Part 2* (1592)

6 The rusty curb of old father antick, the law.
  William Shakespeare 1564–1616: *Henry IV, Part 1* (1597)

7 You have a gift, sir, (thank your education),
  Will never let you want, while there are men,
  And malice, to breed causes.
  Ben Jonson c.1573–1637: *Volpone* (1605) to a lawyer

8 I am ashamed the law is such an ass.
  George Chapman c.1559–1634: *Revenge for Honour* (1654)

9 Ignorance of the law excuses no man; not that all men know
  the law, but because 'tis an excuse every man will plead, and
  no man can tell how to confute him.
  John Selden 1584–1654: *Table Talk* (1689) 'Law'

10 The end of law is, not to abolish or restrain, but to preserve
  and enlarge freedom.
  John Locke 1632–1704: *Second Treatise of Civil Government*
  (1690)

11 Law is a bottomless pit.
  Dr Arbuthnot 1667–1735: *The History of John Bull* (1712)

12 The hungry judges soon the sentence sign,
  And wretches hang that jury-men may dine.
  Alexander Pope 1688–1744: *The Rape of the Lock* (1714)

13 Laws grind the poor, and rich men rule the law.
  Oliver Goldsmith 1730–74: *The Traveller* (1764)

14 People crushed by law have no hopes but from power. If laws
  are their enemies, they will be enemies to laws; and those,
  who have much to hope and nothing to lose, will always be
  dangerous, more or less.
  Edmund Burke 1729–97: letter to Charles James Fox,
  8 October 1777

15 Bad laws are the worst sort of tyranny.
  Edmund Burke 1729–97: *Speech at Bristol, previous to the
  Late Election* (1780)

16 A precedent embalms a principle.
  Lord Stowell 1745–1836: an opinion, while
  Advocate-General, 1788, quoted by Disraeli in House of
  Commons, 22 February 1848

17 In this country...the individual subject...'has nothing to do
with the laws but to obey them.'
   Bishop Samuel Horsley 1733-1806: speech, House of Lords,
   13 November 1795, defending a maxim he had earlier used
   in committee

18 Laws were made to be broken.
   Christopher North 1785-1854: *Blackwood's Magazine* May
   1830

19 'You must not tell us what the soldier, or any other man,
said, sir,' interposed the judge; 'it's not evidence.'
   Charles Dickens 1812-70: *Pickwick Papers* (1837)

20 If the law supposes that...the law is a ass—a idiot.
   Charles Dickens 1812-70: *Oliver Twist* (1838) Bumble

21 If ever there was a case of clearer evidence than this of
persons acting together, this case is that case.
   William Arabin 1773-1841: in H. B. Churchill *Arabiniana*
   (1843)

22 The one great principle of the English law is, to make
business for itself.
   Charles Dickens 1812-70: *Bleak House* (1853)

23 I know no method to secure the repeal of bad or obnoxious
laws so effective as their stringent execution.
   Ulysses S. Grant 1822-85: inaugural address, 4 March 1869

24 The Law is the true embodiment
Of everything that's excellent.
It has no kind of fault or flaw,
And I, my Lords, embody the Law.
   W. S. Gilbert 1836-1911: *Iolanthe* (1882)

25 You may object that it is not a trial at all; you are quite right,
for it is only a trial if I recognize it as such.
   Franz Kafka 1883-1924: *The Trial* (1925)

26 No poet ever interpreted nature as freely as a lawyer
interprets the truth.
   Jean Giraudoux 1882-1944: *La Guerre de Troie n'aura pas
   lieu* (1935) tr. Christopher Fry as *Tiger at the Gates*, 1955

27 A verbal contract isn't worth the paper it is written on.
   Sam Goldwyn 1882-1974: in A. Johnston *The Great Goldwyn*
   (1937)

28 A lawyer with his briefcase can steal more than a hundred men with guns.
   Mario Puzo 1920– : *The Godfather* (1969)

29 No brilliance is needed in the law. Nothing but common sense, and relatively clean finger nails.
   John Mortimer 1923– : *A Voyage Round My Father* (1971)

Leadership

1 If the blind lead the blind, both shall fall into the ditch.
   Bible: St Matthew

2 Be neither saint nor sophist-led, but be a man.
   Matthew Arnold 1822–88: *Empedocles on Etna* (1852)

3 Ah well! I am their leader, I really had to follow them!
   Alexandre Auguste Ledru-Rollin 1807–74: in E. de Mirecourt *Les Contemporains* (1857)

4 The buck stops here.
   Harry S. Truman 1884–1972: unattributed motto on Truman's desk, when President

5 The final test of a leader is that he leaves behind him in other men the conviction and the will to carry on.
   Walter Lippmann 1889–1974: *New York Herald Tribune* 14 April 1945

6 I don't mind how much my Ministers talk, so long as they do what I say.
   Margaret Thatcher 1925– : in *Observer* 27 January 1980

Leisure

1 If all the year were playing holidays,
   To sport would be as tedious as to work;
   But when they seldom come, they wished for come.
   William Shakespeare 1564–1616: *Henry IV, Part 1* (1597)

2 Conspicuous leisure and consumption...In the one case it is a waste of time and effort, in the other it is a waste of goods.
   Thorstein Veblen 1857–1929: *Theory of the Leisure Class* (1899)

3 What is this life if, full of care,
We have no time to stand and stare.
   W. H. Davies 1871–1940: 'Leisure' (1911)

4 To be able to fill leisure intelligently is the last product of
civilization.
   Bertrand Russell 1872–1970: *The Conquest of Happiness*
(1930)

Letters and Letter-writing

1 Sir, more than kisses, letters mingle souls.
   John Donne 1572–1631: 'To Sir Henry Wotton' (1597–8)

2 John Donne, Anne Donne, Un-done.
   John Donne 1572–1631: in a letter to his wife, on being
dismissed from the service of his father-in-law, George
More; in Izaak Walton *Life of Dr Donne* (1640)

3 All letters, methinks, should be free and easy as one's
discourse, not studied as an oration, nor made up of hard
words like a charm.
   Dorothy Osborne 1627–95: letter to William Temple,
September 1653

4 I have made this [letter] longer than usual, only because I
have not had the time to make it shorter.
   Blaise Pascal 1623–62: *Lettres Provinciales* (1657)

5 A woman seldom writes her mind but in her postscript.
   Richard Steele 1672–1729: *The Spectator* 31 May 1711

6 She has made me in love with a cold climate, and frost and
snow, with a northern moonlight.
   Robert Southey 1774–1843: on Mary Wollstonecraft's letters
from Sweden and Norway; letter, 28 April 1797

7 It is wonderful how much news there is when people write
every other day; if they wait for a month, there is nothing
that seems worth telling.
   O. Douglas 1877–1948: *Penny Plain* (1920)

8 Letters of thanks, letters from banks,
Letters of joy from girl and boy,
Receipted bills and invitations
To inspect new stock or to visit relations,
And applications for situations,

And timid lovers' declarations,
And gossip, gossip from all the nations.
  W. H. Auden 1907–73: *Night Mail* (1936)

9 It's very dangerous if you keep love letters from someone
who is not now your husband.
  Diana Dors 1931–84: *Observer* 28 December 1980 'Sayings of
  the Year'

Liberty

1 Stone walls do not a prison make,
Nor iron bars a cage.
  Richard Lovelace 1618–58: 'To Althea, From Prison' (1649)

2 None can love freedom heartily, but good men; the rest love
not freedom, but licence.
  John Milton 1608–74: *The Tenure of Kings and Magistrates*
  (1649)

3 When the people contend for their liberty, they seldom get
anything by their victory but new masters.
  George Savile, Marquess of Halifax 1633–95: *Political,
  Moral, and Miscellaneous Thoughts* (1750)

4 Man was born free, and everywhere he is in chains.
  Jean-Jacques Rousseau 1712–78: *Du Contrat social* (1762)

5 I know not what course others may take; but as for me, give
me liberty, or give me death!
  Patrick Henry 1736–99: speech, 23 March 1775

6 The people never give up their liberties except under some
delusion.
  Edmund Burke 1729–97: speech at County Meeting of
  Buckinghamshire, 1784; attributed

7 The tree of liberty must be refreshed from time to time with
the blood of patriots and tyrants. It is its natural manure.
  Thomas Jefferson 1743–1826: letter to W. S. Smith,
  13 November 1787

8 The condition upon which God hath given liberty to man is
eternal vigilance.
  John Philpot Curran 1750–1817: speech, 10 July 1790

9 O liberty! what crimes are committed in thy name!
   Mme Roland 1754–93: in A. de Lamartine *Histoire des Girondins* (1847)

10 Eternal spirit of the chainless mind!
   Brightest in dungeons, Liberty! thou art.
   Lord Byron 1788–1824: 'Sonnet on Chillon' (1816)

11 If men are to wait for liberty till they become wise and good in slavery, they may indeed wait for ever.
   Lord Macaulay 1800–59: *Essays* (1843) 'Milton'

12 The liberty of the individual must be thus far limited; he must not make himself a nuisance to other people.
   John Stuart Mill 1806–73: *On Liberty* (1859)

13 Liberty means responsibility. That is why most men dread it.
   George Bernard Shaw 1856–1950: *Man and Superman* (1903)

14 Tyranny is always better organised than freedom.
   Charles Péguy 1873–1914: *Basic Verities* (1943)

15 Freedom is always and exclusively freedom for the one who thinks differently.
   Rosa Luxemburg 1871–1919: *Die Russische Revolution* (1918)

16 Liberty is precious—so precious that it must be rationed.
   Lenin 1870–1924: in Sidney and Beatrice Webb *Soviet Communism* (1936)

17 It's often better to be in chains than to be free.
   Franz Kafka 1883–1924: *The Trial* (1925)

18 It is better to die on your feet than to live on your knees.
   Dolores Ibarruri 1895–1989: speech in Paris, 3 September 1936; also attributed to Emiliano Zapata

19 I am condemned to be free.
   Jean-Paul Sartre 1905–80: *L'Être et le néant* (1943)

20 The enemies of Freedom do not argue; they shout and they shoot.
   Dean Inge 1860–1954: *End of an Age* (1948)

21 Freedom is the freedom to say that two plus two make four. If that is granted, all else follows.
   George Orwell 1903–50: *Nineteen Eighty-Four* (1949)

22 A free society is a society where it is safe to be unpopular.
   Adlai Stevenson 1900–65: speech in Detroit, 7 October 1952

23 Liberty is always unfinished business.
  Anonymous: title of Annual Report of the American Civil
  Liberties Union (1956)

24 Liberty is liberty, not equality or fairness or justice or
  human happiness or a quiet conscience.
  Isaiah Berlin 1909- : *Two Concepts of Liberty* (1958)

25 We shall pay any price, bear any burden, meet any hardship,
  support any friend, oppose any foe to assure the survival and
  the success of liberty.
  John F. Kennedy 1917-63: inaugural address, 20 January
  1961

26 Freedom's just another word for nothin' left to lose,
  Nothin' ain't worth nothin', but it's free.
  Kris Kristofferson 1936- : 'Me and Bobby McGee' (1969
  song, with Fred Foster)

27 Of course liberty is not licence. Liberty in my view is
  conforming to majority opinion.
  Hugh Scanlon 1913- : television interview, 9 August 1977

Libraries

See also **Books, Reading**

1 Come, and take choice of all my library,
  And so beguile thy sorrow.
  William Shakespeare 1564-1616: *Titus Andronicus* (1590)

2 No place affords a more striking conviction of the vanity of
  human hopes, than a public library.
  Samuel Johnson 1709-84: *The Rambler* 23 March 1751

3 A man will turn over half a library to make one book.
  Samuel Johnson 1709-84: in James Boswell *Life of Johnson*
  (1791) 6 April 1775

4 Your *borrowers of books*—those mutilators of collections,
  spoilers of the symmetry of shelves, and creators of odd
  volumes.
  Charles Lamb 1775-1834: *Essays of Elia* (1823) 'The Two
  Races of Men'

5 The true University of these days is a collection of books.
Thomas Carlyle 1795–1881: *On Heroes, Hero-Worship, and the Heroic* (1841)

6 A man should keep his little brain attic stocked with all the furniture that he is likely to use, and the rest he can put away in the lumber room of his library, where he can get it if he wants it.
Arthur Conan Doyle 1859–1930: *Adventures of Sherlock Holmes* (1892)

7 A library is thought in cold storage.
Lord Samuel 1870–1963: *A Book of Quotations* (1947)

....

Lies and Lying
....

See also **Truth**

1 The retort courteous...the quip modest...the reply churlish...the reproof valiant...the countercheck quarrelsome...the lie circumstantial...the lie direct.
William Shakespeare 1564–1616: *As You Like It* (1599), of the degrees of a lie

2 Calumnies are answered best with silence.
Ben Jonson c.1573–1637: *Volpone* (1605)

3 He replied that I must needs be mistaken, or that I *said the thing which was not*. (For they have no word in their language to express lying or falsehood.)
Jonathan Swift 1667–1745: *Gulliver's Travels* (1726)

4 Whoever would lie usefully should lie seldom.
Lord Hervey 1696–1743: *Memoirs of the Reign of George II*

5 Falsehood has a perennial spring.
Edmund Burke 1729–97: *On American Taxation* (1775)

6 O what a tangled web we weave,
When first we practise to deceive!
Sir Walter Scott 1771–1832: *Marmion* (1808)

7 And, after all, what is a lie? 'Tis but
The truth in masquerade.
Lord Byron 1788–1824: *Don Juan* (1819–24)

8 It is well said in the old proverb, 'a lie will go round the
world while truth is pulling its boots on'.
   C. H. Spurgeon 1834–92: *Gems from Spurgeon* (1859)

9 The lie in the soul is a true lie.
   Benjamin Jowett 1817–93: introduction to his translation
   (1871) of Plato's *Republic*

10 The cruellest lies are often told in silence.
   Robert Louis Stevenson 1850–94: *Virginibus Puerisque*
   (1881)

11 There are three kinds of lies: lies, damned lies and statistics.
   Benjamin Disraeli 1804–81: attributed to Disraeli in Mark
   Twain *Autobiography* (1924)

12 Take the life-lie away from the average man and straight
away you take away his happiness.
   Henrik Ibsen 1828–1906: *The Wild Duck* (1884)

13 One of the most striking differences between a cat and a lie is
that a cat has only nine lives.
   Mark Twain 1835–1910: *Pudd'nhead Wilson* (1894)

14 There is no worse lie than a truth misunderstood by those
who hear it.
   William James 1842–1910: *Varieties of Religious Experience*
   (1902)

15 The best liar is he who makes the smallest amount of lying
go the longest way.
   Samuel Butler 1835–1902: *The Way of All Flesh* (1903)

16 A little inaccuracy sometimes saves tons of explanation.
   Saki (H. H. Munro) 1870–1916: *The Square Egg* (1924)

17 Without lies humanity would perish of despair and boredom.
   Anatole France 1844–1924: *La Vie en fleur* (1922)

18 That branch of the art of lying which consists in very nearly
deceiving your friends without quite deceiving your enemies.
   Francis M. Cornford 1874–1943: on propaganda;
   Microcosmographia Academica (1922 ed.)

19 The broad mass of a nation...will more easily fall victim to
a big lie than to a small one.
   Adolf Hitler 1889–1945: *Mein Kampf* (1925)

20 She [Lady Desborough] tells enough white lies to ice
a wedding cake.
   Margot Asquith 1864–1945: in *Listener* 11 June 1953

21 An abomination unto the Lord, but a very present help in time of trouble.

   Anonymous: definition of a lie, an amalgamation of Proverbs 12.22 and Psalms 46.1, often attributed to Adlai Stevenson

22 Truth exists; only lies are invented.

   Georges Braque 1882–1963: *Le Jour et la nuit: Cahiers 1917–52*

23 He would, wouldn't he?

   Mandy Rice-Davies 1944– : at the trial of Stephen Ward, 29 June 1963, on hearing that Lord Astor denied her allegations

24 He will lie even when it is inconvenient: the sign of the true artist.

   Gore Vidal 1925– : attributed

Life

See also **Life Sciences, Living**

1 All that a man hath will he give for his life.

   Bible: Job

2 Man that is born of a woman is of few days, and full of trouble.

   Bible: Job

3 Not to be born is, past all prizing, best.

   Sophocles *c.*496–406 BC: *Oedipus Coloneus* (tr. R. C. Jebb)

4 We live, not as we wish to, but as we can.

   Menander 342–*c.*292 BC: *Dis Exapaton*

5 And life is given to none freehold, but it is leasehold for all.

   Lucretius *c.*94–55 BC: *De Rerum Natura*

6 'Such,' he said, 'O King, seems to me the present life of men on earth, in comparison with that time which to us is uncertain, as if when on a winter's night you sit feasting with your ealdormen and thegns,—a single sparrow should fly swiftly into the hall, and coming in at one door, instantly fly out through another'.

   The Venerable Bede AD 673–735: *Ecclesiastical History of the English People*, tr. B. Colgrave

7 Life well spent is long.
  Leonardo da Vinci 1452–1519: E. McCurdy (ed. and trans.)
  Leonardo da Vinci's Notebooks (1906)

8 The ceaseless labour of your life is to build the house of
  death.
  Montaigne 1533–92: *Essais* (1580)

9 Life is as tedious as a twice-told tale,
  Vexing the dull ear of a drowsy man.
  William Shakespeare 1564–1616: *King John* (1591–8)

10 All the world's a stage,
  And all the men and women merely players:
  They have their exits and their entrances;
  And one man in his time plays many parts,
  His acts being seven ages.
  William Shakespeare 1564–1616: *As You Like It* (1599)

11 It is in life as it is in ways, the shortest way is commonly the
  foulest, and surely the fairer way is not much about.
  Francis Bacon 1561–1626: *The Advancement of Learning*
  (1605)

12 Life's but a walking shadow, a poor player,
  That struts and frets his hour upon the stage,
  And then is heard no more; it is a tale
  Told by an idiot, full of sound and fury,
  Signifying nothing.
  William Shakespeare 1564–1616: *Macbeth* (1606)

13 No arts; no letters; no society; and which is worst of all,
  continual fear and danger of violent death; and the life of
  man, solitary, poor, nasty, brutish, and short.
  Thomas Hobbes 1588–1679: *Leviathan* (1651)

14 Life is an incurable disease.
  Abraham Cowley 1618–67: 'To Dr Scarborough' (1656)

15 Life itself is but the shadow of death, and souls departed but
  the shadows of the living.
  Sir Thomas Browne 1605–82: *The Garden of Cyrus* (1658)

16 Man has but three events in his life: to be born, to live, and
  to die. He is not conscious of his birth, he suffers at his death
  and he forgets to live.
  Jean de la Bruyère 1645–96: *The Characters, or The
  Manners of the Age* (1688)

17 Human life is everywhere a state in which much is to be
endured, and little to be enjoyed.
   Samuel Johnson 1709–84: *Rasselas* (1759)

18 Man wants but little here below,
Nor wants that little long.
   Oliver Goldsmith 1730–74: 'Edwin and Angelina, or the
   Hermit' (1766)

19 This world is a comedy to those that think, a tragedy to those
that feel.
   Horace Walpole 1717–97: letter to Anne, Countess of Upper
   Ossory, 16 August 1776

20 Life, like a dome of many-coloured glass,
Stains the white radiance of Eternity,
Until Death tramples it to fragments.
   Percy Bysshe Shelley 1792–1822: *Adonais* (1821)

21 Life is real! Life is earnest!
And the grave is not its goal;
Dust thou art, to dust returnest,
Was not spoken of the soul.
   Henry Wadsworth Longfellow 1807–82: 'A Psalm of Life'
   (1838)

22 I slept, and dreamed that life was beauty;
I woke, and found that life was duty.
   Ellen Sturgis Hooper 1816–41: 'Beauty and Duty' (1840)

23 Life must be understood backwards; but…it must be lived
forwards.
   Sören Kierkegaard 1813–1855: *Journals and Papers* (1843)

24 Youth is a blunder; Manhood a struggle; Old Age a regret.
   Benjamin Disraeli 1804–81: *Coningsby* (1844)

25 Is it so small a thing
To have enjoyed the sun,
To have lived light in the spring,
To have loved, to have thought, to have done.
   Matthew Arnold 1822–88: *Empedocles on Etna* (1852)

26 All the business of war, and indeed all the business of life, is
to endeavour to find out what you don't know by what you
do; that's what I called 'guessing what was at the other side
of the hill'.
   Duke of Wellington 1769–1852: *The Croker Papers* (1885)

27 The mass of men lead lives of quiet desperation.
   Henry David Thoreau 1817–62: *Walden* (1854)

28 Our life is frittered away by detail...Simplify, simplify.
   Henry David Thoreau 1817–62: *Walden* (1854)

29 Life is mostly froth and bubble,
   Two things stand like stone,
   Kindness in another's trouble,
   Courage in your own.
   Adam Lindsay Gordon 1833–70: *Ye Wearie Wayfarer* (1866)

30 Cats and monkeys—monkeys and cats—all human life is
   there!
   Henry James 1843–1916: *The Madonna of the Future* (1879)
   'All human life is there' became the slogan of the *News of
   the World* from the late 1950s

31 *Ah! que la vie est quotidienne.*
   Oh, what a day-to-day business life is.
   Jules Laforgue 1860–87: *Complainte sur certains ennuis*
   (1885)

32 The life of every man is a diary in which he means to write
   one story, and writes another; and his humblest hour is
   when he compares the volume as it is with what he vowed to
   make it.
   J. M. Barrie 1860–1937: *The Little Minister* (1891)

33 Life is like playing a violin solo in public and learning the
   instrument as one goes on
   Samuel Butler 1835–1902: speech, 27 February 1895

34 Life is one long process of getting tired.
   Samuel Butler 1835–1902: *Notebooks* (1912)

35 To live is like to love—all reason is against it, and all healthy
   instinct for it.
   Samuel Butler 1835–1902: *Notebooks* (1912)

36 Life is just one damned thing after another.
   Elbert Hubbard 1859–1915: *Philistine* December 1909, often
   attributed to Frank Ward O'Malley

37 And Life is Colour and Warmth and Light
   And a striving evermore for these;
   And he is dead, who will not fight;
   And who dies fighting has increase.
   Julian Grenfell 1888–1915: 'Into Battle' (1915)

38 Life is a foreign language: all men mispronounce it.
   Christopher Morley 1890–1957: *Thunder on the Left* (1925)

39 Life is not a series of gig lamps symmetrically arranged; life
   is a luminous halo, a semi-transparent envelope surrounding
   us from the beginning of consciousness to the end.
   Virginia Woolf 1882–1941: *The Common Reader* (1925)
   'Modern Fiction'

40 I enjoy almost everything. Yet I have some restless searcher
   in me. Why is there not a discovery in life? Something one
   can lay one's hands on and say "This is it"?
   Virginia Woolf 1882–1941: diary, 27 February 1926

41 Never to have lived is best, ancient writers say;
   Never to have drawn the breath of life, never to have looked
   into the eye of day;
   The second best's a gay goodnight and quickly turn away.
   W. B. Yeats 1865–1939: 'From *Oedipus at Colonus*' (1928)

42 Life is a horizontal fall.
   Jean Cocteau 1889–1963: *Opium* (1930)

43 Life is just a bowl of cherries.
   Lew Brown 1893–1958: title of song (1931)

44 Birth, and copulation, and death.
   That's all the facts when you come to brass tacks.
   T. S. Eliot 1888–1965: *Sweeney Agonistes* (1932)

45 I long ago come to the conclusion that all life is 6 to 5
   against.
   Damon Runyon 1884–1946: *Collier's* 8 September 1934

46 It's a funny old world—a man's lucky if he gets out of it
   alive.
   Walter de Leon and **Paul M. Jones**: *You're Telling Me*
   (1934 film); spoken by W. C. Fields

47 Many men would take the death-sentence without a whimper
   to escape the life-sentence which fate carries in her other
   hand.
   T. E. Lawrence 1888–1935: *The Mint* (1955)

48 Yet we have gone on living,
   Living and partly living.
   T. S. Eliot 1888–1965: *Murder in the Cathedral* (1935)

49 Oh, life is a glorious cycle of song,
   A medley of extemporanea;

And love is a thing that can never go wrong;
And I am Marie of Roumania.
  Dorothy Parker 1893–1967: 'Comment' (1937)

50 What, knocked a tooth out? Never mind, dear, laugh it off,
laugh it off; it's all part of life's rich pageant.
  Arthur Marshall 1910–89: *The Games Mistress* (recorded
  monologue, 1937)

51 All that matters is love and work.
  Sigmund Freud 1856–1939: attributed

52 Life is not having been told that the man has just waxed the
floor.
  Ogden Nash 1902–71: 'You and Me and P. B. Shelley' (1942)

53 Dying is nothing. So start by living. It's less fun and it lasts
longer.
  Jean Anouilh 1910–87: *Roméo et Jeannette* (1946)

54 The cradle rocks above an abyss, and common sense tells us
that our existence is but a brief crack of light between two
eternities of darkness.
  Vladimir Nabokov 1899–1977: *Speak, Memory* (1951)

55 Life is like a sewer. What you get out of it depends on what
you put into it.
  Tom Lehrer 1928– : 'We Will All Go Together When We
  Go' (1953 song), preamble

56 Oh, isn't life a terrible thing, thank God?
  Dylan Thomas 1914–53: *Under Milk Wood* (1954)

57 They give birth astride of a grave, the light gleams an
instant, then it's night once more.
  Samuel Beckett 1906–89: *Waiting for Godot* (1955)

58 When you don't have any money, the problem is food. When
you have money, it's sex. When you have both, it's health.
  J. P. Donleavy 1926– : *The Ginger Man* (1955)

59 Man is born to live, not to prepare for life.
  Boris Pasternak 1890–1960: *Doctor Zhivago* (1958)

60 If it were possible to talk to the unborn, one could never
explain to them how it feels to be alive, for life is washed in
the speechless real.
  Jacques Barzun 1907– : *The House of Intellect* (1959)

61 One's prime is elusive. You little girls, when you grow up,
must be on the alert to recognise your prime at whatever
time of your life it may occur.
   Muriel Spark 1918– : *The Prime of Miss Jean Brodie* (1961)

62 As far as we can discern, the sole purpose of human
existence is to kindle a light in the darkness of mere being.
   Carl Gustav Jung 1875–1961: *Memories, Dreams, Reflections*
   (1962)

63 Life is first boredom, then fear.
   Philip Larkin 1922–85: 'Dockery & Son' (1964)

64 Life is a gamble at terrible odds—if it was a bet, you wouldn't
take it.
   Tom Stoppard 1937– : *Rosencrantz and Guildenstern are
   Dead* (1967)

65 I've looked at life from both sides now,
From win and lose and still somehow
It's life's illusions I recall;
I really don't know life at all.
   Joni Mitchell 1945– : 'Both Sides Now' (1967 song)

66 Expect nothing. Live frugally
on surprise.
   Alice Walker 1944– : 'Expect nothing' (1973)

67 The Answer to the Great Question Of…Life, the Universe
and Everything…[is] Forty-two.
   Douglas Adams 1952– : *The Hitch Hiker's Guide to the
   Galaxy* (1979)

68 It seems that I have spent my entire time trying to make life
more rational and that it was all wasted effort.
   A. J. Ayer 1910–89: in *Observer* 17 August 1986

69 Life is a sexually transmitted disease.
   Anonymous: graffito found on the London Underground

Life Sciences

See also **Science**

1 So, naturalists observe, a flea
Hath smaller fleas that on him prey;

And these have smaller fleas to bite 'em,
And so proceed *ad infinitum*.
   Jonathan Swift 1667–1745: 'On Poetry' (1733)

2 I have called this principle, by which each slight variation, if
useful, is preserved, by the term of Natural Selection.
   Charles Darwin 1809–82: *On the Origin of Species* (1859)

3 Was it through his grandfather or his grandmother that he
claimed his descent from a monkey?
   Bishop Samuel Wilberforce 1805–73: addressed to T. H.
   Huxley in a debate on Darwin's theory of evolution at
   Oxford, June 1860

4 Survival of the fittest implies multiplication of the fittest.
   Herbert Spencer 1820–1903: *Principles of Biology* (1865)

5 It has, I believe, been often remarked that a hen is only an
egg's way of making another egg.
   Samuel Butler 1835–1902: *Life and Habit* (1877)

6 The Microbe is so very small
You cannot make him out at all.
   Hilaire Belloc 1870–1953: 'The Microbe' (1897)

7 Life exists in the universe only because the carbon atom
possesses certain exceptional properties.
   James Jeans 1877–1946: *The Mysterious Universe* (1930)

8 Water is life's *mater* and *matrix*, mother and medium. There
is no life without water.
   Albert von Szent-Györgyi 1893–1986: *Perspectives in
   Biology and Medicine* Winter 1971

9 The essence of life is statistical improbability on a colossal
scale.
   Richard Dawkins 1941– : *The Blind Watchmaker* (1986)

10 Almost all aspects of life are engineered at the molecular
level, and without understanding molecules we can only have
a very sketchy understanding of life itself.
   Francis Crick 1916– : *What Mad Pursuit* (1988)

Literature

See also **Writing**

1 Works of serious purpose and grand promises often have a
  purple patch or two stitched on, to shine far and wide.
  Horace 65-8 BC: *Ars Poetica*

2 'Oh! it is only a novel!...only Cecilia, or Camilla, or Belinda:'
  or, in short, only some work in which the most thorough
  knowledge of human nature, the happiest delineation of its
  varieties, the liveliest effusions of wit and humour are
  conveyed to the world in the best chosen language.
  Jane Austen 1775-1817: *Northanger Abbey* (1818)

3 All tragedies are finished by a death,
  All comedies are ended by a marriage;
  The future states of both are left to faith.
  Lord Byron 1788-1824: *Don Juan* (1819-24)

4 A novel is a mirror which passes over a highway. Sometimes
  it reflects to your eyes the blue of the skies, at others the
  churned-up mud of the road.
  Stendhal 1783-1842: *Le Rouge et le noir* (1830)

5 A losing trade, I assure you, sir: literature is a drug.
  George Borrow 1803-81: *Lavengro* (1851)

6 It takes a great deal of history to produce a little literature.
  Henry James 1843-1916: *Hawthorne* (1879)

7 In *Anna Karenina* and *Onegin* not a single problem is solved,
  but they satisfy you completely just because all their
  problems are correctly presented. The court is obliged to
  submit the case fairly, but let the jury do the deciding, each
  according to its own judgement.
  Anton Chekhov 1860-1904: letter to Alexei Suvorin,
  27 October 1888

8 The good ended happily, and the bad unhappily. That is what
  fiction means.
  Oscar Wilde 1854-1900: *The Importance of Being Earnest*
  (1895)

9 Literature is a luxury; fiction is a necessity.
  G. K. Chesterton 1874-1936: *The Defendant* (1901) 'A
  Defence of Penny Dreadfuls'

10 Never trust the artist. Trust the tale.
  D. H. Lawrence 1885-1930: *Studies in Classic American Literature* (1923)

11 Yes—oh dear yes—the novel tells a story.
  E. M. Forster 1879-1970: *Aspects of the Novel* (1927)

12 Our American professors like their literature clear and cold and pure and very dead.
  Sinclair Lewis 1885-1951: *The American Fear of Literature* (Nobel Prize Address, 12 December 1930)

13 Literature is news that STAYS news.
  Ezra Pound 1885-1972: *The ABC of Reading* (1934)

14 The bad end unhappily, the good unluckily. That is what tragedy means.
  Tom Stoppard 1937- : *Rosencrantz and Guildenstern are Dead* (1967)

Living

See also **Life**

1 Thou shalt love thy neighbour as thyself.
  Bible: Leviticus. See also St Matthew

2 Fear God, and keep his commandments: for this is the whole duty of man.
  Bible: Ecclesiastes

3 A man hath no better thing under the sun, than to eat, and to drink, and to be merry.
  Bible: Ecclesiastes

4 Love and do what you will.
  St Augustine of Hippo AD 354-430: *In Epistolam Joannis ad Parthos* (AD 413)

5 *Quidquid agis, prudenter agas, et respice finem.*
  Whatever you do, do cautiously, and look to the end.
  Anonymous: *Gesta Romanorum*

6 *Fais ce que voudras.*
  Do what you like.
  François Rabelais *c.*1494-*c.*1553: *Gargantua* (1534)

7 *Mon métier et mon art c'est vivre.*
Living is my job and my art.
   Montaigne 1533–92: *Essais* (1580)

8 If I had no duties, and no reference to futurity, I would spend
my life in driving briskly in a post-chaise with a pretty
woman.
   Samuel Johnson 1709–84: in James Boswell *Life of Johnson*
(1791) 19 September 1777

9 Take short views, hope for the best, and trust in God.
   Sydney Smith 1771–1845: in Lady Holland *Memoir* (1855)

10 Believe me! The secret of reaping the greatest fruitfulness
and the greatest enjoyment from life is *to live dangerously*!
   Friedrich Nietzsche 1844–1900: *Die fröhliche Wissenschaft*
(1882)

11 Live all you can; it's a mistake not to. It doesn't so much
matter what you do in particular, so long as you have your
life. If you haven't had that, what *have* you had?
   Henry James 1843–1916: *Ambassadors* (1903)

12 Do what thou wilt shall be the whole of the Law.
   Aleister Crowley 1875–1947: *Book of the Law* (1909)

13 I've lived a life that's full, I've travelled each and ev'ry
highway
And more, much more than this. I did it my way.
   Paul Anka 1941– : *My Way* (1969 song)

....

London
....

1 London, thou art the flower of cities all!
   Anonymous: 'London' previously attributed to William
Dunbar, *c*.1465–*c*.1530

2 The full tide of human existence is at Charing-Cross.
   Samuel Johnson 1709–84: in James Boswell *Life of Johnson*
(1791) 2 April 1775

3 When a man is tired of London, he is tired of life.
   Samuel Johnson 1709–84: in James Boswell *Life of Johnson*
(1791) 20 September 1777

4 Crowds without company, and dissipation without pleasure.
   Edward Gibbon 1737–94: *Memoirs of My Life* (1796)

5 Earth has not anything to show more fair:
Dull would he be of soul who could pass by
A sight so touching in its majesty.
   William Wordsworth 1770–1850: 'Composed upon
   Westminster Bridge' (1807)

6 *Was für Plunder!*
What rubbish!
   Gebhard Lebrecht Blücher 1742–1819: of London as seen
   from the Monument in June 1814, often misquoted '*Was für
   plündern* [What a place to plunder]!'

7 The great wen of all.
   William Cobbett 1762–1835: *Rural Rides* 5 January 1822

8 I thought of London spread out in the sun,
Its postal districts packed like squares of wheat.
   Philip Larkin 1922–85: *The Whitsun Weddings* (1964)

Love

See also **Marriage, Sex**

1 Many waters cannot quench love, neither can the floods
drown it.
   Bible: Song of Solomon

2 *Omnia vincit Amor: et nos cedamus Amori.*
Love conquers all things: let us too give in to Love.
   Virgil 70–19 BC: *Eclogues*

3 Greater love hath no man than this, that a man lay down his
life for his friends.
   Bible: St John

4 Though I speak with the tongues of men and of angels, and
have not charity, I am become as sounding brass, or a
tinkling cymbal.
   And though I have the gift of prophecy, and understand all
mysteries, and all knowledge; and though I have all faith; so
that I could remove mountains; and have not charity, I am
nothing.
   Bible: I Corinthians

5 And now abideth faith, hope, charity, these three; but the
   greatest of these is charity.
      Bible: I Corinthians

6 There is no fear in love; but perfect love casteth out fear.
      Bible: I John

7 Difficult or easy, pleasant or bitter, you are the same you: I
   cannot live with you—or without you.
      Martial AD c.40–c.104: *Epigrammata*

8 *L'amor che muove il sole e l'altre stelle.*
   The love that moves the sun and the other stars.
      Dante Alighieri 1265-1321: *Divina Commedia* 'Paradiso'

9 Love wol nat been constreyned by maistrye.
   When maistrie comth, the God of Love anon
   Beteth his wynges, and farewel, he is gon!
      Geoffrey Chaucer c.1343-1400: *The Canterbury Tales* 'The
      Franklin's Tale'

10 If I am pressed to say why I loved him, I feel it can only be
   explained by replying: 'Because it was he; because it was me.'
      Montaigne 1533-92: *Essais* (1580)

11 Love is a spirit all compact of fire,
   Not gross to sink, but light, and will aspire.
      William Shakespeare 1564-1616: *Venus and Adonis* (1593)

12 Fie, fie! how wayward is this foolish love
   That, like a testy babe, will scratch the nurse
   And presently all humbled kiss the rod!
      William Shakespeare 1564-1616: *The Two Gentlemen of
      Verona* (1592-3)

13 O! how this spring of love resembleth
   The uncertain glory of an April day.
      William Shakespeare 1564-1616: *The Two Gentlemen of
      Verona* (1592-3)

14 Love built on beauty, soon as beauty, dies.
      John Donne 1572-1631: 'The Anagram' (c.1595)

15 For stony limits cannot hold love out,
   And what love can do that dares love attempt.
      William Shakespeare 1564-1616: *Romeo and Juliet* (1595)

16 Love looks not with the eyes, but with the mind,
   And therefore is winged Cupid painted blind.
      William Shakespeare 1564-1616: *A Midsummer Night's
      Dream* (1595-6)

17 The course of true love never did run smooth.
   William Shakespeare 1564–1616: *A Midsummer Night's Dream* (1595–6)

18 Where both deliberate, the love is slight;
   Who ever loved that loved not at first sight?
   Christopher Marlowe 1564–93: *Hero and Leander* (1598)

19 Love sought is good, but giv'n unsought is better.
   William Shakespeare 1564–1616: *Twelfth Night* (1601)

20   To be wise, and love,
   Exceeds man's might.
   William Shakespeare 1564–1616: *Troilus and Cressida* (1602)

21   Then, must you speak
   Of one that loved not wisely but too well.
   William Shakespeare 1564–1616: *Othello* (1602–4)

22 ANTONY: There's beggary in the love that can be reckoned.
   CLEOPATRA: I'll set a bourn how far to be beloved.
   ANTONY: Then must thou needs find out new heaven, new earth.
   William Shakespeare 1564–1616: *Antony and Cleopatra* (1606–7)

23 Let me not to the marriage of true minds
   Admit impediments. Love is not love
   Which alters when it alteration finds.
   William Shakespeare 1564–1616: sonnet 116 (1609)

24 Love is like linen often changed, the sweeter.
   Phineas Fletcher 1582–1650: *Sicelides* (1614)

25 Love, a child, is ever crying:
   Please him and he straight is flying,
   Give him, he the more is craving,
   Never satisfied with having.
   Lady Mary Wroth *c.*1586–*c.*1652: 'Love, a child, is ever crying' (1621)

26 Love is a growing or full constant light;
   And his first minute, after noon, is night.
   John Donne 1572–1631: 'A Lecture in the Shadow'

27 All other things, to their destruction draw,
   Only our love hath no decay;
   This, no tomorrow hath, nor yesterday,

Running it never runs from us away,
But truly keeps his first, last, everlasting day.
   John Donne 1572–1631: 'The Anniversary'

28 Why so pale and wan, fond lover?
   Prithee, why so pale?
   Will, when looking well can't move her,
   Looking ill prevail?
   John Suckling 1609–42: *Aglaura* (1637)

29 To enlarge or illustrate this power and effect of love is to set
a candle in the sun.
   Robert Burton 1577–1640: *Anatomy of Melancholy* (1621–51)

30 Love is the fart
   Of every heart:
   It pains a man when 'tis kept close,
   And others doth offend, when 'tis let loose.
   John Suckling 1609–42: 'Love's Offence' (1646)

31 Love's passives are his activ'st part.
   The wounded is the wounding heart.
   Richard Crashaw *c.*1612–49: 'The Flaming Heart upon the
   Book of Saint Teresa' (1652)

32 And love's the noblest frailty of the mind.
   John Dryden 1631–1700: *The Indian Emperor* (1665)

33 Had we but world enough, and time,
   This coyness, lady, were no crime.
   Andrew Marvell 1621–78: 'To His coy Mistress' (1681)

34 Say what you will, 'tis better to be left than never to have
been loved.
   William Congreve 1670–1729: *The Way of the World* (1700)

35 Love is only one of many passions.
   Samuel Johnson 1709–84: *Plays of William Shakespeare*
   (1765) preface

36 Love and a cottage! Eh, Fanny! Ah, give me indifference and
a coach and six!
   George Colman, the Elder 1732–94 and **David Garrick**
   1717–79: *The Clandestine Marriage* (1766)

37 Friendship is a disinterested commerce between equals; love,
an abject intercourse between tyrants and slaves.
   Oliver Goldsmith 1730–74: *The Good-Natured Man* (1768)

38 Love is the wisdom of the fool and the folly of the wise.
   Samuel Johnson 1709–84: in W. Cooke *Life of Samuel Foote* (1805)

39 Love's pleasure lasts but a moment; love's sorrow lasts all through life.
   Jean-Pierre Claris de Florian 1755–94: *Célestine* (1784)

40 Love seeketh not itself to please,
   Nor for itself hath any care;
   But for another gives its ease,
   And builds a Heaven in Hell's despair.
   William Blake 1757–1827: 'The Clod and the Pebble' (1794)

41 Love seeketh only Self to please,
   To bind another to its delight,
   Joys in another's loss of ease,
   And builds a Hell in Heaven's despite.
   William Blake 1757–1827: 'The Clod and the Pebble' (1794)

42 If I love you, what does that matter to you!
   Johann Wolfgang von Goethe 1749–1832: *Wilhelm Meister's Apprenticeship* (1795–6), tr. R. D. Moon

43 O, my Luve's like a red, red rose
   That's newly sprung in June;
   O my Luve's like the melodie
   That's sweetly play'd in tune.
   Robert Burns 1759–96: 'A Red Red Rose' (1796); derived from various folk-songs

44 No, there's nothing half so sweet in life
   As love's young dream.
   Thomas Moore 1779–1852: 'Love's Young Dream' (1807)

45 Love in a hut, with water and a crust,
   Is—Love, forgive us!—cinders, ashes, dust.
   John Keats 1795–1821: 'Lamia' (1820)

46 My love for Heathcliff resembles the eternal rocks beneath:—a source of little visible delight, but necessary.
   Emily Brontë 1818–48: *Wuthering Heights* (1847)

47 If you could see my legs when I take my boots off, you'd form some idea of what unrequited affection is.
   Charles Dickens 1812–70: *Dombey and Son* (1848) Mr Toots

48 'Tis better to have loved and lost
Than never to have loved at all.
Alfred, Lord Tennyson 1809–92: *In Memoriam A. H. H.*
(1850)

49 Love's like the measles—all the worse when it comes late in
life.
Douglas Jerrold 1803–57: *Wit and Opinions* (1859)

50 We loved, sir—used to meet:
How sad and bad and mad it was—
But then, how it was sweet!
Robert Browning 1812–89: 'Confessions' (1864)

51 O lyric Love, half-angel and half-bird
And all a wonder and a wild desire.
Robert Browning 1812–89: *The Ring and the Book* (1868–9)

52 Love is like any other luxury. You have no right to it unless
you can afford it.
Anthony Trollope 1815–82: *The Way We Live Now* (1875)

53 A lover without indiscretion is no lover at all.
Thomas Hardy 1840–1928: *The Hand of Ethelberta* (1876)

54 Never the time and the place
And the loved one all together!
Robert Browning 1812–89: 'Never the Time and the Place'
(1883)

55 A pity beyond all telling,
Is hid in the heart of love.
W. B. Yeats 1865–1939: 'The Pity of Love' (1893)

56 I am the Love that dare not speak its name.
Lord Alfred Douglas 1870–1945: 'Two Loves' (1896)

57 Yet each man kills the thing he loves,
By each let this be heard,
Some do it with a bitter look,
Some with a flattering word.
The coward does it with a kiss,
The brave man with a sword!
Oscar Wilde 1854–1900: *The Ballad of Reading Gaol* (1898)

58 The fickleness of the women I love is only equalled by the
infernal constancy of the women who love me.
George Bernard Shaw 1856–1950: *The Philanderer* (1898)

59 A woman can be proud and stiff
When on love intent;

But Love has pitched his mansion in
The place of excrement;
For nothing can be sole or whole
That has not been rent.
W. B. Yeats 1865–1939: 'Crazy Jane Talks with the Bishop'
(1932)

60 By the time you say you're his,
Shivering and sighing
And he vows his passion is
Infinite, undying—
Lady, make a note of this:
One of you is lying.
Dorothy Parker 1893–1967: 'Unfortunate Coincidence'
(1937)

61 Life has taught us that love does not consist in gazing at each
other but in looking together in the same direction.
Antoine de Saint-Exupéry 1900–1944: *Terre des Hommes*
(translated as 'Wind, Sand and Stars', 1939)

62 I'll love you, dear, I'll love you
Till China and Africa meet
And the river jumps over the mountain
And the salmon sing in the street.
W. H. Auden 1907–73: 'As I Walked Out One Evening' (1940)

63 How alike are the groans of love to those of the dying.
Malcolm Lowry 1909–57: *Under the Volcano* (1947)

64 Love is the delusion that one woman differs from another.
H. L. Mencken 1880–1956: *Chrestomathy* (1949)

65 You know very well that love is, above all, the gift of oneself!
Jean Anouilh 1910–87: *Ardèle* (1949)

66 Birds do it, bees do it,
Even educated fleas do it.
Let's do it, let's fall in love.
Cole Porter 1891–1964: 'Let's Do It' (1954 song; words added
to the 1928 original)

67 Love means not ever having to say you're sorry.
Erich Segal 1937– : *Love Story* (1970)

Madness

1 Whenever God prepares evil for a man, He first damages his mind, with which he deliberates.
   Anonymous: scholiastic annotation to Sophocles's *Antigone*

2 Though this be madness, yet there is method in't.
   William Shakespeare 1564–1616: *Hamlet* (1601)

3 I am but mad north-north-west; when the wind is southerly, I know a hawk from a handsaw.
   William Shakespeare 1564–1616: *Hamlet* (1601)

4 O! what a noble mind is here o'erthrown.
   William Shakespeare 1564–1616: *Hamlet* (1601)

5 O! let me not be mad, not mad, sweet heaven;
   Keep me in temper; I would not be mad!
   William Shakespeare 1564–1616: *King Lear* (1605–6)

6 *Quem Jupiter vult perdere, dementat prius.*
   Whom God would destroy He first sends mad.
   James Duport 1606–79: *Homeri Gnomologia* (1660)

7 Mad, is he? Then I hope he will *bite* some of my other generals.
   George II 1683–1760: replying to the Duke of Newcastle, who had complained that General Wolfe was a madman

8 Babylon in all its desolation is a sight not so awful as that of the human mind in ruins.
   Scrope Davies *c.*1783–1852: letter to Thomas Raikes, May 1835

9 There was only one catch and that was Catch-22...Orr would be crazy to fly more missions and sane if he didn't, but if he was sane he had to fly them. If he flew them he was crazy and didn't have to; but if he didn't want to he was sane and had to.
   Joseph Heller 1923– : *Catch-22* (1961)

Majorities see Minorities and Majorities

Management

See also **Bureaucracy, Careers**

1 Every time I create an appointment, I create a hundred
malcontents and one ingrate.
   Louis XIV 1638–1715: in Voltaire *Siècle de Louis XIV* (1768
   ed.)

2 *Dans ce pays-ci il est bon de tuer de temps en temps un amiral
pour encourager les autres.*
   In this country [England] it is thought well to kill an admiral
   from time to time to encourage the others.
   Voltaire 1694–1778: *Candide* (1759)

3 The shortest way to do many things is to do only one thing at
once.
   Samuel Smiles 1812–1904: *Self-Help* (1859)

4 A place for everything and everything in its place.
   Mrs Beeton 1836–65: *Book of Household Management* (1861),
   often attributed to Samuel Smiles

5 This island is made mainly of coal and surrounded by fish.
Only an organizing genius could produce a shortage of coal
and fish at the same time.
   Aneurin Bevan 1897–1960: speech at Blackpool, 24 May 1945

6 Committee—a group of men who individually can do nothing
but as a group decide that nothing can be done.
   Fred Allen 1894–1956: attributed

7 Time spent on any item of the agenda will be in inverse
proportion to the sum involved.
   C. Northcote Parkinson 1909–93: *Parkinson's Law* (1958)

8 Perfection of planned layout is achieved only by institutions
on the point of collapse.
   C. Northcote Parkinson 1909–93: *Parkinson's Law* (1958)

9 A problem left to itself dries up or goes rotten. But fertilize a
problem with a solution—you'll hatch out dozens.
   N. F. Simpson 1919– : *A Resounding Tinkle* (1958)

10 You're either part of the solution or you're part of the
problem.
   Eldridge Cleaver 1935– : speech in San Francisco, 1968

11 In a hierarchy every employee tends to rise to his level of
incompetence.
   Laurence Peter 1919- : *The Peter Principle* (1969)

12 Competence, like truth, beauty and contact lenses, is in the
eye of the beholder.
   Laurence Peter 1919- : *The Peter Principle* (1969)

13 There cannot be a crisis next week. My schedule is already
full.
   Henry Kissinger 1923- : in *New York Times Magazine*
   1 June 1969

14 If it ain't broke, don't fix it.
   Bert Lance 1931- : in *Nation's Business* May 1977

15 A camel is a horse designed by a committee.
   Alec Issigonis 1906-88: on his dislike of working in teams

16 Management that wants to change an institution must first
show it loves that institution.
   John Tusa 1936- : *Observer* 27 February 1994 'Sayings of
   the Week'

Manners

See also **Behaviour**

1 Evil communications corrupt good manners.
   Bible: I Corinthians

2 Stand not upon the order of your going.
   William Shakespeare 1564-1616: *Macbeth* (1606)

3 Courts and camps are the only places to learn the world in.
   Lord Chesterfield 1694-1773: *Letters to his Son* (1774)
   2 October 1747

4 Take the tone of the company that you are in.
   Lord Chesterfield 1694-1773: *Letters to his Son* (1774)
   16 October 1747

5 He is the very pineapple of politeness!
   Richard Brinsley Sheridan 1751-1816: *The Rivals* (1775)

6 Most vices may be committed very genteelly: a man may
debauch his friend's wife genteelly: he may cheat at cards
genteelly.
   James Boswell 1740–95: *Life of Samuel Johnson* (1791)

7 Ceremony is an invention to take off the uneasy feeling
which we derive from knowing ourselves to be less the object
of love and esteem with a fellow-creature than some other
person is.
   Charles Lamb 1775–1834: *Essays of Elia* (1823) 'A Bachelor's
   Complaint of the Behaviour of Married People'

8 *L'exactitude est la politesse des rois.*
Punctuality is the politeness of kings.
   Louis XVIII 1755–1824: attributed

9 Curtsey while you're thinking what to say. It saves time.
   Lewis Carroll 1832–98: *Through the Looking-Glass* (1872)

10 Very notable was his distinction between coarseness and
vulgarity (coarseness, revealing something; vulgarity,
concealing something).
   E. M. Forster 1879–1970: *The Longest Journey* (1907)

11 There are few who would not rather be taken in adultery
than in provincialism.
   Aldous Huxley 1894–1963: *Antic Hay* (1923)

12 JUDGE: You are extremely offensive, young man.
SMITH: As a matter of fact, we both are, and the only
difference between us is that I am trying to be, and you can't
help it.
   F. E. Smith 1872–1930: in 2nd Earl of Birkenhead *Earl of
   Birkenhead* (1933)

13 Phone for the fish-knives, Norman
As Cook is a little unnerved;
You kiddies have crumpled the serviettes
And I must have things daintily served.
   John Betjeman 1906–84: 'How to get on in Society' (1954)

14 To Americans, English manners are far more frightening
than none at all.
   Randall Jarrell 1914–65: *Pictures from an Institution*
   (1954)

15 Manners are especially the need of the plain. The pretty can
get away with anything.
   Evelyn Waugh 1903–66: in *Observer* 15 April 1962

Marriage

See also **Love, Sex**

1 Therefore shall a man leave his father and his mother, and
   shall cleave unto his wife: and they shall be one flesh.
      Bible: Genesis

2 What therefore God hath joined together, let not man put
   asunder.
      Bible: St Matthew

3 It is better to marry than to burn.
      Bible: I Corinthians

4 Men are April when they woo, December when they wed:
   maids are May when they are maids, but the sky changes
   when they are wives.
      William Shakespeare 1564–1616: *As You Like It* (1599)

5 A young man married is a man that's marred.
      William Shakespeare 1564–1616: *All's Well that Ends Well*
      (1603–4)

6 Wives are young men's mistresses, companions for middle
   age, and old men's nurses.
      Francis Bacon 1561–1626: *Essays* (1625) 'Of Marriage and
      the Single Life'

7 He was reputed one of the wise men that made answer to the
   question when a man should marry? 'A young man not yet,
   an elder man not at all.'
      Francis Bacon 1561–1626: *Essays* (1625) 'Of Marriage and
      the Single Life'

8 I would be married, but I'd have no wife,
   I would be married to a single life.
      Richard Crashaw *c.*1612–49: 'On Marriage' (1646)

9 Then be not coy, but use your time;
   And while ye may, go marry:
   For having lost but once your prime,
   You may for ever tarry.
      Robert Herrick 1591–1674: 'To the Virgins, to Make Much
      of Time' (1648)

10 Wilt thou love her, comfort her, honour, and keep her in sickness and in health; and, forsaking all other, keep thee only unto her, so long as ye both shall live?
  Book of Common Prayer 1662: *Solemnization of Matrimony*

11 To have and to hold from this day forward, for better for worse, for richer for poorer, in sickness and in health, to love, cherish, and to obey, till death us do part.
  Book of Common Prayer 1662: *Solemnization of Matrimony*

12 A Man may not marry his Mother.
  Book of Common Prayer 1662: *A Table of Kindred and Affinity*

13 Strange to say what delight we married people have to see these poor fools decoyed into our condition.
  Samuel Pepys 1633–1703: diary, 25 December 1665

14 Courtship to marriage, as a very witty prologue to a very dull play.
  William Congreve 1670–1729: *The Old Bachelor* (1693)

15 SHARPER: Thus grief still treads upon the heels of pleasure: Married in haste, we may repent at leisure.
  SETTER: Some by experience find those words mis-placed: At leisure married, they repent in haste.
  William Congreve 1670–1729: *The Old Bachelor* (1693)

16 Oh! how many torments lie in the small circle of a wedding-ring!
  Colley Cibber 1671–1757: *The Double Gallant* (1707)

17 Do you think your mother and I should have lived comfortably so long together, if ever we had been married?
  John Gay 1685–1732: *The Beggar's Opera* (1728)

18 The comfortable estate of widowhood, is the only hope that keeps up a wife's spirits.
  John Gay 1685–1732: *The Beggar's Opera* (1728)

19 One fool at least in every married couple.
  Henry Fielding 1707–54: *Amelia* (1751)

20 Marriage has many pains, but celibacy has no pleasures.
  Samuel Johnson 1709–84: *Rasselas* (1759)

21 I...chose my wife, as she did her wedding gown, not for a fine glossy surface, but such qualities as would wear well.
  Oliver Goldsmith 1730–74: *The Vicar of Wakefield* (1766)

22 O! how short a time does it take to put an end to a woman's liberty!
   Fanny Burney 1752–1840: of a wedding; diary, 20 July 1768

23 The triumph of hope over experience.
   Samuel Johnson 1709–84: of a man who remarried immediately after the death of a wife with whom he had been unhappy, 1770; in James Boswell *Life of Johnson* (1791)

24 Still I can't contradict, what so oft has been said,
   'Though women are angels, yet wedlock's the devil.'
   Lord Byron 1788–1824: 'To Eliza' (1806)

25 It is a truth universally acknowledged, that a single man in possession of a good fortune, must be in want of a wife.
   Jane Austen 1775–1817: *Pride and Prejudice* (1813)

26 There is not one in a hundred of either sex who is not taken in when they marry…it is, of all transactions, the one in which people expect most from others, and are least honest themselves.
   Jane Austen 1775–1817: *Mansfield Park* (1814)

27 Marriage may often be a stormy lake, but celibacy is almost always a muddy horsepond.
   Thomas Love Peacock 1785–1866: *Melincourt* (1817)

28 Think you, if Laura had been Petrarch's wife,
   He would have written sonnets all his life?
   Lord Byron 1788–1824: *Don Juan* (1819–24)

29 Advice to persons about to marry.—'Don't.'
   Punch: 1845

30 My definition of marriage…it resembles a pair of shears, so joined that they cannot be separated; often moving in opposite directions, yet always punishing anyone who comes between them.
   Sydney Smith 1771–1845: in Lady Holland *Memoir* (1855)

31 It doesn't much signify whom one marries, for one is sure to find next morning that it was someone else.
   Samuel Rogers 1763–1855: in A. Dyce (ed.) *Table Talk of Samuel Rogers* (1860)

32 A woman dictates before marriage in order that she may have an appetite for submission afterwards.
   George Eliot 1819–80: *Middlemarch* (1871–2)

33 Marriage is like life in this—that it is a field of battle, and not a bed of roses.
   Robert Louis Stevenson 1850-94: *Virginibus Puerisque* (1881)

34 It was very good of God to let Carlyle and Mrs Carlyle marry one another and so make only two people miserable instead of four.
   Samuel Butler 1835-1902: letter to Miss E. M. A. Savage, 21 November 1884

35 In married life three is company and two none.
   Oscar Wilde 1854-1900: *The Importance of Being Earnest* (1895)

36 If it were not for the presents, an elopement would be preferable.
   George Ade 1866-1944: *Forty Modern Fables* (1901)

37 Marriage is popular because it combines the maximum of temptation with the maximum of opportunity.
   George Bernard Shaw 1856-1950: *Man and Superman* (1903)

38 Being a husband is a whole-time job. That is why so many husbands fail. They cannot give their entire attention to it.
   Arnold Bennett 1867-1931: *The Title* (1918)

39 Chumps always make the best husbands...All the unhappy marriages come from the husbands having brains.
   P. G. Wodehouse 1881-1975: *The Adventures of Sally* (1920)

40 Marriage isn't a word...it's a *sentence*!
   King Vidor 1895-1982: *The Crowd* (1928 film)

41 Marriage always demands the finest arts of insincerity possible between two human beings.
   Vicki Baum 1888-1960: *Zwischenfall in Lohwinckel* (1930), tr. M. Goldsmith as *Results of an Accident* (1931)

42 The deep, deep peace of the double-bed after the hurly-burly of the chaise-longue.
   Mrs Patrick Campbell 1865-1940: on her recent marriage, in A. Woollcott *While Rome Burns* (1934)

43 The critical period in matrimony is breakfast-time.
   A. P. Herbert 1890-1971: *Uncommon Law* (1935)

44 So they were married—to be the more together—
   And found they were never again so much together,
   Divided by the morning tea,

By the evening paper,
By children and tradesmen's bills.
    Louis MacNeice 1907–63: *Plant and Phantom* (1941)

45 Sidney would remark, 'I know just what Beatrice is saying at
this moment. She is saying, "as Sidney always says, marriage
is the waste-paper basket of the emotions."'
    Sidney Webb 1859–1947 and **Beatrice Webb** 1858–1943: in
Bertrand Russell *Autobiography* (1967)

46 It takes two to make a marriage a success and only one
a failure.
    Lord Samuel 1870–1963: *A Book of Quotations* (1947)

47 One doesn't have to get anywhere in a marriage. It's not a
public conveyance.
    Iris Murdoch 1919– : *A Severed Head* (1961)

48 Never marry a man who hates his mother, because he'll end
up hating you.
    Jill Bennett 1931–90: in *Observer* 12 September 1982
'Sayings of the Week'

....

Mathematics
....

1 Let no one enter who does not know geometry [mathematics].
    Anonymous: inscription on Plato's door, probably at the
Academy at Athens

2 There is no 'royal road' to geometry.
    Euclid fl. *c.*300 BC: addressed to Ptolemy I, in Proclus
Commentary on the First Book of Euclid's Elementa

3 Multiplication is vexation,
Division is as bad;
The Rule of Three doth puzzle me,
And Practice drives me mad.
    Anonymous: in *Lean's Collectanea* (1904), possibly
16th-century

4 I have often admired the mystical way of Pythagoras, and the
secret magic of numbers.
    Sir Thomas Browne 1605–82: *Religio Medici* (1643)

5 They are neither finite quantities, or quantities infinitely
small, nor yet nothing. May we not call them the ghosts of
departed quantities?
   Bishop George Berkeley 1685–1753: *The Analyst* (1734), on
   Newton's infinitesimals

6 The most devilish thing is 8 times 8 and 7 times 7 it is what
nature itselfe cant endure.
   Marjory Fleming 1803–11: *Journals, Letters and Verses*
   (1934)

7 What would life be like without arithmetic, but a scene of
horrors?
   Sydney Smith 1771–1845: letter to Miss [Lucie Austen],
   22 July 1835

8 God made the integers, all the rest is the work of man.
   Leopold Kronecker 1823–91: *Jahrsberichte der Deutschen
   Mathematiker Vereinigung* bk. 2

9 I never could make out what those damned dots meant.
   Lord Randolph Churchill 1849–94: on decimal points, in
   W. S. Churchill *Lord Randolph Churchill* (1906)

10 Mathematics, rightly viewed, possesses not only truth, but
supreme beauty—a beauty cold and austere, like that of
sculpture.
   Bertrand Russell 1872–1970: *Philosophical Essays* (1910)

11 Mathematics may be defined as the subject in which we
never know what we are talking about, nor whether what we
are saying is true.
   Bertrand Russell 1872–1970: *Mysticism and Logic* (1918)

12 Beauty is the first test: there is no permanent place in the
world for ugly mathematics.
   Godfrey Harold Hardy 1877–1947: *A Mathematician's
   Apology* (1940)

13 Equations are more important to me, because politics is for
the present, but an equation is something for eternity.
   Albert Einstein 1879–1955: in Stephen Hawking *A Brief
   History of Time* (1988)

14 Someone told me that each equation I included in the book
would halve the sales.
   Stephen Hawking 1942– : *A Brief History of Time* (1988)

Meaning

See also **Words**

1 I pray thee, understand a plain man in his plain meaning.
   William Shakespeare 1564–1616: *The Merchant of Venice*
   (1596–8)

2 God and I both knew what it meant once; now God alone
   knows.
   Friedrich Klopstock 1724–1803: in C. Lombroso *The Man of
   Genius* (1891); also attributed to Browning, apropos
   Sordello, in the form 'When it was written, God and Robert
   Browning knew what it meant; now only God knows'

3 'Then you should say what you mean,' the March Hare went
   on. 'I do,' Alice hastily replied; 'at least—at least I mean what
   I say—that's the same thing, you know.' 'Not the same thing
   a bit!' said the Hatter. 'Why, you might just as well say that
   "I see what I eat" is the same thing as "I eat what I see!" '
   Lewis Carroll 1832–98: *Alice's Adventures in Wonderland*
   (1865)

4 The meaning doesn't matter if it's only idle chatter of a
   transcendental kind.
   W. S. Gilbert 1836–1911: *Patience* (1881)

5 No one means all he says, and yet very few say all they
   mean, for words are slippery and thought is viscous.
   Henry Brooks Adams 1838–1918: *The Education of Henry
   Adams* (1907)

6 The little girl had the making of a poet in her who, being told
   to be sure of her meaning before she spoke, said, 'How can
   I know what I think till I see what I say?'
   Graham Wallas 1858–1932: *The Art of Thought* (1926)

7 It all depends what you mean by...
   C. E. M. Joad 1891–1953: replying to questions on 'The
   Brains Trust' (formerly 'Any Questions'), BBC radio
   (1941–8)

Medicine

See also **Sickness and Health**

1 Honour a physician with the honour due unto him for the
uses which ye may have of him.
   Bible (Apocrypha): Ecclesiasticus

2 He that sinneth before his Maker, let him fall into the hand
of the physician.
   Bible (Apocrypha): Ecclesiasticus

3 Life is short, the art long.
   Hippocrates c.460–357 BC: *Aphorisms*; often quoted '*Ars
   longa, vita brevis*', after Seneca *De Brevitate Vitae*

4 Physician, heal thyself.
   Bible: St Luke

5 Throw physic to the dogs; I'll none of it.
   William Shakespeare 1564–1616: *Macbeth* (1606)

6 Cure the disease and kill the patient.
   Francis Bacon 1561–1626: *Essays* (1625) 'Of Friendship'

7 The remedy is worse than the disease.
   Francis Bacon 1561–1626: *Essays* (1625) 'Of Seditions and
   Troubles'

8 We all labour against our own cure, for death is the cure of
all diseases.
   Sir Thomas Browne 1605–82: *Religio Medici* (1643)

9 GÉRONTE: It seems to me you are locating them wrongly: the
heart is on the left and the liver is on the right.
   SGANARELLE: Yes, in the old days that was so, but we have
   changed all that.
   Molière 1622–73: *Le Médecin malgré lui* (1667)

10 Sciatica: he cured it, by boiling his buttock.
   John Aubrey 1626–97: *Brief Lives* 'Sir Jonas Moore'

11 Ah, well, then, I suppose that I shall have to die beyond my
means.
   Oscar Wilde 1854–1900: at the mention of a huge fee for a
   surgical operation; in R. H. Sherard *Life of Oscar Wilde*
   (1906)

12 Physicians of the Utmost Fame
Were called at once; but when they came

They answered, as they took their Fees,
'There is no Cure for this Disease.'
   Hilaire Belloc 1870–1953: 'Henry King' (1907)

13 There is at bottom only one genuinely scientific treatment for
all diseases, and that is to stimulate the phagocytes.
   George Bernard Shaw 1856–1950: *The Doctor's Dilemma*
   (1911)

14 Every day, in every way, I am getting better and better.
   Émile Coué 1857–1926: to be said 15 to 20 times, morning
   and evening, in *De la suggestion et de ses applications* (1915)

15 One finger in the throat and one in the rectum makes a good
diagnostician.
   William Osler 1849–1919: *Aphorisms from his Bedside
   Teachings* (1961)

16 The wounded surgeon plies the steel
That questions the distempered part;
Beneath the bleeding hands we feel
The sharp compassion of the healer's art
Resolving the enigma of the fever chart.
   T. S. Eliot 1888–1965: *Four Quartets* 'East Coker' (1940)

17 I stuffed their mouths with gold.
   Aneurin Bevan 1897–1960: on his handling of the
   consultants during the establishment of the National
   Health Service, in B. Abel-Smith *The Hospitals 1800–1948*
   (1964)

18 We shall have to learn to refrain from doing things merely
because we know how to do them.
   Theodore Fox 1899–1989: speech to Royal College of
   Physicians, 18 October 1965

19 Formerly, when religion was strong and science weak, men
mistook magic for medicine; now, when science is strong and
religion weak, men mistake medicine for magic.
   Thomas Szasz 1920– : *The Second Sin* (1973) 'Science and
   Scientism'

20 Medicinal discovery,
It moves in mighty leaps,
It leapt straight past the common cold
And gave it us for keeps.
   Pam Ayres 1947– : 'Oh no, I got a cold' (1976)

Meeting and Parting

1 *Atque in perpetuum, frater, ave atque vale.*
And so, my brother, hail, and farewell evermore!
  Catullus *c.*84–*c.*54 BC: *Carmina*

2 Fare well my dear child and pray for me, and I shall for you
and all your friends that we may merrily meet in heaven.
  Sir Thomas More 1478–1535: letter to his daughter
  Margaret, 5 July 1535, on the eve of his execution

3 Good-night, good-night! parting is such sweet sorrow
That I shall say good-night till it be morrow.
  William Shakespeare 1564–1616: *Romeo and Juliet* (1595)

4 Ill met by moonlight, proud Titania.
  William Shakespeare 1564–1616: *A Midsummer Night's
  Dream* (1595–6)

5 When shall we three meet again
In thunder, lightning, or in rain?
  William Shakespeare 1564–1616: *Macbeth* (1606)

6 Farewell! thou art too dear for my possessing.
  William Shakespeare 1564–1616: sonnet 87 (1609)

7 Since there's no help, come let us kiss and part,
Nay, I have done: you get no more of me.
  Michael Drayton 1563–1631: sonnet (1619)

8 You have sat too long here for any good you have been doing.
Depart, I say, and let us have done with you. In the name of
God, go!
  Oliver Cromwell 1599–1658: addressing the Rump
  Parliament, 20 April 1653 (oral tradition; quoted by Leo
  Amery, House of Commons, 7 May 1940)

9 For I, who hold sage Homer's rule the best,
Welcome the coming, speed the going guest.
  Alexander Pope 1688–1744: *Imitations of Horace* (1734)
  ('speed the parting guest' in Pope's translation of *The
  Odyssey* (1725–6))

10 Their meetings made December June,
Their every parting was to die.
  Alfred, Lord Tennyson 1809–92: *In Memoriam A. H. H.*
  (1850)

11 In every parting there is an image of death.
    George Eliot 1819–80: *Scenes of Clerical Life* (1858)

12 Dr Livingstone, I presume?
    Henry Morton Stanley 1841–1904: *How I found Livingstone* (1872)

13 Parting is all we know of heaven,
And all we need of hell.
    Emily Dickinson 1830–86: 'My life closed twice before its close'

14 Yet meet we shall, and part, and meet again
Where dead men meet, on lips of living men.
    Samuel Butler 1835–1902: 'Not on sad Stygian shore' (1904)

15 If you can't leave in a taxi you can leave in a huff. If that's too soon, you can leave in a minute and a huff.
    Bert Kalmar 1884–1947 et al.: *Duck Soup* (1933 film); spoken by Groucho Marx

16 Why don't you come up sometime, and see me?
    Mae West 1892–1980: *She Done Him Wrong* (1933 film); usually quoted 'Why don't you come up and see me sometime?'

17 How long ago Hector took off his plume,
Not wanting that his little son should cry,
Then kissed his sad Andromache goodbye —
And now we three in Euston waiting-room.
    Frances Cornford 1886–1960: 'Parting in Wartime' (1948)

Memory

1 Old men forget: yet all shall be forgot,
But he'll remember with advantages
What feats he did that day.
    William Shakespeare 1564–1616: *Henry V* (1599)

2 There's rosemary, that's for remembrance; pray, love, remember.
    William Shakespeare 1564–1616: *Hamlet* (1601)

3 When to the sessions of sweet silent thought
I summon up remembrance of things past.
    William Shakespeare 1564–1616: sonnet 30 (1609)

4 You may break, you may shatter the vase, if you will,
  But the scent of the roses will hang round it still.
    Thomas Moore 1779–1852: 'Farewell!—but whenever' (1807)

5 For oft, when on my couch I lie
  In vacant or in pensive mood,
  They flash upon that inward eye
  Which is the bliss of solitude;
  And then my heart with pleasure fills,
  And dances with the daffodils.
    William Wordsworth 1770–1850: 'I wandered lonely as a
    cloud' (1815 ed.)

6 Music, when soft voices die,
  Vibrates in the memory—
  Odours, when sweet violets sicken,
  Live within the sense they quicken.
    Percy Bysshe Shelley 1792–1822: 'To—: Music, when soft
    voices die' (1824)

7 In looking on the happy autumn-fields,
  And thinking of the days that are no more.
    Alfred, Lord Tennyson 1809–92: *The Princess* (1847) song
    (added 1850)

8 And we forget because we must
  And not because we will.
    Matthew Arnold 1822–88: 'Absence' (1852)

9 Better by far you should forget and smile
  Than that you should remember and be sad.
    Christina Rossetti 1830–94: 'Remember' (1862)

10 And the best and the worst of this is
   That neither is most to blame,
   If you have forgotten my kisses
   And I have forgotten your name.
     Algernon Charles Swinburne 1837–1909: 'An Interlude'
     (1866)

11 I have forgot much, Cynara! gone with the wind,
   Flung roses, roses, riotously, with the throng,
   Dancing, to put thy pale, lost lilies out of mind.
     Ernest Dowson 1867–1900: 'Non Sum Qualis Eram' (1896)

12 Memories are hunting horns
   Whose sound dies on the wind.
     Guillaume Apollinaire 1880–1918: 'Cors de Chasse' (1912)

13 And suddenly the memory revealed itself. The taste was that
of the little piece of madeleine which...my aunt Léonie used
to give me, dipping it first in her own cup of tea or tisane.
   Marcel Proust 1871–1922: *Swann's Way* (1913)

14 Midnight shakes the memory
As a madman shakes a dead geranium.
   T. S. Eliot 1888–1965: 'Rhapsody on a Windy Night' (1917)

15 In plucking the fruit of memory one runs the risk of spoiling
its bloom.
   Joseph Conrad 1857–1924: *Arrow of Gold* (author's note,
   1920, to 1924 Uniform Edition)

16 Someone said that God gave us memory so that we might
have roses in December.
   J. M. Barrie 1860–1937: Rectorial Address at St Andrew's,
   3 May 1922

17 A cigarette that bears a lipstick's traces,
An airline ticket to romantic places.
   Holt Marvell 1901–69: 'These Foolish Things Remind Me
   of You' (1935 song)

18 Footfalls echo in the memory
Down the passage which we did not take
Towards the door we never opened
Into the rose-garden.
   T. S. Eliot 1888–1965: *Four Quartets* 'Burnt Norton' (1936)

19 Am in Market Harborough. Where ought I to be?
   G. K. Chesterton 1874–1936: telegram said to have been
   sent to his wife; *Autobiography* (1936)

20 Our memories are card-indexes consulted, and then put back
in disorder by authorities whom we do not control.
   Cyril Connolly 1903–74: *The Unquiet Grave* (1944)

21 Memories are not shackles, Franklin, they are garlands.
   Alan Bennett 1934– : *Forty Years On* (1969)

22 I never forget a face, but in your case I'll be glad to make an
exception.
   Groucho Marx 1895–1977: in Leo Rosten *People I have
   Loved, Known or Admired* (1970) 'Groucho'

Men

1 Sigh no more, ladies, sigh no more,
 Men were deceivers ever.
   William Shakespeare 1564–1616: *Much Ado About Nothing*
   (1598–9)

2 Men are but children of a larger growth;
 Our appetites as apt to change as theirs,
 And full as craving too, and full as vain.
   John Dryden 1631–1700: *All for Love* (1678)

3 Man is to be held only by the *slightest* chains, with the idea
 that he can break them at pleasure, he submits to them in
 sport.
   Maria Edgeworth 1768–1849: *Letters for Literary Ladies*
   (1795)

4 Men have had every advantage of us in telling their own
 story. Education has been theirs in so much higher a degree;
 the pen has been in their hands.
   Jane Austen 1775–1817: *Persuasion* (1818)

5 A man…is *so* in the way in the house!
   Elizabeth Gaskell 1810–65: *Cranford* (1853)

6 Man is Nature's sole mistake!
   W. S. Gilbert 1836–1911: *Princess Ida* (1884)

7 The three most important things a man has are, briefly, his
 private parts, his money, and his religious opinions.
   Samuel Butler 1835–1902: *Further Extracts from Notebooks*
   (1934)

8 The natural man has only two primal passions, to get and
 beget.
   William Osler 1849–1919: *Science and Immortality* (1904)

9 A husband is what is left of a lover, after the nerve has been
 extracted.
   Helen Rowland 1875–1950: *A Guide to Men* (1922)

10 Somehow a bachelor never quite gets over the idea that he is
 a thing of beauty and a boy forever.
   Helen Rowland 1875–1950: *A Guide to Men* (1922)

11 It's not the men in my life that counts—it's the life in my
 men.
   Mae West 1892–1980: *I'm No Angel* (1933 film)

12 Why can't a woman be more like a man?
Men are so honest, so thoroughly square;
Eternally noble, historically fair.
   Alan Jay Lerner 1918–86: 'A Hymn to Him' (1956 song)

13 Whatever they may be in public life, whatever their relations
with men, in their relations with women, all men are rapists,
and that's all they are. They rape us with their eyes, their
laws, and their codes.
   Marilyn French 1929– : *The Women's Room* (1977)

14 What makes men so tedious
Is the need to show off and compete.
They'll bore you to death for hours and hours
Before they'll admit defeat.
   Wendy Cope 1945– : 'Men and their boring arguments'
   (1988)

Men and Women

See also **Woman's Role**

1 Is there no way for men to be, but women
Must be half-workers?
   William Shakespeare 1564–1616: *Cymbeline* (1609–10)

2 So court a mistress, she denies you;
Let her alone, she will court you.
Say, are not women truly then
Styled but the shadows of us men?
   Ben Jonson *c*.1573–1637: 'That Women are but Men's
   Shadows' (1616)

3   Just such disparity
As is 'twixt air and angels' purity,
'Twixt women's love, and men's will ever be.
   John Donne 1572–1631: 'Air and Angels'

4 He for God only, she for God in him.
   John Milton 1608–74: *Paradise Lost* (1667)

5 Man's love is of man's life a thing apart,
'Tis woman's whole existence.
   Lord Byron 1788–1824: *Don Juan* (1819–24)

6 What is it men in women do require
  The lineaments of gratified desire
  What is it women do in men require
  The lineaments of gratified desire.
  William Blake 1757–1827: *MS Note-Book*

7 The man's desire is for the woman; but the woman's desire is
  rarely other than for the desire of the man.
  Samuel Taylor Coleridge 1772–1834: *Table Talk* (1835)
  23 July 1827

8 Man is the hunter; woman is his game.
  Alfred, Lord Tennyson 1809–92: *The Princess* (1847)

9 'Tis strange what a man may do, and a woman yet think him
  an angel.
  William Makepeace Thackeray 1811–63: *The History of
  Henry Esmond* (1852)

10 Man dreams of fame while woman wakes to love.
  Alfred, Lord Tennyson 1809–92: *Idylls of the King* 'Merlin
  and Vivien' (1859)

11 The silliest woman can manage a clever man; but it takes a
  very clever woman to manage a fool.
  Rudyard Kipling 1865–1936: *Plain Tales from the Hills*
  (1888)

12 All women become like their mothers. That is their tragedy.
  No man does. That's his.
  Oscar Wilde 1854–1900: *The Importance of Being Earnest*
  (1895)

13 Of all human struggles there is none so treacherous and
  remorseless as the struggle between the artist man and the
  mother woman.
  George Bernard Shaw 1856–1950: *Man and Superman*
  (1903)

14 Hogamus, higamous
  Man is polygamous
  Higamus, hogamous
  Woman monogamous.
  William James 1842–1910: in *Oxford Book of Marriage*
  (1990)

15 The female of the species is more deadly than the male.
  Rudyard Kipling 1865–1936: 'The Female of the Species'
  (1919)

16 A woman can forgive a man for the harm he does her, but she can never forgive him for the sacrifices he makes on her account.

 W. Somerset Maugham 1874–1965: *The Moon and Sixpence* (1919)

17 Women have served all these centuries as looking-glasses possessing the magic and delicious power of reflecting the figure of a man at twice its natural size.

 Virginia Woolf 1882–1941: *A Room of One's Own* (1929)

18 Me Tarzan, you Jane.

 Johnny Weissmuller 1904–84: summing up his role in *Tarzan, the Ape Man* (1932 film); in *Photoplay Magazine* June 1932. The words occur neither in the film nor the original, by Edgar Rice Burroughs

19 Any man has to, needs to, wants to
Once in a lifetime, do a girl in.

 T. S. Eliot 1888–1965: *Sweeney Agonistes* (1932)

20 I admit it is better fun to punt than to be punted, and that a desire to have all the fun is nine-tenths of the law of chivalry.

 Dorothy L. Sayers 1893–1957: *Gaudy Night* (1935)

21 In the sex-war thoughtlessness is the weapon of the male, vindictiveness of the female.

 Cyril Connolly 1903–74: *Unquiet Grave* (1944)

22 Men have a much better time of it than women. For one thing, they marry later. For another thing, they die earlier.

 H. L. Mencken 1880–1956: *Chrestomathy* (1949)

23 There is more difference within the sexes than between them.

 Ivy Compton-Burnett 1884–1969: *Mother and Son* (1955)

24 Women are really much nicer than men:
No wonder we like them.

 Kingsley Amis 1922– : 'A Bookshop Idyll' (1956)

25 Women want mediocre men, and men are working hard to be as mediocre as possible.

 Margaret Mead 1901–78: in *Quote Magazine* 15 June 1958

26 Whatever women do they must do twice as well as men to be thought half as good.

 Charlotte Whitton 1896–1975: in *Canada Month* June 1963

27 Women have very little idea of how much men hate them.

 Germaine Greer 1939– : *The Female Eunuch* (1971)

28 Whereas nature turns girls into women, society has to make boys into men.
   Anthony Stevens: *Archetype* (1982)

29 More and more it appears that, biologically, men are designed for short, brutal lives and women for long miserable ones.
   Estelle Ramey: *Observer* 7 April 1985 'Sayings of the Week'

30 A woman without a man is like a fish without a bicycle.
   Gloria Steinem 1934- : attributed

Middle Age

1 I am past thirty, and three parts iced over.
   Matthew Arnold 1822-88: letter to Arthur Hugh Clough, 12 February 1853

2 Mr Salteena was an elderly man of 42.
   Daisy Ashford 1881-1972: *The Young Visiters* (1919)

3 At eighteen our convictions are hills from which we look; at forty-five they are caves in which we hide.
   F. Scott Fitzgerald 1896-1940: 'Bernice Bobs her Hair' (1920)

4 One of the pleasures of middle age is to *find out* that one WAS right, and that one was much righter than one knew at say 17 or 23.
   Ezra Pound 1885-1972: *ABC of Reading* (1934)

5 Do you think my mind is maturing late,
   Or simply rotted early?
   Ogden Nash 1902-71: 'Lines on Facing Forty' (1942)

6 Years ago we discovered the exact point, the dead centre of middle age. It occurs when you are too young to take up golf and too old to rush up to the net.
   Franklin P. Adams 1881-1960: *Nods and Becks* (1944)

7 At forty-five,
   What next, what next?
   At every corner,
   I meet my Father,
   my age, still alive.
   Robert Lowell 1917-77: 'Middle Age' (1964)

The Mind

1 The mind is its own place, and in itself
Can make a heaven of hell, a hell of heaven.
    John Milton 1608–74: *Paradise Lost* (1667)

2 To give a sex to mind was not very consistent with the
principles of a man [Rousseau] who argued so warmly, and
so well, for the immortality of the soul.
    Mary Wollstonecraft 1759–97: *A Vindication of the Rights
of Woman* (1792), often quoted 'Mind has no sex'

3 What is Matter?—Never mind.
What is Mind?—No matter.
    Punch: 1855

4 On earth there is nothing great but man; in man there is
nothing great but mind.
    William Hamilton 1788–1856: *Lectures on Metaphysics and
Logic* (1859), attributed in a Latin form to Favorinus (2nd
century AD)

5 O the mind, mind has mountains; cliffs of fall
Frightful, sheer, no-man-fathomed.
    Gerard Manley Hopkins 1844–89: 'No worst, there is none'
(written 1885)

6 Personal relations are the important thing for ever and ever,
and not this outer life of telegrams and anger.
    E. M. Forster 1879–1970: *Howards End* (1910)

7 Minds like beds always made up,
(more stony than a shore)
unwilling or unable.
    William Carlos Williams 1883–1963: *Paterson* (1946)

8 Mind in its purest play is like some bat
That beats about in caverns all alone,
Contriving by a kind of senseless wit
Not to conclude against a wall of stone.
    Richard Wilbur 1921– : 'Mind' (1956)

9 That's the classical mind at work, runs fine inside but looks
dingy on the surface.
    Robert M. Pirsig 1928– : *Zen and the Art of Motorcycle
Maintenance* (1974)

10 Consciousness...is the phenomenon whereby the universe's
very existence is made known.
   Roger Penrose 1931– : *The Emperor's New Mind* (1989)

Minorities and Majorities

See also **Democracy**

1 *Nec audiendi qui solent dicere, Vox populi, vox Dei, quum
tumultuositas vulgi semper insaniae proxima sit.*
And those people should not be listened to who keep saying
the voice of the people is the voice of God, since the
riotousness of the crowd is always very close to madness.
   Alcuin *c.*735–804: *Works* (1863) letter 164

2 Nor is the people's judgement always true:
The most may err as grossly as the few.
   John Dryden 1631–1700: *Absalom and Achitophel* (1681)

3 'It's always best on these occasions to do what the mob do.'
'But suppose there are two mobs?' suggested Mr Snodgrass.
'Shout with the largest,' replied Mr Pickwick.
   Charles Dickens 1812–70: *Pickwick Papers* (1837)

4 Minorities...are almost always in the right.
   Sydney Smith 1771–1845: in H. Pearson *The Smith of Smiths*
   (1934)

5 The majority never has right on its side. Never I say! That is
one of the social lies that a free, thinking man is bound to
rebel against. Who makes up the majority in any given
country? Is it the wise men or the fools? I think we must
agree that the fools are in a terrible overwhelming majority,
all the wide world over.
   Henrik Ibsen 1828–1906: *The Master Builder* (1892)

6 The fact that an opinion has been widely held is no evidence
whatever that it is not utterly absurd; indeed in view of the
silliness of the majority of mankind, a widespread belief is
more likely to be foolish than sensible.
   Bertrand Russell 1872–1970: *Marriage and Morals* (1929)

7 Never forget that only dead fish swim with the stream.
   Malcolm Muggeridge 1903–90: quoting a supporter, in
   Radio Times 9 July 1964

Misfortune

1 Man is born unto trouble, as the sparks fly upward.
   Bible: Job

2 For in every ill-turn of fortune the most unhappy sort of
   unfortunate man is the one who has been happy.
   Boethius AD c.476–524: *De Consolatione Philosophiae*

3 ...*Nessun maggior dolore,*
   Che ricordarsi del tempo felice
   Nella miseria.
   There is no greater pain than to remember a happy time
   when one is in misery.
   Dante Alighieri 1265–1321: *Divina Commedia* 'Inferno'

4 Sweet are the uses of adversity,
   Which like the toad, ugly and venomous,
   Wears yet a precious jewel in his head.
   William Shakespeare 1564–1616: *As You Like It* (1599)

5 Misery acquaints a man with strange bedfellows.
   William Shakespeare 1564–1616: *The Tempest* (1611)

6 Prosperity doth best discover vice, but adversity doth best
   discover virtue.
   Francis Bacon 1561–1626: *Essays* (1625) 'Of Adversity'

7 In the misfortune of our best friends, we always find
   something which is not displeasing to us.
   Duc de la Rochefoucauld 1613–80: *Réflexions ou Maximes
   Morales* (1665)

8 When I consider how my light is spent,
   E're half my days, in this dark world and wide,
   And that one talent which is death to hide
   Lodged with me useless.
   John Milton 1608–74: 'When I consider how my light is
   spent' (1673)

9 We are all strong enough to bear the misfortunes of others.
   Duc de la Rochefoucauld 1613–80: *Maximes* (1678)

10 I had never had a piece of toast
   Particularly long and wide,
   But fell upon the sanded floor,
   And always on the buttered side.
   James Payn 1830–98: *Chambers's Journal* 2 February 1884

11 I left the room with silent dignity, but caught my foot in the mat.
> **George Grossmith** 1847–1912 and **Weedon Grossmith** 1854–1919: *Diary of a Nobody* (1894)

12 And always keep a-hold of Nurse
For fear of finding something worse.
> **Hilaire Belloc** 1870–1953: 'Jim' (1907)

13 now and then
there is a person born
who is so unlucky
that he runs into accidents
which started to happen
to somebody else.
> **Don Marquis** 1878–1937: *archys life of mehitabel* (1933)

14 boss there is always
a comforting thought
in time of trouble when
it is not our trouble.
> **Don Marquis** 1878–1937: *archy does his part* (1935)

15 And all my endeavours are unlucky explorers
come back, abandoning the expedition.
> **Keith Douglas** 1920–44: 'On Return from Egypt, 1943–4' (1946)

16　　　　　　　　People will take balls,
Balls will be lost always, little boy,
And no one buys a ball back.
> **John Berryman** 1914–72: 'The Ball Poem' (1948)

17 In the words of one of my more sympathetic correspondents, it has turned out to be an 'annus horribilis'.
> **Elizabeth II** 1926– : speech at Guildhall, London, 24 November 1992

Mistakes

1 I would rather be wrong, by God, with Plato...than be correct with those men.
> **Cicero** 106–43 BC: *Tusculanae Disputationes* (of Pythagoreans)

2 I'm aggrieved when sometimes even excellent Homer nods.
   Horace 65–8 BC: *Ars Poetica*

3 I beseech you, in the bowels of Christ, think it possible you
   may be mistaken.
   Oliver Cromwell 1599–1658: letter to the General Assembly
   of the Kirk of Scotland, 3 August 1650

4 Errors, like straws, upon the surface flow;
   He who would search for pearls must dive below.
   John Dryden 1631–1700: *All for Love* (1678)

5 Crooked things may be as stiff and unflexible as straight: and
   men may be as positive in error as in truth.
   John Locke 1632–1704: *Essay concerning Human
   Understanding* (1690)

6 To err is human; to forgive, divine.
   Alexander Pope 1688–1744: *An Essay on Criticism* (1711)

7 Truth lies within a little and certain compass, but error is
   immense.
   Henry St John, 1st Viscount Bolingbroke1678–1751:
   Reflections upon Exile (1716)

8 A man should never be ashamed to own he has been in the
   wrong, which is but saying, in other words, that he is wiser
   to-day than he was yesterday.
   Alexander Pope 1688–1744: *Miscellanies* (1727) 'Thoughts on
   Various Subjects'

9 It is worse than a crime, it is a blunder.
   Antoine Boulay de la Meurthe 1761–1840: on hearing of
   the execution of the Duc d'Enghien, 1804

10 Error has never approached my spirit.
   Prince Metternich 1773–1859: addressed to Guizot in 1848,
   in F. Guizot *Mémoires* (1858–67)

11 'Forward, the Light Brigade!'
   Was there a man dismayed?
   Not though the soldier knew
   Some one had blundered.
   Alfred, Lord Tennyson 1809–92: 'The Charge of the Light
   Brigade' (1854)

12 The man who makes no mistakes does not usually make
   anything.
   Edward John Phelps 1822–1900: speech, 24 January 1889

13 To lose one parent, Mr Worthing, may be regarded as a misfortune; to lose both looks like carelessness.
   Oscar Wilde 1854–1900: *The Importance of Being Earnest* (1895)

14 Well, if I called the wrong number, why did you answer the phone?
   James Thurber 1894–1961: cartoon caption in *New Yorker* 5 June 1937

15 The weak have one weapon: the errors of those who think they are strong.
   Georges Bidault 1899–1983: in *Observer* 15 July 1962 'Sayings of the Week'

16 Like most of those who study history, he [Napoleon III] learned from the mistakes of the past how to make new ones.
   A. J. P. Taylor 1906–90: *Listener* 6 June 1963

17 An expert is someone who knows some of the worst mistakes that can be made in his subject and who manages to avoid them.
   Werner Heisenberg 1901–76: *Der Teil und das Ganze* (1969) tr. A. J. Pomerans as *Physics and Beyond* (1971)

Moderation

1 Nothing in excess.
   Anonymous: inscribed on the temple of Apollo at Delphi, and variously ascribed to the Seven Wise Men

2 There is moderation in everything.
   Horace 65–8 BC: *Satires*

3 You will go most safely by the middle way.
   Ovid 43 BC–AD c.17: *Metamorphoses*

4 Because thou art lukewarm, and neither cold nor hot, I will spew thee out of my mouth.
   Bible: Revelation

5 To many, total abstinence is easier than perfect moderation.
   St Augustine of Hippo AD 354–430: *On the Good of Marriage* (AD 401)

6 To gild refinèd gold, to paint the lily,
   To throw a perfume on the violet,

To smooth the ice, or add another hue
Unto the rainbow, or with taper light
To seek the beauteous eye of heaven to garnish,
Is wasteful and ridiculous excess.
    William Shakespeare 1564–1616: *King John* (1591–8)

7 They are as sick that surfeit with too much, as they that
starve with nothing.
    William Shakespeare 1564–1616: *The Merchant of Venice*
    (1596–8)

8 By God, Mr Chairman, at this moment I stand astonished at
my own moderation!
    Lord Clive 1725–74: during Parliamentary
    cross-examination, 1773 in G. R. Gleig *Life of Robert, First
    Lord Clive* (1848)

9 Abstinence is as easy to me, as temperance would be difficult.
    Samuel Johnson 1709–84: in W. Roberts (ed.) *Memoirs
    of…Mrs Hannah More* (1834)

10 We know what happens to people who stay in the middle of
the road. They get run down.
    Aneurin Bevan 1897–1960: in *Observer* 6 December 1953

11 I would remind you that extremism in the defence of liberty
is no vice! And let me remind you also that moderation in
the pursuit of justice is no virtue!
    Barry Goldwater 1909– : accepting the presidential
    nomination, 16 July 1964

Money

See also **Poverty, Wealth**

1 Wine maketh merry: but money answereth all things.
    Bible: Ecclesiastes

2 The sinews of war, unlimited money.
    Cicero 106–43 BC: *Fifth Philippic*

3   *Quid non mortalia pectora cogis,
Auri sacra fames!*
To what do you not drive human hearts, cursed craving for
gold!
    Virgil 70–19 BC: *Aeneid*

4 The love of money is the root of all evil.
Bible: I Timothy

5 If possible honestly, if not, somehow, make money.
Horace 65–8 BC: *Epistles*

6 I can get no remedy against this consumption of the purse:
borrowing only lingers and lingers it out, but the disease is
incurable.
William Shakespeare 1564–1616: *Henry IV, Part 2* (1597)

7 Money is like muck, not good except it be spread.
Francis Bacon 1561–1626: *Essays* (1625) 'Of Seditions and
Troubles'

8 But it is pretty to see what money will do.
Samuel Pepys 1633–1703: diary, 21 March 1667

9 Money speaks sense in a language all nations understand.
Aphra Behn 1640–89: *The Rover* pt. 2 (1681)

10 Money is the sinews of love, as of war.
George Farquhar 1678–1707: *Love and a Bottle* (1698)

11 Nothing to be done without a bribe I find, in love as well as
law.
Susannah Centlivre *c.*1669–1723: *The Perjured Husband*
(1700)

12 Take care of the pence, and the pounds will take care of
themselves.
William Lowndes 1652–1724: in Lord Chesterfield *Letters to
his Son* (1774) 5 February 1750

13 Money…is none of the wheels of trade: it is the oil which
renders the motion of the wheels more smooth and easy.
David Hume 1711–76: *Essays: Moral and Political* (1741–2)
'Of Money'

14 An annuity is a very serious business.
Jane Austen 1775–1817: *Sense and Sensibility* (1811)

15 £40,000 a year a moderate income—such a one as a man *might
jog on with*.
John George Lambton 1792–1840: letter, 13 September 1821

16 The almighty dollar is the only object of worship.
Anonymous: *Philadelphia Public Ledger* 2 December 1836

17 Annual income twenty pounds, annual expenditure nineteen
nineteen six, result happiness. Annual income twenty

pounds, annual expenditure twenty pounds ought and six,
result misery.
    Charles Dickens 1812–70: *David Copperfield* (1850) Mr
Micawber

18 Money is like a sixth sense without which you cannot make
a complete use of the other five.
    W. Somerset Maugham 1874–1965: *Of Human Bondage*
(1915)

19 Lenin was right. There is no subtler, no surer means of
overturning the existing basis of society than to debauch the
currency.
    John Maynard Keynes 1883–1946: *Economic Consequences of
the Peace* (1919)

20 'My boy,' he says, 'always try to rub up against money, for if
you rub up against money long enough, some of it may rub
off on you.'
    Damon Runyon 1884–1946: *Cosmopolitan* August 1929

21 We could have saved sixpence. We have saved fivepence.
(*Pause*) But at what cost?
    Samuel Beckett 1906–89: *All That Fall* (1957)

22 A bank is a place that will lend you money if you can prove
that you don't need it.
    Bob Hope 1903– : in A. Harrington *Life in the Crystal
Palace* (1959)

23 Expenditure rises to meet income.
    C. Northcote Parkinson 1909–93: *The Law and the Profits*
(1960)

24 Money, it turned out, was exactly like sex, you thought of
nothing else if you didn't have it and thought of other things
if you did.
    James Baldwin 1924–87: *Esquire* May 1961

25 I want to spend, and spend, and spend.
    Vivian Nicholson 1936– : said to reporters on arriving to
collect football pools winnings of £152,000, 27 September 1961

26 Money couldn't buy friends but you got a better class of
enemy.
    Spike Milligan 1918– : *Puckoon* (1963)

27 For I don't care too much for money,
For money can't buy me love.
> **John Lennon** 1940–80 and **Paul McCartney** 1942– : 'Can't Buy Me Love' (1964 song)

28 Money doesn't talk, it swears.
> **Bob Dylan** 1941– : 'It's Alright, Ma (I'm Only Bleeding)' (1965 song)

29 From now the pound abroad is worth 14 per cent or so less in terms of other currencies. It does not mean, of course, that the pound here in Britain, in your pocket or purse or in your bank, has been devalued.
> **Harold Wilson** 1916– : ministerial broadcast, 19 November 1967

Morality

1 *Cum finis est licitus, etiam media sunt licita.*
The end justifies the means.
> **Hermann Busenbaum** 1600–68: *Medulla Theologiae Moralis* (1650); literally 'When the end is allowed, the means also are allowed'

2 Two things fill the mind with ever new and increasing wonder and awe, the more often and the more seriously reflection concentrates upon them: the starry heaven above me and the moral law within me.
> **Immanuel Kant** 1724–1804: *Critique of Practical Reason* (1788)

3 We do not look in great cities for our best morality.
> **Jane Austen** 1775–1817: *Mansfield Park* (1814)

4 We know no spectacle so ridiculous as the British public in one of its periodical fits of morality.
> **Lord Macaulay** 1800–59: *Essays* (1843) 'Moore's *Life of Lord Byron*'

5 A clever theft was praiseworthy amongst the Spartans; and it is equally so amongst Christians, provided it be on a sufficiently large scale.
> **Herbert Spencer** 1820–1903: *Social Statics* (1850)

6 Morality is the herd-instinct in the individual.
  Friedrich Nietzsche 1844–1900: *Die fröhliche Wissenschaft*
  (1882)

7 Morality is a private and costly luxury.
  Henry Brooks Adams 1838–1918: *The Education of Henry
  Adams* (1907)

8 Moral indignation is jealousy with a halo.
  H. G. Wells 1866–1946: *The Wife of Sir Isaac Harman* (1914)

9 The most useful thing about a principle is that it can always
  be sacrificed to expediency.
  W. Somerset Maugham 1874–1965: *The Circle* (1921)

10 Food comes first, then morals.
  Bertolt Brecht 1898–1956: *The Threepenny Opera* (1928)

11 The last temptation is the greatest treason:
  To do the right deed for the wrong reason.
  T. S. Eliot 1888–1965: *Murder in the Cathedral* (1935)

12 What is morality in any given time or place? It is what the
  majority then and there happen to like, and immorality is
  what they dislike.
  Alfred North Whitehead 1861–1947: *Dialogues* (1954)
  30 August 1941

13 If people want a sense of purpose, they should get it from
  their archbishops. They should not hope to receive it from
  their politicians.
  Harold Macmillan 1894–1986: to Henry Fairlie, 1963; in H.
  Fairlie *The Life of Politics* (1968)

14 Standards are always out of date. That is what makes them
  standards.
  Alan Bennett 1934– : *Forty Years On* (1969)

....

Murder

....

1 Thou shalt not kill.
  Bible: Exodus

2 Mordre wol out; that se we day by day.
  Geoffrey Chaucer *c.*1343–1400: *The Canterbury Tales* 'The
  Nun's Priest's Tale'

3 Murder most foul, as in the best it is;
But this most foul, strange, and unnatural.
William Shakespeare 1564–1616: *Hamlet* (1601)

4 Here's the smell of the blood still: all the perfumes of Arabia
will not sweeten this little hand.
William Shakespeare 1564–1616: *Macbeth* (1606)

5 Killing no murder briefly discourse in three questions.
Edward Sexby d. 1658: title of pamphlet (an apology for
tyrannicide, 1657)

6 Murder considered as one of the fine arts.
Thomas De Quincey 1785–1859: *Blackwood's Magazine*
February 1827 (essay title)

7 Thou shalt not kill; but need'st not strive
Officiously to keep alive.
Arthur Hugh Clough 1819–61: 'The Latest Decalogue'
(1862)

8 Kill a man, and you are an assassin. Kill millions of men,
and you are a conqueror. Kill everyone, and you are a god.
Jean Rostand 1894–1977: *Pensées d'un biologiste* (1939)

Music

See also **Singing**

1   How sour sweet music is,
When time is broke, and no proportion kept!
William Shakespeare 1564–1616: *Richard II* (1595)

2 The man that hath no music in himself,
Nor is not moved with concord of sweet sounds,
Is fit for treasons, stratagems, and spoils.
William Shakespeare 1564–1616: *The Merchant of Venice*
(1596–8)

3 If music be the food of love, play on;
Give me excess of it, that, surfeiting,
The appetite may sicken, and so die.
William Shakespeare 1564–1616: *Twelfth Night* (1601)

4   Their lean and flashy songs
Grate on their scrannel pipes of wretched straw.
John Milton 1608–74: 'Lycidas' (1638)

5 Such sweet compulsion doth in music lie.
   John Milton 1608–74: 'Arcades' (1645)

6 Music has charms to soothe a savage breast.
   William Congreve 1670–1729: *The Mourning Bride* (1697)

7 Difficult do you call it, Sir? I wish it were impossible.
   Samuel Johnson 1709–84: on the performance of a
   celebrated violinist, in W. Seward *Supplement to the
   Anecdotes of Distinguished Persons* (1797)

8 Of music Dr Johnson used to say that it was the only sensual
   pleasure without vice.
   Samuel Johnson 1709–84: in *European Magazine* (1795)

9 Perhaps the self-same song that found a path
   Through the sad heart of Ruth, when, sick for home,
   She stood in tears amid the alien corn;
   The same that oft-times hath
   Charmed magic casements, opening on the foam
   Of perilous seas, in faery lands forlorn.
   John Keats 1795–1821: 'Ode to a Nightingale' (1820)

10 He [Hill] did not see any reason why the devil should have all
   the good tunes.
   Rowland Hill 1744–1833: E. W. Broome *Rowland Hill*
   (1881)

11 Hark, the dominant's persistence till it must be answered to!
   Robert Browning 1812–89: 'A Toccata of Galuppi's' (1855)

12 Please do not shoot the pianist. He is doing his best.
   Anonymous: printed notice in a dancing saloon, in Oscar
   Wilde *Impressions of America* (c.1882–3)

13 Hell is full of musical amateurs: music is the brandy of the
   damned.
   George Bernard Shaw 1856–1950: *Man and Superman*
   (1903)

14 There is music in the air.
   Edward Elgar 1857–1934: in R. J. Buckley *Sir Edward
   Elgar* (1905)

15 It will be generally admitted that Beethoven's Fifth
   Symphony is the most sublime noise that has ever penetrated
   into the ear of man.
   E. M. Forster 1879–1970: *Howards End* (1910)

16 Fortissimo at last!
   Gustav Mahler 1860–1911: on seeing Niagara Falls; in
   K. Blaukopf *Gustav Mahler* (1973)

17 Music is feeling, then, not sound.
   Wallace Stevens 1879–1955: 'Peter Quince at the Clavier'
   (1923)

18 Music begins to atrophy when it departs too far from the
   dance…poetry begins to atrophy when it gets too far from
   music.
   Ezra Pound 1885–1972: *The ABC of Reading* (1934)

19 Down the road someone is practising scales,
   The notes like little fishes vanish with a wink of tails.
   Louis MacNeice 1907–63: 'Sunday Morning' (1935)

20 The whole problem can be stated quite simply by asking, 'Is
   there a meaning to music?' My answer to that would be,
   'Yes.' And 'Can you state in so many words what the
   meaning is?' My answer to that would be, 'No.'
   Aaron Copland 1900–90: *What to Listen for in Music* (1939)

21 Good music is that which penetrates the ear with facility and
   quits the memory with difficulty.
   Thomas Beecham 1879–1961: speech, *c*.1950, in *New York
   Times* 9 March 1961

22 Applause is a receipt, not a note of demand.
   Artur Schnabel 1882–1951: in *Saturday Review of
   Literature* 29 September 1951

23 Too easy for children, and too difficult for artists.
   Artur Schnabel 1882–1951: of Mozart's sonatas, in Nat
   Shapiro (ed.) *Encyclopedia of Quotations about Music*
   (1978). In *My Life and Music* (1961), Schnabel says:
   'Children are given Mozart because of the small *quantity* of
   the notes; grown-ups avoid Mozart because of the great
   quality of the notes'

24 Music is your own experience, your thoughts, your wisdom.
   If you don't live it, it won't come out of your horn.
   Charlie Parker 1920–55: in Nat Shapiro and Nat Hentoff
   Hear Me Talkin' to Ya (1955)

25 The English may not like music, but they absolutely love the
   noise it makes.
   Thomas Beecham 1879–1961: In *New York Herald Tribune*
   9 March 1961

26 There are two golden rules for an orchestra: start together
and finish together. The public doesn't give a damn what
goes on in between.
    Thomas Beecham 1879-1961: in H. Atkins and A. Newman
    Beecham Stories (1978)

27 Two skeletons copulating on a corrugated tin roof.
    Thomas Beecham 1879-1961: describing the harpsichord, in
    H. Atkins and A. Newman *Beecham Stories* (1978)

28 A good composer does not imitate; he steals.
    Igor Stravinsky 1882-1971: in P. Yates *Twentieth Century*
    Music (1967)

29 If you still have to ask...shame on you.
    Louis Armstrong 1901-71: when asked what jazz is, in Max
    Jones et al. *Salute to Satchmo* (1970); sometimes quoted
    'Man, if you gotta ask you'll never know'

30 All music is folk music, I ain't never heard no horse sing a
song.
    Louis Armstrong 1901-71: in *New York Times* 7 July 1971

31 Music is, by its very nature, essentially powerless to *express*
anything at all...music expresses itself.
    Igor Stravinsky 1882-1971: in *Esquire* December 1972

32 Improvisation is too good to leave to chance.
    Paul Simon 1942- : in *Observer* 30 December 1990 'Sayings
    of the Year'

Musicians

1 Wagner has lovely moments but awful quarters of an hour.
    Gioacchino Rossini 1792-1868: in E. Naumann *Italienische*
    Tondichter (1883), April 1867

2 I have been told that Wagner's music is better than it sounds.
    Bill Nye 1850-96: in Mark Twain *Autobiography* (1924)

3 The notes I handle no better than many pianists. But the
pauses between the notes—ah, that is where the art resides!
    Artur Schnabel 1882-1951: in *Chicago Daily News* 11 June
    1958

4 I don't know whether I like it, but it's what I meant.
    Ralph Vaughan Williams 1872-1958: on his 4th symphony,

in C. Headington *Bodley Head History of Western Music* (1974)

5 At a rehearsal I let the orchestra play as they like. At the concert I make them play as *I* like.
   Thomas Beecham 1879–1961: in Neville Cardus *Sir Thomas Beecham* (1961)

6 Too much counterpoint; what is worse, Protestant counterpoint.
   Thomas Beecham 1879–1961: of J. S. Bach; in *Guardian* 8 March 1971

7 A kind of musical Malcolm Sargent.
   Thomas Beecham 1879–1961: of Herbert von Karajan, in H. Atkins and A. Newman *Beecham Stories* (1978)

8 My music is best understood by children and animals.
   Igor Stravinsky 1882–1971: in *Observer* 8 October 1961

9 Whether the angels play only Bach in praising God I am not quite sure; I am sure, however, that en famille they play Mozart.
   Karl Barth 1886–1968: in *New York Times* 11 December 1968

10 Ballads and babies. That's what happened to me.
   Paul McCartney 1942– : on reaching the age of fifty; in *Time* 8 June 1992

Nature

1 Nature does nothing without purpose or uselessly.
   Aristotle 384–322 BC: *Politics*

2 You may drive out nature with a pitchfork, yet she'll be constantly running back.
   Horace 65–8 BC: *Epistles*

3 In her [Nature's] inventions nothing is lacking, and nothing is superfluous.
   Leonardo da Vinci 1452–1519: E. McCurdy (ed. and trans.) *Leonardo da Vinci's Notebooks* (1906)

4 And this our life, exempt from public haunt,
Finds tongues in trees, books in the running brooks,
Sermons in stones, and good in everything.
   William Shakespeare 1564-1616: *As You Like It* (1599)

5 All things are artificial, for nature is the art of God.
   Sir Thomas Browne 1605-82: *Religio Medici* (1643)

6 There was a time when meadow, grove, and stream,
The earth, and every common sight,
To me did seem
Apparelled in celestial light,
The glory and the freshness of a dream.
   William Wordsworth 1770-1850: 'Ode. Intimations of
   Immortality' (1807)

7 To me the meanest flower that blows can give
Thoughts that do often lie too deep for tears.
   William Wordsworth 1770-1850: 'Ode. Intimations of
   Immortality' (1807)

8 There is a pleasure in the pathless woods,
There is a rapture on the lonely shore,
There is society, where none intrudes,
By the deep sea, and music in its roar:
I love not man the less, but nature more.
   Lord Byron 1788-1824: *Childe Harold's Pilgrimage* (1812-18)

9 The roaring of the wind is my wife and the stars through the
window pane are my children.
   John Keats 1795-1821: letter to George and Georgiana
   Keats, 24 October 1818

10 Nature, red in tooth and claw.
   Alfred, Lord Tennyson 1809-92: *In Memoriam A. H. H.*
   (1850)

11 So careful of the type she seems,
So careless of the single life.
   Alfred, Lord Tennyson 1809-92: *In Memoriam A. H. H.*
   (1850), of Nature

12 What a book a devil's chaplain might write on the clumsy,
wasteful, blundering, low, and horridly cruel works of
nature!
   Charles Darwin 1809-82: letter to J. D. Hooker, 13 July
   1856

13 Nature is not a temple, but a workshop, and man's the
workman in it.
Ivan Turgenev 1818–83: *Fathers and Sons* (1862), tr. R.
Edmonds

14 'I play for Seasons; not Eternities!'
Says Nature.
George Meredith 1828–1909: *Modern Love* (1862)

15 In nature there are neither rewards nor punishments—there
are consequences.
Robert G. Ingersoll 1833–99: *Some Reasons Why* (1881)

16 Pile the bodies high at Austerlitz and Waterloo.
Shovel them under and let me work—
I am the grass; I cover all.
Carl Sandburg 1878–1967: 'Grass' (1918)

17 For nature, heartless, witless nature,
Will neither care nor know
What stranger's feet may find the meadow
And trespass there and go.
A. E. Housman 1859–1936: *Last Poems* (1922) no. 40

News and Journalism

1 Tell it not in Gath, publish it not in the streets of Askelon.
Bible: II Samuel

2 As cold waters to a thirsty soul, so is good news from a far
country.
Bible: Proverbs

3 How beautiful upon the mountains are the feet of him that
bringeth good tidings, that publisheth peace.
Bible: Isaiah

4 Ill news hath wings, and with the wind doth go,
Comfort's a cripple and comes ever slow.
Michael Drayton 1563–1631: *The Barons' Wars* (1603)

5 The nature of bad news infects the teller.
William Shakespeare 1564–1616: *Antony and Cleopatra*
(1606–7)

6 The journalists have constructed for themselves a little
wooden chapel, which they also call the Temple of Fame, in

which they put up and take down portraits all day long and make such a hammering you can't hear yourself speak.
Georg Christoph Lichtenberg 1742–99: in A. Leitzmann *Georg Christoph Lichtenberg Aphorismen* (1904)

7 *The Times* has made many ministries.
Walter Bagehot 1826–77: *The English Constitution* (1867)

8 All the news that's fit to print.
Adolph S. Ochs 1858–1935: motto of the *New York Times*, from 1896

9 The report of my death was an exaggeration.
Mark Twain 1835–1910: *New York Journal* 2 June 1897, usually quoted 'Reports of my death have been greatly exaggerated'

10 By office boys for office boys.
Lord Salisbury 1830–1903: of the *Daily Mail*, in H. Hamilton Fyfe *Northcliffe* (1930)

11 The men with the muck-rakes are often indispensable to the well-being of society; but only if they know when to stop raking the muck.
Theodore Roosevelt 1858–1919: speech, 14 April 1906

12 Editor: a person employed by a newspaper, whose business it is to separate the wheat from the chaff, and to see that the chaff is printed.
Elbert Hubbard 1859–1915: *The Roycroft Dictionary* (1914)

13 Journalists say a thing that they know isn't true, in the hope that if they keep on saying it long enough it *will* be true.
Arnold Bennett 1867–1931: *The Title* (1918)

14 When a dog bites a man, that is not news, because it happens so often. But if a man bites a dog, that is news.
John B. Bogart 1848–1921: in F. M. O'Brien *Story of the* [New York] *Sun* (1918), often attributed to Charles A. Dana

15 Christianity, of course...but why journalism?
Arthur James Balfour 1848–1930: replying to Frank Harris's remark that 'all the faults of the age come from Christianity and journalism'; in Margot Asquith *Autobiography* (1920)

16 Comment is free, but facts are sacred.
C. P. Scott 1846–1932: *Manchester Guardian* 5 May 1921

17 Well, all I know is what I read in the papers.
Will Rogers 1879–1935: *New York Times* 30 September 1923

18 You cannot hope
to bribe or twist,
thank God! the
British journalist.
But, seeing what
the man will do
unbribed, there's
no occasion to.
> **Humbert Wolfe** 1886–1940: 'Over the Fire' (1930)

19 Power without responsibility: the prerogative of the harlot
throughout the ages.
> **Rudyard Kipling** 1865–1936: summing up Lord
> Beaverbrook's political standpoint *vis-à-vis* the *Daily
> Express*; quoted by Stanley Baldwin, 18 March 1931

20 The art of newspaper paragraphing is to stroke a platitude
until it purrs like an epigram.
> **Don Marquis** 1878–1937: in E. Anthony *O Rare Don
> Marquis* (1962)

21 News is what a chap who doesn't care much about anything
wants to read. And it's only news until he's read it. After that
it's dead.
> **Evelyn Waugh** 1903–66: *Scoop* (1938)

22 Small earthquake in Chile. Not many dead.
> **Claud Cockburn** 1904–81: winning entry for a dullest head-
> line competition at *The Times*; *In Time of Trouble* (1956)

23 I read the newspapers avidly. It is my one form of continuous
fiction.
> **Aneurin Bevan** 1897–1960: in *The Times* 29 March 1960

24 A good newspaper, I suppose, is a nation talking to itself.
> **Arthur Miller** 1915– : in *Observer* 26 November 1961

25 Freedom of the press in Britain means freedom to print
such of the proprietor's prejudices as the advertisers don't
object to.
> **Hannen Swaffer** 1879–1962: in Tom Driberg *Swaff* (1974)

26 Success in journalism can be a form of failure. Freedom
comes from lack of possessions. The truth-divulging paper
must imitate the tramp and sleep under a hedge.
> **Graham Greene** 1904–91: *New Statesman* 31 May 1968

27 Comment is free but facts are on expenses.
> **Tom Stoppard** 1937– : *Night and Day* (1978)

28 Rock journalism is people who can't write interviewing people who can't talk for people who can't read.
  Frank Zappa 1940–93: in L. Botts *Loose Talk* (1980)

29 We must try to find ways to starve the terrorist and the hijacker of the oxygen of publicity on which they depend.
  Margaret Thatcher 1925– : speech to American Bar Association in London, 15 July 1985

30 Blood sport is brought to its ultimate refinement in the gossip columns.
  Bernard Ingham 1932– : speech, 5 February 1986

31 An odious exhibition of journalists dabbling their fingers in the stuff of other people's souls.
  Lord McGregor 1921– : on press coverage of the marriage of the Prince and Princess of Wales; *The Times* 9 June 1992

Night see Day and Night

Old Age

1 Then shall ye bring down my grey hairs with sorrow to the grave.
  Bible: Genesis

2 The days of our age are threescore years and ten; and though men be so strong that they come to fourscore years: yet is their strength then but labour and sorrow; so soon passeth it away, and we are gone.
  Bible: Psalm 90

3 How ill white hairs become a fool and jester!
  William Shakespeare 1564–1616: *Henry IV, Part 2* (1597)

4   The sixth age shifts
Into the lean and slippered pantaloon,
With spectacles on nose and pouch on side.
  William Shakespeare 1564–1616: *As You Like It* (1599)

5 Second childishness, and mere oblivion,
Sans teeth, sans eyes, sans taste, sans everything.
  William Shakespeare 1564–1616: *As You Like It* (1599)

6 Unregarded age in corners thrown.
  William Shakespeare 1564–1616: *As You Like It* (1599)

7 Therefore my age is as a lusty winter,
Frosty, but kindly.
William Shakespeare 1564–1616: *As You Like It* (1599)

8 I have lived long enough: my way of life
Is fall'n into the sear, the yellow leaf.
William Shakespeare 1564–1616: *Macbeth* (1606)

9 Age will not be defied.
Francis Bacon 1561–1626: *Essays* (1625) 'Of Regimen of
Health'

10 Every man desires to live long; but no man would be old.
Jonathan Swift 1667–1745: *Thoughts on Various Subjects*
(1727 ed.)

11 See how the world its veterans rewards!
A youth of frolics, an old age of cards.
Alexander Pope 1688–1744: *Epistles to Several Persons* 'To a
Lady' (1735)

12 Old-age, a second child, by Nature cursed
With more and greater evils than the first,
Weak, sickly, full of pains; in ev'ry breath
Railing at life, and yet afraid of death.
Charles Churchill 1731–64: *Gotham* (1764)

13 How happy he who crowns in shades like these,
A youth of labour with an age of ease.
Oliver Goldsmith 1730–74: *The Deserted Village* (1770)

14 Time has shaken me by the hand and death is not far behind.
John Wesley 1703–91: letter to Ezekiel Cooper, 1 February
1791

15 There's a fascination frantic
In a ruin that's romantic;
Do you think you are sufficiently decayed?
W. S. Gilbert 1836–1911: *The Mikado* (1885)

16 When you are old and grey and full of sleep,
And nodding by the fire, take down this book
And slowly read and dream of the soft look
Your eyes had once, and of their shadows deep.
W. B. Yeats 1865–1939: 'When You Are Old' (1893)

17 I grow old...I grow old...
I shall wear the bottoms of my trousers rolled.
T. S. Eliot 1888–1965: 'Love Song of J. Alfred Prufrock'
(1917)

18 Oh, to be seventy again!
> **Georges Clemenceau** 1841-1929: on seeing a pretty girl on
> his eightieth birthday; in James Agate's diary, 19 April
> 1938

19 An aged man is but a paltry thing,
A tattered coat upon a stick, unless
Soul clap its hands and sing, and louder sing
For every tatter in its mortal dress.
> **W. B. Yeats** 1865-1939: 'Sailing to Byzantium' (1928)

20 From the earliest times the old have rubbed it into the young
that they are wiser than they, and before the young had
discovered what nonsense this was they were old too, and it
profited them to carry on the imposture.
> **W. Somerset Maugham** 1874-1965: *Cakes and Ale* (1930)

21 There is more felicity on the far side of baldness than young
men can possibly imagine.
> **Logan Pearsall Smith** 1865-1946: *Afterthoughts* (1931) 'Age
> and Death'

22 Nothing really wrong with him—only anno domini, but that's
the most fatal complaint of all, in the end.
> **James Hilton** 1900-54: *Goodbye, Mr Chips* (1934)

23 Old age is the most unexpected of all things that happen to
a man.
> **Leon Trotsky** 1879-1940: diary, 8 May 1935

24 You think it horrible that lust and rage
Should dance attendance upon my old age;
They were not such a plague when I was young;
What else have I to spur me into song?
> **W. B. Yeats** 1865-1939: 'The Spur' (1938)

25 You will recognize, my boy, the first sign of old age: it is
when you go out into the streets of London and realize for
the first time how young the policemen look.
> **Seymour Hicks** 1871-1949: in C. R. D. Pulling *They Were
> Singing* (1952)

26 Do not go gentle into that good night,
Old age should burn and rave at close of day;
Rage, rage against the dying of the light.
> **Dylan Thomas** 1914-53: 'Do Not Go Gentle into that Good
> Night' (1952)

27 Conversation is imperative if gaps are to be filled, and old age, it is the last gap but one.
   Patrick White 1912-90: *The Tree of Man* (1955)

28 To me old age is always fifteen years older than I am.
   Bernard Baruch 1870-1965: in *Newsweek* 29 August 1955

29 When one has reached 81…one likes to sit back and let the world turn by itself, without trying to push it.
   Sean O'Casey 1880-1964: *New York Times* 25 September 1960

30 Considering the alternative, it's not too bad at all.
   Maurice Chevalier 1888-1972: when asked what he felt about the advancing years on his 72nd birthday; in M. Freedland *Maurice Chevalier* (1981)

31 In a dream you are never eighty.
   Anne Sexton 1928-74: 'Old' (1962)

32 Will you still need me, will you still feed me,
When I'm sixty four?
   John Lennon 1940-80 and **Paul McCartney** 1942- : 'When I'm Sixty Four' (1967 song)

33 The man who works and is not bored is never old.
   Pablo Casals 1876-1973: in J. Lloyd Webber (ed.) *Song of the Birds* (1985)

34 Growing old is like being increasingly penalized for a crime you haven't committed.
   Anthony Powell 1905- : *Temporary Kings* (1973)

35 Perhaps being old is having lighted rooms
Inside your head, and people in them, acting.
People you know, yet can't quite name.
   Philip Larkin 1922-85: 'The Old Fools' (1974)

36 If I'd known I was gonna live this long, I'd have taken better care of myself.
   Eubie Blake 1883-1983: on reaching the age of 100; in *Observer* 13 February 1983 'Sayings of the Week'

37 Alun's life was coming to consist more and more exclusively of being told at dictation speed what he knew.
   Kingsley Amis 1922- : *The Old Devils* (1986)

Opening Lines

1 *Arma virumque cano.*
I sing of arms and the man.
  Virgil 70–19 BC: *Aeneid*

2 *Nel mezzo del cammin di nostra vita.*
Midway along the path of our life.
  Dante Alighieri 1265–1321: *Divina Commedia* 'Inferno'

3 O! for a Muse of fire, that would ascend
The brightest heaven of invention.
  William Shakespeare 1564–1616: *Henry V* (1599)

4 Yet once more, O ye laurels, and once more
Ye myrtles brown, with ivy never sere.
  John Milton 1608–74: 'Lycidas' (1638)

5 Of man's first disobedience, and the fruit
Of that forbidden tree, whose mortal taste
Brought death into the world, and all our woe,
With loss of Eden.
  John Milton 1608–74: *Paradise Lost* (1667)

6 Oh, what can ail thee knight at arms
Alone and palely loitering?
  John Keats 1795–1821: 'La belle dame sans merci' (1820)

7 It was a dark and stormy night.
  Edward Bulwer-Lytton 1803–73: *Paul Clifford* (1830)

8 The boy stood on the burning deck
Whence all but he had fled.
  Felicia Hemans 1793–1835: 'Casabianca' (1849)

9 It was the best of times, it was the worst of times.
  Charles Dickens 1812–70: *A Tale of Two Cities* (1859)

10 'Is there anybody there?' said the Traveller,
Knocking on the moonlit door.
  Walter de la Mare 1873–1956: 'The Listeners' (1912)

11 When Gregor Samsa awoke one morning from uneasy
dreams he found himself transformed in his bed into
a gigantic insect.
  Franz Kafka 1883–1924: *The Metamorphosis* (1915)

12 Last night I dreamt I went to Manderley again.
  Daphne Du Maurier 1907–89: *Rebecca* (1938)

13 It was a bright cold day in April, and the clocks were striking thirteen.
   George Orwell 1903–50: *Nineteen Eighty-Four* (1949)

14 Lolita, light of my life, fire of my loins. My sin, my soul. Lo-lee-ta: the tip of the tongue taking a trip of three steps down the palate to tap, at three, on the teeth. Lo. Lee. Ta.
   Vladimir Nabokov 1899–1977: *Lolita* (1955)

15 'Take my camel, dear,' said my aunt Dot, as she climbed down from this animal on her return from High Mass.
   Rose Macaulay 1881–1958: *The Towers of Trebizond* (1956)

16 It was the afternoon of my eighty-first birthday, and I was in bed with my catamite when Ali announced that the archbishop had come to see me.
   Anthony Burgess 1917–93: *Earthly Powers* (1980)

Opinion

1 There are as many opinions as there are people: each has his own correct way.
   Terence *c.*190–159 BC: *Phormio*

2 Opinion in good men is but knowledge in the making.
   John Milton 1608–74: *Areopagitica* (1644)

3 They that approve a private opinion, call it opinion; but they that mislike it, heresy: and yet heresy signifies no more than private opinion.
   Thomas Hobbes 1588–1679: *Leviathan* (1651)

4 He that complies against his will,
   Is of his own opinion still.
   Samuel Butler 1612–80: *Hudibras* pt. 3 (1680)

5 New opinions are always suspected, and usually opposed, without any other reason but because they are not already common.
   John Locke 1632–1704: *Essay concerning Human Understanding* (1690)

6 Some praise at morning what they blame at night;
   But always think the last opinion right.
   Alexander Pope 1688–1744: *An Essay on Criticism* (1711)

7 Every man has a right to utter what he thinks truth, and
every other man has a right to knock him down for it.
Martyrdom is the test.
   Samuel Johnson 1709–84: in James Boswell *Life of Johnson*
   (1791) 1780

8 A man can brave opinion, a woman must submit to it.
   Mme de Staël 1766–1817: *Delphine* (1802)

9 There are nine and sixty ways of constructing tribal lays,
And—every—single—one—of—them—is—right!
   Rudyard Kipling 1865–1936: 'In the Neolithic Age' (1893)

Optimism and Pessimism

See also **Hope and Despair**

1 Sin is behovely, but all shall be well and all shall be well and
all manner of thing shall be well.
   Julian of Norwich 1343–after 1416: *Revelations of Divine
   Love*

2 In this best of possible worlds…all is for the best.
   Voltaire 1694–1778: *Candide* (1759); usually quoted 'All is
   for the best in the best of all possible worlds'

3 The lark's on the wing;
The snail's on the thorn:
God's in his heaven—
All's right with the world!
   Robert Browning 1812–89: *Pippa Passes* (1841)

4 I have known him come home to supper with a flood of tears,
and a declaration that nothing was now left but a jail; and go
to bed making a calculation of the expense of putting
bow-windows to the house, 'in case anything turned up,'
which was his favourite expression.
   Charles Dickens 1812–70: *David Copperfield* (1850) of Mr
   Micawber

5 Where everything is bad it must be good to know the worst.
   F. H. Bradley 1846–1924: *Appearance and Reality* (1893)

6 Nothing to do but work,
Nothing to eat but food,

Nothing to wear but clothes
To keep one from going nude.
Benjamin Franklin King 1857–94: 'The Pessimist'

7 Cheer up! the worst is yet to come!
Philander Chase Johnson 1866–1939: *Everybody's Magazine*
May 1920

8 The optimist proclaims that we live in the best of all possible
worlds; and the pessimist fears this is true.
James Branch Cabell 1879–1958: *The Silver Stallion* (1926)

9 an optimist is a guy
that has never had
much experience.
Don Marquis 1878–1937: *archy and mehitabel* (1927)

10 'Twixt the optimist and pessimist
The difference is droll:
The optimist sees the doughnut
But the pessimist sees the hole.
McLandburgh Wilson 1892– : *Optimist and Pessimist*

11 Man hands on misery to man.
It deepens like a coastal shelf.
Get out as early as you can,
And don't have any kids yourself.
Philip Larkin 1922–85: 'This Be The Verse' (1974)

12 If we see light at the end of the tunnel,
It's the light of the oncoming train.
Robert Lowell 1917–77: 'Since 1939' (1977)

13 I don't consider myself a pessimist. I think of a pessimist as
someone who is waiting for it to rain. And I feel soaked to
the skin.
Leonard Cohen 1934– : in *Observer* 2 May 1993 'Sayings of
the Week'

Painting and Drawing

1 The King found her [Anne of Cleves] so different from her
picture…that…he swore they had brought him a Flanders
mare.
Henry VIII 1491–1547: Tobias Smollett *Complete History of
England* (3rd ed., 1759)

2 Good painters imitate nature, bad ones spew it up.
   Cervantes 1547–1616: *El Licenciado Vidriera* in *Novelas Ejemplares* (1613)

3 Remark all these roughnesses, pimples, warts, and everything as you see me; otherwise I will never pay a farthing for it.
   Oliver Cromwell 1599–1658: to Lely, on the painting of his portrait; in Horace Walpole *Anecdotes of Painting in England* (1763) (commonly quoted 'warts and all')

4 In Claude's landscape all is lovely—all amiable—all is amenity and repose;—the calm sunshine of the heart.
   John Constable 1776–1837: lecture, 2 June 1836

5 *Le dessin est la probité de l'art.*
   Drawing is the true test of art.
   J. A. D. Ingres 1780–1867: *Pensées d'Ingres* (1922)

6 She is older than the rocks among which she sits.
   Walter Pater 1839–94: of the *Mona Lisa*; *Studies in the History of the Renaissance* (1873)

7 I have seen, and heard, much of Cockney impudence before now; but never expected to hear a coxcomb ask two hundred guineas for flinging a pot of paint in the public's face.
   John Ruskin 1819–1900: on Whistler's *Nocturne in Black and Gold*; *Fors Clavigera* (1871–84) Letter 79, 18 June 1877

8 No, I ask it for the knowledge of a lifetime.
   James McNeill Whistler 1834–1903: in his case against Ruskin, replying to the question: 'For two days' labour, you ask two hundred guineas?'; in D. C. Seitz *Whistler Stories* (1913)

9 Yes madam, Nature is creeping up.
   James McNeill Whistler 1834–1903: to a lady who had been reminded of his work by an 'exquisite haze in the atmosphere'; in D. C. Seitz *Whistler Stories* (1913)

10 Art does not reproduce the visible; rather, it makes visible.
   Paul Klee 1879–1940: 'Creative Credo' (1920)

11 An active line on a walk, moving freely without a goal. A walk for walk's sake.
   Paul Klee 1879–1940: *Pedagogical Sketchbook* (1925)

12 Every time I paint a portrait I lose a friend.
   John Singer Sargent 1856–1925: in N. Bentley and E. Esar *Treasury of Humorous Quotations* (1951)

13 I am a painter and I nail my pictures together.
   Kurt Schwitters 1887–1948: in R. Hausmann *Am Anfang war Dada* (1972)

14 Painting is saying "Ta" to God.
   Stanley Spencer 1891–1959: in letter from Spencer's daughter Shirin, *Observer* 7 February 1988

15 I paint objects as I think them, not as I see them.
   Pablo Picasso 1881–1973: in John Golding *Cubism* (1959)

16 A product of the untalented, sold by the unprincipled to the utterly bewildered.
   Al Capp 1907–79: on abstract art, in *National Observer* 1 July 1963

Parents

See also **Children, The Family**

1 Honour thy father and thy mother.
   Bible: Exodus

2 A wise son maketh a glad father: but a foolish son is the heaviness of his mother.
   Bible: Proverbs

3 Or what man is there of you, whom if his son ask bread, will he give him a stone?
   Bible: St Matthew

4 Parents love their children more than children love their parents.
   Auctoritates Aristotelis: a compilation of medieval propositions

5 It is a wise father that knows his own child.
   William Shakespeare 1564–1616: *The Merchant of Venice* (1596–8)

6 The joys of parents are secret, and so are their griefs and fears.
   Francis Bacon 1561–1626: *Essays* (1625) 'Of Parents and Children'

7 A slavish bondage to parents cramps every faculty of the mind.
   Mary Wollstonecraft 1759-97: *A Vindication of the Rights of Woman* (1792)

8 The hand that rocks the cradle
   Is the hand that rules the world.
   William Ross Wallace d. 1881: 'What rules the world' (1865)

9 If I were damned of body and soul,
   I know whose prayers would make me whole,
   Mother o' mine, O mother o' mine.
   Rudyard Kipling 1865-1936: *The Light That Failed* (1891)

10 Children begin by loving their parents; after a time they judge them; rarely, if ever, do they forgive them.
   Oscar Wilde 1854-1900: *A Woman of No Importance* (1893)

11 And mothers of large families (who claim to common sense)
   Will find a Tiger well repay the trouble and expense.
   Hilaire Belloc 1870-1953: *A Bad Child's Book of Beasts* (1896) 'The Tiger'

12 Few misfortunes can befall a boy which bring worse consequences than to have a really affectionate mother.
   W. Somerset Maugham 1874-1965: *A Writer's Notebook* (1949) (written in 1896)

13 The parent who could see his boy as he really is, would shake his head and say: 'Willie is no good; I'll sell him.'
   Stephen Leacock 1869-1944: *Essays and Literary Studies* (1916)

14 The natural term of the affection of the human animal for its offspring is six years.
   George Bernard Shaw 1856-1950: *Heartbreak House* (1919)

15 Your children are not your children.
   They are the sons and daughters of Life's longing for itself.
   They came through you but not from you
   And though they are with you yet they belong not to you.
   Kahlil Gibran 1883-1931: *The Prophet* (1923) 'On Children'

16 The fundamental defect of fathers, in our competitive society, is that they want their children to be a credit to them.
   Bertrand Russell 1872-1970: *Sceptical Essays* (1928)

17 Children aren't happy with nothing to ignore,
And that's what parents were created for.
Ogden Nash 1902–71: 'The Parent' (1933)

18 Oh, what a tangled web do parents weave
When they think that their children are naïve.
Ogden Nash 1902–71: 'Baby, What Makes the Sky Blue'
(1940)

19 Parentage is a very important profession, but no test of
fitness for it is ever imposed in the interest of the children.
George Bernard Shaw 1856–1950: *Everybody's Political
What's What?* (1944)

20 Parents—especially step-parents—are sometimes a bit of
a disappointment to their children. They don't fulfil the
promise of their early years.
Anthony Powell 1905– : *A Buyer's Market* (1952)

21 The value of marriage is not that adults produce children but
that children produce adults.
Peter De Vries 1910– : *The Tunnel of Love* (1954)

22 Parents learn a lot from their children about coping with life.
Muriel Spark 1918– : *The Comforters* (1957)

23 The thing that impresses me most about America is the way
parents obey their children.
Edward VIII 1894–1972: *Look* 5 March 1957

24 A Jewish man with parents alive is a fifteen-year-old boy,
and will remain a fifteen-year-old boy until *they die*!
Philip Roth 1933– : *Portnoy's Complaint* (1967)

25 No matter how old a mother is she watches her middle-aged
children for signs of improvement.
Florida Scott-Maxwell: *Measure of my Days* (1968)

26 They fuck you up, your mum and dad.
They may not mean to, but they do.
They fill you with the faults they had
And add some extra, just for you.
Philip Larkin 1922–85: 'This Be The Verse' (1974)

The Past

1 Even a god cannot change the past.
   Agathon b. *c.*445 BC: in Aristotle *Nicomachaean Ethics*
   (literally 'The one thing which even a god cannot do is to
   make undone what has been done')

2 *Mais où sont les neiges d'antan?*
   But where are the snows of yesteryear?
   François Villon b. 1431: 'Ballade des dames du temps
   jadis' (1461), tr. D. G. Rossetti

3 O! call back yesterday, bid time return.
   William Shakespeare 1564–1616: *Richard II* (1595)

4 Antiquities are history defaced, or some remnants of history
   which have casually escaped the shipwreck of time.
   Francis Bacon 1561–1626: *The Advancement of Learning*
   (1605)

5 What's done cannot be undone.
   William Shakespeare 1564–1616: *Macbeth* (1606)

6 What's gone and what's past help
   Should be past grief.
   William Shakespeare 1564–1616: *The Winter's Tale*
   (1610–11)

7 Ancient times were the youth of the world.
   Francis Bacon 1561–1626: *De Dignitate et Augmentis
   Scientiarum* (1623)

8 There never was a merry world since the fairies left off
   dancing, and the Parson left conjuring.
   John Selden 1584–1654: *Table Talk* (1689)

9 Think of it, soldiers; from the summit of these pyramids,
   forty centuries look down upon you.
   Napoléon I 1769–1821: speech before the Battle of the
   Pyramids, 21 July 1798

10 The moving finger writes; and, having writ,
   Moves on: nor all thy piety nor wit
   Shall lure it back to cancel half a line,
   Nor all thy tears wash out a word of it.
   Edward Fitzgerald 1809–83: *The Rubáiyát of Omar
   Khayyám* (1859)

11 What are those blue remembered hills,
What spires, what farms are those?

That is the land of lost content,
I see it shining plain,
The happy highways where I went
And cannot come again.
A. E. Housman 1859-1936: *A Shropshire Lad* (1896)

12 Those who cannot remember the past are condemned to
repeat it.
George Santayana 1863-1952: *The Life of Reason* (1905)

13 O God! Put back Thy universe and give me yesterday.
Henry Arthur Jones 1851-1929 and **Henry Herman**
1832-94: *The Silver King* (1907)

14 Stands the Church clock at ten to three?
And is there honey still for tea?
Rupert Brooke 1887-1915: 'The Old Vicarage, Grantchester'
(1915)

15 The past is the only dead thing that smells sweet.
Edward Thomas 1878-1917: 'Early one morning in May I set
out' (1917)

16 I tell you the past is a bucket of ashes.
Carl Sandburg 1878-1967: 'Prairie' (1918)

17 Things ain't what they used to be.
Ted Persons: title of song (1941)

18 In every age 'the good old days' were a myth. No one ever
thought they were good at the time. For every age has
consisted of crises that seemed intolerable to the people who
lived through them.
Brooks Atkinson 1894-1984: *Once Around the Sun* (1951)

19 The past is a foreign country: they do things differently
there.
L. P. Hartley 1895-1972: *The Go-Between* (1953)

20 People who are always praising the past
And especially the times of faith as best
Ought to go and live in the Middle Ages
And be burnt at the stake as witches and sages.
Stevie Smith 1902-71: 'The Past' (1957)

21 I have heard tell of a Professor of Economics who has a sign
on the wall of his study, reading 'the future is not what it

was'. The sentiment was admirable; unfortunately, the past is not getting any better either.
Bernard Levin 1928– : *Sunday Times* 22 May 1977

22 Nostalgia isn't what it used to be.
Anonymous: graffito; taken as title of book by Simone Signoret, 1978

Patriotism

1 *Dulce et decorum est pro patria mori.*
Lovely and honourable it is to die for one's country.
Horace 65–8 BC: *Odes*

2 Never was patriot yet, but was a fool.
John Dryden 1631–1700: *Absalom and Achitophel* (1681)

3   What pity is it
That we can die but once to serve our country!
Joseph Addison 1672–1719: *Cato* (1713)

4   Be England what she will,
With all her faults, she is my country still.
Charles Churchill 1731–64: *The Farewell* (1764)

5 The more foreigners I saw, the more I loved my homeland.
De Belloy 1727–75: *Le Siège de Calais* (1765)

6 Patriotism is the last refuge of a scoundrel.
Samuel Johnson 1709–84: in James Boswell *Life of Johnson* (1791) 7 April 1775

7 I only regret that I have but one life to lose for my country.
Nathan Hale 1755–76: prior to his execution by the British for spying, 22 September 1776

8 These are the times that try men's souls. The summer soldier and the sunshine patriot will, in this crisis, shrink from the service of their country; but he that stands it *now*, deserves the love and thanks of men and women.
Thomas Paine 1737–1809: *The Crisis* (December 1776)

9 True patriots we; for be it understood,
We left our country for our country's good.
Henry Carter d. 1806: prologue, written for, but not recited at, the opening of the Playhouse, Sydney, New South Wales, 16 January 1796, when the actors were principally

convicts. Previously attributed to George Barrington
(b. 1755)

10 Breathes there the man, with soul so dead,
Who never to himself hath said,
This is my own, my native land!
Sir Walter Scott 1771–1832: *The Lay of the Last Minstrel*
(1805)

11 Our country! In her intercourse with foreign nations, may
she always be in the right; but our country, right or wrong.
Stephen Decatur 1779–1820: toast at Norfolk, Virginia,
April 1816

12 My toast would be, may our country be always successful,
but whether successful or otherwise, always right.
John Quincy Adams 1767–1848: letter to John Adams,
1 August 1816

13 A steady patriot of the world alone,
The friend of every country but his own.
George Canning 1770–1827: of the Jacobin, in 'New
Morality' (1821)

14 That kind of patriotism which consists in hating all other
nations.
Elizabeth Gaskell 1810–65: *Sylvia's Lovers* (1863)

15 My country, right or wrong; if right, to be kept right; and if
wrong, to be set right!
Carl Schurz 1829–1906: speech, US Senate, 29 February
1872

16 Patriotism is not enough. I must have no hatred or bitterness
towards anyone.
Edith Cavell 1865–1915: on the eve of her execution, in *The
Times* 23 October 1915

17 I vow to thee, my country—all earthly things above—
Entire and whole and perfect, the service of my love.
Cecil Spring-Rice 1859–1918: 'I Vow to Thee, My Country'
(1918)

18 You'll never have a quiet world till you knock the patriotism
out of the human race.
George Bernard Shaw 1856–1950: *O'Flaherty V.C.* (1919)

19 Patriotism is a lively sense of collective responsibility.
Nationalism is a silly cock crowing on its own dunghill.
    Richard Aldington 1892–1962: *The Colonel's Daughter*
(1931)

20 If I had to choose between betraying my country and
betraying my friend, I hope I should have the guts to betray
my country.
    E. M. Forster 1879–1970: *Two Cheers for Democracy* (1951)

21 I would die for my country but I would never let my country
die for me.
    Neil Kinnock 1942– : speech at Labour party conference,
30 September 1986

22 The cricket test—which side do they cheer for?...Are you
still looking back to where you came from or where you are?
    Norman Tebbit 1931– : on the loyalties of Britain's
immigrant population; interview in *Los Angeles Times*,
reported in *Daily Telegraph* 20 April 1990

Peace

1 They shall beat their swords into plowshares, and their
spears into pruninghooks: nation shall not lift up sword
against nation, neither shall they learn war any more.
    Bible: Isaiah

2 The peace of God, which passeth all understanding, shall
keep your hearts and minds through Christ Jesus.
    Bible: Philippians

3 They make a wilderness and call it peace.
    Tacitus AD *c.*56–after 117: *Agricola*

4 *Qui desiderat pacem, praeparet bellum.*
Let him who desires peace, prepare for war.
    Vegetius fourth century AD: *Epitoma Rei Militaris*, usually
quoted '*Si vis pacem, para bellum* [If you want peace,
prepare for war]'

5 *E'n la sua volontade è nostra pace.*
In His will is our peace.
    Dante Alighieri 1265–1321: *Divina Commedia* 'Paradiso'

6 ...The naked, poor, and manglèd Peace,
Dear nurse of arts, plenties, and joyful births.
   William Shakespeare 1564–1616: *Henry V* (1599)

7 ...Peace hath her victories
No less renowned than war.
   John Milton 1608–74: 'To the Lord General Cromwell'
   (written 1652)

8 Give peace in our time, O Lord.
   Book of Common Prayer 1662: *Morning Prayer*

9 Lord Salisbury and myself have brought you back peace—but
a peace I hope with honour.
   Benjamin Disraeli 1804–81: speech on returning from the
   Congress of Berlin, 16 July 1878

10 PEACE, *n*. In international affairs, a period of cheating
between two periods of fighting.
   Ambrose Bierce 1842–*c*.1914: *The Devil's Dictionary* (1911)

11 This is the second time in our history that there has come
back from Germany to Downing Street peace with honour. I
believe it is peace for our time.
   Neville Chamberlain 1869–1940: speech from 10 Downing
   Street, 30 September 1938

12 I think that people want peace so much that one of these days
governments had better get out of the way and let them have
it.
   Dwight D. Eisenhower 1890–1969: broadcast discussion,
   31 August 1959

13 Give peace a chance.
   John Lennon 1940–80 and **Paul McCartney** 1942– : title of
   song (1969)

14 There is no such thing as inner peace. There is only
nervousness or death.
   Fran Lebowitz 1946– : *Metropolitan Life* (1978)

People

See also **Musicians, Poets, Politicians, Writers**

1 As time requireth, a man of marvellous mirth and pastimes, and sometime of as sad gravity, as who say: a man for all seasons.
    Robert Whittington: of Sir Thomas More, in *Vulgaria* (1521)

2 He had a head to contrive, a tongue to persuade, and a hand to execute any mischief.
    Edward Hyde, Earl of Clarendon 1609–74: of Hampden, *History of the Rebellion* (1703)

3 He snatched the lightning shaft from heaven, and the sceptre from tyrants.
    A. R. J. Turgot 1727–81: inscription for a bust of Benjamin Franklin, inventor of the lightning conductor

4 As he rose like a rocket, he fell like the stick.
    Thomas Paine 1737–1809: on Edmund Burke losing the debate on the French Revolution to Charles James Fox, in the House of Commons; in *Letter to the Addressers on the late Proclamation* (1792)

5 Mad, bad, and dangerous to know.
    Lady Caroline Lamb 1785–1828: of Byron; diary, March 1812

6 An Archangel a little damaged.
    Charles Lamb 1775–1834: of Coleridge; letter to Wordsworth, 26 April 1816

7 He rather hated the ruling few than loved the suffering many.
    Jeremy Bentham 1748–1832: of James Mill, in H. N. Pym (ed.) *Memories of Old Friends* (1882)

8 The seagreen Incorruptible.
    Thomas Carlyle 1795–1881: of Robespierre, *History of the French Revolution* (1837)

9 Macaulay is well for a while, but one wouldn't *live* under Niagara.
    Thomas Carlyle 1795–1881: in R. M. Milnes *Notebook* (1838)

10 Thou large-brained woman and large-hearted man.
    Elizabeth Barrett Browning 1806–61: 'To George Sand—
    A Desire' (1844)

11 Who saw life steadily, and saw it whole:
    The mellow glory of the Attic stage;
    Singer of sweet Colonus, and its child.
    Matthew Arnold 1822–88: 'To a Friend' (1849), of Sophocles

12   The statue stood
    Of Newton, with his prism, and silent face:
    The marble index of a mind for ever
    Voyaging through strange seas of Thought, alone.
    William Wordsworth 1770–1850: *The Prelude* (1850)

13 He [Bernard Shaw] hasn't an enemy in the world, and none
of his friends like him.
    Oscar Wilde 1854–1900: in Bernard Shaw *Sixteen Self
    Sketches* (1949)

14 Her conception of God was certainly not orthodox. She felt
towards Him as she might have felt towards a glorified
sanitary engineer; and in some of her speculations she seems
hardly to distinguish between the Deity and the Drains.
    Lytton Strachey 1880–1932: *Eminent Victorians* (1918)
    'Florence Nightingale'

15 A good man fallen among Fabians.
    Lenin 1870–1924: of G. B. Shaw, in A. Ransome *Six Weeks in
    Russia in 1919* (1919) 'Notes of Conversations with Lenin'

16 He was no striped frieze; he was shot silk.
    Lytton Strachey 1880–1932: of Francis Bacon, *Elizabeth
    and Essex* (1928)

17 He seemed at ease and to have the look of the last gentleman
in Europe.
    Ada Leverson 1865–1936: of Oscar Wilde, *Letters to the
    Sphinx* (1930)

18 Victor Hugo was a madman who thought he was Victor
Hugo.
    Jean Cocteau 1889–1963: *Opium* (1930)

19 To us he is no more a person
now but a whole climate of opinion.
    W. H. Auden 1907–73: 'In Memory of Sigmund Freud' (1940)

20 Beaverbrook is so pleased to be in the Government that he is
like the town tart who has finally married the Mayor!
   Beverley Baxter 1891-1964: in Henry 'Chips' Channon's
   diary, 12 June 1940

21 The candle in that great turnip has gone out.
   Winston Churchill 1874-1965: of Stanley Baldwin, in
   Harold Nicolson's diary, 17 August 1950

22 Rousseau was the first militant lowbrow.
   Isaiah Berlin 1909- : *Observer* 9 November 1952

23 The mama of dada.
   Clifton Fadiman 1904- : of Gertrude Stein, *Party of One*
   (1955)

24 An elderly fallen angel travelling incognito.
   Peter Quennell 1905-93: of André Gide, *The Sign of the
   Fish* (1960)

25 Forty years ago he was Slightly in *Peter Pan*, and you might
say that he has been wholly in *Peter Pan* ever since.
   Kenneth Tynan 1927-80: of Noël Coward, *Curtains* (1961)

26 What, when drunk, one sees in other women, one sees in
Garbo sober.
   Kenneth Tynan 1927-80: *Curtains* (1961)

27 She would rather light a candle than curse the darkness, and
her glow has warmed the world.
   Adlai Stevenson 1900-65: on learning of Eleanor
   Roosevelt's death; in *New York Times* 8 November 1962

28 In defeat unbeatable: in victory unbearable.
   Winston Churchill 1874-1965: of Viscount Montgomery, in
   E. Marsh *Ambrosia and Small Beer* (1964)

29 A doormat in a world of boots.
   Jean Rhys c.1890-1979: describing herself; in *Guardian*
   6 December 1990

30 Every word she writes is a lie, including 'and' and 'the'.
   Mary McCarthy 1912-89: quoting herself on Lillian
   Hellman in *New York Times* 16 February 1980

Perfection

1 How many things by season seasoned are
  To their right praise and true perfection!
  William Shakespeare 1564–1616: *The Merchant of Venice*
  (1596–8)

2 Perfection is the child of Time.
  Bishop Joseph Hall 1574–1656: *Works* (1625)

3 Whoever thinks a faultless piece to see,
  Thinks what ne'er was, nor is, nor e'er shall be.
  Alexander Pope 1688–1744: *An Essay on Criticism* (1711)

4 *Le mieux est l'ennemi du bien.*
  The best is the enemy of the good.
  Voltaire 1694–1778: *Contes* (1772), deriving from an Italian
  proverb

5 Pictures of perfection as you know make me sick and wicked.
  Jane Austen 1775–1817: letter to Fanny Knight, 23 March
  1817

6 No one can be perfectly free till all are free; no one can be
  perfectly moral till all are moral; no one can be perfectly
  happy till all are happy.
  Herbert Spencer 1820–1903: *Social Statics* (1850)

7   What's come to perfection perishes.
  Things learned on earth, we shall practise in heaven:
  Works done least rapidly, Art most cherishes.
  Robert Browning 1812–89: 'Old Pictures in Florence' (1855)

8 Faultily faultless, icily regular, splendidly null,
  Dead perfection, no more.
  Alfred, Lord Tennyson 1809–92: *Maud* (1855)

9 He is all fault who hath no fault at all:
  For who loves me must have a touch of earth.
  Alfred, Lord Tennyson 1809–92: *Idylls of the King*
  'Lancelot and Elaine' (1859)

10 Faultless to a fault.
  Robert Browning 1812–89: *The Ring and the Book* (1868–9)

11 The pursuit of perfection, then, is the pursuit of sweetness
  and light…He who works for sweetness and light united,
  works to make reason and the will of God prevail.
  Matthew Arnold 1822–88: *Culture and Anarchy* (1869)

12 The best is the best, though a hundred judges have declared it so.
  Arthur Quiller-Couch 1863-1944: *Oxford Book of English Verse* (1900)

13 Finality is death. Perfection is finality.
  Nothing is perfect. There are lumps in it.
  James Stephens 1882-1950: *The Crock of Gold* (1912)

14 The intellect of man is forced to choose
  Perfection of the life, or of the work.
  W. B. Yeats 1865-1939: 'Coole Park and Ballylee, 1932' (1933)

Pessimism see Optimism and Pessimism

Philosophy

1 The unexamined life is not worth living.
  Socrates 469-399 BC: in Plato *Apology*

2 There is nothing so absurd but some philosopher has said it.
  Cicero 106-43 BC: *De Divinatione*

3 How charming is divine philosophy!
  Not harsh and crabbèd, as dull fools suppose,
  But musical as is Apollo's lute,
  John Milton 1608-74: *Comus* (1637)

4 I refute it *thus*.
  Samuel Johnson 1709-84: kicking a large stone by way of refuting Bishop Berkeley's theory of the non-existence of matter; in James Boswell *Life of Johnson* (1791) 6 August 1763

5 Philosophy will clip an Angel's wings.
  John Keats 1795-1821: 'Lamia' (1820)

6 When philosophy paints its grey on grey, then has a shape of life grown old. By philosophy's grey on grey it cannot be rejuvenated but only understood. The owl of Minerva spreads its wings only with the falling of the dusk.
  G. W. F. Hegel 1770-1831: *Philosophy of Right* (1821) tr. T. M. Knox

7 If it was so, it might be; and if it were so, it would be: but as it isn't, it ain't. That's logic.
 Lewis Carroll 1832-98: *Through the Looking-Glass* (1872)

8 Metaphysics is the finding of bad reasons for what we believe upon instinct.
 F. H. Bradley 1846-1924: *Appearance and Reality* (1893)

9 The Socratic manner is not a game at which two can play.
 Max Beerbohm 1872-1956: *Zuleika Dobson* (1911)

10 The safest general characterization of the European philosophical tradition is that it consists of a series of footnotes to Plato.
 Alfred North Whitehead 1861-1947: *Process and Reality* (1929)

11 Philosophy is a battle against the bewitchment of our intelligence by means of language.
 Ludwig Wittgenstein 1889-1951: *Philosophische Untersuchungen* (1953)

12 What is your aim in philosophy?—To show the fly the way out of the fly-bottle.
 Ludwig Wittgenstein 1889-1951: *Philosophische Untersuchungen* (1953)

Places

See also **America, Britain, England, Europe, France, Ireland, London, Scotland, Wales**

1 *Semper aliquid novi Africam adferre.*
 Africa always brings [us] something new.
 Pliny the Elder AD 23-79: *Historia Naturalis* (often quoted '*Ex Africa semper aliquid novi* [Always something new out of Africa]')

2 Once did she hold the gorgeous East in fee,
 And was the safeguard of the West.
 William Wordsworth 1770-1850: 'On the Extinction of the Venetian Republic' (1807)

3 One has no great hopes from Birmingham. I always say there is something direful in the sound.
 Jane Austen 1775-1817: *Emma* (1816)

4 Sun-girt city, thou hast been
Ocean's child, and then his queen;
Now is come a darker day,
And thou soon must be his prey.
   Percy Bysshe Shelley 1792–1822: of Venice, 'Lines written
   amongst the Euganean Hills' (1818)

5 While stands the Coliseum, Rome shall stand;
When falls the Coliseum, Rome shall fall;
And when Rome falls—the World.
   Lord Byron 1788–1824: *Childe Harold's Pilgrimage* (1812–18)

6 Let there be light! said Liberty,
And like sunrise from the sea,
Athens arose!
   Percy Bysshe Shelley 1792–1822: *Hellas* (1822)

7 The isles of Greece, the isles of Greece!
Where burning Sappho loved and sung,
Where grew the arts of war and peace,
Where Delos rose, and Phoebus sprung!
Eternal summer gilds them yet,
But all, except their sun, is set!
   Lord Byron 1788–1824: *Don Juan* (1819–24)

8 It is from the midst of this putrid sewer that the greatest
river of human industry springs up and carries fertility to
the whole world. From this foul drain pure gold flows forth.
   Alexis de Tocqueville 1805–59: of Manchester, *Voyage en
   Angleterre et en Irlande de 1835* (1958)

9 Kent, sir—everybody knows Kent—apples, cherries, hops,
and women.
   Charles Dickens 1812–70: *Pickwick Papers* (1837) Jingle

10 That temple of silence and reconciliation where the enmities
of twenty generations lie buried.
   Lord Macaulay 1800–59: of Westminster Abbey, *Essays*
   (1843)

11 Italy is a geographical expression.
   Prince Metternich 1773–1859: discussing the Italian
   question with Palmerston in 1847

12 Russia has two generals in whom she can confide—Generals
Janvier [January] and Février [February].
   Emperor Nicholas I of Russia 1796–1855: attributed

13 Earth is here so kind, that just tickle her with a hoe and she laughs with a harvest.
   Douglas Jerrold 1803–57: of Australia, *Wit and Opinions* (1859) 'A Land of Plenty'

14 Whispering from her towers the last enchantments of the Middle Age...Home of lost causes, and forsaken beliefs.
   Matthew Arnold 1822–88: of Oxford, *Essays in Criticism* (1865)

15 That sweet City with her dreaming spires.
   Matthew Arnold 1822–88: of Oxford, 'Thyrsis' (1866)

16 Towery city and branchy between towers.
   Gerard Manley Hopkins 1844–89: 'Duns Scotus's Oxford' (written 1879)

17 And this is good old Boston,
   The home of the bean and the cod,
   Where the Lowells talk to the Cabots
   And the Cabots talk only to God.
   John Collins Bossidy 1860–1928: verse spoken at Holy Cross College alumni dinner in Boston, Massachusetts, 1910

18 Great God! this is an awful place.
   Robert Falcon Scott 1868–1912: of the South Pole; diary, 17 January 1912

19 For Cambridge people rarely smile,
   Being urban, squat, and packed with guile.
   Rupert Brooke 1887–1915: 'The Old Vicarage, Grantchester' (1915)

20 Poor Mexico, so far from God and so close to the United States.
   Porfirio Diaz 1830–1915: attributed

21 Hog Butcher for the World,
   Tool Maker, Stacker of Wheat,
   Player with Railroads and the Nation's Freight Handler;
   Stormy, husky, brawling,
   City of the Big Shoulders.
   Carl Sandburg 1878–1967: 'Chicago' (1916)

22 STREETS FLOODED. PLEASE ADVISE.
   Robert Benchley 1889–1945: telegraph message on arriving in Venice

23 I cannot forecast to you the action of Russia. It is a riddle
wrapped in a mystery inside an enigma.
   Winston Churchill 1874–1965: radio broadcast, 1 October
   1939

24 The last time I saw Paris
Her heart was warm and gay,
I heard the laughter of her heart in ev'ry street café.
   Oscar Hammerstein II 1895–1960: 'The Last Time I saw
   Paris' (1940 song)

25 A big hard-boiled city with no more personality than a paper
cup.
   Raymond Chandler 1888–1959: of Los Angeles, *The Little
   Sister* (1949)

26 A trip through a sewer in a glass-bottomed boat.
   Wilson Mizner 1876–1933: of Hollywood, in A. Johnston *The
   Legendary Mizners* (1953)

27 Venice is like eating an entire box of chocolate liqueurs in
one go.
   Truman Capote 1924–84: in *Observer* 26 November 1961

28 Paris is a movable feast.
   Ernest Hemingway 1899–1961: *A Movable Feast* (1964)

Pleasure

1 *Trahit sua quemque voluptas.*
Everyone is dragged on by their favourite pleasure.
   Virgil 70–19 BC: *Eclogues*

2 Who loves not woman, wine, and song
Remains a fool his whole life long.
   Martin Luther 1483–1546: attributed (later inscribed, in
   German, in the Luther room in the Wartburg)

3 Pleasure is nothing else but the intermission of pain.
   John Selden 1584–1654: *Table Talk* (1689) 'Pleasure'

4 Remorse, the fatal egg by pleasure laid.
   William Cowper 1731–1800: 'The Progress of Error' (1782)

5 One half of the world cannot understand the pleasures of the
other.
   Jane Austen 1775–1817: *Emma* (1816)

6 Ever let the fancy roam,
Pleasure never is at home.
     John Keats 1795–1821: 'Fancy' (1820)

7 Pleasure's a sin, and sometimes sin's a pleasure.
     Lord Byron 1788–1824: *Don Juan* (1819–24)

8 Let us have wine and women, mirth and laughter,
Sermons and soda-water the day after.
     Lord Byron 1788–1824: *Don Juan* (1819–24)

9 The greatest pleasure I know, is to do a good action by
stealth, and to have it found out by accident.
     Charles Lamb 1775–1834: 'Table Talk by the late Elia' in
     The Athenaeum 4 January 1834

10 The Puritan hated bear-baiting, not because it gave pain to
the bear, but because it gave pleasure to the spectators.
     Lord Macaulay 1800–59: *History of England* vol. 1 (1849)

11 Life would be very pleasant if it were not for its enjoyments.
     R. S. Surtees 1805–64: *Mr Facey Romford's Hounds* (1865)

12 I'm tired of Love: I'm still more tired of Rhyme.
But Money gives me pleasure all the time.
     Hilaire Belloc 1870–1953: 'Fatigued' (1923)

13 All the things I really like to do are either illegal, immoral,
or fattening.
     Alexander Woollcott 1887–1943: in R. E. Drennan *Wit's
     End* (1973)

14 There's no greater bliss in life than when the plumber
eventually comes to unblock your drains. No writer can give
that sort of pleasure.
     Victoria Glendinning 1937– : *Observer* 3 January 1993

Poetry

1 Skilled or unskilled, we all scribble poems.
     Horace 65–8 BC: *Epistles*

2 [The poet] cometh unto you, with a tale which holdeth
children from play, and old men from the chimney corner.
     Philip Sidney 1554–86: *The Defence of Poetry* (1595)

3 Rhyme being...but the invention of a barbarous age, to set
off wretched matter and lame metre.
   John Milton 1608–74: *Paradise Lost* (1667) 'The Verse'
   (preface, 1668)

4   Wit will shine
Through the harsh cadence of a rugged line.
   John Dryden 1631–1700: 'To the Memory of Mr Oldham'
   (1684)

5 [BOSWELL:] Sir, what is poetry?
   [JOHNSON:] Why Sir, it is much easier to say what it is not. We
   all *know* what light is; but it is not easy to *tell* what it is.
   Samuel Johnson 1709–84: in James Boswell *Life of Johnson*
   (1791) 12 April 1776

6 Poetry is the spontaneous overflow of powerful feelings: it
takes its origin from emotion recollected in tranquillity.
   William Wordsworth 1770–1850: *Lyrical Ballads* (2nd ed.,
   1802) preface

7 That willing suspension of disbelief for the moment, which
constitutes poetic faith.
   Samuel Taylor Coleridge 1772–1834: *Biographia Literaria*
   (1817)

8   Most wretched men
Are cradled into poetry by wrong:
They learn in suffering what they teach in song.
   Percy Bysshe Shelley 1792–1822: 'Julian and Maddalo'
   (1818)

9 If poetry comes not as naturally as the leaves to a tree it had
better not come at all.
   John Keats 1795–1821: letter to Taylor, 27 February 1818

10 Poetry is the record of the best and happiest moments of the
happiest and best minds.
   Percy Bysshe Shelley 1792–1822: *A Defence of Poetry*
   (written 1821)

11 Poets are the unacknowledged legislators of the world.
   Percy Bysshe Shelley 1792–1822: *A Defence of Poetry*
   (written 1821)

12 Prose = words in their best order;—poetry = the *best* words
in the best order.
   Samuel Taylor Coleridge 1772–1834: *Table Talk* (1835)
   12 July 1827

13 Prose is when all the lines except the last go on to the end.
Poetry is when some of them fall short of it.
> **Jeremy Bentham** 1748–1832: in M. St. J. Packe *Life of John Stuart Mill* (1954)

14 Poetry is a subject as precise as geometry.
> **Gustave Flaubert** 1821–80: letter to Louise Colet, 14 August 1853

15 The difference between genuine poetry and the poetry of Dryden, Pope, and all their school, is briefly this: their poetry is conceived and composed in their wits, genuine poetry is conceived and composed in the soul.
> **Matthew Arnold** 1822–88: *Essays in Criticism* (1888)

16 I said 'a line will take us hours maybe,
Yet if it does not seem a moment's thought
Our stitching and unstitching has been naught.'
> **W. B. Yeats** 1865–1939: 'Adam's Curse' (1904)

17 Poetry must be *as well written as prose.*
> **Ezra Pound** 1885–1972: letter to Harriet Monroe, January 1915

18 All a poet can do today is warn.
> **Wilfred Owen** 1893–1918: *Poems* (1963) preface (written 1918)

19 We make out of the quarrel with others, rhetoric, but of the quarrel with ourselves, poetry.
> **W. B. Yeats** 1865–1939: *Essays* (1924)

20 A poem should not mean
But be.
> **Archibald MacLeish** 1892–1982: 'Ars Poetica' (1926)

21 Of all the literary scenes
Saddest this sight to me:
The graves of little magazines
Who died to make verse free.
> **Keith Preston** 1884–1927: 'The Liberators'

22 As soon as war is declared it will be impossible to hold the poets back. Rhyme is still the most effective drum.
> **Jean Giraudoux** 1882–1944: *La Guerre de Troie n'aura pas lieu* (1935) tr. Christopher Fry as *Tiger at the Gates*, 1955

23 Writing a book of poetry is like dropping a rose petal down
the Grand Canyon and waiting for the echo.
   Don Marquis 1878–1937: in E. Anthony *O Rare Don
   Marquis* (1962)

24 Like a piece of ice on a hot stove the poem must ride on its
own melting. A poem may be worked over once it is in being,
but may not be worried into being.
   Robert Frost 1874–1963: *Collected Poems* (1939) 'The Figure
   a Poem Makes'

25 It is the logic of our times,
No subject for immortal verse—
That we who lived by honest dreams
Defend the bad against the worse.
   C. Day-Lewis 1904–72: 'Where are the War Poets?' (1943)

26 I'd as soon write free verse as play tennis with the net down.
   Robert Frost 1874–1963: in E. Lathem *Interviews with
   Robert Frost* (1966)

27 Most people ignore most poetry
because
most poetry ignores most people.
   Adrian Mitchell 1932– : *Poems* (1964)

28 A poet's hope: to be,
like some valley cheese,
local, but prized elsewhere.
   W. H. Auden 1907–73: 'Shorts II' (1976)

Poets

1 Dr Donne's verses are like the peace of God; they pass all
understanding.
   James I 1566–1625: remark recorded by Archdeacon Plume
   (1630–1704)

2 All poets are mad.
   Robert Burton 1577–1640: *Anatomy of Melancholy* (1621–51)
   'Democritus to the Reader'

3 He invades authors like a monarch; and what would be theft
in other poets, is only victory in him.
   John Dryden 1631–1700: of Ben Jonson; *Essay of Dramatic
   Poesy* (1668)

4 'Tis sufficient to say [of Chaucer], according to the proverb, that here is God's plenty.
   John Dryden 1631–1700: *Fables Ancient and Modern* (1700)

5 Ev'n copious Dryden, wanted, or forgot,
   The last and greatest art, the art to blot.
   Alexander Pope 1688–1744: *Imitations of Horace* (1737)

6 Milton, Madam, was a genius that could cut a Colossus from a rock; but could not carve heads upon cherry-stones.
   Samuel Johnson 1709–84: to Hannah More, who had expressed a wonder that the poet who had written *Paradise Lost* should write such poor sonnets; in James Boswell *Life of Johnson* (1791) 13 June 1784

7 The reason Milton wrote in fetters when he wrote of Angels and God, and at liberty when of Devils and Hell, is because he was a true Poet, and of the Devil's party without knowing it.
   William Blake 1757–1827: *The Marriage of Heaven and Hell* (1790–3)

8 With Donne, whose muse on dromedary trots,
   Wreathe iron pokers into true-love knots.
   Samuel Taylor Coleridge 1772–1834: 'On Donne's Poetry' (1818)

9 A cloud-encircled meteor of the air,
   A hooded eagle among blinking owls.
   Percy Bysshe Shelley 1792–1822: of Coleridge, 'Letter to Maria Gisborne' (1820)

10 We learn from Horace, Homer sometimes sleeps;
   We feel without him: Wordsworth sometimes wakes.
   Lord Byron 1788–1824: *Don Juan* (1819–24)

11 Out-babying Wordsworth and out-glittering Keats.
   Edward Bulwer-Lytton 1803–73: of Tennyson, in *The New Timon* (1846)

12 He spoke, and loosed our heart in tears.
   He laid us as we lay at birth
   On the cool flowery lap of earth.
   Matthew Arnold 1822–88: of Wordsworth, 'Memorial Verses, April 1850' (1852)

13 In poetry, no less than in life, he is 'a beautiful and
ineffectual angel, beating in the void his luminous wings in
vain'.
   Matthew Arnold 1822–88: *Essays in Criticism* (1888)
   'Shelley'

14 Immature poets imitate; mature poets steal.
   T. S. Eliot 1888–1965: *The Sacred Wood* (1920)

15 Poets in our civilization, as it exists at present, must be
difficult.
   T. S. Eliot 1888–1965: 'The Metaphysical Poets' (1921)

16 The poet is always indebted to the universe, paying interest
and fines on sorrow.
   Vladimir Mayakovsky 1893–1930: 'Conversation with an
   Inspector of Taxes about Poetry' (1926), tr. D. Obolensky

17 You were silly like us; your gift survived it all:
The parish of rich women, physical decay,
Yourself. Mad Ireland hurt you into poetry.
   W. H. Auden 1907–73: 'In Memory of W. B. Yeats' (1940)

18 [*The Waste Land*] was only the relief of a personal and wholly
insignificant grouse against life; it is just a piece of
rhythmical grumbling.
   T. S. Eliot 1888–1965: *The Waste Land* (ed. Valerie Eliot,
   1971) epigraph

19 Self-contempt, well-grounded.
   F. R. Leavis 1895–1978: on the foundation of T. S. Eliot's
   work, in *Times Literary Supplement* 21 October 1988

20 I used to think all poets were Byronic.
They're mostly wicked as a ginless tonic
And wild as pension plans.
   Wendy Cope 1945– : 'Triolet' (1986)

Political Comment

See also **Government, Political Parties, Politics**

1 Caesar had his Brutus—Charles the First, his Cromwell—and George the Third—('Treason,' cried the Speaker)...*may profit by their example.* If *this* be treason, make the most of it.
   Patrick Henry 1736–99: speech in the Virginia assembly, May 1765

2 The Commons, faithful to their system, remained in a wise and masterly inactivity.
   James Mackintosh 1765–1832: *Vindiciae Gallicae* (1791)

3 The compact which exists between the North and the South is 'a covenant with death and an agreement with hell'.
   William Lloyd Garrison 1805–79: resolution adopted by the Massachusetts Anti-Slavery Society, 27 January 1843

4 I am for 'Peace, retrenchment, and reform', the watchword of the great Liberal party 30 years ago.
   John Bright 1811–89: speech at Birmingham, 28 April 1859

5 Meddle and muddle.
   Edward Stanley, 14th Earl of Derby 1799–1869: summarizing Earl Russell's foreign policy, in Speech on the Address, House of Lords, 4 February 1864

6 [Palmerston] once said that only three men in Europe had ever understood [the Schleswig-Holstein question], and of these the Prince Consort was dead, a Danish statesman (unnamed) was in an asylum, and he himself had forgotten it.
   Lord Palmerston 1784–1865: in R. W. Seton-Watson *Britain in Europe 1789–1914* (1937)

7 With malice toward none; with charity for all; with firmness in the right, as God gives us to see the right, let us strive on to finish the work we are in.
   Abraham Lincoln 1809–65: second inaugural address, 4 March 1865

8 This policy cannot succeed through speeches, and shooting-matches, and songs; it can only be carried out through blood and iron.
   Otto von Bismarck 1815–98: speech in the Prussian House

of Deputies, 28 January 1886. In an earlier speech,
30 September 1862, Bismarck used the form 'iron and blood'

9 We are all socialists now.
   William Harcourt 1827–1904: during the passage of the
   1894 budget, which equalized death duties on real and
   personal property (attributed)

10 A mastiff? It is the right hon. Gentleman's poodle.
   David Lloyd George 1863–1945: on the House of Lords and
   Lord Balfour respectively; speech, House of Commons,
   26 June 1907

11 We had better wait and see.
   Herbert Asquith 1852–1928: referring to the rumour that
   the House of Lords was to be flooded with new Liberal
   peers to ensure the passage of the Finance Bill, 1910

12 There are three classes which need sanctuary more than
   others—birds, wild flowers, and Prime Ministers.
   Stanley Baldwin 1867–1947: in *Observer* 24 May 1925

13 The most conservative man in this world is the British Trade
   Unionist when you want to change him.
   Ernest Bevin 1881–1951: speech at Trades Union Congress,
   8 September 1927

14 Do not run up your nose dead against the Pope or the NUM!
   Stanley Baldwin 1867–1947: in Lord Butler *The Art of
   Memory* (1982)

15 My [foreign] policy is to be able to take a ticket at Victoria
   Station and go anywhere I damn well please.
   Ernest Bevin 1881–1951: in *Spectator* 20 April 1951

16 If you carry this resolution you will send Britain's Foreign
   Secretary naked into the conference chamber.
   Aneurin Bevan 1897–1960: speech at Labour Party
   Conference, 3 October 1957, against a motion proposing
   unilateral nuclear disarmament by the UK

17 Let us be frank about it: most of our people have never had it
   so good.
   Harold Macmillan 1894–1986: speech at Bedford, 20 July
   1957 ('You Never Had It So Good' was the Democratic Party
   slogan during the 1952 US election campaign)

18 I thought the best thing to do was to settle up these little
local difficulties, and then turn to the wider vision of the
Commonwealth.
   Harold Macmillan 1894–1986: statement at London airport
   on leaving for a Commonwealth tour, 7 January 1958,
   following the resignation of the Chancellor of the
   Exchequer and others

19 The wind of change is blowing through this continent, and,
whether we like it or not, this growth of [African] national
consciousness is a political fact.
   Harold Macmillan 1894–1986: speech at Cape Town,
   3 February 1960

20 And so, my fellow Americans: ask not what your country can
do for you—ask what you can do for your country.
   John F. Kennedy 1917–63: inaugural address, 20 January
   1961

21 Greater love hath no man than this, that he lay down his
friends for his life.
   Jeremy Thorpe 1929– : on Harold Macmillan sacking seven
   of his Cabinet on 13 July 1962

22 I was determined that no British government should be
brought down by the action of two tarts.
   Harold Macmillan 1894–1986: comment on the Profumo
   affair, July 1963

23 A week is a long time in politics.
   Harold Wilson 1916– : probably first said at the time of
   the 1964 sterling crisis. See Nigel Rees *Sayings of the
   Century* (1984)

24 Think of it! A second Chamber selected by the Whips. A
seraglio of eunuchs.
   Michael Foot 1913– : speech, House of Commons,
   3 February 1969

25 The unpleasant and unacceptable face of capitalism.
   Edward Heath 1916– : speech, House of Commons, 15 May
   1973, on the Lonrho affair

26 We shall not be diverted from our course. To those waiting
with bated breath for that favourite media catch-phrase, the

U-turn, I have only this to say. 'You turn if you want; the
lady's not for turning.'
  Margaret Thatcher 1925– : speech at Conservative Party
  Conference, 10 October 1980

27 There are three bodies no sensible man directly challenges:
the Roman Catholic Church, the Brigade of Guards and the
National Union of Mineworkers.
  Harold Macmillan 1894–1986: in *Observer* 22 February
  1981

28 First of all the Georgian silver goes, and then all that
nice furniture that used to be in the saloon. Then the
Canalettos go.
  Harold Macmillan 1894–1986: speech on privatization to
  the Tory Reform Group, 8 November 1985

Political Parties

See also **Politicians, Politics**

1 Party-spirit, which at best is but the madness of many for the
gain of a few.
  Alexander Pope 1688–1744: letter to E. Blount, 27 August
  1714

2 A Conservative Government is an organized hypocrisy.
  Benjamin Disraeli 1804–81: speech, House of Commons
  17 March 1845

3 Party is organized opinion.
  Benjamin Disraeli 1804–81: speech at Oxford, 25 November
  1864

4 Damn your principles! Stick to your party.
  Benjamin Disraeli 1804–81: believed to have been said to
  Edward Bulwer-Lytton; attributed in E. Latham *Famous
  Sayings and their Authors* (1904)

5 CONSERVATIVE, *n.* A statesman who is enamoured of existing
evils, as distinguished from the Liberal, who wishes to
replace them with others.
  Ambrose Bierce 1842–*c.*1914: *The Cynic's Word Book* (1906)

6 The more you read and observe about this Politics thing, you
   got to admit that each party is worse than the other. The one
   that's out always looks the best.
   Will Rogers 1879–1935: *Illiterate Digest* (1924)

7 The mules of politics: without pride of ancestry, or hope of
   posterity.
   John O'Connor Power b. 1846: of the Liberal Unionists, in
   H. H. Asquith *Memories and Reflections* (1928)

8 The language of priorities is the religion of Socialism.
   Aneurin Bevan 1897–1960: speech at Labour Party
   Conference, 8 June 1949

9 If they [the Republicans] will stop telling lies about the
   Democrats, we will stop telling the truth about them.
   Adlai Stevenson 1900–65: speech during 1952 Presidential
   campaign

10 There are some of us...who will fight and fight and fight
   again to save the Party we love.
   Hugh Gaitskell 1906–63: speech at Labour Party
   Conference, 5 October 1960

11 Loyalty is the Tory's secret weapon.
   Lord Kilmuir 1900–67: in Anthony Sampson *Anatomy of
   Britain* (1962)

12 A great party is not to be brought down because of a scandal
   by a woman of easy virtue and a proved liar.
   Lord Hailsham 1907– : BBC television interview on the
   Profumo affair; in *The Times* 14 June 1963

Politicians

See also **Political Comment, Politics**

1   Get thee glass eyes;
   And, like a scurvy politician, seem
   To see the things thou dost not.
   William Shakespeare 1564–1616: *King Lear* (1605–6)

2 The greatest art of a politician is to render vice serviceable to
   the cause of virtue.
   Henry St John, 1st Viscount Bolingbroke 1678–1751:

comment (c.1728), in Joseph Spence *Observations,*
Anecdotes, and Characters (1820)

3 All those men have their price.
   Robert Walpole 1676-1745: of fellow parliamentarians; in
   W. Coxe *Memoirs of Sir Robert Walpole* (1798)

4 Your representative owes you, not his industry only, but his
   judgement; and he betrays, instead of serving you, if he
   sacrifices it to your opinion.
   Edmund Burke 1729-97: speech, 3 November 1774

5 Not merely a chip of the old 'block', but the old block itself.
   Edmund Burke 1729-97: on the younger Pitt's maiden
   speech, February 1781

6 If a due participation of office is a matter of right, how are
   vacancies to be obtained? Those by death are few; by
   resignation none.
   Thomas Jefferson 1743-1826: letter to E. Shipman and
   others, 12 July 1801 (usually quoted 'Few die and none
   resign')

7 When a man assumes a public trust, he should consider
   himself as public property.
   Thomas Jefferson 1743-1826: to Baron von Humboldt, 1807,
   in B. L. Rayner *Life of Jefferson* (1834)

8 What I want is men who will support me when I am in the
   wrong.
   Lord Melbourne 1779-1848: replying to a politician who
   said 'I will support you as long as you are in the right'; in
   Lord David Cecil *Lord M* (1954)

9 A constitutional statesman is in general a man of common
   opinion and uncommon abilities.
   Walter Bagehot 1826-77: *Biographical Studies* (1881)

10 The prospect of a lot
   Of dull MPs in close proximity,
   All thinking for themselves is what
   No man can face with equanimity.
   W. S. Gilbert 1836-1911: *Iolanthe* (1882)

11 A lath of wood painted to look like iron.
   Otto von Bismarck 1815-98: describing Lord Salisbury;
   attributed, but vigorously denied by Sidney Whitman in
   Personal Reminiscences of Prince Bismarck (1902)

12 He knows nothing; and he thinks he knows everything. That
points clearly to a political career.
  George Bernard Shaw 1856–1950: *Major Barbara* (1907)

13 'Do you pray for the senators, Dr Hale?' 'No, I look at the
senators and I pray for the country.'
  Edward Everett Hale 1822–1909: Van Wyck Brooks *New
  England Indian Summer* (1940)

14 He [Labouchere] did not object to the old man always having
a card up his sleeve, but he did object to his insinuating that
the Almighty had placed it there.
  Henry Labouchere 1831–1912: on Gladstone's 'frequent
  appeals to a higher power'; in Earl Curzon *Modern
  Parliamentary Eloquence* (1913)

15 We all know that Prime Ministers are wedded to the truth,
but like other married couples they sometimes live apart.
  Saki (H. H. Munro) 1870–1916: *The Unbearable Bassington*
  (1912)

16 For twenty years he [H. H. Asquith] has held a season-ticket
on the line of least resistance and has gone wherever the
train of events has carried him, lucidly justifying his position
at whatever point he has happened to find himself.
  Leo Amery 1873–1955: *Quarterly Review* July 1914

17 They [parliament] are a lot of hard-faced men who look as if
they had done very well out of the war.
  Stanley Baldwin 1867–1947: in J. M. Keynes *Economic
  Consequences of the Peace* (1919)

18 I thought he was a young man of promise, but it appears he
is a young man of promises.
  Arthur James Balfour 1848–1930: describing Churchill, in
  Winston Churchill *My Early Life* (1930)

19 I have waited 50 years to see the boneless wonder [Ramsay
Macdonald] sitting on the Treasury Bench.
  Winston Churchill 1874–1965: speech, House of Commons,
  28 January 1931

20 The time has come for all good men to rise above principle.
  Huey Long 1893–1935: attributed

21 a politician is an arse upon
which everyone has sat except a man.
  e. e. cummings 1894–1962: *1 x 1* (1944) no. 10

22 The voice we heard was that of Mr Churchill but the mind
was that of Lord Beaverbrook.
   Clement Attlee 1883–1967: speech on radio, 5 June 1945

23 [Winston Churchill] does not talk the language of the 20th
century but that of the 18th. He is still fighting Blenheim all
over again. His only answer to a difficult situation is send
a gun-boat.
   Aneurin Bevan 1897–1960: speech at Labour Party
   Conference, 2 October 1951

24 Damn it all, you can't have the crown of thorns *and* the
thirty pieces of silver.
   Aneurin Bevan 1897–1960: on his position in the Labour
   Party, *c.*1956; in Michael Foot *Aneurin Bevan* vol. 2 (1973)

25 Forever poised between a cliché and an indiscretion.
   Harold Macmillan 1894–1986: on the life of a Foreign
   Secretary; in *Newsweek* 30 April 1956

26 I am not going to spend any time whatsoever in attacking the
Foreign Secretary…If we complain about the tune, there is
no reason to attack the monkey when the organ grinder is
present.
   Aneurin Bevan 1897–1960: during a debate on the Suez
   crisis, House of Commons, 16 May 1957

27 A statesman is a politician who's been dead 10 or 15 years.
   Harry S. Truman 1884–1972: in *New York World Telegram
   and Sun* 12 April 1958

28 Listening to a speech by Chamberlain is like paying a visit to
Woolworth's: everything in its place and nothing above
sixpence.
   Aneurin Bevan 1897–1960: in Michael Foot *Aneurin Bevan*
   vol. 1 (1962)

29 Too clever by half.
   Lord Salisbury 1893–1972: of Iain Macleod, Colonial
   Secretary; speech, House of Lords, 7 March 1961

30 It is the ability to foretell what is going to happen tomorrow,
next week, next month, and next year. And to have the
ability afterwards to explain why it didn't happen.
   Winston Churchill 1874–1965: on the qualifications for
   becoming a politician, in B. Adler *Churchill Wit* (1965)

31 A sheep in sheep's clothing.
   Winston Churchill 1874–1965: of Clement Attlee, in Lord
   Home *The Way the Wind Blows* (1976)

32 The Stag at Bay with the mentality of a fox at large.
   Bernard Levin 1928– : of Harold Macmillan, in *The
   Pendulum Years* (1970)

33 A statesman is a politician who places himself at the service
   of the nation. A politician is a statesman who places the
   nation at his service.
   Georges Pompidou 1911–74: in *Observer* 30 December 1973
   'Sayings of the Year'

34 This is a rotten argument, but it should be good enough for
   their lordships on a hot summer afternoon.
   Anonymous: annotation to a ministerial brief, said to have
   been read out inadvertently in the House of Lords; in Lord
   Home *The Way the Wind Blows* (1976)

35 It is not necessary that every time he rises he should give his
   famous imitation of a semi-house-trained polecat.
   Michael Foot 1913– : of Norman Tebbit; speech, House of
   Commons, 2 March 1978

36 Like being savaged by a dead sheep.
   Denis Healey 1917– : on being criticized by Geoffrey Howe
   in the House of Commons, 14 June 1978

37 It is, I think, good evidence of life after death.
   Lord Soper 1903– : on the quality of debate in the House of
   Lords, in *Listener* 17 August 1978

38 A triumph of the embalmer's art.
   Gore Vidal 1925– : of Ronald Reagan, in *Observer* 26 April
   1981

39 The only safe pleasure for a parliamentarian is a bag of
   boiled sweets.
   Julian Critchley 1930– : *Listener* 10 June 1982

40 Comrades, this man has a nice smile, but he's got iron teeth.
   Andrei Gromyko 1909–89: on Mikhail Gorbachev; speech to
   Soviet Communist Party Central Committee, 11 March 1985

41 There are no true friends in politics. We are all sharks
   circling, and waiting, for traces of blood to appear in the
   water.
   Alan Clark 1928– : diary, 30 November 1990

42 I could name eight people—half of those eight are barmy.
How many apples short of a picnic?
    John Major 1943- : on Tory critics, 19 September 1993

43 Being an MP is the sort of job all working-class parents want
for their children—clean, indoors and no heavy lifting.
    Diane Abbott 1953- : *Observer* 23 January 1994 'Sayings of
the Week'

Politics

See also **Democracy, Government, Political
Comment, Political Parties, Politicians,
Voting**

1 Man is by nature a political animal.
    Aristotle 384–322 BC: *Politics*

2 Most schemes of political improvement are very laughable
things.
    Samuel Johnson 1709–84: in James Boswell *Life of Johnson*
(1791) 26 October 1769

3 Magnanimity in politics is not seldom the truest wisdom; and
a great empire and little minds go ill together.
    Edmund Burke 1729–97: *On Conciliation with America* (1775)

4 In politics the middle way is none at all.
    John Adams 1735–1826: letter to Horatio Gates, 23 March
1776

5 In politics, what begins in fear usually ends in folly.
    Samuel Taylor Coleridge 1772–1834: *Table Talk* (1835)
5 October 1830

6 'Two nations; between whom there is no intercourse and no
sympathy; who are as ignorant of each other's habits,
thoughts, and feelings, as if they were dwellers in different
zones, or inhabitants of different planets...' 'You speak of—'
said Egremont, hesitatingly, 'THE RICH AND THE POOR.'
    Benjamin Disraeli 1804–81: *Sybil* (1845)

7 What is a communist? One who hath yearnings
For equal division of unequal earnings.
    Ebenezer Elliott 1781–1849: 'Epigram' (1850)

8 Politics is the art of the possible.
   Otto von Bismarck 1815–98: in conversation with Meyer
   von Waldeck, 11 August 1867

9 Politics is perhaps the only profession for which no
   preparation is thought necessary.
   Robert Louis Stevenson 1850–94: *Familiar Studies of Men
   and Books* (1882)

10 Politics...has always been the systematic organization of
   hatreds.
   Henry Brooks Adams 1838–1918: *The Education of Henry
   Adams* (1907)

11 Practical politics consists in ignoring facts.
   Henry Brooks Adams 1838–1918: *The Education of Henry
   Adams* (1907)

12 If you want to succeed in politics, you must keep your
   conscience well under control.
   David Lloyd George 1863–1945: in Lord Riddell's diary,
   23 April 1919

13 Who? Whom?
   Lenin 1870–1924: definition of political science, meaning
   'Who will outstrip whom?'; in *Polnoe Sobranie Sochinenii*
   (1979) 17 October 1921, and elsewhere

14 I do not know which makes a man more conservative—to
   know nothing but the present, or nothing but the past.
   John Maynard Keynes 1883–1946: *The End of Laissez-Faire*
   (1926)

15 I never dared be radical when young
   For fear it would make me conservative when old.
   Robert Frost 1874–1963: 'Precaution' (1936)

16 Politics is war without bloodshed while war is politics with
   bloodshed.
   Mao Tse-tung 1893–1976: lecture, 1938, in *Selected Works*
   (1965)

17 Politics is the art of preventing people from taking part in
   affairs which properly concern them.
   Paul Valéry 1871–1945: *Tel Quel 2* (1943)

18 Political language…is designed to make lies sound truthful
and murder respectable, and to give an appearance of solidity
to pure wind.
   George Orwell 1903–50: *Shooting an Elephant* (1950)
   'Politics and the English Language'

19 [Russian Communism is] the illegitimate child of Karl Marx
and Catherine the Great.
   Clement Attlee 1883–1967: speech at Aarhus University,
   11 April 1956

20 Politics is not the art of the possible. It consists in choosing
between the disastrous and the unpalatable.
   J. K. Galbraith 1908– : letter to President Kennedy,
   2 March 1962

21 The great nations have always acted like gangsters, and the
small nations like prostitutes.
   Stanley Kubrick 1928– : in *Guardian* 5 June 1963

22 Socialism can only arrive by bicycle.
   José Antonio Viera Gallo 1943– : in Ivan Illich *Energy
   and Equity* (1974) epigraph

Pollution

See also **Environment**

1 Woe to her that is filthy and polluted, to the oppressing city!
   Bible: Zephaniah

2 It goes so heavily with my disposition that this goodly frame,
the earth, seems to me a sterile promóntory; this most
excellent canopy, the air, look you, this brave o'erhanging
firmament, this majestical roof fretted with golden fire, why,
it appears no other thing to me but a foul and pestilent
congregation of vapours.
   William Shakespeare 1564–1616: *Hamlet* (1601)

3 The river Rhine, it is well known,
Doth wash your city of Cologne;
But tell me, Nymphs, what power divine
Shall henceforth wash the river Rhine?
   Samuel Taylor Coleridge 1772–1834: 'Cologne' (1834)

4 And all is seared with trade; bleared, smeared with toil;
And wears man's smudge and shares man's smell.
  Gerard Manley Hopkins 1844–89: 'God's Grandeur'
  (written 1877)

5 Man has been endowed with reason, with the power to
create, so that he can add to what he's been given. But up to
now he hasn't been a creator, only a destroyer. Forests keep
disappearing, rivers dry up, wild life's become extinct, the
climate's ruined and the land grows poorer and uglier every
day.
  Anton Chekhov 1860–1904: *Uncle Vanya* (1897)

6 NOISE, *n*. A stench in the ear...The chief product and
authenticating sign of civilization.
  Ambrose Bierce 1842–?1914: *Devil's Dictionary* (1911)

7 The sanitary and mechanical age we are now entering makes
up for the mercy it grants to our sense of smell by the
ferocity with which it assails our sense of hearing. As usual,
what we call 'progress' is the exchange of one nuisance for
another nuisance.
  Havelock Ellis 1859–1939: *Impressions and Comments*
  (1914)

8 Clear the air! clean the sky! wash the wind!
  T. S. Eliot 1888–1965: *Murder in the Cathedral* (1935)

Poverty

1 What mean ye that ye beat my people to pieces, and grind the
faces of the poor?
  Bible: Isaiah

2 The misfortunes of poverty carry with them nothing harder
to bear than that it makes men ridiculous.
  Juvenal AD *c*.60–*c*.130: *Satires*

3 I want there to be no peasant in my kingdom so poor that he
is unable to have a chicken in his pot every Sunday.
  Henri IV 1553–1610: in H. de Péréfixe *Histoire de Henri le
  Grand* (1681)

4 Come away; poverty's catching.
  Aphra Behn 1640–89: *The Rover* pt. 2 (1681)

5 There is no scandal like rags, nor any crime so shameful as poverty.
   George Farquhar 1678-1707: *The Beaux' Stratagem* (1707)

6 Give me not poverty lest I steal.
   Daniel Defoe 1660-1731: *Moll Flanders* (1721)

7 This mournful truth is ev'rywhere confessed,
   Slow rises worth, by poverty depressed.
   Samuel Johnson 1709-84: *London* (1738)

8 Resolve not to be poor: whatever you have, spend less.
   Poverty is a great enemy to human happiness; it certainly
   destroys liberty, and it makes some virtues impracticable,
   and others extremely difficult.
   Samuel Johnson 1709-84: letter to James Boswell,
   7 December 1782

9 The murmuring poor, who will not fast in peace.
   George Crabbe 1754-1832: 'The Newspaper' (1785)

10 The poor are Europe's blacks.
   Nicolas-Sébastien Chamfort 1741-94: *Maximes et Pensées*
   (1796)

11 Oh! God! that bread should be so dear,
   And flesh and blood so cheap!
   Thomas Hood 1799-1845: 'The Song of the Shirt' (1843)

12 Poverty is no disgrace to a man, but it is confoundedly
   inconvenient.
   Sydney Smith 1771-1845: in J. Potter Briscoe *Sidney Smith:
   His Wit and Wisdom* (1900)

13 They [the poor] have to labour in the face of the majestic
   equality of the law, which forbids the rich as well as the poor
   to sleep under bridges, to beg in the streets, and to steal
   bread.
   Anatole France 1844-1924: *Le Lys rouge* (1894)

14 The greatest of evils and the worst of crimes is poverty.
   George Bernard Shaw 1856-1950: *Major Barbara* (1907)
   preface

15 There's nothing surer,
   The rich get rich and the poor get children.
   Gus Kahn 1886-1941 and **Raymond B. Egan** 1890-1952: 'Ain't
   We Got Fun' (1921 song)

16 Battles and sex are the only free diversions in slum life.
   Couple them with drink, which costs money, and you have

the three principal outlets for that escape complex which is
for ever working in the tenement dweller's subconscious
mind.

Alexander McArthur and **H. Kingsley Long**: *No Mean
City* (1935)

17 People don't resent having nothing nearly as much as too
little.

Ivy Compton-Burnett 1884–1969: *A Family and a Fortune*
(1939)

18 Sixteen tons, what do you get?
Another day older and deeper in debt.
Say brother, don't you call me 'cause I can't go
I owe my soul to the company store.

Merle Travis 1917–83: 'Sixteen Tons' (1947 song)

19 Anyone who has ever struggled with poverty knows how
extremely expensive it is to be poor.

James Baldwin 1924–87: *Nobody Knows My Name* (1961)

Power

1   Man, proud man,
Drest in a little brief authority.

William Shakespeare 1564–1616: *Measure for Measure*
(1604)

2 Men in great place are thrice servants: servants of the
sovereign or state, servants of fame, and servants of business.

Francis Bacon 1561–1626: *Essays* (1625) 'Of Great Place'

3 All rising to great place is by a winding stair.

Francis Bacon 1561–1626: *Essays* (1625) 'Of Great Place'

4 Power is so apt to be insolent and Liberty to be saucy, that
they are very seldom upon good terms.

George Savile, Marquess of Halifax 1633–95: *Political,
Moral, and Miscellaneous Thoughts* (1750)

5 Nature has left this tincture in the blood,
That all men would be tyrants if they could.

Daniel Defoe 1660–1731: *The History of the Kentish Petition*
(1712–13)

6 The strongest poison ever known
Came from Caesar's laurel crown.
   William Blake 1757–1827: 'Auguries of Innocence' (*c.*1803)

7 Power tends to corrupt and absolute power corrupts
absolutely.
   Lord Acton 1834–1902: letter to Bishop Mandell Creighton,
   3 April 1887

8 Whatever happens we have got
The Maxim Gun, and they have not.
   Hilaire Belloc 1870–1953: *The Modern Traveller* (1898)

9 A man may build himself a throne of bayonets, but he cannot
sit on it.
   Dean Inge 1860–1954: *Philosophy of Plotinus* (1923), quoted
   by Boris Yeltsin at the time of the failed military coup in
   Russia, August 1991

10 The Pope! How many divisions has *he* got?
   Joseph Stalin 1879–1953: on being asked to encourage
   Catholicism in Russia by way of conciliating the Pope,
   13 May 1935

11 The hand that signed the treaty bred a fever,
And famine grew, and locusts came;
Great is the hand that holds dominion over
Man by a scribbled name.
   Dylan Thomas 1914–53: 'The hand that signed the paper
   felled a city' (1936)

12 Political power grows out of the barrel of a gun.
   Mao Tse-tung 1893–1976: speech, 6 November 1938

13 When he laughed, respectable senators burst with laughter,
And when he cried the little children died in the streets
   W. H. Auden 1907–73: 'Epitaph on a Tyrant' (1940)

14 Who controls the past controls the future: who controls the
present controls the past.
   George Orwell 1903–50: *Nineteen Eighty-Four* (1949)

15 You only have power over people as long as you don't take
everything away from them. But when you've robbed a man
of *everything* he's no longer in your power—he's free again.
   Alexander Solzhenitsyn 1918– : *The First Circle* (1968)

16 I'll make him an offer he can't refuse.
   Mario Puzo 1920– : *The Godfather* (1969)

17 Power is the great aphrodisiac.
   Henry Kissinger 1923- : in *New York Times* 19 January
   1971

Practicality

1 Common sense is the best distributed commodity in the
   world, for every man is convinced that he is well supplied
   with it.
   René Descartes 1596-1650: *Le Discours de la méthode* (1637)

2 'Tis use alone that sanctifies expense,
   And splendour borrows all her rays from sense.
   Alexander Pope 1688-1744: 'To Lord Burlington' (1731)

3 Whenever our neighbour's house is on fire, it cannot be
   amiss for the engines to play a little on our own.
   Edmund Burke 1729-97: *Reflections on the Revolution in
   France* (1790)

4 Put your trust in God, my boys, and keep your powder dry.
   Valentine Blacker 1728-1823: 'Oliver's Advice' (1856),
   often attributed to Oliver Cromwell himself

5 It's grand, and you canna expect to be baith grand and
   comfortable.
   J. M. Barrie 1860-1937: *The Little Minister* (1891)

6 So I really think that American gentlemen are the best after
   all, because kissing your hand may make you feel very very
   good but a diamond and safire bracelet lasts forever.
   Anita Loos 1893-1981: *Gentlemen Prefer Blondes* (1925)

7 Praise the Lord and pass the ammunition.
   Howell Forgy 1908-83: at Pearl Harbor, 7 December 1941,
   while sailors passed ammunition by hand to the deck; later
   title of song by Frank Loesser, 1942

8 Life is too short to stuff a mushroom.
   Shirley Conran 1932- : *Superwoman* (1975)

Praise

1 But when I tell him he hates flatterers,
   He says he does, being then most flattered.
   William Shakespeare 1564-1616: *Julius Caesar* (1599)

2 It has been well said that 'the arch-flatterer with whom all
   the petty flatterers have intelligence is a man's self.'
   Francis Bacon 1561-1626: *Essays* (1625) 'Of Love'

3 He who discommendeth others obliquely commendeth
   himself.
   Sir Thomas Browne 1605-82: *Christian Morals* (1716)

4 Damn with faint praise, assent with civil leer,
   And without sneering, teach the rest to sneer.
   Alexander Pope 1688-1744: 'An Epistle to Dr Arbuthnot'
   (1735)

5 All censure of a man's self is oblique praise. It is in order to
   shew how much he can spare.
   Samuel Johnson 1709-84: in James Boswell *Life of Johnson*
   (1791) 25 April 1778

6 Imitation is the sincerest of flattery.
   Charles Caleb Colton 1780-1832: *Lacon* (1820)

7 No flowers, by request.
   Alfred Ainger 1837-1904: speech summarizing the
   principle of conciseness for contributors to the *Dictionary
   of National Biography*, 8 July 1897

8 The advantage of doing one's praising for oneself is that one
   can lay it on so thick and exactly in the right places.
   Samuel Butler 1835-1902: *The Way of All Flesh* (1903)

9 I suppose flattery hurts no one, that is, if he doesn't inhale.
   Adlai Stevenson 1900-65: television broadcast, 30 March
   1952

Prayer

1 Ask, and it shall be given you; seek, and ye shall find; knock,
   and it shall be opened unto you.
   Bible: St Matthew

2 My words fly up, my thoughts remain below:
Words without thoughts never to heaven go.
  William Shakespeare 1564–1616: *Hamlet* (1601)

3 I throw myself down in my Chamber, and I call in, and invite
God, and his Angels thither, and when they are there, I
neglect God and his Angels, for the noise of a fly, for the
rattling of a coach, for the whining of a door.
  John Donne 1572–1631: sermon, 12 December 1626 'At the
  Funeral of Sir William Cokayne'

4 O Lord! thou knowest how busy I must be this day: if I forget
thee, do not thou forget me.
  Jacob Astley 1579–1652: prayer before the Battle of
  Edgehill

5 No praying, it spoils business.
  Thomas Otway 1652–85: *Venice Preserved* (1682)

6 O God, if there be a God, save my soul, if I have a soul!
  Anonymous: prayer of a common soldier before the battle
  of Blenheim (1704)

7 One single grateful thought raised to heaven is the most
perfect prayer.
  G. E. Lessing 1729–81: *Minna von Barnhelm* (1767)

8 He prayeth best, who loveth best
All things both great and small.
  Samuel Taylor Coleridge 1772–1834: 'The Rime of the
  Ancient Mariner' (1798)

9 And lips say, 'God be pitiful,'
Who ne'er said, 'God be praised.'
  Elizabeth Barrett Browning 1806–61: 'The Cry of the
  Human' (1844)

10 I am just going to pray for you at St Paul's, but with no very
lively hope of success.
  Sydney Smith 1771–1845: in H. Pearson *The Smith of Smiths*
  (1934)

11 If thou shouldst never see my face again,
Pray for my soul. More things are wrought by prayer
Than this world dreams of.
  Alfred, Lord Tennyson 1809–92: *Idylls of the King* 'The
  Passing of Arthur' (1869)

12 Whatever a man prays for, he prays for a miracle. Every
prayer reduces itself to this: Great God, grant that twice two
be not four.
   Ivan Turgenev 1818–83: *Poems in Prose* (1881) 'Prayer'

13 To lift up the hands in prayer gives God glory, but a man
with a dungfork in his hand, a woman with a slop-pail, give
him glory too.
   Gerard Manley Hopkins 1844–89: 'The Principle or
   Foundation' (1882)

14 Bernard always had a few prayers in the hall and some
whiskey afterwards as he was rarther pious but Mr Salteena
was not very addicted to prayers so he marched up to bed.
   Daisy Ashford 1881–1972: *The Young Visiters* (1919)

15 The wish for prayer is a prayer in itself.
   Georges Bernanos 1888–1948: *Journal d'un curé de
   campagne* (1936)

16 The family that prays together stays together.
   Al Scalpone: motto devised for the Roman Catholic Family
   Rosary Crusade, 1947

Prejudice

See also **Race**

1 You call me misbeliever, cut-throat dog,
And spit upon my Jewish gabardine,
And all for use of that which is mine own.
   William Shakespeare 1564–1616: *The Merchant of Venice*
   (1596–8)

2 Drive out prejudices through the door, and they will return
through the window.
   Frederick the Great 1712–86: letter to Voltaire, 19 March
   1771

3 Am I not a man and a brother.
   Josiah Wedgwood 1730–95: legend on Wedgwood cameo,
   depicting a kneeling Negro slave in chains; reproduced in
   facsimile in E. Darwin *The Botanic Garden* pt. 1 (1791)

4 Prejudice is the child of ignorance.
   William Hazlitt 1778–1830: 'On Prejudice' (1830)

5 Without the aid of prejudice and custom, I should not be able
to find my way across the room.
William Hazlitt 1778-1830: 'On Prejudice' (1830)

6 Who's 'im, Bill?
A stranger!
'Eave 'arf a brick at 'im.
Punch: 1854

7 The only good Indian is a dead Indian.
Philip Henry Sheridan 1831-88: at Fort Cobb, January 1869
(attributed)

8 Bigotry may be roughly defined as the anger of men who
have no opinions.
G. K. Chesterton 1874-1936: *Heretics* (1905)

9 PREJUDICE, *n*. A vagrant opinion without visible means of
support.
Ambrose Bierce 1842-*c*.1914: *The Devil's Dictionary* (1911)

10 Minds are like parachutes. They only function when they are
open.
James Dewar 1842-1923: attributed

11 How odd
Of God
To choose
The Jews.
William Norman Ewer 1885-1976: in *Week-End Book* (1924)

12 But not so odd
As those who choose
A Jewish God,
But spurn the Jews.
Cecil Browne 1932- : reply to verse by William Norman
Ewer

13 I decline utterly to be impartial as between the fire brigade
and the fire.
Winston Churchill 1874-1965: replying to complaints of his
bias in editing the *British Gazette* during the General
Strike; House of Commons, 7 July 1926

14 Bigotry tries to keep truth safe in its hand
With a grip that kills it.
Rabindranath Tagore 1861-1941: *Fireflies* (1928)

15 And wherefore is he wearing such a conscience-stricken air?
Oh they're taking him to prison for the colour of his hair.
  A. E. Housman 1859–1936: *Collected Poems* (1939) 'Additional Poems' no. 18

16 Four legs good, two legs bad.
  George Orwell 1903–50: *Animal Farm* (1945)

17 Being a star has made it possible for me to get insulted in places where the average Negro could never *hope* to go and get insulted.
  Sammy Davis Jnr. 1925–90: in *Yes I Can* (1965)

18 It comes as a great shock around the age of 5, 6 or 7 to discover that the flag to which you have pledged allegiance, along with everybody else, has not pledged allegiance to you. It comes as a great shock to see Gary Cooper killing off the Indians and, although you are rooting for Gary Cooper, that the Indians are you.
  James Baldwin 1924–87: speech at Cambridge University, 17 February 1965

The Present

1 *Carpe diem, quam minimum credula postero.*
Seize the day, put no trust in the future.
  Horace 65–8 BC: *Odes*

2 Take therefore no thought for the morrow: for the morrow shall take thought for the things of itself. Sufficient unto the day is the evil thereof.
  Bible: St Matthew

3 Can ye not discern the signs of the times?
  Bible: St Matthew

4 What is love? 'tis not hereafter;
Present mirth hath present laughter;
What's to come is still unsure.
  William Shakespeare 1564–1616: *Twelfth Night* (1601)

5 Praise they that will times past, I joy to see
My self now live: this age best pleaseth me.
  Robert Herrick 1591–1674: 'The Present Time Best Pleaseth' (1648)

6 The present is the funeral of the past,
And man the living sepulchre of life.
   John Clare 1793-1864: 'The present is the funeral of the
   past' (written 1845)

7 Ah, fill the cup:—what boots it to repeat
How time is slipping underneath our feet:
Unborn TO-MORROW, and dead YESTERDAY,
Why fret about them if TO-DAY be sweet!
   Edward Fitzgerald 1809-83: *The Rubáiyát of Omar
   Khayyám* (1859)

8 The rule is, jam to-morrow and jam yesterday—but never
jam today.
   Lewis Carroll 1832-98: *Through the Looking-Glass* (1872)

9 He abhorred plastics, Picasso, sunbathing and
jazz—everything in fact that had happened in his own
lifetime.
   Evelyn Waugh 1903-66: *The Ordeal of Gilbert Pinfold* (1957)

Pride

1 Pride goeth before destruction, and an haughty spirit before
a fall.
   Bible: Proverbs

2 For whosoever exalteth himself shall be abased; and he that
humbleth himself shall be exalted.
   Bible: St Luke. See also St Matthew

3 He that is down needs fear no fall,
He that is low no pride.
He that is humble ever shall
Have God to be his guide.
   John Bunyan 1628-88: *The Pilgrim's Progress* (1684)
   'Shepherd Boy's Song'

4 And the Devil did grin, for his darling sin
Is pride that apes humility.
   Samuel Taylor Coleridge 1772-1834: 'The Devil's
   Thoughts' (1799)

5 We are so very 'umble.
   Charles Dickens 1812-70: *David Copperfield* (1850) Uriah
   Heep

6 As for conceit, what man will do any good who is not
   conceited? Nobody holds a good opinion of a man who has a
   low opinion of himself.
   Anthony Trollope 1815–82: *Orley Farm* (1862)

7 I can trace my ancestry back to a protoplasmal primordial
   atomic globule. Consequently, my family pride is something
   in-conceivable. I can't help it. I was born sneering.
   W. S. Gilbert 1836–1911: *The Mikado* (1885)

8 The tumult and the shouting dies—
   The captains and the kings depart—
   Still stands Thine ancient Sacrifice,
   An humble and a contrite heart.
   Lord God of Hosts, be with us yet,
   Lest we forget—lest we forget!
   Rudyard Kipling 1865–1936: 'Recessional' (1897)

9 PLEASE ACCEPT MY RESIGNATION. I DON'T WANT TO BELONG TO ANY
   CLUB THAT WILL ACCEPT ME AS A MEMBER.
   Groucho Marx 1895–1977: *Groucho and Me* (1959)

10 No one can make you feel inferior without your consent.
   Eleanor Roosevelt 1884–1962: in *Catholic Digest* August
   1960

11 In 1969 I published a small book on Humility. It was a
   pioneering work which has not, to my knowledge, been
   superseded.
   Lord Longford 1905– : *Tablet* 22 January 1994

Progress

1 The thing that hath been, it is that which shall be; and that
  which is done is that which shall be done: and there is no
  new thing under the sun.
  Bible: Ecclesiastes

2 We are like dwarfs on the shoulders of giants, so that we can
  see more than they, and things at a greater distance, not by
  virtue of any sharpness of sight on our part, or any physical
  distinction, but because we are carried high and raised up by
  their giant size.
  Bernard of Chartres d. *c.*1130: in John of Salisbury *The
  Metalogicon* (1159)

3 If I have seen further it is by standing on the shoulders of
giants.
Isaac Newton 1642–1727: letter to Robert Hooke, 5 February
1676

4 And he gave it for his opinion, that whoever could make two
ears of corn or two blades of grass to grow upon a spot of
ground where only one grew before, would deserve better of
mankind, and do more essential service to his country than
the whole race of politicians put together.
Jonathan Swift 1667–1745: *Gulliver's Travels* (1726)

5 Progress, therefore, is not an accident, but a necessity…It is
a part of nature.
Herbert Spencer 1820–1903: *Social Statics* (1850)

6 Progress, man's distinctive mark alone,
Not God's, and not the beasts': God is, they are,
Man partly is and wholly hopes to be.
Robert Browning 1812–89: 'A Death in the Desert' (1864)

7 Belief in progress is a doctrine of idlers and Belgians. It is
the individual relying upon his neighbours to do his work.
Charles Baudelaire 1821–67: *Journaux intimes* (1887), tr.
Christopher Isherwood

8 The reasonable man adapts himself to the world: the
unreasonable one persists in trying to adapt the world to
himself. Therefore all progress depends on the unreasonable
man.
George Bernard Shaw 1856–1950: *Man and Superman*
(1903)

9 Want is one only of five giants on the road of
reconstruction…the others are Disease, Ignorance, Squalor
and Idleness.
William Henry Beveridge 1879–1963: *Social Insurance and
Allied Services* (1942)

10 pity this busy monster, manunkind,
not. Progress is a comfortable disease.
e. e. cummings 1894–1962: *1 x 1* (1944) no. 14

11 Is it progress if a cannibal uses knife and fork?
Stanislaw Lec 1909–66: *Unkempt Thoughts* (1962)

Punishment see Crime and Punishment

Quotations

1 Some for renown on scraps of learning dote,
   And think they grow immortal as they quote.
   Edward Young 1683–1765: *The Love of Fame* (1725–8)

2 Every quotation contributes something to the stability or
   enlargement of the language.
   Samuel Johnson 1709–84: on citations of usage in a
   dictionary; *Dictionary of the English Language* (1755)
   preface

3 Classical quotation is the *parole* of literary men all over the
   world.
   Samuel Johnson 1709–84: in James Boswell *Life of Johnson*
   (1791) 8 May 1781

4 I hate quotation. Tell me what you know.
   Ralph Waldo Emerson 1803–82: diary, May 1849

5 Next to the originator of a good sentence is the first quoter of
   it.
   Ralph Waldo Emerson 1803–82: *Letters and Social Aims*
   (1876)

6 OSCAR WILDE: How I wish I had said that.
   WHISTLER: You will, Oscar, you will.
   James McNeill Whistler 1834–1903: in R. Ellman *Oscar
   Wilde* (1987)

7 What a good thing Adam had. When he said a good thing he
   knew nobody had said it before.
   Mark Twain 1835–1910: *Notebooks* (1935)

8 An anthology is like all the plums and orange peel picked out
   of a cake.
   Walter Raleigh 1861–1922: letter to Mrs Robert Bridges,
   15 January 1915

9 It is a good thing for an uneducated man to read books of
   quotations.
   Winston Churchill 1874–1965: *My Early Life* (1930)

10 The surest way to make a monkey of a man is to quote him.
   Robert Benchley 1889–1945: *My Ten Years in a Quandary*
   (1936)

11 Famous remarks are very seldom quoted correctly.
   Simeon Strunsky 1879–1948: *No Mean City* (1944)

12 The nice thing about quotes is that they give us a nodding
acquaintance with the originator which is often socially
impressive.
   Kenneth Williams 1926–88: *Acid Drops* (1980)

....

Race
....

See also **Equality, Prejudice**

1 My mother bore me in the southern wild,
And I am black, but O! my soul is white;
White as an angel is the English child:
But I am black as if bereaved of light.
   William Blake 1757–1827: 'The Little Black Boy' (1789)

2 I, too, sing America.

I am the darker brother.
They send me to eat in the kitchen
When company comes.
   Langston Hughes 1902–67: 'I, Too' in *Survey Graphic*
   March 1925

3 I herewith commission you to carry out all preparations with
regard to ... a *total solution* of the Jewish question in those
territories of Europe which are under German influence.
   Hermann Goering 1893–1946: instructions to Heydrich,
   31 July 1941

4 I want to be the white man's brother, not his brother-in-law.
   Martin Luther King 1929–68: in *New York
   Journal-American* 10 September 1962

5 I have a dream that my four little children will one day live
in a nation where they will not be judged by the colour of
their skin but by the content of their character.
   Martin Luther King 1929–68: speech at Civil Rights March
   in Washington, 28 August 1963

6 There are no 'white' or 'coloured' signs on the foxholes or
graveyards of battle.
   John F. Kennedy 1917–63: message to Congress on proposed
   Civil Rights Bill, 19 June 1963

7 Black is beautiful.
   Anonymous: slogan of American civil rights campaigners, mid-1960s

Reading

See also **Books**

1 POLONIUS: What do you read, my lord?
   HAMLET: Words, words, words.
   William Shakespeare 1564–1616: *Hamlet* (1601)

2 Choose an author as you choose a friend.
   Wentworth Dillon, Earl of Roscommon *c.*1633–1685: *Essay on Translated Verse* (1684)

3 He was wont to say that if he had read as much as other men, he should have known no more than other men.
   John Aubrey 1626–97: *Brief Lives* 'Thomas Hobbes'

4 Reading is to the mind what exercise is to the body.
   Richard Steele 1672–1729: *The Tatler* 18 March 1710

5 The bookful blockhead, ignorantly read,
   With loads of learned lumber in his head.
   Alexander Pope 1688–1744: *An Essay on Criticism* (1711)

6 A man ought to read just as inclination leads him; for what he reads as a task will do him little good.
   Samuel Johnson 1709–84: in James Boswell *Life of Johnson* (1791) 14 July 1763

7 Digressions, incontestably, are the sunshine;—they are the life, the soul of reading.
   Laurence Sterne 1713–68: *Tristram Shandy* (1759–67)

8 Much have I travelled in the realms of gold,
   And many goodly states and kingdoms seen.
   John Keats 1795–1821: 'On First Looking into Chapman's Homer' (1817)

9 The reading or non-reading a book—will never keep down a single petticoat.
   Lord Byron 1788–1824: letter to Richard Hoppner, 29 October 1819

10 In science, read, by preference, the newest works; in
literature, the oldest.
  Edward Bulwer-Lytton 1803–73: *Caxtoniana* (1863) 'Hints
  on Mental Culture'

11 People say that life is the thing, but I prefer reading.
  Logan Pearsall Smith 1865–1946: *Afterthoughts* (1931)
  'Myself'

Reality

1 All theory, dear friend, is grey, but the golden tree of actual
life springs ever green.
  Johann Wolfgang von Goethe 1749–1832: *Faust* pt. 1 (1808)

2 It's as large as life, and twice as natural!
  Lewis Carroll 1832–98: *Through the Looking-Glass* (1872)

3 Between the idea
And the reality
Between the motion
And the act
Falls the Shadow.
  T. S. Eliot 1888–1965: 'The Hollow Men' (1925)

4   Human kind
Cannot bear very much reality.
  T. S. Eliot 1888–1965: *Four Quartets* 'Burnt Norton' (1936)

5 The camera makes everyone a tourist in other people's
reality, and eventually in one's own.
  Susan Sontag 1933– : *New York Review of Books* 18 April
  1974

Religion

See also **The Bible, The Church, God, Prayer**

1 Is that which is holy loved by the gods because it is holy, or
is it holy because it is loved by the gods?
  Plato 429–347 BC: *Euthyphro*

2 *Tantum religio potuit suadere malorum.*
So much wrong could religion induce.
Lucretius *c.*94–55 BC: *De Rerum Natura*

3 It is convenient that there be gods, and, as it is convenient,
let us believe that there are.
Ovid 43 BC–AD *c.*17: *Ars Amatoria*

4 Render therefore unto Caesar the things which are Caesar's;
and unto God the things that are God's.
Bible: St Matthew

5 Faith is the substance of things hoped for, the evidence of
things not seen.
Bible: Hebrews

6 I count religion but a childish toy,
And hold there is no sin but ignorance.
Christopher Marlowe 1564–93: *The Jew of Malta* (*c.*1592)

7 'Twas only fear first in the world made gods.
Ben Jonson *c.*1573–1637: *Sejanus* (1603)

8 Had I but served my God with half the zeal
I served my king, he would not in mine age
Have left me naked to mine enemies.
William Shakespeare 1564–1616: *Henry VIII* (with John
Fletcher, 1613)

9 A servant with this clause
Makes drudgery divine:
Who sweeps a room as for Thy laws
Makes that and th' action fine.
George Herbert 1593–1633: 'The Elixir' (1633)

10 A verse may find him, who a sermon flies,
And turn delight into a sacrifice.
George Herbert 1593–1633: 'The Church Porch' (1633)

11 One religion is as true as another.
Robert Burton 1577–1640: *Anatomy of Melancholy* (1621–51)

12 Persecution is a bad and indirect way to plant religion.
Sir Thomas Browne 1605–82: *Religio Medici* (1643)

13 As for those wingy mysteries in divinity and airy subtleties
in religion, which have unhinged the brains of better heads,
they never stretched the *pia mater* of mine; methinks there
be not impossibilities enough in religion for an active faith.
Sir Thomas Browne 1605–82: *Religio Medici* (1643)

14 Men have lost their reason in nothing so much as their religion, wherein stones and clouts make martyrs.

    Sir Thomas Browne 1605–82: *Hydriotaphia* (Urn Burial, 1658)

15 They are for religion when in rags and contempt; but I am for him when he walks in his golden slippers, in the sunshine and with applause.

    John Bunyan 1628–88: *The Pilgrim's Progress* (1678) Mr By-Ends

16 'Men of sense are really but of one religion.' ... 'Pray, my lord, what religion is that which men of sense agree in?' 'Madam,' says the earl immediately, 'men of sense never tell it.'

    1st Earl of Shaftesbury 1621–83: in Bishop Gilbert Burnet *History of My Own Time* vol. 1 (1724)

17 Wherever God erects a house of prayer,
The Devil always builds a chapel there;
And 'twill be found, upon examination,
The latter has the largest congregation.

    Daniel Defoe 1660–1731: *The True-Born Englishman* (1701)

18 We have just enough religion to make us hate, but not enough to make us love one another.

    Jonathan Swift 1667–1745: *Thoughts on Various Subjects* (1711)

19 I went to America to convert the Indians; but oh, who shall convert me?

    John Wesley 1703–91: diary, 24 January 1738

20 In all ages of the world, priests have been enemies of liberty.

    David Hume 1711–76: *Essays, Moral, Political, and Literary* (1875) 'Of the Parties of Great Britain' (1741–2)

21 Putting moral virtues at the highest, and religion at the lowest, religion must still be allowed to be a collateral security, at least, to virtue; and every prudent man will sooner trust to two securities than to one.

    Lord Chesterfield 1694–1773: *Letters to his Son* (1774) 8 January 1750

22 Orthodoxy is my doxy; heterodoxy is another man's doxy.

    Bishop William Warburton 1698–1779: to Lord Sandwich, in Joseph Priestley *Memoirs* (1807)

23 The various modes of worship, which prevailed in the Roman world, were all considered by the people as equally true; by

the philosopher, as equally false; and by the magistrate, as
equally useful. And thus toleration produced not only mutual
indulgence, but even religious concord.
   Edward Gibbon 1737–94: *Decline and Fall of the Roman
   Empire* (1776–88)

24 My country is the world, and my religion is to do good.
   Thomas Paine 1737–1809: *The Rights of Man* pt. 2 (1792)

25 Any system of religion that has any thing in it that shocks
the mind of a child cannot be a true system.
   Thomas Paine 1737–1809: *The Age of Reason* pt. 1 (1794)

26 The dust of creeds outworn.
   Percy Bysshe Shelley 1792–1822: *Prometheus Unbound*
   (1820)

27 In vain with lavish kindness
The gifts of God are strown;
The heathen in his blindness
Bows down to wood and stone.
   Bishop Reginald Heber 1783–1826: 'From Greenland's icy
   mountains' (1821 hymn)

28 Christians have burnt each other, quite persuaded
That all the Apostles would have done as they did.
   Lord Byron 1788–1824: *Don Juan* (1819–24)

29 He who begins by loving Christianity better than Truth will
proceed by loving his own sect or church better than
Christianity, and end by loving himself better than all.
   Samuel Taylor Coleridge 1772–1834: *Aids to Reflection*
   (1825)

30 Religion…is the opium of the people.
   Karl Marx 1818–83: *A Contribution to the Critique of
   Hegel's Philosophy of Right* (1843–4)

31 Things have come to a pretty pass when religion is allowed
to invade the sphere of private life.
   Lord Melbourne 1779–1848: on hearing an evangelical
   sermon; in G. W. E. Russell *Collections and Recollections*
   (1898)

32 Thou shalt have one God only; who
Would be at the expense of two?
   Arthur Hugh Clough 1819–61: 'The Latest Decalogue'
   (1862)

33 If I am obliged to bring religion into after-dinner toasts
(which indeed does not seem quite the thing) I shall
drink...to Conscience first, and to the Pope afterwards.
   Cardinal Newman 1801–90: *Letter Addressed to the Duke of
   Norfolk...* (1875)

34 Scratch the Christian and you find the pagan—spoiled.
   Israel Zangwill 1864–1926: *Children of the Ghetto* (1892)

35 I can't talk religion to a man with bodily hunger in his eyes.
   George Bernard Shaw 1856–1950: *Major Barbara* (1907)

36 Wot prawce Selvytion nah?
   George Bernard Shaw 1856–1950: *Major Barbara* (1907)

37 A Christian is a man who feels
Repentance on a Sunday
For what he did on Saturday
And is going to do on Monday.
   Thomas Russell Ybarra b. 1880: 'The Christian' (1909)

38 The Christian ideal has not been tried and found wanting. It
has been found difficult; and left untried.
   G. K. Chesterton 1874–1936: *What's Wrong with the World*
   (1910)

39 SAINT, *n*. A dead sinner revised and edited.
   Ambrose Bierce 1842–c.1914: *The Devil's Dictionary* (1911)

40 There is no expeditious road
To pack and label men for God,
And save them by the barrel-load.
Some may perchance, with strange surprise,
Have blundered into Paradise.
   Francis Thompson 1859–1907: 'A Judgement in Heaven'
   (1913)

41 So many gods, so many creeds,
So many paths that wind and wind,
While just the art of being kind
Is all the sad world needs.
   Ella Wheeler Wilcox 1855–1919: 'The World's Need'

42 Religion is the frozen thought of men out of which they build
temples.
   Jiddu Krishnamurti d. 1986: in *Observer* 22 April 1928
   'Sayings of the Week'

43 Christianity is the most materialistic of all great religions.
Archbishop William Temple 1881-1944: *Readings in St John's Gospel* (1939)

44 Better authentic mammon than a bogus god.
Louis MacNeice 1907-63: *Autumn Journal* (1939)

45 Science without religion is lame, religion without science is blind.
Albert Einstein 1879-1955: *Science, Philosophy and Religion* (1941)

Revenge

1 Vengeance is mine; I will repay, saith the Lord.
Bible: Romans

2 Men should be either treated generously or destroyed, because they take revenge for slight injuries—for heavy ones they cannot.
Niccolò Machiavelli 1469-1527: *The Prince* (1513)

3 Revenge is a kind of wild justice, which the more man's nature runs to, the more ought law to weed it out.
Francis Bacon 1561-1626: *Essays* (1625) 'Of Revenge'

4 Heaven has no rage, like love to hatred turned,
Nor Hell a fury, like a woman scorned.
William Congreve 1670-1729: *The Mourning Bride* (1697)

5 Sweet is revenge—especially to women.
Lord Byron 1788-1824: *Don Juan* (1819-24)

6 The Germans...are going to be squeezed as a lemon is squeezed—until the pips squeak.
Eric Geddes 1875-1937: speech at Cambridge, 10 December 1918

Revolution and Rebellion

1 A desperate disease requires a dangerous remedy.
Guy Fawkes 1570-1606: 6 November 1605

2 Rebellion to tyrants is obedience to God.
John Bradshaw 1602-59: supposititious epitaph

3 *Après nous le déluge.*
After us the deluge.
   Madame de Pompadour 1721–64: in Mme du Hausset
   Mémoires (1824)

4 A little rebellion now and then is a good thing.
   Thomas Jefferson 1743–1826: letter to James Madison,
   30 January 1787

5 How much the greatest event it is that ever happened in the
world! and how much the best!
   Charles James Fox 1749–1806: on the fall of the Bastille;
   letter to R. Fitzpatrick, 30 July 1789

6 Kings will be tyrants from policy when subjects are rebels
from principle.
   Edmund Burke 1729–97: *Reflections on the Revolution in
   France* (1790)

7 Bliss was it in that dawn to be alive,
But to be young was very heaven!
   William Wordsworth 1770–1850: 'The French Revolution,
   as it Appeared to Enthusiasts' (1809); also *The Prelude*
   (1850)

8 A share in two revolutions is living to some purpose.
   Thomas Paine 1737–1809: in E. Foner *Tom Paine and
   Revolutionary America* (1976)

9 Maximilien Robespierre was nothing but the hand of Jean
Jacques Rousseau, the bloody hand that drew from the womb
of time the body whose soul Rousseau had created.
   Heinrich Heine 1797–1856: *Zur Geschichte der Religion und
   Philosophie in Deutschland* (1834)

10 *J'ai vécu.*
I survived.
   Abbé Emmanuel Joseph Sieyès 1748–1836: when asked what
   he had done during the French Revolution

11 I will die like a true-blue rebel. Don't waste any time in
mourning—organize.
   Joe Hill 1879–1915: farewell telegram prior to his death by
   firing squad; in *Salt Lake* (Utah) *Tribune* 19 November 1915

12 While there is a lower class, I am in it; while there is a criminal element, I am of it; while there is a soul in prison, I am not free.

  Eugene Victor Debs 1855–1926: speech at his trial for sedition in Cleveland, Ohio, 14 September 1918

13 I have seen the future; and it works.

  Lincoln Steffens 1866–1936: following a visit to the Soviet Union in 1919, in *Letters* (1938)

14 All civilization has from time to time become a thin crust over a volcano of revolution.

  Havelock Ellis 1859–1939: *Little Essays of Love and Virtue* (1922)

15 'There won't be any revolution in America,' said Isadore. Nikitin agreed. 'The people are all too clean. They spend all their time changing their shirts and washing themselves. You can't feel fierce and revolutionary in a bathroom.'

  Eric Linklater 1899–1974: *Juan in America* (1931)

16 What is a rebel? A man who says no.

  Albert Camus 1913–60: *The Rebel* (1953)

17 All modern revolutions have ended in a reinforcement of the State.

  Albert Camus 1913–60: *The Rebel* (1953)

18 The most radical revolutionary will become a conservative on the day after the revolution.

  Hannah Arendt 1906–75: *New Yorker* 12 September 1970

19 Revolutions are celebrated when they are no longer dangerous.

  Pierre Boulez 1925– : *Guardian* 13 January 1989

Royalty

1 I know I have the body of a weak and feeble woman, but I have the heart and stomach of a king, and of a king of England too.

  Elizabeth I 1533–1603: speech to the troops at Tilbury on the approach of the Armada, 1588

2 Not all the water in the rough rude sea
Can wash the balm from an anointed king.

  William Shakespeare 1564–1616: *Richard II* (1595)

3 Uneasy lies the head that wears a crown.
　　William Shakespeare 1564–1616: *Henry IV, Part 2* (1597)

4 And what have kings that privates have not too,
　Save ceremony, save general ceremony?
　　William Shakespeare 1564–1616: *Henry V* (1599)

5 There's such divinity doth hedge a king,
　That treason can but peep to what it would.
　　William Shakespeare 1564–1616: *Hamlet* (1601)

6 He is the fountain of honour.
　　Francis Bacon 1561–1626: *An Essay of a King* (1642)

7 *L'État c'est moi.*
　I am the State.
　　Louis XIV 1638–1715: before the Parlement de Paris,
　　13 April 1655; probably apocryphal

8 I see it is impossible for the King to have things done as
　cheap as other men.
　　Samuel Pepys 1633–1703: diary, 21 July 1662

9 Titles are shadows, crowns are empty things,
　The good of subjects is the end of kings.
　　Daniel Defoe 1660–1731: *The True-Born Englishman* (1701)

10 The Right Divine of Kings to govern wrong.
　　Alexander Pope 1688–1744: *The Dunciad* (1742)

11 Born and educated in this country, I glory in the name of
　Briton.
　　George III 1738–1820: *The King's Speech on Opening the
　　Session*, 18 November 1760

12 The influence of the Crown has increased, is increasing, and
　ought to be diminished.
　　John Dunning 1731–83: resolution passed in the House of
　　Commons, 6 April 1780

13 I will be good.
　　Queen Victoria 1819–1901: on being shown a chart of the
　　line of succession, 11 March 1830; in Theodore Martin *The
　　Prince Consort* (1875)

14 It has been said, not truly, but with a possible approximation
　to truth, that in 1802 every hereditary monarch was insane.
　　Walter Bagehot 1826–77: *The English Constitution* (1867)

15 The Sovereign has, under a constitutional monarchy such as
ours, three rights—the right to be consulted, the right to
encourage, the right to warn.
   Walter Bagehot 1826–77: *The English Constitution* (1867)

16 We must not let in daylight upon magic.
   Walter Bagehot 1826–77: *The English Constitution* (1867)

17 Everyone likes flattery; and when you come to Royalty you
should lay it on with a trowel.
   Benjamin Disraeli 1804–81: to Matthew Arnold, in G. W. E.
   Russell *Collections and Recollections* (1898)

18 George the Third
Ought never to have occurred.
One can only wonder
At so grotesque a blunder.
   Edmund Clerihew Bentley 1875–1956: 'George the Third'
   (1929)

19 Soon there will be only five Kings left—the King of England,
the King of Spades, the King of Clubs, the King of Hearts and
the King of Diamonds.
   King Farouk 1920–65: comment in Cairo, 1948

20 For seventeen years he did nothing at all but kill animals
and stick in stamps.
   Harold Nicolson 1886–1968: of King George V; diary,
   17 August 1949

21 Royalty is the gold filling in a mouthful of decay.
   John Osborne 1929– : 'They call it cricket' in T. Maschler
   (ed.) *Declaration* (1957)

Satisfaction and Discontent

1 He is well paid that is well satisfied.
   William Shakespeare 1564–1616: *The Merchant of Venice*
   (1596–8)

2 'Tis just like a summer birdcage in a garden; the birds that
are without despair to get in, and the birds that are within
despair, and are in a consumption, for fear they shall never
get out.
   John Webster c.1580–c.1625: *The White Devil* (1612)

3 Plain living and high thinking are no more:
  The homely beauty of the good old cause
  Is gone.
    William Wordsworth 1770–1850: 'O friend! I know not
    which way I must look' (1807)

4 A book of verses underneath the bough,
  A jug of wine, a loaf of bread—and Thou
  Beside me singing in the wilderness—
  And wilderness were paradise enow.
    Edward Fitzgerald 1809–83: *The Rubáiyát of Omar
    Khayyám* (1879 ed.)

5 Content is disillusioning to behold: what is there to be
  content about?
    Virginia Woolf 1882–1941: diary, 5 May 1920

6 He spoke with a certain what-is-it in his voice, and I could
  see that, if not actually disgruntled, he was far from being
  gruntled.
    P. G. Wodehouse 1881–1975: *The Code of the Woosters* (1938)

7 If one cannot catch the bird of paradise, better take a wet
  hen.
    Nikita Khrushchev 1894–1971: in *Time* 6 January 1958

8 These are the days when men of all social disciplines and all
  political faiths seek the comfortable and the accepted...in
  minor modification of the scriptural parable, the bland lead
  the bland.
    J. K. Galbraith 1908– : *The Affluent Society* (1958)

Science

See also **Inventions and Discoveries, Life
Sciences, Technology**

1 *Felix qui potuit rerum cognoscere causas.*
  Lucky is he who has been able to understand the causes of
  things.
    Virgil 70–19 BC: *Georgics*

2 That all things are changed, and that nothing really perishes, and that the sum of matter remains exactly the same, is sufficiently certain.
 Francis Bacon 1561–1626: *Cogitationes de Natura Rerum*

3 He had been eight years upon a project for extracting sun-beams out of cucumbers, which were to be put into vials hermetically sealed, and let out to warm the air in raw inclement summers.
 Jonathan Swift 1667–1745: *Gulliver's Travels* (1726)

4 It may be so, there is no arguing against facts and experiments.
 Isaac Newton 1642–1727: when told of an experiment which appeared to destroy his theory, as reported by John Conduit, 1726; in D. Brewster *Memoirs of Sir Isaac Newton* (1855)

5 Nature, and Nature's laws lay hid in night.
 God said, *Let Newton be!* and all was light.
 Alexander Pope 1688–1744: 'Epitaph: Intended for Sir Isaac Newton' (1730)

6 If ignorance of nature gave birth to the Gods, knowledge of nature is destined to destroy them.
 Paul Henri, Baron d'Holbach 1723–89: *Système de la Nature* (1770)

7 Science moves, but slowly slowly, creeping on from point to point.
 Alfred, Lord Tennyson 1809–92: 'Locksley Hall' (1842)

8 Where observation is concerned, chance favours only the prepared mind.
 Louis Pasteur 1822–95: address, 7 December 1854

9 Science is nothing but trained and organized common sense, differing from the latter only as a veteran may differ from a raw recruit: and its methods differ from those of common sense only as far as the guardsman's cut and thrust differ from the manner in which a savage wields his club.
 T. H. Huxley 1825–95: *Collected Essays* (1893–4) 'The Method of Zadig'

10 The great tragedy of Science—the slaying of a beautiful hypothesis by an ugly fact.
 T. H. Huxley 1825–95: *Collected Essays* (1893–4) 'Biogenesis and Abiogenesis'

11 Science is built up of facts, as a house is built of stones; but an accumulation of facts is no more a science than a heap of stones is a house.

Henri Poincaré 1854-1912: *Science and Hypothesis* (1905)

12 The outcome of any serious research can only be to make two questions grow where one question grew before.

Thorstein Veblen 1857-1929: *University of California Chronicle* (1908)

13 In science the credit goes to the man who convinces the world, not to the man to whom the idea first occurs.

Francis Darwin 1848-1925: *Eugenics Review* April 1914 'Francis Galton'

14 There was a young lady named Bright,
Whose speed was far faster than light;
She set out one day
In a relative way
And returned on the previous night.

Arthur Buller 1874-1944: 'Relativity' (1923)

15 It did not last: the Devil howling 'Ho!
Let Einstein be!' restored the status quo.

J. C. Squire 1884-1958: 'In continuation of Pope on Newton' (1926)

16 We believe a scientist because he can substantiate his remarks, not because he is eloquent and forcible in his enunciation. In fact, we distrust him when he seems to be influencing us by his manner.

I. A. Richards 1893-1979: *Science and Poetry* (1926)

17 I ask you to look both ways. For the road to a knowledge of the stars leads through the atom; and important knowledge of the atom has been reached through the stars.

Arthur Eddington 1882-1944: *Stars and Atoms* (1928)

18 If someone points out to you that your pet theory of the universe is in disagreement with Maxwell's equations—then so much the worse for Maxwell's equations. If it is found to be contradicted by observation—well, these experimentalists do bungle things sometimes. But if your theory is found to be against the second law of thermodynamics I can give you no hope; there is nothing for it but to collapse in deepest humiliation.

Arthur Eddington 1882-1944: *The Nature of the Physical World* (1928)

19 It is much easier to make measurements than to know exactly what you are measuring.
J. W. N. Sullivan 1886–1937: comment, 1928; in R. L. Weber *More Random Walks in Science* (1982)

20 Science means simply the aggregate of all the recipes that are always successful. The rest is literature.
Paul Valéry 1871–1945: *Moralités* (1932)

21 All science is either physics or stamp collecting.
Ernest Rutherford 1871–1937: in J. B. Birks *Rutherford at Manchester* (1962)

22 We haven't got the money, so we've got to think!
Ernest Rutherford 1871–1937: in *Bulletin of the Institute of Physics* (1962), as recalled by R. V. Jones

23 It was quite the most incredible event that has ever happened to me in my life. It was almost as incredible as if you fired a 15-inch shell at a piece of tissue paper and it came back and hit you.
Ernest Rutherford 1871–1937: on the back-scattering effect of metal foil on alpha-particles, in E. N. da C. Andrade *Rutherford and the Nature of the Atom* (1964)

24 The aim of science is not to open the door to infinite wisdom, but to set a limit to infinite error.
Bertolt Brecht 1898–1956: *Life of Galileo* (1939)

25 Science without religion is lame, religion without science is blind.
Albert Einstein 1879–1955: *Science, Philosophy and Religion* (1941)

26 Now who is responsible for this work of development on which so much depends? To whom must the praise be given? To the boys in the back rooms. They do not sit in the limelight. But they are the men who do the work.
Lord Beaverbrook 1879–1964: *Listener* 27 March 1941

27 The physicists have known sin; and this is a knowledge which they cannot lose.
J. Robert Oppenheimer 1904–67: lecture at Massachusetts Institute of Technology, 25 November 1947

28 A new scientific truth does not triumph by convincing its opponents and making them see the light, but rather because its opponents eventually die, and a new generation grows up that is familiar with it.

Max Planck 1858–1947: *A Scientific Autobiography* (1949) tr. F. Gaynor

29 Aristotle maintained that women have fewer teeth than men; although he was twice married, it never occurred to him to verify this statement by examining his wives' mouths.

Bertrand Russell 1872–1970: *Impact of Science on Society* (1952)

30 We do not know why they [elementary particles] have the masses they do; we do not know why they transform into another the way they do; we do not know anything! The one concept that stands like the Rock of Gibraltar in our sea of confusion is the Pauli [exclusion] principle.

George Gamow 1904–68: *Scientific American* July 1959

31 When I find myself in the company of scientists, I feel like a shabby curate who has strayed by mistake into a drawing room full of dukes.

W. H. Auden 1907–73: *The Dyer's Hand* (1963)

32 It is more important to have beauty in one's equations than to have them fit experiment.

Paul Dirac 1902–84: *Scientific American* May 1963

33 If politics is the art of the possible, research is surely the art of the soluble. Both are immensely practical-minded affairs.

Peter Medawar 1915–87: *New Statesman* 19 June 1964

34 It is a good morning exercise for a research scientist to discard a pet hypothesis every day before breakfast.

Konrad Lorenz 1903–89: *On Aggression* (1966), tr. M. Latzke

35 If an elderly but distinguished scientist says that something is possible he is almost certainly right, but if he says that it is impossible he is very probably wrong.

Arthur C. Clarke 1917– : in *New Yorker* 9 August 1969

36 Basic research is what I am doing when I don't know what I am doing.

Wernher von Braun 1912–77: in R. L. Weber *A Random Walk in Science* (1973)

37 The essence of science: ask an impertinent question, and you are on the way to a pertinent answer.

Jacob Bronowski 1908–74: *The Ascent of Man* (1973)

Scotland and the Scots

1 It came with a lass, and it will pass with a lass.
  James V 1512–42: of the crown of Scotland, on learning of
  the birth of Mary Queen of Scots, December 1542; in Robert
  Lindsay of Pitscottie (*c.*1500–65) *History of Scotland* (1728)

2 Now there's ane end of ane old song.
  James Ogilvy, 1st Earl of Seafield 1664–1730: as he signed
  the engrossed exemplification of the Act of Union, 1706, in
  The Lockhart Papers (1817)

3 The noblest prospect which a Scotchman ever sees, is the
  high road that leads him to England!
  Samuel Johnson 1709–84: in James Boswell *Life of Johnson*
  (1791) 6 July 1763

4 A Scotchman must be a very sturdy moralist, who does not
  love Scotland better than truth.
  Samuel Johnson 1709–84: *A Journey to the Western Islands
  of Scotland* (1775)

5 My heart's in the Highlands, my heart is not here;
  My heart's in the Highlands a-chasing the deer.
  Robert Burns 1759–96: 'My Heart's in the Highlands' (1790)

6 Scots, wha hae wi' Wallace bled,
  Scots, wham Bruce has aften led,
  Welcome to your gory bed,—
  Or to victorie.
  Robert Burns 1759–96: 'Robert Bruce's March to
  Bannockburn' (1799)

7 O Caledonia! stern and wild,
  Meet nurse for a poetic child!
  Sir Walter Scott 1771–1832: *The Lay of the Last Minstrel*
  (1805)

8 A land of meanness, sophistry, and mist.
  Lord Byron 1788–1824: 'The Curse of Minerva' (1812)

9 From the lone shieling of the misty island
  Mountains divide us, and the waste of seas—
  Yet still the blood is strong, the heart is Highland,
  And we in dreams behold the Hebrides!
  John Galt 1779–1839: 'Canadian Boat Song', attributed

10 That knuckle-end of England—that land of Calvin, oat-cakes,
and sulphur.
  Sydney Smith 1771–1845: in Lady Holland *Memoir* (1855)

11 There are few more impressive sights in the world than
a Scotsman on the make.
  J. M. Barrie 1860–1937: *What Every Woman Knows* (1908)

12 Scotland, land of the omnipotent No.
  Alan Bold 1943– : 'A Memory of Death' (1969)

The Sea

1 One deep calleth another, because of the noise of the
water-pipes: all thy waves and storms are gone over me.
  Bible: Psalm 42

2 They that go down to the sea in ships: and occupy their
business in great waters.
  Bible: Psalm 107

3 Now would I give a thousand furlongs of sea for an acre of
barren ground.
  William Shakespeare 1564–1616: *The Tempest* (1611)

4 Full fathom five thy father lies;
Of his bones are coral made:
Those are pearls that were his eyes:
Nothing of him that doth fade,
But doth suffer a sea-change
Into something rich and strange.
  William Shakespeare 1564–1616: *The Tempest* (1611)

5 Be pleased to receive into thy Almighty and most gracious
protection the persons of us thy servants, and the Fleet in
which we serve.
  Book of Common Prayer 1662: *Forms of Prayer to be Used
at Sea*

6 No man will be a sailor who has contrivance enough to get
himself into a jail; for being in a ship is being in a jail, with
the chance of being drowned…A man in a jail has more
room, better food, and commonly better company.
  Samuel Johnson 1709–84: in James Boswell *Life of Johnson*
(1791) 16 March 1759

7 Water, water, everywhere,
And all the boards did shrink;
Water, water, everywhere,
Nor any drop to drink.
   Samuel Taylor Coleridge 1772–1834: 'The Rime of the
   Ancient Mariner' (1798)

8 A willing foe and sea room.
   Anonymous: naval toast in the time of Nelson

9 Roll on, thou deep and dark blue Ocean—roll!
Ten thousand fleets sweep over thee in vain;
Man marks the earth with ruin—his control
Stops with the shore.
   Lord Byron 1788–1824: *Childe Harold's Pilgrimage* (1812–18)

10 If blood be the price of admiralty,
Lord God, we ha' paid in full!
   Rudyard Kipling 1865–1936: 'The Song of the Dead' (1896)

11 I must go down to the sea again, to the lonely sea and the
sky,
And all I ask is a tall ship and a star to steer her by.
   John Masefield 1878–1967: 'Sea Fever' (misprinted 'I must
   down to the seas' in the 1902 original)

12 A ship, an isle, a sickle moon—
With few but with how splendid stars
The mirrors of the sea are strewn
Between their silver bars!
   James Elroy Flecker 1884–1915: 'A Ship, an Isle, and a
   Sickle Moon' (1913)

13 Don't talk to me about naval tradition. It's nothing but rum,
sodomy, and the lash.
   Winston Churchill 1874–1965: in P. Gretton *Former Naval
   Person* (1968)

....

The Seasons
....

1 Sumer is icumen in,
Lhude sing cuccu!
Groweth sed, and bloweth med,
And springeth the wude nu.
   Anonymous: 'Cuckoo Song' (*c.*1250)

2 At Christmas I no more desire a rose
Than wish a snow in May's new-fangled mirth;
But like of each thing that in season grows.
   William Shakespeare 1564–1616: *Love's Labour's Lost* (1595)

3 When icicles hang by the wall,
And Dick the shepherd blows his nail,
And Tom bears logs into the hall,
And milk comes frozen home in pail.
   William Shakespeare 1564–1616: *Love's Labour's Lost* (1595)

4 That time of year thou mayst in me behold
When yellow leaves, or none, or few, do hang
Upon those boughs which shake against the cold,
Bare ruined choirs, where late the sweet birds sang.
   William Shakespeare 1564–1616: sonnet 73 (1609)

5 It was no summer progress. A cold coming they had of it, at
this time of the year; just, the worst time of the year, to take
a journey, and specially a long journey, in. The ways deep,
the weather sharp, the days short, the sun farthest off *in
solstitio brumali*, the very dead of Winter.
   Bishop Lancelot Andrewes 1555–1626: *Of the Nativity* (1622)
   Sermon 15

6 Sweet spring, full of sweet days and roses,
A box where sweets compacted lie.
   George Herbert 1593–1633: 'Virtue' (1633)

7 I sing of brooks, of blossoms, birds, and bowers:
Of April, May, of June, and July-flowers.
I sing of May-poles, Hock-carts, wassails, wakes,
Of bride-grooms, brides, and of their bridal-cakes.
   Robert Herrick 1591–1674: *Hesperides* (1648)

8 The way to ensure summer in England is to have it framed
and glazed in a comfortable room.
   Horace Walpole 1717–97: letter to Revd William Cole,
   28 May 1774

9 Snowy, Flowy, Blowy,
Showery, Flowery, Bowery,
Hoppy, Croppy, Droppy,
Breezy, Sneezy, Freezy.
   George Ellis 1753–1815: 'The Twelve Months'

10 O wild West Wind, thou breath of Autumn's being,
Thou, from whose unseen presence the leaves dead

Are driven, like ghosts from an enchanter fleeing,

Yellow, and black, and pale, and hectic red,
Pestilence-stricken multitudes.
　　Percy Bysshe Shelley 1792–1822: 'Ode to the West Wind'
　　(1819)

11 Season of mists and mellow fruitfulness,
　　Close bosom-friend of the maturing sun;
　　Conspiring with him how to load and bless
　　With fruit the vines that round the thatch-eaves run.
　　　John Keats 1795–1821: 'To Autumn' (1820)

12 The English winter—ending in July,
　　To recommence in August.
　　　Lord Byron 1788–1824: *Don Juan* (1819–24)

13 Summer has set in with its usual severity.
　　　Samuel Taylor Coleridge 1772–1834: quoted in letter from
　　　Charles Lamb to Vincent Novello, 9 May 1826

14 No sun—no moon!
　　No morn—no noon
　　No dawn—no dusk—no proper time of day…
　　No shade, no shine, no butterflies, no bees,
　　No fruits, no flowers, no leaves, no birds,—
　　November!
　　　Thomas Hood 1799–1845: 'No!' (1844)

15 When the hounds of spring are on winter's traces,
　　The mother of months in meadow or plain
　　Fills the shadows and windy places
　　With lisp of leaves and ripple of rain;
　　　Algernon Charles Swinburne 1837–1909: *Atalanta in
　　　Calydon* (1865)

16 Coldly, sadly descends
　　The autumn evening. The Field
　　Strewn with its dank yellow drifts
　　Of withered leaves, and the elms,
　　Fade into dimness apace.
　　　Matthew Arnold 1822–88: 'Rugby Chapel, November 1857'
　　　(1867)

17 May is a pious fraud of the almanac.
　　　James Russell Lowell 1819–91: 'Under the Willows' (1869)

18 In the bleak mid-winter
　　Frosty wind made moan,

Earth stood hard as iron,
Water like a stone.
   Christina Rossetti 1830–94: 'Mid-Winter' (1875)

19 Though worlds of wanwood leafmeal lie.
   Gerard Manley Hopkins 1844–89: 'Spring and Fall: to a young child' (written 1880)

20 In winter I get up at night
And dress by yellow candle-light.
In summer, quite the other way,—
I have to go to bed by day.
   Robert Louis Stevenson 1850–94: 'Bed in Summer' (1885)

21 Loveliest of trees, the cherry now
Is hung with bloom along the bough,
And stands about the woodland ride
Wearing white for Eastertide.
   A. E. Housman 1859–1936: *A Shropshire Lad* (1896)

22 Winter is icummen in,
Lhude sing Goddamm,
Raineth drop and staineth slop,
And how the wind doth ramm!
   Ezra Pound 1885–1972: 'Ancient Music' (1917)

23 April is the cruellest month, breeding
Lilacs out of the dead land.
   T. S. Eliot 1888–1965: *The Waste Land* (1922)

24 The autumn always gets me badly, as it breaks into colours.
I want to go south, where there is no autumn, where the cold
doesn't crouch over one like a snow-leopard waiting to
pounce. The heart of the North is dead, and the fingers of
cold are corpse fingers.
   D. H. Lawrence 1885–1930: letter to J. Middleton Murry,
3 October 1924

25 Summer time an' the livin' is easy,
Fish are jumpin' an' the cotton is high.
   Du Bose Heyward 1885–1940 and **Ira Gershwin** 1896–1983:
'Summertime' (1935 song)

26 In fact, it is about five o'clock in an evening that the first
hour of spring strikes—autumn arrives in the early morning,
but spring at the close of a winter day.
   Elizabeth Bowen 1899–1973: *Death of the Heart* (1938)

27 June is bustin' out all over.
  Oscar Hammerstein II 1895-1960: title of song (1945)

28 What of October, that ambiguous month, the month of tension, the unendurable month?
  Doris Lessing 1919- : *Martha Quest* (1952)

29 August is a wicked month.
  Edna O'Brien 1936- : title of novel (1965)

Secrets

1 Stolen waters are sweet, and bread eaten in secret is pleasant.
  Bible: Proverbs

2 I would not open windows into men's souls.
  Elizabeth I 1533-1603: oral tradition, the words possibly originating in a letter drafted by Bacon

3 Love and a cough cannot be hid.
  George Herbert 1593-1633: *Outlandish Proverbs* (1640)

4 For secrets are edged tools,
  And must be kept from children and from fools.
  John Dryden 1631-1700: *Sir Martin Mar-All* (1667)

5 It is public scandal that constitutes offence, and to sin in secret is not to sin at all.
  Molière 1622-73: *Le Tartuffe* (1669)

6 Love ceases to be a pleasure, when it ceases to be a secret.
  Aphra Behn 1640-89: *The Lover's Watch* (1686)

7 I know that's a secret, for it's whispered every where.
  William Congreve 1670-1729: *Love for Love* (1695)

8 I shall be but a short time tonight. I have seldom spoken with greater regret, for my lips are not yet unsealed. Were these troubles over I would make a case, and I guarantee that not a man would go into the lobby against us.
  Stanley Baldwin 1867-1947: speech, House of Commons, 10 December 1935, on the Abyssinian crisis (usually quoted 'My lips are sealed')

9 We dance round in a ring and suppose,
  But the Secret sits in the middle and knows.
  Robert Frost 1874-1963: 'The Secret Sits' (1942)

10 Once the toothpaste is out of the tube, it is awfully hard to get it back in.

> **H. R. Haldeman** 1929-93 : comment to John Wesley Dean on Watergate affair, 8 April 1973

The Self

1 Who is it that can tell me who I am?
> **William Shakespeare** 1564-1616: *King Lear* (1605-6)

2 The self is hateful.
> **Blaise Pascal** 1623-62: *Pensées* (1670)

3 Thus God and nature linked the gen'ral frame,
And bade self-love and social be the same.
> **Alexander Pope** 1688-1744: *An Essay on Man* Epistle 3 (1733)

4 It is not contrary to reason to prefer the destruction of the whole world to the scratching of my finger.
> **David Hume** 1711-76: *A Treatise upon Human Nature* (1739)

5 If a man does not keep pace with his companions, perhaps it is because he hears a different drummer. Let him step to the music which he hears, however measured or far away.
> **Henry David Thoreau** 1817-62: *Walden* (1854)

6 Do I contradict myself?
Very well then I contradict myself,
(I am large, I contain multitudes.)
> **Walt Whitman** 1819-92: 'Song of Myself' (written 1855)

7 It is easy—terribly easy—to shake a man's faith in himself. To take advantage of that to break a man's spirit is devil's work.
> **George Bernard Shaw** 1856-1950: *Candida* (1898)

8 Rose is a rose is a rose is a rose, is a rose.
> **Gertrude Stein** 1874-1946: *Sacred Emily* (1913)

9 We are all serving a life-sentence in the dungeon of self.
> **Cyril Connolly** 1903-74: *The Unquiet Grave* (1944)

10 The image of myself which I try to create in my own mind in order that I may love myself is very different from the image

which I try to create in the minds of others in order that they
may love me.

    W. H. Auden 1907–73: *The Dyer's Hand* (1963)

11 Some thirty inches from my nose
The frontier of my Person goes,
And all the untilled air between
Is private *pagus* or demesne.

    W. H. Auden 1907–73: 'Prologue: the Birth of Architecture'
    (1966)

12 My one regret in life is that I am not someone else.

    Woody Allen 1935– : epigraph to Eric Lax *Woody Allen
    and his Comedy* (1975)

Self-Knowledge

1 Know thyself.

    Anonymous: inscribed on the temple of Apollo at Delphi;
    Plato ascribes the saying to the Seven Wise Men

2 I do not know whether I was then a man dreaming I was
a butterfly, or whether I am now a butterfly dreaming I am
a man.

    Chuang-tzu (or Zhuangzi) *c.*369–286 BC: *Chuang Tzu* (1889)
    tr. H. A. Giles

3 Why beholdest thou the mote that is in thy brother's eye, but
considerest not the beam that is in thine own eye?

    Bible: St Matthew

4 For the good that I would I do not: but the evil which I would
not, that I do.

    Bible: Romans

5 The greatest thing in the world is to know how to be oneself.

    Montaigne 1533–92: *Essais* (1580)

6 This above all: to thine own self be true,
And it must follow, as the night the day,
Thou canst not then be false to any man.

    William Shakespeare 1564–1616: *Hamlet* (1601)

7 But I do nothing upon my self, and yet I am mine own
Executioner.

    John Donne 1572–1631: *Devotions upon Emergent Occasions*
    (1624)

8 All our knowledge is, ourselves to know.
   Alexander Pope 1688–1744: *An Essay on Man* Epistle 4
   (1734)

9 O wad some Pow'r the giftie gie us
   To see oursels as others see us!
   It wad frae mony a blunder free us,
   And foolish notion.
   Robert Burns 1759–96: 'To a Louse' (1786)

10 The Vision of Christ that thou dost see
   Is my vision's greatest enemy
   Thine has a great hook nose like thine
   Mine has a snub nose like to mine.
   William Blake 1757–1827: *The Everlasting Gospel* (c.1818)

11 How little do we know that which we are!
   How less what we may be!
   Lord Byron 1788–1824: *Don Juan* (1819–24)

12 I do not know myself, and God forbid that I should.
   Johann Wolfgang von Goethe 1749–1832: J. P. Eckermann
   Gespräche mit Goethe (1836–48) 10 April 1829

13 The tragedy of a man who has found himself out.
   J. M. Barrie 1860–1937: *What Every Woman Knows* (1908)

14 Between the ages of twenty and forty we are engaged in the
   process of discovering who we are, which involves learning
   the difference between accidental limitations which it is our
   duty to outgrow and the necessary limitations of our nature
   beyond which we cannot trespass with impunity.
   W. H. Auden 1907–73: *The Dyer's Hand* (1963)

15 There are few things more painful than to recognise one's
   own faults in others.
   John Wells 1936– : *Observer* 23 May 1982 'Sayings of the
   Week'

Sex

See also **Love, Marriage**

1 Someone asked Sophocles, 'How is your sex-life now? Are you
   still able to have a woman?' He replied, 'Hush, man; most

gladly indeed am I rid of it all, as though I had escaped from
a mad and savage master.'
   Sophocles c.496–406 BC: in Plato *Republic*

2 Delight of lust is gross and brief
And weariness treads on desire.
   Petronius d. AD 65: in A. Baehrens *Poetae Latini Minores*
   (1882), tr. H. Waddell

3 Give me chastity and continency—but not yet!
   St Augustine of Hippo AD 354–430: *Confessions* (AD 397–8)

4 Licence my roving hands, and let them go,
Behind, before, above, between, below.
O my America, my new found land,
My kingdom, safeliest when with one man manned.
   John Donne 1572–1631: 'To His Mistress Going to Bed'
   (c.1595)

5 Is it not strange that desire should so many years outlive
performance?
   William Shakespeare 1564–1616: *Henry IV, Part 2* (1597)

6 This is the monstruosity in love, lady, that the will is
infinite, and the execution confined; that the desire is
boundless, and the act a slave to limit.
   William Shakespeare 1564–1616: *Troilus and Cressida*
   (1602)

7   Die: die for adultery! No:
The wren goes to't, and the small gilded fly
Does lecher in my sight.
Let copulation thrive.
   William Shakespeare 1564–1616: *King Lear* (1605–6)

8 The expense of spirit in a waste of shame
Is lust in action.
   William Shakespeare 1564–1616: sonnet 129 (1609)

9 This trivial and vulgar way of coition; it is the foolishest act
a wise man commits in all his life, nor is there any thing that
will more deject his cooled imagination, when he shall
consider what an odd and unworthy piece of folly he hath
committed.
   Sir Thomas Browne 1605–82: *Religio Medici* (1643)

10 He in a few minutes ravished this fair creature, or at least would have ravished her, if she had not, by a timely compliance, prevented him.
   Henry Fielding 1707–54: *Jonathan Wild* (1743)

11 The Duke returned from the wars today and did pleasure me in his top-boots.
   Sarah, Duchess of Marlborough 1660–1744: attributed in various forms. See I. Butler *Rule of Three* (1967)

12 I'll come no more behind your scenes, David; for the silk stockings and white bosoms of your actresses excite my amorous propensities.
   Samuel Johnson 1709–84: in James Boswell *Life of Johnson* (1791) 1750

13 The pleasure is momentary, the position ridiculous, and the expense damnable.
   Lord Chesterfield 1694–1773: of sex; attributed

14 'Tisn't beauty, so to speak, nor good talk necessarily. It's just It. Some women'll stay in a man's memory if they once walked down a street.
   Rudyard Kipling 1865–1936: *Traffics and Discoveries* (1904)

15 When I hear his steps outside my door I lie down on my bed, close my eyes, open my legs, and think of England.
   Lady Hillingdon 1857–1940: diary, 1912

16 Chastity—the most unnatural of all the sexual perversions.
   Aldous Huxley 1894–1963: *Eyeless in Gaza* (1936)

17 Pornography is the attempt to insult sex, to do dirt on it.
   D. H. Lawrence 1885–1930: *Phoenix* (1936) 'Pornography and Obscenity'

18 But did thee feel the earth move?
   Ernest Hemingway 1899–1961: *For Whom the Bell Tolls* (1940)

19 It doesn't matter what you do in the bedroom as long as you don't do it in the street and frighten the horses.
   Mrs Patrick Campbell 1865–1940: in D. Fielding *Duchess of Jermyn Street* (1964)

20 Continental people have sex life; the English have hot-water bottles.
   George Mikes 1912– : *How to be an Alien* (1946)

21 He said it was artificial respiration, but now I find I am to have his child.
Anthony Burgess 1917–93: *Inside Mr Enderby* (1963)

22 I have heard some say ...[homosexual] practices are allowed in France and in other NATO countries. We are not French, and we are not other nationals. We are British, thank God!
Field Marshal Montgomery 1887–1976: speaking on the 2nd reading of the Sexual Offences Bill; House of Lords, 24 May 1965

23 Literature is mostly about having sex and not much about having children. Life is the other way round.
David Lodge 1935– : *The British Museum is Falling Down* (1965)

24 The orgasm has replaced the Cross as the focus of longing and the image of fulfilment.
Malcolm Muggeridge 1903–90: *Tread Softly* (1966)

25 You were born with your legs apart. They'll send you to the grave in a Y-shaped coffin.
Joe Orton 1933–67: *What the Butler Saw* (1969)

26 Is sex dirty? Only if it's done right.
Woody Allen 1935– : *Everything You Always Wanted to Know about Sex* (1972 film)

27 Sexual intercourse began
In nineteen sixty-three
(Which was rather late for me)—
Between the end of the *Chatterley* ban
And the Beatles' first LP.
Philip Larkin 1922–85: 'Annus Mirabilis' (1974)

28 On bisexuality: It immediately doubles your chances for a date on Saturday night.
Woody Allen 1935– : *New York Times* 1 December 1975

29 Seduction is often difficult to distinguish from rape. In seduction, the rapist bothers to buy a bottle of wine.
Andrea Dworkin 1946– : speech to women at *Harper & Row*, 1976; in *Letters from a War Zone* (1988)

30 That [sex] was the most fun I ever had without laughing.
Woody Allen 1935– : *Annie Hall* (1977 film, with Marshall Brickman)

31 Don't knock masturbation. It's sex with someone I love.
Woody Allen 1935– : *Annie Hall* (1977 film, with Marshall Brickman)

....

Shakespeare

....

See also **Acting and the Theatre**

1   Reader, look
Not on his picture, but his book.
Ben Jonson c.1573–1637: 'On the Portrait of Shakespeare' (1623)

2 He was not of an age, but for all time!
Ben Jonson c.1573–1637: 'To the Memory of…Shakespeare' (1623)

3 His mind and hand went together: And what he thought, he uttered with that easiness, that we have scarce received from him a blot.
John Heming 1556–1630 and **Henry Condell** d. 1627: First Folio Shakespeare (1623) preface

4 Whatsoever he [Shakespeare] penned, he never blotted out a line. My answer hath been 'Would he had blotted a thousand.'
Ben Jonson c.1573–1637: *Timber* (1641)

5 Was there ever such stuff as great part of Shakespeare? Only one must not say so!
George III 1738–1820: in Fanny Burney's diary, 19 December 1785

6 Others abide our question. Thou art free.
We ask and ask: Thou smilest and art still,
Out-topping knowledge.
Matthew Arnold 1822–88: 'Shakespeare' (1849)

7 He had read Shakespeare and found him weak in chemistry.
H. G. Wells 1866–1946: 'Lord of the Dynamos' (1927)

8 When I read Shakespeare I am struck with wonder
That such trivial people should muse and thunder
In such lovely language.
D. H. Lawrence 1885–1930: 'When I Read Shakespeare' (1929)

9 Shakespeare is so tiring. You never get a chance to sit down
unless you're a king.
  Josephine Hull ?1886–1957: in *Time* 16 November 1953

Sickness and Health

See also **Medicine**

1 Life's not just being alive, but being well.
  Martial AD *c.*40–*c.*104: *Epigrammata*

2 *Mens sana in corpore sano.*
A sound mind in a sound body.
  Juvenal AD *c.*60–*c.*130: *Satires*

3   Diseases desperate grown,
By desperate appliances are relieved
Or not at all.
  William Shakespeare 1564–1616: *Hamlet* (1601)

4   Bid them wash their faces,
And keep their teeth clean.
  William Shakespeare 1564–1616: *Coriolanus* (1608)

5 Look to your health; and if you have it, praise God, and value
it next to a good conscience; for health is the second blessing
that we mortals are capable of; a blessing that money cannot
buy.
  Izaak Walton 1593–1683: *The Compleat Angler* (1653)

6 Cured yesterday of my disease,
I died last night of my physician.
  Matthew Prior 1664–1721: 'The Remedy Worse than the
Disease' (1727)

7 If a lot of cures are suggested for a disease, it means that the
disease is incurable.
  Anton Chekhov 1860–1904: *The Cherry Orchard* (1904), tr.
E. Fen

8 Does it matter?—losing your sight?...
There's such splendid work for the blind;
And people will always be kind,
As you sit on the terrace remembering
And turning your face to the light.
  Siegfried Sassoon 1886–1967: 'Does it Matter?' (1918)

9 Human nature seldom walks up to the word 'cancer'.
   Rudyard Kipling 1865-1936: *Debits and Credits* (1926)

10 Early to rise and early to bed makes a male healthy and
   wealthy and dead.
   James Thurber 1894-1961: 'The Shrike and the Chipmunks'
   in *New Yorker* 18 February 1939

11 Coughs and sneezes spread diseases. Trap the germs in your
   handkerchief.
   Anonymous: Second World War health slogan (1942)

12 Venerable Mother Toothache
   Climb down from the white battlements,
   Stop twisting in your yellow fingers
   The fourfold rope of nerves.
   John Heath-Stubbs 1918- : 'A Charm Against the
   Toothache' (1954)

13 I know the colour rose, and it is lovely,
   But not when it ripens in a tumour;
   And healing greens, leaves and grass, so springlike,
   In limbs that fester are not springlike.
   Dannie Abse 1923- : 'Pathology of Colours' (1968)

14 Illness is the night-side of life, a more onerous citizenship.
   Everyone who is born holds dual citizenship, in the kingdom
   of the well and in the kingdom of the sick.
   Susan Sontag 1933- : *New York Review of Books*
   26 January 1978

15 [AIDS was] an illness in stages, a very long flight of steps
   that led assuredly to death, but whose every step represented
   a unique apprenticeship. It was a disease that gave death
   time to live and its victims time to die, time to discover time,
   and in the end to discover life.
   Hervé Guibert 1955-91: *To the Friend who did not Save my
   Life* (1991) tr. Linda Coverdale

Silence

1 Silence is the virtue of fools.
   Francis Bacon 1561-1626: *De Dignitate et Augmentis
   Scientiarum* (1623)

2 Thou still unravished bride of quietness,
Thou foster-child of silence and slow time.
    John Keats 1795–1821: 'Ode on a Grecian Urn' (1820)

3 Elected Silence, sing to me
And beat upon my whorlèd ear.
    Gerard Manley Hopkins 1844–89: 'The Habit of Perfection'
    (written 1866)

4 If we had a keen vision and feeling of all ordinary human
life, it would be like hearing the grass grow and the
squirrel's heart beat, and we should die of that roar which
lies on the other side of silence.
    George Eliot 1819–80: *Middlemarch* (1871–2)

5   Deep is the silence, deep
On moon-washed apples of wonder.
    John Drinkwater 1882–1937: 'Moonlit Apples' (1917)

6 People talking without speaking
People hearing without listening…
'Fools,' said I, 'You do not know
Silence like a cancer grows.'
    Paul Simon 1942– : 'Sound of Silence' (1964 song)

Singing

See also **Music**

1 If a man were permitted to make all the ballads, he need not
care who should make the laws of a nation.
    Andrew Fletcher of Saltoun 1655–1716: 'Conversation
    concerning a Right Regulation of Government…' (1704)

2 Today if something is not worth saying, people sing it.
    Pierre-Augustin Caron de Beaumarchais 1732–99: *The
    Barber of Seville* (1775)

3 Swans sing before they die: 'twere no bad thing
Should certain persons die before they sing.
    Samuel Taylor Coleridge 1772–1834: 'On a Volunteer
    Singer' (1834)

4 You think that's noise—you ain't heard nuttin' yet!
    Al Jolson 1886–1950: in a café, competing with the din
    from a neighbouring building site, 1906

5 An unalterable and unquestioned law of the musical world
required that the German text of French operas sung by
Swedish artists should be translated into Italian for the
clearer understanding of English-speaking audiences.
  Edith Wharton 1862–1937: *The Age of Innocence* (1920)

6 Sing 'em muck! It's all they can understand!
  Dame Nellie Melba 1861–1931: advice to Dame Clara Butt,
  prior to her departure for Australia; in W. H. Ponder *Clara
  Butt* (1928)

7 Opera is when a guy gets stabbed in the back and, instead of
bleeding, he sings.
  Ed Gardner 1901–63: in *Duffy's Tavern* (US radio
  programme, 1940s)

The Skies

1 　　　　　The moon's an arrant thief,
And her pale fire she snatches from the sun.
  William Shakespeare 1564–1616: *Timon of Athens* (1607)

2 Busy old fool, unruly sun,
Why dost thou thus,
Through windows, and through curtains call on us?
  John Donne 1572–1631: 'The Sun Rising'

3 *Eppur si muove.*
But it does move.
  Galileo Galilei 1564–1642: attributed to Galileo after his
  recantation, that the earth moves around the sun, in 1632

4 The eternal silence of these infinite spaces [the heavens]
terrifies me.
  Blaise Pascal 1623–62: *Pensées* (1670)

5 …The evening star,
Love's harbinger.
  John Milton 1608–74: *Paradise Lost* (1667)

6 And like a dying lady, lean and pale,
Who totters forth, wrapped in a gauzy veil.
  Percy Bysshe Shelley 1792–1822: 'The Waning Moon' (1824)

7 Look at the stars! look, look up at the skies!
O look at all the fire-folk sitting in the air!
The bright boroughs, the circle-citadels there!
   Gerard Manley Hopkins 1844–89: 'The Starlight Night'
   (written 1877)

8 Slowly, silently, now the moon
Walks the night in her silver shoon.
   Walter de la Mare 1873–1956: 'Silver' (1913)

9 Stars scribble on our eyes the frosty sagas,
The gleaming cantos of unvanquished space.
   Hart Crane 1899–1932: 'Cape Hatteras' (1930)

10 Houston, Tranquillity Base here. The Eagle has landed.
   Buzz Aldrin 1930– : on landing on the moon, 21 July 1969

Sleep and Dreams

1 The sleep of a labouring man is sweet.
   Bible: Ecclesiastes

2 Care-charmer Sleep, son of the sable Night,
Brother to Death, in silent darkness born.
   Samuel Daniel 1563–1619: *Delia* (1592) sonnet 54

3 O God! I could be bounded in a nut-shell, and count myself a
king of infinite space, were it not that I have bad dreams.
   William Shakespeare 1564–1616: *Hamlet* (1601)

4 Methought I heard a voice cry, 'Sleep no more!
Macbeth does murder sleep,' the innocent sleep,
Sleep that knits up the ravelled sleave of care.
   William Shakespeare 1564–1616: *Macbeth* (1606)

5 What hath night to do with sleep?
   John Milton 1608–74: *Comus* (1637)

6 We term sleep a death, and yet it is waking that kills us, and
destroys those spirits which are the house of life.
   Sir Thomas Browne 1605–82: *Religio Medici* (1643)

7 And so to bed.
   Samuel Pepys 1633–1703: diary, 20 April 1660

8 That children dream not in the first half year, that men
 dream not in some countries, are to me sick men's dreams,
 dreams out of the ivory gate, and visions before midnight.
  Sir Thomas Browne 1605–82: 'On Dreams'

9 Tired Nature's sweet restorer, balmy sleep!
  Edward Young 1683–1765: *Night Thoughts* (1742–5)

10 The dream of reason produces monsters.
  Goya 1746–1828: *Los Caprichos* (1799)

11   The quick Dreams,
 The passion-wingèd Ministers of thought.
  Percy Bysshe Shelley 1792–1822: *Adonais* (1821)

12 When you're lying awake with a dismal headache, and repose
  is taboo'd by anxiety,
 I conceive you may use any language you choose to indulge
  in, without impropriety.
  W. S. Gilbert 1836–1911: *Iolanthe* (1882)

13 The interpretation of dreams is the royal road to a knowledge
 of the unconscious activities of the mind.
  Sigmund Freud 1856–1939: *The Interpretation of Dreams*
  (2nd ed., 1909) often quoted 'Dreams are the royal road to
  the unconscious'

14 ...The cool kindliness of sheets, that soon
 Smooth away trouble; and the rough male kiss
 Of blankets.
  Rupert Brooke 1887–1915: 'The Great Lover' (1914)

15 The armoured cars of dreams, contrived to let us do
 so many a dangerous thing.
  Elizabeth Bishop 1911–79: 'Sleeping Standing Up' (1946)

16 All the things one has forgotten scream for help in dreams.
  Elias Canetti 1905–94 : *Die Provinz der Menschen* (1973)

Society

1 No man is an Island, entire of it self.
  John Donne 1572–1631: *Devotions upon Emergent Occasions*
  (1624)

2 During the time men live without a common power to keep
them all in awe, they are in that condition which is called
war; and such a war as is of every man against every man.
    Thomas Hobbes 1588–1679: *Leviathan* (1651)

3 That action is best, which procures the greatest happiness for
the greatest numbers.
    Francis Hutcheson 1694–1746: *Inquiry into the Original*...
    (1725)

4 Society is indeed a contract...it becomes a partnership not
only between those who are living, but between those who
are living, those who are dead, and those who are to be born.
    Edmund Burke 1729–97: *Reflections on the Revolution in
    France* (1790)

5 Only in the state does man have a rational existence...Man
owes his entire existence to the state, and has his being
within it alone.
    G. W. F. Hegel 1770–1831: *Lectures on the Philosophy of
    World History: Introduction* (1830), tr. H. B. Nisbet

6 The greatest happiness of the greatest number is the
foundation of morals and legislation.
    Jeremy Bentham 1748–1832: *Commonplace Book*. Bentham
    claimed that either Joseph Priestley (1733–1804) or Cesare
    Beccaria (1738–94) passed on 'the sacred truth'

7 *La propriété c'est le vol.*
Property is theft.
    Pierre-Joseph Proudhon 1809–65: *Qu'est-ce que la
    propriété?* (1840)

8 From each according to his abilities, to each according to his
needs.
    Karl Marx 1818–83: *Critique of the Gotha Programme*
    (written 1875, but of earlier origin). See Morelly *Code de la
    nature* (1755), and J. Blanc *Organisation du travail* (1839)

9 The Social Contract is nothing more or less than a vast
conspiracy of human beings to lie to and humbug themselves
and one another for the general Good. Lies are the mortar
that bind the savage individual man into the social masonry.
    H. G. Wells 1866–1946: *Love and Mr Lewisham* (1900)

10 Hunger allows no choice
To the citizen or the police;
We must love one another or die.
   W. H. Auden 1907–73: 'September 1, 1939' (1940)

11 We shall have to walk and live a Woolworth life hereafter.
   Harold Nicolson 1886–1968: anticipating the aftermath of
   the Second World War; diary, 4 June 1941

12 The city is not a concrete jungle, it is a human zoo.
   Desmond Morris 1928– : *The Human Zoo* (1969)

13 We started off trying to set up a small anarchist community,
but people wouldn't obey the rules.
   Alan Bennett 1934– : *Getting On* (1972)

14 In a consumer society there are inevitably two kinds of
slaves: the prisoners of addiction and the prisoners of envy.
   Ivan Illich 1926– : *Tools for Conviviality* (1973)

15 There is no such thing as Society. There are individual men
and women, and there are families.
   Margaret Thatcher 1925– : in *Woman's Own* 31 October
   1987

Solitude

1 It is not good that the man should be alone; I will make him
an help meet for him.
   Bible: Genesis

2 He who is unable to live in society, or who has no need
because he is sufficient for himself, must be either a beast or
a god.
   Aristotle 384–322 BC: *Politics*

3 A man should keep for himself a little back shop, all his own,
quite unadulterated, in which he establishes his true freedom
and chief place of seclusion and solitude.
   Montaigne 1533–92: *Essais* (1580)

4 If you are idle, be not solitary; if you are solitary, be not idle.
   Samuel Johnson 1709–84: letter to Boswell, 27 October 1779

5 I am monarch of all I survey,
My right there is none to dispute.
  William Cowper 1731–1800: 'Verses Supposed to be Written
  by Alexander Selkirk' (1782)

6 To fly from, need not be to hate, mankind.
  Lord Byron 1788–1824: *Childe Harold's Pilgrimage* (1812–18)

7 Never less alone than when alone.
  Samuel Rogers 1763–1855: 'Human Life' (1819)

8 I long for scenes where man hath never trod
A place where woman never smiled or wept
There to abide with my Creator God.
  John Clare 1793–1864: 'I Am' (1848)

9 Yes! in the sea of life enisled,
With echoing straits between us thrown,
Dotting the shoreless watery wild,
We mortal millions live *alone*.
  Matthew Arnold 1822–88: 'To Marguerite—Continued'
  (1852)

10 Ships that pass in the night, and speak each other in passing;
Only a signal shown and a distant voice in the darkness;
So on the ocean of life we pass and speak one another,
Only a look and a voice; then darkness again and a silence.
  Henry Wadsworth Longfellow 1807–82: *Tales of a Wayside
  Inn* pt. 3 (1874)

11 Down to Gehenna or up to the Throne,
He travels the fastest who travels alone.
  Rudyard Kipling 1865–1936: *The Story of the Gadsbys* (1890)

12 Before I built a wall I'd ask to know
What I was walling in or walling out,
And to whom I was like to give offence.
  Robert Frost 1874–1963: 'Mending Wall' (1914)

13 Laugh and the world laughs with you;
Weep, and you weep alone;
For the sad old earth must borrow its mirth,
But has trouble enough of its own.
  Ella Wheeler Wilcox 1855–1919: 'Solitude'

14 I want to be alone.
  Greta Garbo 1905–90: *Grand Hotel* (1932 film)

15 God created man and, finding him not sufficiently alone, gave
him a companion to make him feel his solitude more keenly.
Paul Valéry 1871–1945: *Tel Quel 1* (1941)

16 He [Barrymore] would quote from Genesis the text which
says, 'It is not good for man to be alone,' and then add, 'But O
my God, what a relief.'
John Barrymore 1882–1942: A. Power-Waters *John
Barrymore* (1941)

17 All the lonely people, where do they all come from?
John Lennon 1940–80 and **Paul McCartney** 1942– :
'Eleanor Rigby' (1966 song)

18 Thirty years is a very long time to live alone and life doesn't
get any nicer.
Frances Partridge 1900– : on widowhood, at the age of 92;
in G. Kinnock and F. Miller *By Faith and Daring* (1993)

Sorrow

See also **Suffering**

1 By the waters of Babylon we sat down and wept: when we
remembered thee, O Sion.
Bible: Psalm 137

2 O my son Absalom, my son, my son Absalom! would God I
had died for thee, O Absalom, my son, my son!
Bible: II Samuel

3 *Sunt lacrimae rerum et mentem mortalia tangunt.*
There are tears shed for things and mortality touches the
heart.
Virgil 70–19 BC: *Aeneid*

4 Silence augmenteth grief, writing increaseth rage,
Staled are my thoughts, which loved and lost, the wonder of
our age.
Edward Dyer d. 1607: 'Elegy on the Death of Sir Philip
Sidney' (1593); formerly attributed to Fulke Greville,
1554–1628

5 Grief fills the room up of my absent child,
Lies in his bed, walks up and down with me.
William Shakespeare 1564–1616: *King John* (1591–8)

6 Every one can master a grief but he that has it.
   William Shakespeare 1564-1616: *Much Ado About Nothing*
   (1598-9)

7 When sorrows come, they come not single spies,
   But in battalions.
   William Shakespeare 1564-1616: *Hamlet* (1601)

8 Give sorrow words: the grief that does not speak
   Whispers the o'er-fraught heart, and bids it break.
   William Shakespeare 1564-1616: *Macbeth* (1606)

9 He first deceased; she for a little tried
   To live without him: liked it not, and died.
   Henry Wotton 1568-1639: 'Upon the Death of Sir Albertus
   Moreton's Wife' (1651)

10 Grief is a species of idleness.
   Samuel Johnson 1709-84: letter to Mrs Thrale, 17 March
   1773

11 For a tear is an intellectual thing;
   And a sigh is the sword of an Angel King.
   William Blake 1757-1827: *Jerusalem* (1815)

12 Then glut thy sorrow on a morning rose.
   John Keats 1795-1821: 'Ode on Melancholy' (1820)

13 Ah, woe is me! Winter is come and gone,
   But grief returns with the revolving year.
   Percy Bysshe Shelley 1792-1822: *Adonais* (1821)

14 I tell you, hopeless grief is passionless.
   Elizabeth Barrett Browning 1806-61: 'Grief' (1844)

15 Tears, idle tears, I know not what they mean,
   Tears from the depth of some divine despair.
   Alfred, Lord Tennyson 1809-92: *The Princess* (1847) song
   (added 1850)

16 For of all sad words of tongue or pen,
   The saddest are these: 'It might have been!'
   John Greenleaf Whittier 1807-92: 'Maud Muller' (1854)

17 We do not expect people to be deeply moved by what is not
   unusual. That element of tragedy which lies in the very fact
   of frequency, has not yet wrought itself into the coarse
   emotion of mankind.
   George Eliot 1819-80: *Middlemarch* (1871-2)

18 Tragedy ought really to be a great kick at misery.
> **D. H. Lawrence** 1885-1930: letter to A. W. McLeod,
> 6 October 1912

19 Now laughing friends deride tears I cannot hide,
So I smile and say 'When a lovely flame dies,
Smoke gets in your eyes.'
> **Otto Harbach** 1873-1963: 'Smoke Gets in your Eyes' (1933
> song)

20 Sob, heavy world,
Sob as you spin
Mantled in mist, remote from the happy.
> **W. H. Auden** 1907-73: *The Age of Anxiety* (1947)

21 He felt the loyalty we all feel to unhappiness—the sense that
that is where we really belong.
> **Graham Greene** 1904-91: *The Heart of the Matter* (1948)

···

Speech and Speeches
···

See also **Conversation**

1 Friends, Romans, countrymen, lend me your ears.
> **William Shakespeare** 1564-1616: *Julius Caesar* (1599)

2 I am no orator, as Brutus is;
But, as you know me all, a plain, blunt man,
That love my friend.
> **William Shakespeare** 1564-1616: *Julius Caesar* (1599)

3 I do not much dislike the matter, but
The manner of his speech.
> **William Shakespeare** 1564-1616: *Antony and Cleopatra*
> (1606-7)

4 But all was false and hollow; though his tongue
Dropped manna, and could make the worse appear
The better reason.
> **John Milton** 1608-74: *Paradise Lost* (1667)

5 And adepts in the speaking trade
Keep a cough by them ready made.
> **Charles Churchill** 1731-64: *The Ghost* (1763)

6 If I reprehend any thing in this world, it is the use of my
oracular tongue, and a nice derangement of epitaphs!
Richard Brinsley Sheridan 1751–1816: *The Rivals* (1775)

7 Mr Speaker, I smell a rat; I see him forming in the air and
darkening the sky; but I'll nip him in the bud.
Boyle Roche 1743–1807: attributed

8 A...sharp tongue is the only edged tool that grows keener
with constant use.
Washington Irving 1783–1859: *The Sketch Book* (1820) 'Rip
Van Winkle'

9 When you have nothing to say, say nothing.
Charles Caleb Colton *c.*1780–1832: *Lacon* (1820)

10 The brilliant chief, irregularly great,
Frank, haughty, rash,—the Rupert of Debate!
Edward Bulwer-Lytton 1803–73: of Edward Stanley, 14th
Earl of Derby, in *The New Timon* (1846)

11 Human speech is like a cracked kettle on which we tap crude
rhythms for bears to dance to, while we long to make music
that will melt the stars.
Gustave Flaubert 1821–80: *Madame Bovary* (1857)

12 Speech is the small change of silence.
George Meredith 1828–1909: *The Ordeal of Richard Feverel*
(1859)

13 To Trinity Church, Dorchester. The rector in his sermon
delivers himself of mean images in a very sublime voice, and
the effect is that of a glowing landscape in which clothes are
hung up to dry.
Thomas Hardy 1840–1928: *Notebooks* 1 February 1874

14 A sophistical rhetorician, inebriated with the exuberance of
his own verbosity.
Benjamin Disraeli 1804–81: of Gladstone, in *The Times*
29 July 1878

15 I absorb the vapour and return it as a flood.
W. E. Gladstone 1809–98: on public speaking, in Lord
Riddell *Some Things That Matter* (1927 ed.)

16 He [Lord Charles Beresford] is one of those orators of whom
it was well said, 'Before they get up, they do not know what
they are going to say; when they are speaking, they do not

know what they are saying; and when they have sat down,
they do not know what they have said.'
   Winston Churchill 1874–1965: speech, House of Commons,
   20 December 1912

17 It is impossible for an Englishman to open his mouth without
making some other Englishman hate or despise him.
   George Bernard Shaw 1856–1950: *Pygmalion* (1916)

18 What can be said at all can be said clearly; and whereof one
cannot speak thereof one must be silent.
   Ludwig Wittgenstein 1889–1951: *Tractatus
   Logico-Philosophicus* (1922)

19   Speech impelled us
To purify the dialect of the tribe.
   T. S. Eliot 1888–1965: *Four Quartets* 'Little Gidding' (1942)

20 He [Winston Churchill] mobilized the English language and
sent it into battle to steady his fellow countrymen and
hearten those Europeans upon whom the long dark night of
tyranny had descended.
   Ed Murrow 1908–65: broadcast, 30 November 1954

21 It was the nation and the race dwelling all round the globe
that had the lion's heart. I had the luck to be called upon to
give the roar.
   Winston Churchill 1874–1965: speech at Westminster Hall,
   30 November 1954

22 I do not object to people looking at their watches when I am
speaking. But I strongly object when they start shaking them
to make certain they are still going.
   Lord Birkett 1883–1962: in *Observer* 30 October 1960

23 A speech from Ernest Bevin on a major occasion had all the
horrific fascination of a public execution. If the mind was left
immune, eyes and ears and emotions were riveted.
   Michael Foot 1913– : *Aneurin Bevan* vol. 1 (1962)

24 Humming, Hawing and Hesitation are the three Graces of
contemporary Parliamentary oratory.
   Julian Critchley 1930– : *Westminster Blues* (1985)

Sport

1 ...*Duas tantum res anxius optat,*
Panem et circenses.
Only two things does he [the modern citizen] anxiously wish
for—bread and the big match.
Juvenal AD *c.*60–*c.*130: *Satires*, usually quoted 'bread and
circuses'

2 There is plenty of time to win this game, and to thrash the
Spaniards too.
Francis Drake *c.*1540–96: attributed

3 When we have matched our rackets to these balls,
We will in France, by God's grace, play a set
Shall strike his father's crown into the hazard.
William Shakespeare 1564–1616: *Henry V* (1599)

4 As no man is born an artist, so no man is born an angler.
Izaak Walton 1593–1683: *The Compleat Angler* (1653)

5 Chaos umpire sits,
And by decision more embroils the fray.
John Milton 1608–74: *Paradise Lost* (1667)

6 Eclipse first, the rest nowhere.
Dennis O'Kelly *c.*1720–87: comment at Epsom, 3 May 1769

7 Fly fishing may be a very pleasant amusement; but angling
or float fishing I can only compare to a stick and a string,
with a worm at one end and a fool at the other.
Samuel Johnson 1709–84: attributed, in Hawker
Instructions to Young Sportsmen (1859); attributed to
Jonathan Swift in *The Indicator* 27 October 1819

8 It's more than a game. It's an institution.
Thomas Hughes 1822–96: of cricket; *Tom Brown's
Schooldays* (1857)

9 There's a breathless hush in the Close to-night—
Ten to make and the match to win—
A bumping pitch and a blinding light,
An hour to play and the last man in.
Henry Newbolt 1862–1938: 'Vitaï Lampada' (1897)

10 Play up! play up! and play the game!
Henry Newbolt 1862–1938: 'Vitaï Lampada' (1897)

11 The bigger they are, the further they have to fall.
   Robert Fitzsimmons 1862–1917: prior to a boxing match, in
   Brooklyn Daily Eagle 11 August 1900 (similar forms found
   in proverbs since the 15th century)

12 The flannelled fools at the wicket or the muddied oafs at the
   goals.
   Rudyard Kipling 1865–1936: 'The Islanders' (1903)

13 As the race wore on...his oar was dipping into the water
   nearly *twice* as often as any other.
   Desmond Coke 1879–1931: *Sandford of Merton* (1903), usually
   misquoted 'All rowed fast, but none so fast as stroke'

14 The important thing in life is not the victory but the contest;
   the essential thing is not to have won but to have fought well.
   Baron Pierre de Coubertin 1863–1937: speech in London
   on the Olympic Games; 24 July 1908

15 To play billiards well is a sign of an ill-spent youth.
   Charles Roupell: attributed, in D. Duncan *Life of Herbert
   Spencer* (1908)

16 A decision of the courts decided that the game of golf may be
   played on Sunday, not being a game within the view of the
   law, but being a form of moral effort.
   Stephen Leacock 1869–1944: *Over the Footlights* (1923)

17 Honey, I just forgot to duck.
   Jack Dempsey 1895–1983: to his wife, on losing the World
   Heavyweight title, 23 September 1926. After a failed attempt
   on his life in 1981, Ronald Reagan quipped 'I forgot to duck'

18 To say that these men paid their shillings to watch
   twenty-two hirelings kick a ball is merely to say that a violin
   is wood and catgut, that *Hamlet* is so much paper and ink.
   For a shilling the Bruddersford United AFC offered you
   Conflict and Art.
   J. B. Priestley 1894–1984: *The Good Companions* (1929)

19 We was robbed!
   Joe Jacobs 1896–1940: after Jack Sharkey beat Max
   Schmeling (of whom Jacobs was manager) in the
   heavyweight title fight, 21 June 1932

20 I should of stood in bed.
   Joe Jacobs 1896–1940: after leaving his sickbed to attend
   the World Baseball Series in Detroit, 1935, and betting on
   the losers

21 For when the One Great Scorer comes to mark against your
name,
He writes—not that you won or lost—but how you played the
Game.
Grantland Rice 1880–1954: 'Alumnus Football' (1941)

22 A sportsman is a man who, every now and then, simply has
to get out and kill something. Not that he's cruel. He
wouldn't hurt a fly. It's not big enough.
Stephen Leacock 1869–1944: *My Remarkable Uncle* (1942)

23 Personally, I have always looked on cricket as organized
loafing.
Archbishop William Temple 1881–1944: attributed

24 Love-thirty, love-forty, oh! weakness of joy,
The speed of a swallow, the grace of a boy,
With carefullest carelessness, gaily you won,
I am weak from your loveliness, Joan Hunter Dunn.
John Betjeman 1906–84: 'A Subaltern's Love-Song' (1945)

25 Nice guys. Finish last.
Leo Durocher 1906–91: casual remark at a practice
ground, July 1946; in *Nice Guys Finish Last* (as the remark
generally is quoted, 1975)

26 Sure, winning isn't everything. It's the only thing.
Henry 'Red' Sanders: in *Sports Illustrated* 26 December
1955 (often attributed to Vince Lombardi)

27 Oh, he's football crazy, he's football mad
And the football it has robbed him o' the wee bit sense he
had.
And it would take a dozen skivvies, his clothes to wash and
scrub,
Since our Jock became a member of that terrible football
club.
Jimmy McGregor: 'Football Crazy' (1960 song)

28 I'm the greatest.
Muhammad Ali 1942– : catch-phrase used from 1962

29 Float like a butterfly, sting like a bee.
Muhammad Ali 1942– : summary of his boxing strategy, in
G. Sullivan *Cassius Clay Story* (1964), probably originated
by Drew 'Bundini' Brown

30 Cricket—a game which the English, not being a spiritual
people, have invented in order to give themselves some
conception of eternity.
  Lord Mancroft 1914–87 : *Bees in Some Bonnets* (1979)

31 Some people think football is a matter of life and
death…I can assure them it is much more serious than that.
  Bill Shankly 1914–81: in *Sunday Times* 4 October 1981

32 The thing about sport, any sport, is that swearing is very
much part of it.
  Jimmy Greaves 1940– : *Observer* 1 January 1989 'Sayings of
the Year'

33 Boxing's just showbusiness with blood.
  Frank Bruno 1961– : in *Observer* 29 December 1991
'Sayings of the Year'

Statistics

1 A witty statesman said, you might prove anything by figures.
  Thomas Carlyle 1795–1881: *Chartism* (1839)

2 Every moment dies a man,
Every moment one is born.
  Alfred, Lord Tennyson 1809–92: 'The Vision of Sin' (1842)

3 Every moment dies a man,
Every moment 1$\frac{1}{16}$ is born.
  Charles Babbage 1792–1871: parody of Tennyson's 'Vision
of Sin' in an unpublished letter to the poet

4 There are three kinds of lies: lies, damned lies and statistics.
  Benjamin Disraeli 1804–81: attributed to Disraeli in Mark
Twain *Autobiography* (1924)

5 He uses statistics as a drunken man uses lampposts—for
support rather than for illumination.
  Andrew Lang 1844–1912: attributed

6 [The War Office kept three sets of figures:] one to mislead the
public, another to mislead the Cabinet, and the third to
mislead itself.
  Herbert Asquith 1852–1928: in A. Horne *Price of Glory*
(1962)

7 From the fact that there are 400,000 species of beetles on this planet, but only 8,000 species of mammals, he [Haldane] concluded that the Creator, if He exists, has a special preference for beetles.
  J. B. S. Haldane 1892–1964: report of lecture, 7 April 1951

Style

1 I strive to be brief, and I become obscure.
  Horace 65–8 BC: *Ars Poetica*

2 When we see a natural style, we are quite surprised and delighted, for we expected to see an author and we find a man.
  Blaise Pascal 1623–62: *Pensées* (1670)

3 One had as good be out of the world, as out of the fashion.
  Colley Cibber 1671–1757: *Love's Last Shift* (1696)

4 Style is the dress of thought; a modest dress,
  Neat, but not gaudy, will true critics please.
  Samuel Wesley 1662–1735: 'An Epistle to a Friend concerning Poetry' (1700)

5 True wit is Nature to advantage dressed,
  What oft was thought, but ne'er so well expressed.
  Alexander Pope 1688–1744: *An Essay on Criticism* (1711)

6 Proper words in proper places, make the true definition of a style.
  Jonathan Swift 1667–1745: *Letter to a Young Gentleman lately entered into Holy Orders* (9 January 1720)

7 Style is the man.
  Comte de Buffon 1707–88: *Discours sur le style* (address given to the Académie Française, 25 August 1753)

8 It is charming to totter into vogue.
  Horace Walpole 1717–97: letter to George Selwyn, 2 December 1765

9 Dr Johnson's sayings would not appear so extraordinary, were it not for his bow-wow way.
  Henry Herbert, 10th Earl of Pembroke 1734–94: in James Boswell *Life of Samuel Johnson* (1791) 27 March 1775

10 Too many flowers…too little fruit.
   Sir Walter Scott 1771–1832: of Felicia Hemans's literary style; letter to Joanna Baillie, 18 July 1823

11 It is rustic all through. It is moorish, and wild, and knotty as a root of heath.
   Charlotte Brontë 1816–55: on the setting of Emily Brontë's *Wuthering Heights*, in her own preface to the 1850 edition

12 Style is life! It is the very life-blood of thought!
   Gustave Flaubert 1821–80: letter to Louise Colet, 7 September 1853

13 Have something to say, and say it as clearly as you can. That is the only secret of style.
   Matthew Arnold 1822–88: in G. W. E. Russell *Collections and Recollections* (1898)

14 The Mandarin style…is beloved by literary pundits, by those who would make the written word as unlike as possible to the spoken one.
   Cyril Connolly 1903–74: *Enemies of Promise* (1938)

Success and Failure

1 The race is not to the swift, nor the battle to the strong.
   Bible: Ecclesiastes

2 *Veni, vidi, vici.*
   I came, I saw, I conquered.
   Julius Caesar 100–44 BC: inscription displayed in Caesar's Pontic triumph, according to Suetonius *Lives of the Caesars*; or, according to Plutarch *Parallel Lives*, written in a letter by Caesar, announcing the victory of Zela which concluded the Pontic campaign

3 The only safe course for the defeated is to expect no safety.
   Virgil 70–19 BC: *Aeneid*

4 These success encourages: they can because they think they can.
   Virgil 70–19 BC: *Aeneid*

5 *Vae victis.*
   Down with the defeated!
   Livy 59 BC–AD 17: cry (already proverbial) of the Gallic

King, Brennus, on capturing Rome in 390 BC; in *Ab Urbe Condita*

6 For what shall it profit a man, if he shall gain the whole world, and lose his own soul?
   Bible: St Mark. See also St Matthew

7 *Deos fortioribus adesse.*
   The gods are on the side of the stronger.
   Tacitus AD c.56–after 117: *Histories*

8   We fail!
   But screw your courage to the sticking-place,
   And we'll not fail.
   William Shakespeare 1564–1616: *Macbeth* (1606)

9 'Tis not in mortals to command success,
   But we'll do more, Sempronius; we'll deserve it.
   Joseph Addison 1672–1719: *Cato* (1713)

10 The conduct of a losing party never appears right: at least it never can possess the only infallible criterion of wisdom to vulgar judgements—success.
   Edmund Burke 1729–97: *Letter to a Member of the National Assembly* (1791)

11 The sublime and the ridiculous are often so nearly related, that it is difficult to class them separately. One step above the sublime, makes the ridiculous; and one step above the ridiculous, makes the sublime again.
   Thomas Paine 1737–1809: *The Age of Reason* pt. 2 (1795)

12 There is only one step from the sublime to the ridiculous.
   Napoléon I 1769–1821: following the retreat from Moscow in 1812; in D. G. De Pradt *Histoire de l'Ambassade dans le grand-duché de Varsovie en 1812* (1815).

13 I have climbed to the top of the greasy pole.
   Benjamin Disraeli 1804–81: on becoming Prime Minister, in W. Monypenny and G. Buckle *Life of Disraeli* (1916)

14 To burn always with this hard, gemlike flame, to maintain this ecstasy, is success in life.
   Walter Pater 1839–94: *Studies in the History of the Renaissance* (1873)

15 All you need in this life is ignorance and confidence; then success is sure.
   Mark Twain 1835–1910: letter to Mrs Foote, 2 December 1887

16 We are not interested in the possibilities of defeat; they do not exist.
  Queen Victoria 1819–1901: on the Boer War during 'Black Week', December 1899

17 The moral flabbiness born of the exclusive worship of the bitch-goddess *success*.
  William James 1842–1910: letter to H. G. Wells, 11 September 1906

18 If you can meet with triumph and disaster
And treat those two imposters just the same.
  Rudyard Kipling 1865–1936: 'If—' (1910)

19 History to the defeated
May say Alas but cannot help or pardon.
  W. H. Auden 1907–73: 'Spain 1937' (1937)

20 Success is relative:
It is what we can make of the mess we have made of things.
  T. S. Eliot 1888–1965: *The Family Reunion* (1939)

21 You ask, what is our aim? I can answer in one word: Victory, victory at all costs, victory in spite of all terror; victory, however long and hard the road may be; for without victory, there is no survival.
  Winston Churchill 1874–1965: speech, House of Commons, 13 May 1940

22 Trying to learn to use words, and every attempt
Is a wholly new start, and a different kind of failure.
  T. S. Eliot 1888–1965: *Four Quartets* 'East Coker' (1940)

23 *La vittoria trova cento padri, e nessuno vuole riconoscere l'insuccesso.*
Victory has a hundred fathers, but defeat is an orphan.
  Count Galeazzo Ciano 1903–44: diary, 9 September 1942 (literally 'no-one wants to recognise defeat as his own')

24 If *A* is a success in life, then *A* equals *x* plus *y* plus *z*. Work is *x*; *y* is play; and *z* is keeping your mouth shut.
  Albert Einstein 1879–1955: in *Observer* 15 January 1950

25 Be nice to people on your way up because you'll meet 'em on your way down.
  Wilson Mizner 1876–1933: in A. Johnston *The Legendary Mizners* (1953)

26 She knows there's no success like failure
And that failure's no success at all.
Bob Dylan 1941- : 'Love Minus Zero / No Limit' (1965 song)

27 For a writer, success is always temporary, success is only a delayed failure. And it is incomplete.
Graham Greene 1904–91: *A Sort of Life* (1971)

28 Whenever a friend succeeds, a little something in me dies.
Gore Vidal 1925- : in *Sunday Times Magazine* 16 September 1973

29 It is not enough to succeed. Others must fail.
Gore Vidal 1925- : in G. Irvine *Antipanegyric for Tom Driberg* 8 December 1976

Suffering

1 O you who have borne even heavier things, God will grant an end to these too.
Virgil 70–19 BC: *Aeneid*

2 Nothing happens to anybody which he is not fitted by nature to bear.
Marcus Aurelius AD 121–80: *Meditations*

3 He jests at scars, that never felt a wound.
William Shakespeare 1564–1616: *Romeo and Juliet* (1595)

4 But I have that within which passeth show;
These but the trappings and the suits of woe.
William Shakespeare 1564–1616: *Hamlet* (1601)

5 But yet the pity of it, Iago! O! Iago, the pity of it, Iago!
William Shakespeare 1564–1616: *Othello* (1602-4)

6   I am a man
More sinned against than sinning.
William Shakespeare 1564–1616: *King Lear* (1605–6)

7   The worst is not,
So long as we can say, 'This is the worst.'
William Shakespeare 1564–1616: *King Lear* (1605–6)

8 The oldest hath borne most: we that are young,
Shall never see so much, nor live so long.
William Shakespeare 1564–1616: *King Lear* (1605–6)

9 To each his suff'rings, all are men,
   Condemned alike to groan;
   The tender for another's pain,
   Th' unfeeling for his own.
   Thomas Gray 1716–71: *Ode on a Distant Prospect of Eton College* (1747)

10 Hides from himself his state, and shuns to know,
   That life protracted is protracted woe.
   Samuel Johnson 1709–84: *The Vanity of Human Wishes* (1749)

11 Thank you, madam, the agony is abated.
   Lord Macaulay 1800–59: aged four, having had hot coffee spilt over his legs; in G. O. Trevelyan *Life and Letters of Lord Macaulay* (1876)

12 If suffer we must, let's suffer on the heights.
   Victor Hugo 1802–85: *Contemplations* (1856)

13 Those who have courage to love should have courage to suffer.
   Anthony Trollope 1815–82: *The Bertrams* (1859)

14 Nothing begins, and nothing ends,
   That is not paid with moan;
   For we are born in other's pain,
   And perish in our own.
   Francis Thompson 1859–1907: 'Daisy' (1913)

15 It is not true that suffering ennobles the character; happiness does that sometimes, but suffering, for the most part, makes men petty and vindictive.
   W. Somerset Maugham 1874–1965: *Moon and Sixpence* (1919)

16 Too long a sacrifice
   Can make a stone of the heart.
   W. B. Yeats 1865–1939: 'Easter, 1916' (1921)

17 We can't all be happy, we can't all be rich, we can't all be lucky...Some must cry so that others may be able to laugh the more heartily.
   Jean Rhys c.1890–1979: *Good Morning, Midnight* (1939)

18 Even the dreadful martyrdom must run its course
   Anyhow in a corner, some untidy spot
   Where the dogs go on with their doggy life and the torturer's

horse
Scratches its innocent behind on a tree.
   W. H. Auden 1907–73: 'Musée des Beaux Arts' (1940)

The Supernatural

1 Then a spirit passed before my face; the hair of my flesh
stood up.
   Bible: Job

2 GLENDOWER: I can call spirits from the vasty deep.
HOTSPUR: Why, so can I, or so can any man;
But will they come when you do call for them?
   William Shakespeare 1564–1616: *Henry IV, Part 1* (1597)

3 Is this a dagger which I see before me,
The handle toward my hand?
   William Shakespeare 1564–1616: *Macbeth* (1606)

4 Double, double toil and trouble;
Fire burn and cauldron bubble.
   William Shakespeare 1564–1616: *Macbeth* (1606)

5 Superstition sets the whole world in flames; philosophy
quenches them.
   Voltaire 1694–1778: *Dictionnaire philosophique* (1764)

6 I wants to make your flesh creep.
   Charles Dickens 1812–70: *Pickwick Papers* (1837) The Fat
   Boy

7 Up the airy mountain,
Down the rushy glen,
We daren't go a-hunting,
For fear of little men.
   William Allingham 1824–89: 'The Fairies' (1850)

8 From ghoulies and ghosties and long-leggety beasties
And things that go bump in the night,
Good Lord, deliver us!
   Anonymous: 'The Cornish or West Country Litany', in F. T.
   Nettleinghame *Polperro Proverbs and Others* (1926)

9 I always knew the living talked rot, but it's nothing to the rot
the dead talk.
   Margot Asquith 1864–1945: on spiritualism, in Henry
   'Chips' Channon, diary, 20 December 1937

Taxes

1 *Pecunia non olet.*
  Money has no smell.
  > **Emperor Vespasian** AD 9–79: quashing an objection to a tax on public lavatories, in Suetonius *Lives of the Caesars*

2 *Excise.* A hateful tax levied upon commodities.
  > **Samuel Johnson** 1709–84: *Dictionary of the English Language* (1755)

3 Taxation without representation is tyranny.
  > **James Otis** 1725–83: watchword (coined *c.*1761) of the American Revolution

4 To tax and to please, no more than to love and to be wise, is not given to men.
  > **Edmund Burke** 1729–97: *On American Taxation* (1775)

5 There is no art which one government sooner learns of another than that of draining money from the pockets of the people.
  > **Adam Smith** 1723–90: *Wealth of Nations* (1776)

6 In this world nothing can be said to be certain, except death and taxes.
  > **Benjamin Franklin** 1706–90: letter to Jean Baptiste Le Roy, 13 November 1789

7 The Chancellor of the Exchequer is a man whose duties make him more or less of a taxing machine. He is intrusted with a certain amount of misery which it is his duty to distribute as fairly as he can.
  > **Robert Lowe** 1811–92: speech, House of Commons, 11 April 1870

8 Income Tax has made more Liars out of the American people than Golf.
  > **Will Rogers** 1879–1935: *The Illiterate Digest* (1924)

9 Death and taxes and childbirth! There's never any convenient time for any of them.
  > **Margaret Mitchell** 1900–49: *Gone with the Wind* (1936)

10 Only the little people pay taxes.
  > **Leona Helmsley** *c.*1920– : addressed to her housekeeper in 1983, and reported at her trial for tax evasion; in *New York Times* 12 July 1989

11 Read my lips: no new taxes.
   George Bush 1924- : campaign pledge on taxation, in *New York Times* 19 August 1988

Teaching

See also **Education**

1 For precept must be upon precept, precept upon precept; line upon line, line upon line; here a little, and there a little.
   Bible: Isaiah

2 *Homines dum docent discunt.*
   Even while they teach, men learn.
   Seneca ('the Younger') c.4 BC–AD 65: *Epistulae Morales*

3 There is no such whetstone, to sharpen a good wit and encourage a will to learning, as is praise.
   Roger Ascham 1515–68: *The Schoolmaster* (1570)

4 We loved the doctrine for the teacher's sake.
   Daniel Defoe 1660–1731: 'Character of the late Dr S. Annesley' (1697)

5 Men must be taught as if you taught them not,
   And things unknown proposed as things forgot.
   Alexander Pope 1688–1744: *An Essay on Criticism* (1711)

6 Delightful task! to rear the tender thought,
   To teach the young idea how to shoot.
   James Thomson 1700–48: *The Seasons* (1746) 'Spring'

7 Be a governess! Better be a slave at once!
   Charlotte Brontë 1816–55: *Shirley* (1849)

8 He who can, does. He who cannot, teaches.
   George Bernard Shaw 1856–1950: *Man and Superman* (1903)

9 A teacher affects eternity; he can never tell where his influence stops.
   Henry Brooks Adams 1838–1918: *The Education of Henry Adams* (1907)

10 For every person who wants to teach there are approximately thirty who don't want to learn—much.

> **W. C. Sellar** 1898–1951 and **R. J. Yeatman** 1898–1968: *And Now All This* (1932)

11 Give me a girl at an impressionable age, and she is mine for life.

> **Muriel Spark** 1918– : *The Prime of Miss Jean Brodie* (1961)

12 *You* have not had thirty years' experience... *You* have had one year's experience 30 times.

> **J. L. Carr** 1912– : *The Harpole Report* (1972)

Technology

See also **Inventions and Discoveries, Science**

1 Give me but one firm spot on which to stand, and I will move the earth.

> **Archimedes** *c*.287–212 BC: on the action of a lever, in Pappus *Synagoge*

2 I sell here, Sir, what all the world desires to have—POWER.

> **Matthew Boulton** 1728–1809: speaking to Boswell of his engineering works; in James Boswell *Life of Samuel Johnson* (1791)

3 One machine can do the work of fifty ordinary men. No machine can do the work of one extraordinary man.

> **Elbert Hubbard** 1859–1915: *Thousand and One Epigrams* (1911)

4 Your worship is your furnaces,
> Which, like old idols, lost obscenes,
> Have molten bowels; your vision is
> Machines for making more machines.

> **Gordon Bottomley** 1874–1948: 'To Ironfounders and Others' (1912)

5 Communism is Soviet power plus the electrification of the whole country.

> **Lenin** 1870–1924: Report to 8th Congress, 1920, in *Collected Works*

6 Machines are worshipped because they are beautiful, and valued because they confer power; they are hated because they are hideous, and loathed because they impose slavery.
   Bertrand Russell 1872–1970: *Sceptical Essays* (1928)

7 Her own mother lived the latter years of her life in the horrible suspicion that electricity was dripping invisibly all over the house.
   James Thurber 1894–1961: *My Life and Hard Times* (1933)

8 This is not the age of pamphleteers. It is the age of the engineers. The spark-gap is mightier than the pen.
   Lancelot Hogben 1895–1975: *Science for the Citizen* (1938)

9 Technology…the knack of so arranging the world that we need not experience it.
   Max Frisch 1911– : *Homo Faber* (1957)

10 The new electronic interdependence recreates the world in the image of a global village.
   Marshall McLuhan 1911–80: *The Gutenberg Galaxy* (1962)

11 The Britain that is going to be forged in the white heat of this revolution will be no place for restrictive practices or for outdated methods on either side of industry.
   Harold Wilson 1916– : speech at the Labour Party Conference, 1 October 1963; usually quoted 'the white heat of the technological revolution'

12 The medium is the message.
   Marshall McLuhan 1911–80: *Understanding Media* (1964)

13 To err is human but to really foul things up requires a computer.
   Anonymous: *Farmers' Almanac for 1978*

14 A modern computer hovers between the obsolescent and the nonexistent.
   Sydney Brenner 1927– : attributed in *Science* 5 January 1990

Temptation

1 Watch and pray, that ye enter not into temptation: the spirit indeed is willing but the flesh is weak.
   Bible: St Matthew

2 From all the deceits of the world, the flesh, and the devil,
Good Lord, deliver us.
  Book of Common Prayer 1662: *The Litany*

3 Then gently scan your brother man,
Still gentler sister woman;
Tho' they may gang a kennin wrang,
To step aside is human.
  Robert Burns 1759–96: 'Address to the Unco Guid' (1787)

4 What's done we partly may compute,
But know not what's resisted.
  Robert Burns 1759–96: 'Address to the Unco Guid' (1787)

5 I can resist everything except temptation.
  Oscar Wilde 1854–1900: *Lady Windermere's Fan* (1892)

6 There are several good protections against temptations, but
the surest is cowardice.
  Mark Twain 1835–1910: *Following the Equator* (1897)

7 The Devil, having nothing else to do,
Went off to tempt My Lady Poltagrue.
My Lady, tempted by a private whim,
To his extreme annoyance, tempted him.
  Hilaire Belloc 1870–1953: 'On Lady Poltagrue' (1923)

The Theatre see Acting and the Theatre

Thinking

See also **Ideas, The Mind**

1 To change your mind and to follow him who sets you right is
to be nonetheless the free agent that you were before.
  Marcus Aurelius AD 121–80: *Meditations*

2 Reasons are not like garments, the worse for wearing.
  Robert Devereux, 2nd Earl of Essex 1566–1601: letter to
  Lord Willoughby, 4 January 1599

3 Yond Cassius has a lean and hungry look;
He thinks too much: such men are dangerous.
  William Shakespeare 1564–1616: *Julius Caesar* (1599)

4 *Cogito, ergo sum.*
I think, therefore I am.
   René Descartes 1596-1650: *Le Discours de la méthode* (1637)

5 How comes it to pass, then, that we appear such cowards in
reasoning, and are so afraid to stand the test of ridicule?
   3rd Earl of Shaftesbury 1671-1713: *A Letter Concerning
   Enthusiasm* (1708)

6 I'll not listen to reason...Reason always means what
someone else has got to say.
   Elizabeth Gaskell 1810-65: *Cranford* (1853)

7 How often misused words generate misleading thoughts.
   Herbert Spencer 1820-1903: *Principles of Ethics* (1879)

8 Logical consequences are the scarecrows of fools and the
beacons of wise men.
   T. H. Huxley 1825-95: *Science and Culture and Other Essays*
   (1881)

9 It is a capital mistake to theorize before you have all the
evidence. It biases the judgement.
   Arthur Conan Doyle 1859-1930: *A Study in Scarlet* (1888)

10 Heretics are the only bitter remedy against the entropy of
human thought.
   Yevgeny Zamyatin 1884-1937: 'Literature, Revolution and
   Entropy' quoted in *The Dragon and other Stories* (1967, tr.
   M. Ginsberg) introduction

11 *Doublethink* means the power of holding two contradictory
beliefs in one's mind simultaneously, and accepting both of
them.
   George Orwell 1903-50: *Nineteen Eighty-Four* (1949)

12 What was once thought can never be unthought.
   Friedrich Dürrenmatt 1921- : *The Physicists* (1962)

13 The real question is not whether machines think but whether
men do.
   B. F. Skinner 1904-90: *Contingencies of Reinforcement* (1969)

Time

1 For a thousand years in thy sight are but as yesterday:
seeing that is past as a watch in the night.
   Bible: Psalm 90

2 To every thing there is a season, and a time to every purpose
under the heaven:
   A time to be born, and a time to die…
   A time to weep, and a time to laugh; a time to mourn, and
   a time to dance.
   Bible: Ecclesiastes

3 *Sed fugit interea, fugit inreparabile tempus.*
   But meanwhile it is flying, irretrievable time is flying.
   Virgil 70–19 BC: *Georgics* (usually quoted '*tempus fugit*
   [time flies]')

4 *Tempus edax rerum.*
   Time the devourer of everything.
   Ovid 43 BC–AD *c.*17: *Metamorphoses*

5 Time is a violent torrent; no sooner is a thing brought to
sight than it is swept by and another takes its place.
   Marcus Aurelius AD 121–80: *Meditations*

6 Every instant of time is a pinprick of eternity.
   Marcus Aurelius AD 121–80: *Meditations*

7 Time is the measure of movement.
   Auctoritates Aristotelis: a compilation of medieval
   propositions

8 Time is…Time was…Time is past.
   Robert Greene *c.*1560–92: *Friar Bacon and Friar Bungay*
   (1594)

9 I wasted time, and now doth time waste me.
   William Shakespeare 1564–1616: *Richard II* (1595)

10 Time hath, my lord, a wallet at his back,
   Wherein he puts alms for oblivion.
   William Shakespeare 1564–1616: *Troilus and Cressida*
   (1602)

11   Come what come may,
   Time and the hour runs through the roughest day.
   William Shakespeare 1564–1616: *Macbeth* (1606)

12 To-morrow, and to-morrow, and to-morrow,
Creeps in this petty pace from day to day,
To the last syllable of recorded time;
And all our yesterdays have lighted fools
The way to dusty death.
    William Shakespeare 1564–1616: *Macbeth* (1606)

13   What seest thou else
In the dark backward and abysm of time?
    William Shakespeare 1564–1616: *The Tempest* (1611)

14 Even such is Time, which takes in trust
Our youth, our joys, and all we have,
And pays us but with age and dust.
    Walter Ralegh *c*.1552–1618: written the night before his
death

15 Fly envious Time, till thou run out thy race,
Call on the lazy leaden-stepping hours.
    John Milton 1608–74: 'On Time' (1645)

16 I saw Eternity the other night,
Like a great ring of pure and endless light.
    Henry Vaughan 1622–95: *Silex Scintillans* (1650–5)

17 But at my back I always hear
Time's wingèd chariot hurrying near:
And yonder all before us lie
Deserts of vast eternity.
    Andrew Marvell 1621–78: 'To His Coy Mistress' (1681)

18 Time, like an ever-rolling stream,
Bears all its sons away.
    Isaac Watts 1674–1748: 'O God, our help in ages past' (1719
hymn)

19 What's not destroyed by Time's devouring hand?
Where's Troy, and where's the Maypole in the Strand?
    James Bramston *c*.1694–1744: *The Art of Politics* (1729)

20 I recommend to you to take care of minutes: for hours will
take care of themselves.
    Lord Chesterfield 1694–1773: *Letters to his Son* (1774)
6 November 1747

21 Eternity is in love with the productions of time.
    William Blake 1757–1827: *The Marriage of Heaven and Hell*
(1790–3) 'Proverbs of Hell'

22 Nothing puzzles me more than time and space; and yet
nothing troubles me less, as I never think about them.
   Charles Lamb 1775–1834: letter to Thomas Manning,
   2 January 1810

23 Men talk of killing time, while time quietly kills them.
   Dion Boucicault 1820–90: *London Assurance* (1841)

24 As if you could kill time without injuring eternity.
   Henry David Thoreau 1817–62: *Walden* (1854)

25 He said, 'What's time? Leave Now for dogs and apes!
Man has Forever.'
   Robert Browning 1812–89: 'A Grammarian's Funeral' (1855)

26 The woods decay, the woods decay and fall,
The vapours weep their burthen to the ground,
Man comes and tills the field and lies beneath,
And after many a summer dies the swan.
   Alfred, Lord Tennyson 1809–92: 'Tithonus' (1860, revised
   1864)

27 Time goes, you say? Ah no!
Alas, Time stays, *we* go.
   Henry Austin Dobson 1840–1921: 'The Paradox of Time'
   (1877)

28 Time, you old gipsy man,
Will you not stay,
Put up your caravan
Just for one day?
   Ralph Hodgson 1871–1962: 'Time, You Old Gipsy Man'
   (1917)

29 I have measured out my life with coffee spoons.
   T. S. Eliot 1888–1965: 'Love Song of J. Alfred Prufrock'
   (1917)

30 Ah! the clock is always slow;
It is later than you think.
   Robert W. Service 1874–1958: 'It Is Later Than You Think'
   (1921)

31 *In the long run* we are all dead.
   John Maynard Keynes 1883–1946: *A Tract on Monetary
   Reform* (1923)

32 I shall use the phrase 'time's arrow' to express this one-way
property of time which has no analogue in space.
   Arthur Eddington 1882–1944: *The Nature of the Physical
   World* (1928)

33 Half our life is spent trying to find something to do with the
time we have rushed through life trying to save.
   Will Rogers 1879–1935: letter in *New York Times* 29 April
   1930

34 Time present and time past
Are both perhaps present in time future,
And time future contained in time past.
   T. S. Eliot 1888–1965: *Four Quartets* 'Burnt Norton' (1936)

35 Three o'clock is always too late or too early for anything you
want to do.
   Jean-Paul Sartre 1905–80: *La Nausée* (Nausea, 1938)

36 I am a sundial, and I make a botch
Of what is done much better by a watch.
   Hilaire Belloc 1870–1953: 'On a Sundial' (1938)

37 The sunlight on the garden
Hardens and grows cold,
We cannot cage the minute
Within its net of gold.
   Louis MacNeice 1907–63: 'Sunlight on the Garden' (1938)

38 VLADIMIR: That passed the time.
ESTRAGON: It would have passed in any case.
VLADIMIR: Yes, but not so rapidly.
   Samuel Beckett 1906–89: *Waiting for Godot* (1955)

Titles

1 But let a Lord once own the happy lines,
How the wit brightens! how the style refines!
   Alexander Pope 1688–1744: *An Essay on Criticism* (1711)

2 The rank is but the guinea's stamp,
The man's the gowd for a' that!
   Robert Burns 1759–96: 'For a' that and a' that' (1790)

3 Kind hearts are more than coronets,
  And simple faith than Norman blood.
    Alfred, Lord Tennyson 1809–92: 'Lady Clara Vere de Vere'
    (1842)

4 Titles distinguish the mediocre, embarrass the superior, and
  are disgraced by the inferior.
    George Bernard Shaw 1856–1950: *Man and Superman*
    (1903)

5 A fully-equipped duke costs as much to keep up as two
  Dreadnoughts; and dukes are just as great a terror and they
  last longer.
    David Lloyd George 1863–1945: speech at Newcastle,
    9 October 1909

6 When I want a peerage, I shall buy it like an honest man.
    Lord Northcliffe 1865–1922: in Tom Driberg *Swaff* (1974)

7 An aristocracy in a republic is like a chicken whose head has
  been cut off: it may run about in a lively way, but in fact it is
  dead.
    Nancy Mitford 1904–73: *Noblesse Oblige* (1956)

8 There is no stronger craving in the world than that of the
  rich for titles, except perhaps that of the titled for riches.
    Hesketh Pearson 1887–1964: *The Pilgrim Daughters* (1961)

9 What harm have I ever done to the Labour Party?
    R. H. Tawney 1880–1962: on declining the offer of a peerage,
    in *Evening Standard* 18 January 1962

10 Even as it [Great Britain] walked out on you and joined the
   Common Market, you were still looking for your MBEs and
   your knighthoods, and all the rest of the regalia that comes
   with it. You would take Australia right back down the time
   tunnel to the cultural cringe where you have always come
   from.
    Paul Keating 1944– : addressing Australian Conservative
    supporters of Great Britain, 27 February 1992

The Town see The Country and the Town

Transience

1 Like that of leaves is a generation of men.
  Homer 8th century BC: *The Iliad*

2 Vanity of vanities; all is vanity.
  Bible: Ecclesiastes

3 All flesh is as grass, and all the glory of man as the flower of
  grass. The grass withereth, and the flower thereof falleth
  away.
  Bible: I Peter

4 *Sic transit gloria mundi.*
  Thus passes the glory of the world.
  Anonymous: said at the coronation of a new Pope, while
  flax is burned; used at the coronation of Alexander V, 1409,
  but earlier in origin

5 Gather ye rosebuds while ye may,
  Old Time is still a-flying:
  And this same flower that smiles to-day,
  To-morrow will be dying.
  Robert Herrick 1591–1674: 'To the Virgins, to Make Much
  of Time' (1648)

6 A little rule, a little sway,
  A sunbeam in a winter's day,
  Is all the proud and mighty have
  Between the cradle and the grave.
  John Dyer 1700–58: *Grongar Hill* (1726)

7 The rainbow comes and goes,
  And lovely is the rose.
  William Wordsworth 1770–1850: 'Ode. Intimations of
  Immortality' (1807)

8 He who binds to himself a joy
  Doth the winged life destroy
  But he who kisses the joy as it flies
  Lives in Eternity's sunrise.
  William Blake 1757–1827: *MS Note-Book*

9 A rainbow and a cuckoo's song
  May never come together again;

May never come
This side the tomb.
   W. H. Davies 1871–1940: 'A Great Time' (1914)

10 Look thy last on all things lovely,
   Every hour.
   Walter de la Mare 1873–1956: 'Fare Well' (1918)

Transport

1 Sir, Saturday morning, although recurring at regular and
   well-foreseen intervals, always seems to take this railway by
   surprise.
   W. S. Gilbert 1836–1911: letter to the station-master at
   Baker Street, on the Metropolitan line; in John Julius
   Norwich *Christmas Crackers* (1980)

2 There is *nothing*—absolutely nothing—half so much worth
   doing as simply messing about in boats.
   Kenneth Grahame 1859–1932: *The Wind in the Willows*
   (1908)

3 The poetry of motion! The *real* way to travel! The *only* way to
   travel! Here today—in next week tomorrow!
   Kenneth Grahame 1859–1932: on the car; *The Wind in the
   Willows* (1908)

4 Railway termini. They are our gates to the glorious and the
   unknown. Through them we pass out into adventure and
   sunshine, to them, alas! we return.
   E. M. Forster 1879–1970: *Howards End* (1910)

5 Before the Roman came to Rye or out to Severn strode,
   The rolling English drunkard made the rolling English road.
   G. K. Chesterton 1874–1936: 'The Rolling English Road'
   (1914)

6 To George F. Babbitt, as to most prosperous citizens of
   Zenith, his motor car was poetry and tragedy, love and
   heroism. The office was his pirate ship but the car his
   perilous excursion ashore.
   Sinclair Lewis 1885–1951: *Babbitt* (1922)

7 [There are] only two classes of pedestrians in these days of
reckless motor traffic—the quick, and the dead.
    Lord Dewar 1864-1930: in George Robey *Looking Back on
Life* (1933)

8 After the first powerful plain manifesto
The black statement of pistons, without more fuss
But gliding like a queen, she leaves the station.
    Stephen Spender 1909- : 'The Express' (1933)

9 This is the Night Mail crossing the Border,
Bringing the cheque and the postal order,
Letters for the rich, letters for the poor,
The shop at the corner, the girl next door.
    W. H. Auden 1907-73: 'Night Mail' (1936)

10 Beneath this slab
John Brown is stowed.
He watched the ads,
And not the road.
    Ogden Nash 1902-71: 'Lather as You Go' (1942)

11 That monarch of the road,
Observer of the Highway Code,
That big six-wheeler
Scarlet-painted
London Transport
Diesel-engined
Ninety-seven horse power
Omnibus!
    Michael Flanders 1922-75 and **Donald Swann** 1923-94: 'A
Transport of Delight' (c.1956 song)

12 I think that cars today are almost the exact equivalent of the
great Gothic cathedrals: I mean the supreme creation of an
era, conceived with passion by unknown artists, and
consumed in image if not in usage by a whole population
which appropriates them as a purely magical object.
    Roland Barthes 1915-80: *Mythologies* (1957), tr. A. Lavers

13 The car has become an article of dress without which we feel
uncertain, unclad and incomplete in the urban compound.
    Marshall McLuhan 1911-80: *Understanding Media* (1964)

14 Commuter—one who spends his life
In riding to and from his wife;

A man who shaves and takes a train,
And then rides back to shave again.

    E. B. White 1899–1985: 'The Commuter' (1982)

Travel

1 Travel, in the younger sort, is a part of education; in the
elder, a part of experience. He that travelleth into a country
before he hath some entrance into the language, goeth to
school, and not to travel.

    Francis Bacon 1561–1626: *Essays* (1625) 'Of Travel'

2 I always love to begin a journey on Sundays, because I shall
have the prayers of the church, to preserve all that travel by
land, or by water.

    Jonathan Swift 1667–1745: *Polite Conversation* (1738)

3 So it is in travelling; a man must carry knowledge with him,
if he would bring home knowledge.

    Samuel Johnson 1709–84: in James Boswell *Life of Johnson*
(1791) 17 April 1778

4 Worth seeing, yes; but not worth going to see.

    Samuel Johnson 1709–84: of the Giant's Causeway; in
James Boswell *Life of Johnson* (1791) 12 October 1779

5 Of all noxious animals, too, the most noxious is a tourist.
And of all tourists the most vulgar, ill-bred, offensive and
loathsome is the British tourist.

    Francis Kilvert 1840–79: diary, 5 April 1870

6 For my part, I travel not to go anywhere, but to go. I travel
for travel's sake. The great affair is to move.

    Robert Louis Stevenson 1850–94: *Travels with a Donkey*
(1879)

7 To travel hopefully is a better thing than to arrive, and the
true success is to labour.

    Robert Louis Stevenson 1850–94: *Virginibus Puerisque*
(1881)

8 Clay lies still, but blood's a rover;
Breath's a ware that will not keep.
Up, lad: when the journey's over
There'll be time enough to sleep.

    A. E. Housman 1859–1936: *A Shropshire Lad* (1896)

9 A man travels the world in search of what he needs and
returns home to find it.
George Moore 1852–1933: *The Brook Kerith* (1916)

10 Whenever I prepare for a journey I prepare as though for
death. Should I never return, all is in order.
Katherine Mansfield 1888–1923: diary, 29 January 1922

11 A cold coming we had of it,
Just the worst time of the year
For a journey, and such a long journey:
The ways deep and the weather sharp,
The very dead of winter.
T. S. Eliot 1888–1965: 'Journey of the Magi' (1927)

12 Abroad is unutterably bloody and foreigners are fiends.
Nancy Mitford 1904–73: *The Pursuit of Love* (1945)

Trust and Treachery

1 He that is surety for a stranger shall smart for it.
Bible: Proverbs

2   *Equo ne credite, Teucri,*
Quidquid est, timeo Danaos et dona ferentes.
Do not trust the horse, Trojans. Whatever it is, I fear the
Greeks even when they bring gifts.
Virgil 70–19 BC: *Aeneid*

3 *Quis custodiet ipsos custodes?*
Who is to guard the guards themselves?
Juvenal AD *c.*60–*c.*130: *Satires*

4 I know what it is to be a subject, and what to be a Sovereign.
Good neighbours I have had, and I have met with bad: and in
trust I have found treason.
Elizabeth I 1533–1603: speech to a Parliamentary
deputation at Richmond, 12 November 1586, as reported in
Camden's *Annals* (1615). A report 'which the queen herself
heavily amended in her own hand' omits the concluding
words

5 Treason doth never prosper, what's the reason?
For if it prosper, none dare call it treason.
John Harington 1561–1612: *Epigrams* (1618)

6 Just for a handful of silver he left us,
Just for a riband to stick in his coat.
    Robert Browning 1812–89: 'The Lost Leader' (1845), of
    Wordsworth

7 And trust me not at all or all in all.
    Alfred, Lord Tennyson 1809–92: *Idylls of the King* 'Merlin
    and Vivien' (1859)

8 And I said to the man who stood at the gate of the year: 'Give
me a light that I may tread safely into the unknown.' And he
replied: 'Go out into the darkness and put your hand into the
Hand of God. That shall be to you better than light and safer
than a known way.'
    Minnie Louise Haskins 1875–1957: 'God Knows' (1908);
    quoted by George VI in his Christmas broadcast, 1939

9 To betray, you must first belong.
    Kim Philby 1912–88: in *Sunday Times* 17 December 1967

10 Having watched the form of our traitors for a number of
years, I cannot think that espionage can be recommended as
a technique for building an impressive civilization. It's a
lout's game.
    Rebecca West 1892–1983: *The Meaning of Treason* (1982 ed.)

Truth

See also **Lies and Lying**

1 But, my dearest Agathon, it is truth which you cannot
contradict; you can without any difficulty contradict
Socrates.
    Socrates 469–399 BC: in Plato *Symposium*

2 Plato is dear to me, but dearer still is truth.
    Aristotle 384–322 BC: attributed

3 Great is Truth, and mighty above all things.
    Bible (Apocrypha): I Esdras

4 And ye shall know the truth, and the truth shall make you
free.
    Bible: St John

5 Honesty is praised and left to shiver.
    Juvenal AD c.60–c.130: *Satires* tr. G. Ramsay

6 Truth will come to light; murder cannot be hid long.
   William Shakespeare 1564-1616: *The Merchant of Venice*
   (1596-8)

7 What is truth? said jesting Pilate; and would not stay for an
   answer.
   Francis Bacon 1561-1626: *Essays* (1625) 'Of Truth'

8 Who says that fictions only and false heir
   Become a verse? Is there in truth no beauty?
   Is all good structure in a winding stair?
   George Herbert 1593-1633: 'Jordan (1)' (1633)

9 Many from...an inconsiderate zeal unto truth, have too
   rashly charged the troops of error, and remain as trophies
   unto the enemies of truth.
   Sir Thomas Browne 1605-82: *Religio Medici* (1643)

10 True and False are attributes of speech, not of things. And
   where speech is not, there is neither Truth nor Falsehood.
   Thomas Hobbes 1588-1679: *Leviathan* (1651)

11 It is one thing to show a man that he is in error, and another
   to put him in possession of truth.
   John Locke 1632-1704: *Essay concerning Human
   Understanding* (1690)

12 Truth is the cry of all, but the game of the few.
   Bishop George Berkeley 1685-1753: *Siris* (1744)

13 It is commonly said, and more particularly by Lord
   Shaftesbury, that ridicule is the best test of truth.
   Lord Chesterfield 1694-1773: *Letters to his Son* (1774)
   6 February 1752

14 In lapidary inscriptions a man is not upon oath.
   Samuel Johnson 1709-84: in James Boswell *Life of Johnson*
   (1791) 1775

15 I can't tell a lie, Pa; you know I can't tell a lie. I did cut it
   with my hatchet.
   George Washington 1732-99: in M. L. Weems *Life of George
   Washington* (10th ed., 1810)

16 A truth that's told with bad intent
   Beats all the lies you can invent.
   William Blake 1757-1827: 'Auguries of Innocence' (*c.*1803)

17 'Tis strange—but true; for truth is always strange;
   Stranger than fiction.
   Lord Byron 1788-1824: *Don Juan* (1819-24)

18 'But the Emperor has nothing on at all!' cried a little child.
   Hans Christian Andersen 1805–75: *Danish Fairy Legends and Tales* (1846) 'The Emperor's New Clothes'

19 What I tell you three times is true.
   Lewis Carroll 1832–98: *The Hunting of the Snark* (1876)

20 It is the customary fate of new truths to begin as heresies and to end as superstitions.
   T. H. Huxley 1825–95: *Science and Culture and Other Essays* (1881) 'The Coming of Age of the Origin of Species'

21 Irrationally held truths may be more harmful than reasoned errors.
   T. H. Huxley 1825–95: *Science and Culture and Other Essays* (1881) 'The Coming of Age of the Origin of Species'

22 There was things which he stretched, but mainly he told the truth.
   Mark Twain 1835–1910: *The Adventures of Huckleberry Finn* (1884)

23 When you have eliminated the impossible, whatever remains, *however improbable*, must be the truth.
   Arthur Conan Doyle 1859–1930: *The Sign of Four* (1890)

24 The truth is rarely pure, and never simple.
   Oscar Wilde 1854–1900: *The Importance of Being Earnest* (1895)

25 Truth is the most valuable thing we have. Let us economize it.
   Mark Twain 1835–1910: *Following the Equator* (1897)

26 A thing is not necessarily true because a man dies for it.
   Oscar Wilde 1854–1900: *Sebastian Melmoth* (1904 ed.)

27 A platitude is simply a truth repeated until people get tired of hearing it.
   Stanley Baldwin 1867–1947: speech, House of Commons, 29 May 1924

28 An exaggeration is a truth that has lost its temper.
   Kahlil Gibran 1883–1931: *Sand and Foam* (1926)

29 I maintain that Truth is a pathless land, and you cannot approach it by any path whatsoever, by any religion, by any sect.
   Jiddu Krishnamurti d. 1986: remark, 1929, in L. Heber *Krishnamurti* (1931)

30 The truth is often a terrible weapon of aggression. It is possible to lie, and even to murder, for the truth.
  Alfred Adler 1870–1937: *The Problems of Neurosis* (1929)

31 The truth which makes men free is for the most part the truth which men prefer not to hear.
  Herbert Agar 1897–1980: *A Time for Greatness* (1942)

32 There are no whole truths; all truths are half-truths. It is trying to treat them as whole truths that plays the devil.
  Alfred North Whitehead 1861–1947: *Dialogues* (1954)

33 Nagging is the repetition of unpalatable truths.
  Edith Summerskill 1901–80: speech to the Married Women's Association, 14 July 1960

34 One of the favourite maxims of my father was the distinction between the two sorts of truths, profound truths recognized by the fact that the opposite is also a profound truth, in contrast to trivialities where opposites are obviously absurd.
  Niels Bohr 1885–1962: in S. Rozental *Niels Bohr* (1967)

35 It contains a misleading impression, not a lie. It was being economical with the truth.
  Robert Armstrong 1927– : during the 'Spycatcher' trial, Supreme Court, New South Wales, in *Daily Telegraph* 19 November 1986

Unbelief see Belief and Unbelief

The Universe

1 Had I been present at the Creation, I would have given some useful hints for the better ordering of the universe.
  Alfonso 'the Wise', King of Castile 1221–84: on studying the Ptolemaic system (attributed)

2 There are more things in heaven and earth, Horatio,
  Than are dreamt of in your philosophy.
  William Shakespeare 1564–1616: *Hamlet* (1601)

3 'Gad! she'd better!'
  Thomas Carlyle 1795–1881: on hearing that Margaret Fuller 'accept[ed]' the universe; in William James *Varieties of Religious Experience* (1902)

4 The world is the best of all possible worlds, and everything in it is a necessary evil.
   F. H. Bradley 1846–1924: *Appearance and Reality* (1893)

5 The world is disgracefully managed, one hardly knows to whom to complain.
   Ronald Firbank 1886–1926: *Vainglory* (1915)

6 The world is everything that is the case.
   Ludwig Wittgenstein 1889–1951: *Tractatus Logico-Philosophicus* (1922)

7 Now, my own suspicion is that the universe is not only queerer than we suppose, but queerer than we *can* suppose.
   J. B. S. Haldane 1892–1964: *Possible Worlds* (1927)

8 From the intrinsic evidence of his creation, the Great Architect of the Universe now begins to appear as a pure mathematician.
   James Jeans 1877–1946: *The Mysterious Universe* (1930)

9 This, now, is the judgement of our scientific age—the third reaction of man upon the universe! This universe is not hostile, nor yet is it friendly. It is simply indifferent.
   John H. Holmes 1879–1964: *The Sensible Man's View of Religion* (1932)

10 For one of those gnostics, the visible universe was an illusion or, more precisely, a sophism. Mirrors and fatherhood are abominable because they multiply it and extend it.
   Jorge Luis Borges 1899–1986: *Tlön, Uqbar, Orbis Tertius* (1941)

11 We milk the cow of the world, and as we do
   We whisper in her ear, 'You are not true.'
   Richard Wilbur 1921– : 'Epistemology' (1950)

12 If we find the answer to that [why it is that we and the universe exist], it would be the ultimate triumph of human reason—for then we would know the mind of God.
   Stephen Hawking 1942– : *A Brief History of Time* (1988)

Vice see **Virtue and Vice**

Violence

1   Who overcomes
By force, hath overcome but half his foe.
   John Milton 1608–74: *Paradise Lost* (1667)

2 Beware of the man who does not return your blow: he
neither forgives you nor allows you to forgive yourself.
   George Bernard Shaw 1856–1950: *Man and Superman*
   (1903)

3 If you strike a child take care that you strike it in anger,
even at the risk of maiming it for life. A blow in cold blood
neither can nor should be forgiven.
   George Bernard Shaw 1856–1950: *Man and Superman*
   (1903)

4 Where force is necessary, there it must be applied boldly,
decisively and completely. But one must know the limitations
of force; one must know when to blend force with
a manoeuvre, a blow with an agreement.
   Leon Trotsky 1879–1940: *What Next?* (1932)

5 Pale Ebenezer thought it wrong to fight,
But Roaring Bill (who killed him) thought it right.
   Hilaire Belloc 1870–1953: 'The Pacifist' (1938)

6 A riot is at bottom the language of the unheard.
   Martin Luther King 1929–68: *Where Do We Go From Here?*
   (1967)

7 I say violence is necessary. It is as American as cherry pie.
   H. Rap Brown 1943– : speech, 27 July 1967

8 Keep violence in the mind
Where it belongs.
   Brian Aldiss 1925– : 'Charteris' (1969)

9 The quietly pacifist peaceful
always die
to make room for men
who shout.
   Alice Walker 1944– : 'The QPP' (1973)

10 Not hard enough.
   Zsa Zsa Gabor 1919– : when asked how hard she had
   slapped a policeman; in *Independent* 21 September 1989

Virtue and Vice

See also **Good and Evil**

1 He that is without sin among you, let him first cast a stone at her.
   Bible: St John

2 For the good that I would I do not: but the evil which I would not, that I do.
   Bible: Romans

3 No one ever suddenly became depraved.
   Juvenal AD c.60–c.130: *Satires*

4 Would that we had spent one whole day well in this world!
   Thomas à Kempis c.1380–1471: *De Imitatione Christi*

5 How far that little candle throws his beams!
   So shines a good deed in a naughty world.
   William Shakespeare 1564–1616: *The Merchant of Venice* (1596–8)

6 How oft the sight of means to do ill deeds
   Makes ill deeds done!
   William Shakespeare 1564–1616: *King John* (1591–8)

7 Dost thou think, because thou art virtuous, there shall be no more cakes and ale?
   William Shakespeare 1564–1616: *Twelfth Night* (1601)

8 Virtue is like a rich stone, best plain set.
   Francis Bacon 1561–1626: *Essays* (1625) 'Of Beauty'

9 Virtue could see to do what Virtue would
   By her own radiant light, though sun and moon
   Were in the flat sea sunk.
   John Milton 1608–74: *Comus* (1637)

10 Vice came in always at the door of necessity, not at the door of inclination.
    Daniel Defoe 1660–1731: *Moll Flanders* (1721)

11 Virtue she finds too painful an endeavour,
    Content to dwell in decencies for ever.
    Alexander Pope 1688–1744: 'To a Lady' (1735)

12 But if he does really think that there is no distinction
between virtue and vice, why, Sir, when he leaves our
houses, let us count our spoons.
   Samuel Johnson 1709–84: in James Boswell *Life of Johnson*
(1791) 14 July 1763

13 Virtue knows to a farthing what it has lost by not having
been vice.
   Horace Walpole 1717–97: in L. Kronenberger *The
Extraordinary Mr Wilkes* (1974)

14 Be good, sweet maid, and let who will be clever.
   Charles Kingsley 1819–75: 'A Farewell' (1858)

15   Change in a trice
The lilies and languors of virtue
For the raptures and roses of vice.
   Algernon Charles Swinburne 1837–1909: 'Dolores' (1866)

16 What is virtue but the Trade Unionism of the married?
   George Bernard Shaw 1856–1950: *Man and Superman*
(1903)

17   What after all
Is a halo? It's only one more thing to keep clean.
   Christopher Fry 1907– : *The Lady's not for Burning* (1949)

18 An orgy looks particularly alluring seen through the mists of
righteous indignation.
   Malcolm Muggeridge 1903–90: *The Most of Malcolm
Muggeridge* (1966)

Voting

See also **Democracy**

1 Vote early and vote often.
   Anonymous: US election slogan, already current when
quoted by William Porcher Miles in the House of
Representatives, 31 March 1858

2 To give victory to the right, not bloody bullets, but peaceful
ballots only, are necessary.
   Abraham Lincoln 1809–65: speech, 18 May 1858; usually
quoted 'The ballot is stronger than the bullet'

3 An election is coming. Universal peace is declared, and the foxes have a sincere interest in prolonging the lives of the poultry.
 George Eliot 1819–80: *Felix Holt* (1866)

4 I always voted at my party's call,
 And I never thought of thinking for myself at all.
 W. S. Gilbert 1836–1911: *HMS Pinafore* (1878)

5 The accursed power which stands on Privilege
 (And goes with Women, and Champagne, and Bridge)
 Broke—and Democracy resumed her reign:
 (Which goes with Bridge, and Women and Champagne).
 Hilaire Belloc 1870–1953: 'On a Great Election' (1923)

6 Elections are won by men and women chiefly because most people vote against somebody rather than for somebody.
 Franklin P. Adams 1881–1960: *Nods and Becks* (1944)

7 Hell, I never vote *for* anybody. I always vote *against*.
 W. C. Fields 1880–1946: in R. L. Taylor *W. C. Fields* (1950)

8 Vote for the man who promises least; he'll be the least disappointing.
 Bernard Baruch 1870–1965: in M. Berger *New York* (1960)

9 It's not the voting that's democracy, it's the counting.
 Tom Stoppard 1937– : *Jumpers* (1972)

10 You won the elections, but I won the count.
 Anastasio Somoza 1925–80: replying to an accusation of ballot-rigging, in *Guardian* 17 June 1977

Wales

1 Though it appear a little out of fashion,
 There is much care and valour in this Welshman.
 William Shakespeare 1564–1616: *Henry V* (1599)

2 The land of my fathers. My fathers can have it.
 Dylan Thomas 1914–53: in *Adam* December 1953

3 There is no present in Wales,
 And no future;
 There is only the past,
 Brittle with relics...
 And an impotent people,

Sick with inbreeding,
Worrying the carcase of an old song.
　R. S. Thomas 1913- : 'Welsh Landscape' (1955)

4 There are still parts of Wales where the only concession to
gaiety is a striped shroud.
　Gwyn Thomas 1913- : *Punch* 18 June 1958

5 It profits a man nothing to give his soul for the whole
world...But for Wales—!
　Robert Bolt 1924- : *A Man for All Seasons* (1960)

War

See also **The Army**

1 We make war that we may live in peace.
　Aristotle 384–322 BC: *Nicomachean Ethics*

2 Laws are silent in time of war.
　Cicero 106–43 BC: *Pro Milone*

3 Once more unto the breach, dear friends, once more;
Or close the wall up with our English dead!
In peace there's nothing so becomes a man
As modest stillness and humility:
But when the blast of war blows in our ears,
Then imitate the action of the tiger;
Stiffen the sinews, summon up the blood,
Disguise fair nature with hard-favoured rage.
　William Shakespeare 1564–1616: *Henry V* (1599)

4 Happy is that city which in time of peace thinks of war.
　Anonymous: inscription found in the armoury of Venice, in
Robert Burton *Anatomy of Melancholy* (1621–51)

5 For as the nature of foul weather, lieth not in a shower or
two of rain; but in an inclination thereto of many days
together: so the nature of war consisteth not in actual
fighting, but in the known disposition thereto during all the
time there is no assurance to the contrary.
　Thomas Hobbes 1588–1679: *Leviathan* (1651)

6 As you know, God is usually on the side of the big squadrons against the small.
  Comte de Bussy-Rabutin 1618–93: letter to the Comte de Limoges, 18 October 1677

7 One to destroy, is murder by the law;
  And gibbets keep the lifted hand in awe;
  To murder thousands, takes a specious name,
  'War's glorious art', and gives immortal fame.
  Edward Young 1683–1765: *The Love of Fame* (1725–8)

8 Among the calamities of war may be jointly numbered the diminution of the love of truth, by the falsehoods which interest dictates and credulity encourages.
  Samuel Johnson 1709–84: *The Idler* 11 November 1758; possibly the source of 'When war is declared, Truth is the first casualty', epigraph to Arthur Ponsonby's *Falsehood in Wartime* (1928); attributed also to Hiram Johnson, speaking in the US Senate, 1918

9 There never was a good war, or a bad peace.
  Benjamin Franklin 1706–90: letter to Josiah Quincy, 11 September 1783

10 Next to a battle lost, the greatest misery is a battle gained.
  Duke of Wellington 1769–1852: in *Diary of Frances, Lady Shelley 1787–1817* (ed. R. Edgcumbe)

11 I used to say of him [Napoleon] that his presence on the field made the difference of forty thousand men.
  Duke of Wellington 1769–1852: in Philip Henry Stanhope *Notes of Conversations with the Duke of Wellington* (1888) 2 November 1831

12 War is nothing but a continuation of politics with the admixture of other means.
  Karl von Clausewitz 1780–1831: *On War* (1832–4) commonly rendered 'War is the continuation of politics by other means'

13 Everything is very simple in war, but the simplest thing is difficult. These difficulties accumulate and produce a friction which no man can imagine exactly who has not seen war.
  Karl von Clausewitz 1780–1831: *On War* (1832–4), tr. J. Graham

14 It is well that war is so terrible. We should grow too fond
of it.
> **Robert E. Lee** 1807–70: after the battle of Fredericksburg,
> December 1862 (attributed)

15 There is many a boy here to-day who looks on war as all
glory, but, boys, it is all hell.
> **General Sherman** 1820–91: speech at Columbus, Ohio,
> 11 August 1880

16 The essence of war is violence. Moderation in war is
imbecility.
> **John Arbuthnot Fisher** 1841–1920: lecture notes 1899–1902

17 A man who is good enough to shed his blood for the country
is good enough to be given a square deal afterwards.
> **Theodore Roosevelt** 1858–1919: speech, 4 June 1903

18 BATTLE, *n.* A method of untying with the teeth a political knot
that would not yield to the tongue.
> **Ambrose Bierce** 1842–*c.*1914: *The Cynic's Word Book* (1906)

19 Yes; quaint and curious war is!
You shoot a fellow down
You'd treat if met where any bar is,
Or help to half-a-crown.
> **Thomas Hardy** 1840–1928: 'The Man he Killed' (1909)

20 War is hell, and all that, but it has a good deal to recommend
it. It wipes out all the small nuisances of peace-time.
> **Ian Hay** 1876–1952: *The First Hundred Thousand* (1915)

21 My subject is War, and the pity of War.
The Poetry is in the pity.
> **Wilfred Owen** 1893–1918: *Poems* (1963) preface (written
> 1918)

22 Waste of Blood, and waste of Tears,
Waste of youth's most precious years,
Waste of ways the saints have trod,
Waste of Glory, waste of God,
War!
> **G. A. Studdert Kennedy** 1883–1929: 'Waste' (1919)

23 It is easier to make war than to make peace.
> **Georges Clemenceau** 1841–1929: speech at Verdun, 20 July
> 1919

24 When we, the Workers, all demand: 'What are WE fighting
for?' …

Then, then we'll end that stupid crime, that devil's
madness—War.
Robert W. Service 1874–1958: 'Michael' (1921)

25 War hath no fury like a non-combatant.
C. E. Montague 1867–1928: *Disenchantment* (1922)

26 When war enters a country
It produces lies like sand.
Anonymous: epigraph to A. Ponsonby *Falsehood in
Wartime* (1928)

27 War is too serious a matter to entrust to military men.
Georges Clemenceau 1841–1929: attributed to Clemenceau,
e.g. in H. Jackson *Clemenceau and the Third Republic*
(1946), but also to Briand and Talleyrand

28 I am not only a pacifist but a militant pacifist. I am willing to
fight for peace. Nothing will end war unless the people
themselves refuse to go to war.
Albert Einstein 1879–1955: interview with G. S. Viereck,
January 1931

29 The bomber will always get through. The only defence is in
offence, which means that you have to kill more women and
children more quickly than the enemy if you want to save
yourselves.
Stanley Baldwin 1867–1947: speech, House of Commons,
10 November 1932

30 Since the day of the air, the old frontiers are gone. When you
think of the defence of England you no longer think of the
chalk cliffs of Dover; you think of the Rhine.
Stanley Baldwin 1867–1947: speech, House of Commons,
30 July 1934

31 The sword is the axis of the world and its power is absolute.
Charles de Gaulle 1890–1970: *Vers l'armée de métier* (1934)

32 If we are attacked we can only defend ourselves with guns
not with butter.
Joseph Goebbels 1897–1945: speech in Berlin, 17 January
1936

33 Would you rather have butter or guns?…preparedness
makes us powerful. Butter merely makes us fat.
Hermann Goering 1893–1946: speech at Hamburg, 1936, in
W. Frischauer *Goering* (1951).

34 Little girl...Sometime they'll give a war and nobody will come.
  Carl Sandburg 1878–1967: *The People, Yes* (1936); 'Suppose They Gave a War and Nobody Came?' was the title of a 1970 film

35 In war, whichever side may call itself the victor, there are no winners, but all are losers.
  Neville Chamberlain 1869–1940: speech at Kettering, 3 July 1938

36 They have gone too long without a war here. Where is morality to come from in such a case, I ask? Peace is nothing but slovenliness, only war creates order.
  Bertolt Brecht 1898–1956: *Mother Courage* (1939)

37 A bayonet is a weapon with a worker at each end.
  Anonymous: British pacifist slogan (1940)

38 Probably the battle of Waterloo *was* won on the playing-fields of Eton, but the opening battles of all subsequent wars have been lost there.
  George Orwell 1903–50: *The Lion and the Unicorn* (1941)

39   And as for war, my wars
Were global from the start.
  Henry Reed 1914–86: 'Lessons of the War: 3, Unarmed Combat' (1946)

40 I have never met anyone who wasn't against war. Even Hitler and Mussolini were, according to themselves.
  David Low 1891–1963: *New York Times Magazine* 10 February 1946

41 The quickest way of ending a war is to lose it.
  George Orwell 1903–50: *Polemic* May 1946

42 This world in arms is not spending money alone. It is spending the sweat of its labourers, the genius of its scientists, the hopes of its children.
  Dwight D. Eisenhower 1890–1969: speech in Washington, 16 April 1953

43 Spare us all word of the weapons, their force and range, The long numbers that rocket the mind.
  Richard Wilbur 1921– : 'Advice to a Prophet' (1961)

44 Dead battles, like dead generals, hold the military mind in their dead grip and Germans, no less than other peoples, prepare for the last war.
  Barbara W. Tuchman 1912–89: *August 1914* (1962)

45 Rule 1, on page 1 of the book of war, is: 'Do not march on Moscow'...[Rule 2] is: 'Do not go fighting with your land armies in China.'
  Field Marshal Montgomery 1887–1976: speech, House of Lords, 30 May 1962

46 History is littered with the wars which everybody knew would never happen.
  Enoch Powell 1912– : speech, 19 October 1967

47 War is capitalism with the gloves off.
  Tom Stoppard 1937– : *Travesties* (1975)

48 I question the right of that great Moloch, national sovereignty, to burn its children to save its pride.
  Anthony Meyer 1920– : speaking against the Falklands War, 1982; in *Listener* 27 September 1990

Wars

1 They now *ring* the bells, but they will soon *wring* their hands.
  Robert Walpole 1676–1745: on the declaration of war with Spain, 1739; in W. Coxe *Memoirs of Sir Robert Walpole* (1798)

2 I have only one eye,—I have a right to be blind sometimes...I really do not see the signal!
  Horatio, Lord Nelson 1758–1805: at the battle of Copenhagen, in R. Southey *Life of Nelson* (1813)

3 *Guerra a cuchillo.*
War to the knife.
  José de Palafox 1780–1847: at the siege of Saragossa, 4 August 1808, replying to the suggestion that he should surrender (as reported). He actually said '*Guerra y cuchillo* [War and the knife]'

4 Up Guards and at them!
  Duke of Wellington 1769–1852: in *The Battle of Waterloo*

by a Near Observer [J. Booth] (1815), later denied by
Wellington

5 Hard pounding this, gentlemen; let's see who will pound
longest.
Duke of Wellington 1769–1852: at the Battle of Waterloo;
in Sir Walter Scott *Paul's Letters* (1816)

6 The battle of Waterloo was won on the playing fields of Eton.
Duke of Wellington 1769–1852: oral tradition, but not
found in this form of words. See C. F. R. Montalembert *De
l'avenir politique de l'Angleterre* (1856)

7 The angel of death has been abroad throughout the land; you
may almost hear the beating of his wings.
John Bright 1811–89: on the effects of the Crimean war;
speech, House of Commons, 23 February 1855

8 All quiet along the Potomac.
General George B. McClellan 1826–85: said at the time of
the American Civil War (attributed)

9 If there is ever another war in Europe, it will come out of
some damned silly thing in the Balkans.
Otto von Bismarck 1815–98: quoted in the House of
Commons, 16 August 1945

10 My centre is giving way, my right is retreating, situation
excellent, I am attacking.
Ferdinand Foch 1851–1929: message during the first Battle
of the Marne, September 1914

11 In Flanders fields the poppies blow
Between the crosses, row on row.
John McCrae 1872–1918: 'In Flanders Fields' (1915)

12 *Ils ne passeront pas*.
They shall not pass.
Anonymous: slogan of the French army at the defence of
Verdun, 1916; variously attributed to Marshal Pétain and to
General Robert Nivelle

13 My home policy: I wage war; my foreign policy: I wage war.
All the time I wage war.
Georges Clemenceau 1841–1929: speech to French Chamber
of Deputies, 8 March 1918

14 I hope we may say that thus, this fateful morning, came to an end all wars.

> **David Lloyd George** 1863–1945: speech, House of Commons, 11 November 1918

15 This is not a peace treaty, it is an armistice for twenty years.

> **Ferdinand Foch** 1851–1929: at the signing of the Treaty of Versailles, 1919; in P. Reynaud *Mémoires* (1963)

16 *No pasarán.*
They shall not pass.

> **Dolores Ibarruri** 1895–1989: radio broadcast, Madrid, 19 July 1936

17 I have nothing to offer but blood, toil, tears and sweat.

> **Winston Churchill** 1874–1965: speech, House of Commons, 13 May 1940

18 We shall not flag or fail. We shall go on to the end. We shall fight in France, we shall fight on the seas and oceans, we shall fight with growing confidence and growing strength in the air, we shall defend our island, whatever the cost may be. We shall fight on the beaches, we shall fight on the landing grounds, we shall fight in the fields and in the streets, we shall fight in the hills; we shall never surrender.

> **Winston Churchill** 1874–1965: speech, House of Commons, 4 June 1940

19 Let us therefore brace ourselves to our duty, and so bear ourselves that, if the British Empire and its Commonwealth lasts for a thousand years, men will still say, 'This was their finest hour.'

> **Winston Churchill** 1874–1965: speech, House of Commons, 18 June 1940

20 Never in the field of human conflict was so much owed by so many to so few.

> **Winston Churchill** 1874–1965: on the Battle of Britain; speech, House of Commons, 20 August 1940

21 I'm glad we've been bombed. It makes me feel I can look the East End in the face.

> **Queen Elizabeth, the Queen Mother** 1900– : to a London policeman, 13 September 1940

22 We must be the great arsenal of democracy.

> **Franklin D. Roosevelt** 1882–1945: broadcast, 29 December 1940

23 Give us the tools and we will finish the job.
   Winston Churchill 1874–1965: radio broadcast, 9 February
   1941

24 I think we might be going a bridge too far.
   Frederick Browning 1896–1965: expressing reservations
   about the Arnhem 'Market Garden' operation,
   10 September 1944

25 The First World War had begun—imposed on the statesmen
   of Europe by railway timetables.
   A. J. P. Taylor 1906–90: *The First World War* (1963)

26 We're going to bomb them back into the Stone Age.
   Curtis E. LeMay 1906–90: on the North Vietnamese, in
   Mission with LeMay (1965)

27 Anyone who isn't confused doesn't really understand the
   situation.
   Ed Murrow 1908–65: on the Vietnam War, in Walter Bryan
   The Improbable Irish (1969)

28 It became necessary to destroy the town to save it.
   Anonymous: statement issued by US Army, referring to
   Ben Tre in Vietnam; in *New York Times* 8 February 1968

29 I counted them all out and I counted them all back.
   Brian Hanrahan 1949– : on the number of British
   aeroplanes joining the raid on Port Stanley; BBC broadcast
   report, 1 May 1982

30 The Falklands thing was a fight between two bald men over
   a comb.
   Jorge Luis Borges 1899–1986: in *Time* 14 February 1983

Wealth

See also **Money**

1 How many things I can do without!
   Socrates 469–399 BC: on looking at a multitude of wares
   exposed for sale, in Diogenes Laertius *Lives of the
   Philosophers*

2 It is easier for a camel to go through the eye of a needle, than
   for a rich man to enter into the kingdom of God.
   Bible: St Matthew

3 Riches are a good handmaid, but the worst mistress.
   Francis Bacon 1561-1626: *De Dignitate et Augmentis Scientiarum* (1623)

4   Let none admire
That riches grow in hell; that soil may best
Deserve the precious bane.
   John Milton 1608-74: *Paradise Lost* (1667)

5 It was very prettily said, that we may learn the little value of fortune by the persons on whom heaven is pleased to bestow it.
   Richard Steele 1672-1729: *The Tatler* 27 July 1710

6 We are all Adam's children but silk makes the difference.
   Thomas Fuller 1654-1734: *Gnomologia* (1732)

7 The chief enjoyment of riches consists in the parade of riches.
   Adam Smith 1723-90: *Wealth of Nations* (1776)

8 We are not here to sell a parcel of boilers and vats, but the potentiality of growing rich, beyond the dreams of avarice.
   Samuel Johnson 1709-84: at the sale of Thrale's brewery; in James Boswell *Life of Johnson* (1791) 6 April 1781

9 The man who dies...rich dies disgraced.
   Andrew Carnegie 1835-1919: *North American Review* June 1889

10 In every well-governed state, wealth is a sacred thing; in democracies it is the only sacred thing.
   Anatole France 1844-1924: *L'Île des pingouins* (1908)

11 Let me tell you about the very rich. They are different from you and me.
   F. Scott Fitzgerald 1896-1940: to which Ernest Hemingway replied, 'Yes, they have more money'; *All the Sad Young Men* (1926)

12 To suppose, as we all suppose, that we could be rich and not behave as the rich behave, is like supposing that we could drink all day and keep absolutely sober.
   Logan Pearsall Smith 1865-1946: *Afterthoughts* (1931)

13 If all the rich people in the world divided up their money among themselves there wouldn't be enough to go round.
   Christina Stead 1902-83: *House of All Nations* (1938)

14 A kiss on the hand may be quite continental,
But diamonds are a girl's best friend.
   Leo Robin 1900- : 'Diamonds are a Girl's Best Friend' (1949
   song); from the film *Gentlemen Prefer Blondes*

15 The greater the wealth, the thicker will be the dirt.
   J. K. Galbraith 1908- : *The Affluent Society* (1958)

16 Will the people in the cheaper seats clap your hands? All the
rest of you, if you'll just rattle your jewellery.
   John Lennon 1940-80: at Royal Variety Performance,
   4 November 1963

17 I've been rich and I've been poor: rich is better.
   Sophie Tucker c.1884-1966: attributed

Weather

1 So foul and fair a day I have not seen.
   William Shakespeare 1564-1616: *Macbeth* (1606)

2 When two Englishmen meet, their first talk is of the weather.
   Samuel Johnson 1709-84: *The Idler* 24 June 1758

3 The best sun we have is made of Newcastle coal.
   Horace Walpole 1717-97: letter to George Montagu,
   15 June 1768

4 The frost performs its secret ministry,
Unhelped by any wind.
   Samuel Taylor Coleridge 1772-1834: 'Frost at Midnight'
   (1798)

5 It is impossible to live in a country which is continually
under hatches...Rain! Rain! Rain!
   John Keats 1795-1821: letter to Reynolds from Devon,
   10 April 1818

6 St Agnes' Eve—Ah, bitter chill it was!
The owl, for all his feathers, was a-cold.
   John Keats 1795-1821: 'The Eve of St Agnes' (1820)

7 This is a London particular...A fog, miss.
   Charles Dickens 1812-70: *Bleak House* (1853)

8 When men were all asleep the snow came flying,
In large white flakes falling on the city brown,

Stealthily and perpetually settling and loosely lying,
Hushing the latest traffic of the drowsy town.
    Robert Bridges 1844-1930: 'London Snow' (1890)

9 The rain, it raineth on the just
And also on the unjust fella:
But chiefly on the just, because
The unjust steals the just's umbrella.
    Lord Bowen 1835-94: in W. Sichel *Sands of Time* (1923)

10 The fog comes
on little cat feet. It sits looking
over harbour and city
on silent haunches
and then moves on.
    Carl Sandburg 1878-1967: 'Fog' (1916)

11 The yellow fog that rubs its back upon the window-panes.
    T. S. Eliot 1888-1965: 'Love Song of J. Alfred Prufrock'
(1917)

12 This is the weather the cuckoo likes,
And so do I;
When showers betumble the chestnut spikes,
And nestlings fly.
    Thomas Hardy 1840-1928: 'Weathers' (1922)

13 Children are dumb to say how hot the day is,
How hot the scent is of the summer rose.
    Robert Graves 1895-1985: 'The Cool Web' (1927)

14 Every time it rains, it rains
Pennies from heaven.
Don't you know each cloud contains
Pennies from heaven?
    Johnny Burke 1908-64: 'Pennies from Heaven' (1936 song)

15 It was the wrong kind of snow.
    Terry Worrall: explaining disruption on British Rail, in
The Independent 16 February 1991

Woman's Role

See also **Men and Women**

1 The First Blast of the Trumpet Against the Monstrous
  Regiment of Women.
    John Knox c.1505–72: title of pamphlet (1558)

2 Be to her virtues very kind;
  Be to her faults a little blind;
  Let all her ways be unconfined;
  And clap your padlock—on her mind.
    Matthew Prior 1664–1721: 'An English Padlock' (1705)

3 If all men are born free, how is it that all women are born
  slaves?
    Mary Astell 1668–1731: *Some Reflections upon Marriage*
    (1706 ed.)

4 A woman's preaching is like a dog's walking on his hinder
  legs. It is not done well; but you are surprised to find it done
  at all.
    Samuel Johnson 1709–84: in James Boswell *Life of Johnson*
    (1791) 31 July 1763

5 How much it is to be regretted, that the British ladies should
  ever sit down contented to polish, when they are able to
  reform; to entertain, when they might instruct; and to dazzle
  for an hour, when they are candidates for eternity!
    Hannah More 1745–1833: *Essays on Various Subjects…for
    Young Ladies* (1777) 'On Dissipation'

6 Can anything be more absurd than keeping women in a state
  of ignorance, and yet so vehemently to insist on their
  resisting temptation?
    Vicesimus Knox 1752–1821: in Mary Wollstonecraft *A
    Vindication of the Rights of Woman* (1792)

7 I do not wish them [women] to have power over men; but
  over themselves.
    Mary Wollstonecraft 1759–97: *A Vindication of the Rights
    of Woman* (1792)

8 The Queen is most anxious to enlist every one who can speak
  or write to join in checking this mad, wicked folly of
  'Woman's Rights', with all its attendant horrors, on which

her poor feeble sex is bent, forgetting every sense of womanly feeling and propriety.

    Queen Victoria 1819-1901: letter to Theodore Martin, 29 May 1870

9 The one point on which all women are in furious secret rebellion against the existing law is the saddling of the right to a child with the obligation to become the servant of a man.

    George Bernard Shaw 1856-1950: *Getting Married* (1911)

10 The worker is the slave of capitalist society, the female worker is the slave of that slave.

    James Connolly 1868-1916: *The Re-conquest of Ireland* (1915)

11 One is not born a woman: one becomes one.

    Simone de Beauvoir 1908-86: *The Second Sex* (1949)

12 The only position for women in SNCC is prone.

    Stokely Carmichael 1941- : response to a question about the position of women at a Student Nonviolent Coordinating Committee conference, November 1964

13 But if God had wanted us to think just with our wombs, why did He give us a brain?

    Clare Booth Luce 1903- : *Life* 16 October 1970

14 I didn't fight to get women out from behind the vacuum cleaner to get them onto the board of Hoover.

    Germaine Greer 1939- : in *Guardian* 27 October 1986

15 Feminism is the most revolutionary idea there has ever been. Equality for women demands a change in the human psyche more profound then anything Marx dreamed of. It means valuing parenthood as much as we value banking.

    Polly Toynbee 1946- : *Guardian* 19 January 1987

....

Women

....

See also **Men and Women**

1 Who can find a virtuous woman? for her price is far above rubies.

    Bible: Proverbs

2 The greatest glory of a woman is to be least talked about by
men.
  Pericles c.495-429 BC: in Thucydides *History of the
  Peloponnesian War*, tr. R. Warner

3   *Varium et mutabile semper*
Femina.
Fickle and changeable always is woman.
  Virgil 70-19 BC: *Aeneid*

4 She is a woman, therefore may be wooed;
She is a woman, therefore may be won.
  William Shakespeare 1564-1616: *Titus Andronicus* (1590)

5 Frailty, thy name is woman!
  William Shakespeare 1564-1616: *Hamlet* (1601)

6 Age cannot wither her, nor custom stale
Her infinite variety; other women cloy
The appetites they feed, but she makes hungry
Where most she satisfies.
  William Shakespeare 1564-1616: *Antony and Cleopatra*
  (1606-7)

7 The weaker sex, to piety more prone.
  William Alexander, Earl of Stirling c.1567-1640:
  'Doomsday' 5th Hour (1637)

8 *Elle flotte, elle hésite; en un mot, elle est femme.*
She floats, she hesitates; in a word, she's a woman.
  Jean Racine 1639-99: *Athalie* (1691)

9 When once a woman has given you her heart, you can never
get rid of the rest of her body.
  John Vanbrugh 1664-1726: *The Relapse* (1696)

10 She knows her man, and when you rant and swear,
Can draw you to her *with a single hair*.
  John Dryden 1631-1700: translation of Persius *Satires*

11 Women, then, are only children of a larger growth.
  Lord Chesterfield 1694-1773: *Letters to his Son* (1774)
  5 September 1748

12 Here's to the maiden of bashful fifteen
Here's to the widow of fifty
Here's to the flaunting, extravagant quean;
And here's to the housewife that's thrifty.
  Richard Brinsley Sheridan 1751-1816: *The School for
  Scandal* (1777)

13 O Woman! in our hours of ease,
Uncertain, coy, and hard to please,
And variable as the shade
By the light quivering aspen made;
When pain and anguish wring the brow,
A ministering angel thou!
    Sir Walter Scott 1771–1832: *Marmion* (1808)

14 All the privilege I claim for my own sex...is that of loving
longest, when existence or when hope is gone.
    Jane Austen 1775–1817: *Persuasion* (1818)

15 I have met with women whom I really think would like to be
married to a poem and to be given away by a novel.
    John Keats 1795–1821: letter to Fanny Brawne, 8 July 1819

16 In her first passion woman loves her lover,
In all the others all she loves is love.
    Lord Byron 1788–1824: *Don Juan* (1819–24)

17 Eternal Woman draws us upward.
    Johann Wolfgang von Goethe 1749–1832: *Faust* pt. 2 (1832)

18 I expect that Woman will be the last thing civilized by Man.
    George Meredith 1828–1909: *The Ordeal of Richard Feverel*
(1859)

19 The happiest women, like the happiest nations, have no
history.
    George Eliot 1819–80: *The Mill on the Floss* (1860)

20 Half the sorrows of women would be averted if they could
repress the speech they know to be useless; nay, the speech
they have resolved not to make.
    George Eliot 1819–80: *Felix Holt* (1866)

21 Women—one half the human race at least—care fifty times
more for a marriage than a ministry.
    Walter Bagehot 1826–77: *The English Constitution* (1867)

22 Woman was God's second blunder.
    Friedrich Nietzsche 1844–1900: *Der Antichrist* (1888)

23 One should never trust a woman who tells one her real age.
A woman who would tell one that, would tell one anything.
    Oscar Wilde 1854–1900: *A Woman of No Importance* (1893)

24 Vitality in a woman is a blind fury of creation.
    George Bernard Shaw 1856–1950: *Man and Superman*
(1903)

25 The prime truth of woman, the universal mother...that if a
thing is worth doing, it is worth doing badly.
> **G. K. Chesterton** 1874–1936: *What's Wrong with the World*
> (1910)

26 A woman will always sacrifice herself if you give her the
opportunity. It is her favourite form of self-indulgence.
> **W. Somerset Maugham** 1874–1965: *Circle* (1921)

27 Women have no wilderness in them,
They are provident instead,
Content in the tight hot cell of their hearts
To eat dusty bread.
> **Louise Bogan** 1897–1970: 'Women' (1923)

28 So this gentleman said a girl with brains ought to do
something with them besides think.
> **Anita Loos** 1893–1981: *Gentlemen Prefer Blondes* (1925)

29 The perpetual hunger to be beautiful and that thirst to be
loved which is the real curse of Eve.
> **Jean Rhys** *c.*1890–1979: *The Left Bank* (1927)

30 The great and almost only comfort about being a woman is
that one can always pretend to be more stupid than one is
and no one is surprised.
> **Freya Stark** 1893–1993: *The Valleys of the Assassins* (1934)

31 What does a woman want?
> **Sigmund Freud** 1856–1939: letter to Marie Bonaparte, in E.
> Jones *Sigmund Freud* (1955)

32 She's the sort of woman who lives for others—you can
always tell the others by their hunted expression.
> **C. S. Lewis** 1898–1963: *The Screwtape Letters* (1942)

33 Slamming their doors, stamping their high heels, banging
their irons and saucepans—the eternal flaming racket of the
female.
> **John Osborne** 1929– : *Look Back in Anger* (1956)

34 Every woman adores a Fascist,
The boot in the face, the brute
Brute heart of a brute like you.
> **Sylvia Plath** 1932–63: 'Daddy' (1963)

35 From birth to 18 a girl needs good parents. From 18 to 35,
she needs good looks. From 35 to 55, good personality. From
55 on, she needs good cash.
> **Sophie Tucker** 1884–1966: in M. Freedland *Sophie* (1978)

36 Woman is the nigger of the world.
   Yoko Ono 1933- : interview for *Nova* magazine (1968);
   adopted by John Lennon as song title (1972)

37 Being a woman is of special interest only to aspiring male
   transsexuals. To actual women, it is merely a good excuse
   not to play football.
   Fran Lebowitz 1946- : *Metropolitan Life* (1978)

38 We are becoming the men we wanted to marry.
   Gloria Steinem 1934- : *Ms* July/August 1982

39 Good women always think it is their fault when someone else
   is being offensive. Bad women never take the blame for
   anything.
   Anita Brookner 1938- : *Hotel du Lac* (1984)

Words

See also **Language, Meaning**

1 And once sent out, a word takes wing beyond recall.
   Horace 65-8 BC: *Epistles*

2 Woord is but wynd; leff woord and tak the dede.
   John Lydgate c.1370-c.1451: *Secrets of Old Philosophers*

3 What's in a name? that which we call a rose
   By any other name would smell as sweet.
   William Shakespeare 1564-1616: *Romeo and Juliet* (1595)

4 The words of Mercury are harsh after the songs of Apollo.
   William Shakespeare 1564-1616: *Love's Labour's Lost* (1595)

5 But words are words; I never yet did hear
   That the bruised heart was piercèd through the ear.
   William Shakespeare 1564-1616: *Othello* (1602-4)

6 Words are the tokens current and accepted for conceits, as
   moneys are for values.
   Francis Bacon 1561-1626: *The Advancement of Learning*
   (1605)

7 Thou whoreson zed! thou unnecessary letter!
   William Shakespeare 1564-1616: *King Lear* (1605-6)

8 Syllables govern the world.
   John Selden 1584-1654: *Table Talk* (1689) 'Power: State'

9 A man who could make so vile a pun would not scruple to
pick a pocket.
John Dennis 1657-1734: *The Gentleman's Magazine* (1781),
editorial note

10 *Lexicographer*. A writer of dictionaries, a harmless drudge.
Samuel Johnson 1709-84: *Dictionary of the English
Language* (1755)

11 I am not yet so lost in lexicography as to forget that words
are the daughters of earth, and that things are the sons of
heaven. Language is only the instrument of science, and
words are but the signs of ideas.
Samuel Johnson 1709-84: *Dictionary of the English
Language* (1755) preface

12 'When *I* use a word,' Humpty Dumpty said in a rather
scornful tone, 'it means just what I choose it to
mean—neither more nor less.'
Lewis Carroll 1832-98: *Through the Looking-Glass* (1872)

13 Dialect words—those terrible marks of the beast to the truly
genteel.
Thomas Hardy 1840-1928: *The Mayor of Casterbridge* (1886)

14 Some word that teems with hidden meaning—like
Basingstoke.
W. S. Gilbert 1836-1911: *Ruddigore* (1887)

15 It cannot in the opinion of His Majesty's Government be
classified as slavery in the extreme acceptance of the word
without some risk of terminological inexactitude.
Winston Churchill 1874-1965: speech, House of Commons,
22 February 1906

16 Words are, of course, the most powerful drug used by
mankind.
Rudyard Kipling 1865-1936: speech, 14 Febuary 1923

17 I gotta use words when I talk to you.
T. S. Eliot 1888-1965: *Sweeney Agonistes* (1932)

18   Words strain,
Crack and sometimes break, under the burden,
Under the tension, slip, slide, perish,
Decay with imprecision, will not stay in place,
Will not stay still.
T. S. Eliot 1888-1965: *Four Quartets* 'Burnt Norton' (1936)

Work

1 In the sweat of thy face shalt thou eat bread.
   Bible: Genesis

2 For the labourer is worthy of his hire.
   Bible: St Luke

3 If any would not work, neither should he eat.
   Bible: II Thesssalonians

4 I have had my labour for my travail.
   William Shakespeare 1564–1616: *Troilus and Cressida* (1602)

5 The labour we delight in physics pain.
   William Shakespeare 1564–1616: *Macbeth* (1606)

6 We spend our midday sweat, our midnight oil;
   We tire the night in thought, the day in toil.
   Francis Quarles 1592–1644: *Emblems* (1635)

7 If you have great talents, industry will improve them: if you have but moderate abilities, industry will supply their deficiency.
   Joshua Reynolds 1723–92: *Discourses on Art* (11 December 1769)

8 The world is too much with us; late and soon,
   Getting and spending, we lay waste our powers.
   William Wordsworth 1770–1850: 'The world is too much with us' (1807)

9 Blessèd are the horny hands of toil!
   James Russell Lowell 1819–91: 'A Glance Behind the Curtain' (1844)

10 Which of us...is to do the hard and dirty work for the rest—and for what pay? Who is to do the pleasant and clean work, and for what pay?
   John Ruskin 1819–1900: *Sesame and Lilies* (1865)

11 Life without industry is guilt, and industry without art is brutality.
   John Ruskin 1819–1900: *Lectures on Art* (1870)

12 I like work: it fascinates me. I can sit and look at it for hours. I love to keep it by me: the idea of getting rid of it nearly breaks my heart.
   Jerome K. Jerome 1859–1927: *Three Men in a Boat* (1889)

13 Work is the curse of the drinking classes.
   Oscar Wilde 1854–1900: in H. Pearson *Life of Oscar Wilde*
   (1946)

14 Work is love made visible.
   Kahlil Gibran 1883–1931: *The Prophet* (1923)

15 Perfect freedom is reserved for the man who lives by his own
   work and in that work does what he wants to do.
   R. G. Collingwood 1889–1943: *Speculum Mentis* (1924)

16 That state is a state of slavery in which a man does what he
   likes to do in his spare time and in his working time that
   which is required of him.
   Eric Gill 1882–1940: *Art-nonsense and Other Essays* (1929)
   'Slavery and Freedom'.

17 One of the symptoms of approaching nervous breakdown is
   the belief that one's work is terribly important, and that to
   take a holiday would bring all kinds of disaster.
   Bertrand Russell 1872–1970: *Conquest of Happiness* (1930)

18 Work is of two kinds: first, altering the position of matter at
   or near the earth's surface relatively to other such matter;
   second, telling other people to do so. The first kind is
   unpleasant and ill paid; the second is pleasant and highly
   paid.
   Bertrand Russell 1872–1970: 'In Praise of Idleness' (1932)

19 A professional is a man who can do his job when he doesn't
   feel like it. An amateur is a man who can't do his job when
   he does feel like it.
   James Agate 1877–1947: diary, 19 July 1945

20 Why should I let the toad *work*
   Squat on my life?
   Can't I use my wit as a pitchfork
   And drive the brute off?
   Philip Larkin 1922–85: 'Toads' (1955)

21 Work expands so as to fill the time available for its
   completion.
   C. Northcote Parkinson 1909–93: *Parkinson's Law* (1958)

22 It's true hard work never killed anybody, but I figure why
   take the chance?
   Ronald Reagan 1911– : interview, *Guardian*
   31 March 1987

23 I have long been of the opinion that if work were such a splendid thing the rich would have kept more of it for themselves.

Bruce Grocott 1940– : *Observer* 22 May 1988 'Sayings of the Week'

Writers

See also **Poets, Shakespeare**

1 No man but a blockhead ever wrote, except for money.

Samuel Johnson 1709–84: in James Boswell *Life of Johnson* (1791) 5 April 1776

2 Another damned, thick, square book! Always scribble, scribble, scribble! Eh! Mr Gibbon?

Duke of Gloucester 1743–1805: in Henry Best *Personal and Literary Memorials* (1829) also attributed to the Duke of Cumberland and George III

3 Johnson hewed passages through the Alps, while Gibbon levelled walks through parks and gardens.

George Colman, the Younger 1762–1836: *Random Records* (1830)

4 Writers, like teeth, are divided into incisors and grinders.

Walter Bagehot 1826–77: *Estimates of some Englishmen and Scotchmen* (1858)

5 The work of Henry James has always seemed divisible by a simple dynastic arrangement into three reigns: James I, James II, and the Old Pretender.

Philip Guedalla 1889–1944: *Supers and Supermen* (1920)

6 When I am dead, I hope it may be said:
'His sins were scarlet, but his books were read.'

Hilaire Belloc 1870–1953: 'On His Books' (1923)

7 A dogged attempt to cover the universe with mud, an inverted Victorianism, an attempt to make crossness and dirt succeed where sweetness and light failed.

E. M. Forster 1879–1970: of James Joyce's *Ulysses*; *Aspects of the Novel* (1927)

8 A woman must have money and a room of her own if she is
to write fiction.
   Virginia Woolf 1882-1941: *A Room of One's Own* (1929)

9 English literature's performing flea.
   Sean O'Casey 1880-1964: in P. G. Wodehouse *Performing
   Flea* (1953), describing the author

10 The writer's only responsibility is to his art. He will be
completely ruthless if he is a good one…If a writer has to
rob his mother, he will not hesitate; the *Ode on a Grecian
Urn* is worth any number of old ladies.
   William Faulkner 1897-1962: in *Paris Review* Spring 1956

11 I think like a genius, I write like a distinguished author, and
I speak like a child.
   Vladimir Nabokov 1899-1977: *Strong Opinions* (1973)

12 The shelf life of the modern hardback writer is somewhere
between the milk and the yoghurt.
   Calvin Trillin 1935- : in *Sunday Times* 9 June 1991
   (attributed)

....

Writing
....

See also **Books, Literature, Poetry, Style**

1 Biting my truant pen, beating myself for spite,
'Fool,' said my Muse to me; 'look in thy heart and write.'
   Philip Sidney 1554-86: *Astrophil and Stella* (1591)

2 And, as imagination bodies forth
The forms of things unknown, the poet's pen
Turns them to shapes, and gives to airy nothing
A local habitation and a name.
   William Shakespeare 1564-1616: *A Midsummer Night's
   Dream* (1595-6)

3 So all my best is dressing old words new,
Spending again what is already spent.
   William Shakespeare 1564-1616: sonnet 76 (1609)

4   What in me is dark
Illumine, what is low raise and support;
That to the height of this great argument

I may assert eternal providence,
And justify the ways of God to men.
  John Milton 1608–74: *Paradise Lost* (1667)

5 Things unattempted yet in prose or rhyme.
  John Milton 1608–74: *Paradise Lost* (1667)

6 We must beat the iron while it is hot, but we may polish it at leisure.
  John Dryden 1631–1700: *Aeneis* (1697)

7 Eye Nature's walks, shoot Folly as it flies,
And catch the Manners living as they rise.
Laugh where we must, be candid where we can;
But vindicate the ways of God to man.
  Alexander Pope 1688–1744: *An Essay on Man* Epistle 1 (1733)

8 But those who cannot write, and those who can,
All rhyme, and scrawl, and scribble, to a man.
  Alexander Pope 1688–1744: *Imitations of Horace* (1737)

9 A man may write at any time, if he will set himself doggedly to it.
  Samuel Johnson 1709–84: in James Boswell *Life of Johnson* (1791) March 1750

10 You write with ease, to show your breeding,
But easy writing's vile hard reading.
  Richard Brinsley Sheridan 1751–1816: 'Clio's Protest' (written 1771)

11 Read over your compositions, and where ever you meet with a passage which you think is particularly fine, strike it out.
  Samuel Johnson 1709–84: in James Boswell *Life of Johnson* (1791) 30 April 1773; quoting a college tutor

12 The composition of a tragedy requires *testicles*.
  Voltaire 1694–1778: on being asked why no woman had ever written 'a tolerable tragedy'; letter from Byron to John Murray, 2 April 1817

13 What is written without effort is in general read without pleasure.
  Samuel Johnson 1709–84: in W. Seward *Biographia* (1799)

14 Never forget what I believe was observed to you by Coleridge, that every great and original writer, in proportion

as he is great and original, must himself create the taste by
which he is to be relished.
  William Wordsworth 1770–1850: letter to Lady Beaumont,
  21 May 1807

15 Let other pens dwell on guilt and misery. I quit such odious
   subjects as soon as I can.
   Jane Austen 1775–1817: *Mansfield Park* (1814)

16 The little bit (two inches wide) of ivory on which I work with
   so fine a brush, as produces little effect after much labour?
   Jane Austen 1775–1817: letter to J. Edward Austen,
   16 December 1816

17 All clean and comfortable I sit down to write.
   John Keats 1795–1821: letter to George and Georgiana
   Keats, 17 September 1819

18 The Big Bow-Wow strain I can do myself like any now going;
   but the exquisite touch, which renders ordinary
   commonplace things and characters interesting, from the
   truth of the description and the sentiment, is denied to me.
   Sir Walter Scott 1771–1832: on Jane Austen; diary,
   14 March 1826

19 Beneath the rule of men entirely great
   The pen is mightier than the sword.
   Edward Bulwer-Lytton 1803–73: *Richelieu* (1839)

20 When once the itch of literature comes over a man, nothing
   can cure it but the scratching of a pen.
   Samuel Lover 1797–1868: *Handy Andy* (1842)

21 Not that the story need be long, but it will take a long while
   to make it short.
   Henry David Thoreau 1817–62: letter to Harrison Blake,
   16 November 1857

22 They shut me up in prose—
   As when a little girl
   They put me in the closet—
   Because they liked me 'still'.
   Emily Dickinson 1830–86: 'They shut me up in prose'
   (*c.*1862)

23 As to the Adjective: when in doubt, strike it out.
   Mark Twain 1835–1910: *Pudd'nhead Wilson* (1894)

24 To give an accurate and exhaustive account of the period
would need a far less brilliant pen than mine.
   Max Beerbohm 1872–1956: *Yellow Book* (1895)

25 Only connect!…Only connect the prose and the passion.
   E. M. Forster 1879–1970: *Howards End* (1910)

26 The test of a round character is whether it is capable of
surprising in a convincing way. If it never surprises, it is
flat. If it does not convince, it is flat pretending to be round.
   E. M. Forster 1879–1970: *Aspects of the Novel* (1927)

27 You praise the firm restraint with which they write—
   I'm with you there, of course:
   They use the snaffle and the curb all right,
   But where's the bloody horse?
   Roy Campbell 1901–57: 'On Some South African Novelists'
   (1930)

28 If you try to nail anything down in the novel, either it kills
the novel, or the novel gets up and walks away with the nail.
   D. H. Lawrence 1885–1930: *Phoenix* (1936) 'Morality and the
   Novel'

29 Morality in the novel is the trembling instability of the
balance. When the novelist puts his thumb in the scale, to
pull down the balance to his own predilection, that is
immorality.
   D. H. Lawrence 1885–1930: *Phoenix* (1936) 'Morality and the
   Novel'

30 If you steal from one author, it's plagiarism; if you steal from
many, it's research.
   Wilson Mizner 1876–1933: in A. Johnston *The Legendary
   Mizners* (1953)

31 A writer's ambition should be…to trade a hundred
contemporary readers for ten readers in ten years' time and
for one reader in a hundred years.
   Arthur Koestler 1905–83: in *New York Times Book Review*
   1 April 1951

32 Writing is not a profession but a vocation of unhappiness.
   Georges Simenon 1903–89: interview in *Paris Review*
   Summer 1955

Youth

See also **The Generation Gap**

1 Whom the gods love dies young.
   Menander 342–c.292 BC: *Dis Exapaton*

2   My salad days,
   When I was green in judgement.
   William Shakespeare 1564–1616: *Antony and Cleopatra*
   (1606–7)

3 Two lads that thought there was no more behind
   But such a day to-morrow as to-day,
   And to be boy eternal.
   William Shakespeare 1564–1616: *The Winter's Tale*
   (1610–11)

4 The atrocious crime of being a young man...I shall neither
   attempt to palliate nor deny.
   William Pitt 1708–78: speech, House of Commons, 2 March
   1741

5 In gallant trim the gilded vessel goes;
   Youth on the prow, and Pleasure at the helm.
   Thomas Gray 1716–71: 'The Bard' (1757)

6 Heaven lies about us in our infancy!
   Shades of the prison-house begin to close
   Upon the growing boy.
   William Wordsworth 1770–1850: 'Ode. Intimations of
   Immortality' (1807)

7 A boy's will is the wind's will
   And the thoughts of youth are long, long thoughts.
   Henry Wadsworth Longfellow 1807–82: 'My Lost Youth'
   (1858)

8 Youth would be an ideal state if it came a little later in life.
   Herbert Asquith 1852–1928: in *Observer* 15 April 1923

9 It is better to waste one's youth than to do nothing with it at
   all.
   Georges Courteline 1858–1929: *La Philosophie de Georges
   Courteline* (1948)

10 What music is more enchanting than the voices of young people, when you can't hear what they say?
  Logan Pearsall Smith 1865-1946: *Afterthoughts* (1931)

11 The force that through the green fuse drives the flower
  Drives my green age.
  Dylan Thomas 1914-53: 'The force that through the green fuse' (1934)

12 Youth is something very new: twenty years ago no one mentioned it.
  Coco Chanel 1883-1971: in M. Haedrich *Coco Chanel, Her Life, Her Secrets* (1971)

13 Youth is vivid rather than happy, but memory always remembers the happy things.
  Bernard Lovell 1913- : in *The Times* 20 August 1993

Index of Authors

Abbott, Diane (1953–)
  Politicians 43
Abse, Dannie (1923–)
  Sickness 13
Accius (170–c.86 BC)
  Government 1
Ace, Goodman
(1899–1982)
  Broadcasting 3
Acheson, Dean
(1893–1971)
  Britain 7
  Bureaucracy 6
  Careers 8
Acton, Lord
(1834–1902)
  Power 7
Adams, Abigail
(1744–1818)
  Character 8
Adams, Douglas
(1952–)
  Life 67
Adams, Franklin P.
(1881–1960)
  Middle Age 6
  Voting 6
Adams, Henry
Brooks (1838–1918)
  Education 19, 20
  Experience 5
  Meaning 5
  Morality 7
  Politics 10, 11
  Teaching 9
Adams, John
(1735–1826)
  Government 10, 11
  Politics 4

Adams, John
Quincy (1767–1848)
  Patriotism 12
Adams, Samuel
(1722–1803)
  Business 10
Adamson, Harold
(1906–80)
  Crises 4
Addison, Joseph
(1672–1719)
  Business 5
  Fame 5
  Future 3
  Gardens 5
  Happiness 4
  Humour 7
  Patriotism 3
  Success 9
Ade, George
(1866–1944)
  Alcohol 13
  Marriage 36
Adenauer, Konrad
(1876–1967)
  Character 17
Adler, Alfred
(1870–1937)
  Truth 30
Agar, Herbert
(1897–1980)
  Truth 31
Agate, James
(1877–1947)
  Certainty 15
  Work 19
Agathon (b. c.445 BC)
  Past 1
Ainger, Alfred
(1837–1904)
  Praise 7

Alain (1868–1951)
  Ideas 6
Alcuin (c.735–804)
  Minorities 1
Aldington, Richard
(1892–1962)
  Patriotism 19
Aldiss, Brian (1925–)
  Violence 8
Aldrin, Buzz (1930–)
  Skies 10
Alexander, Cecil
Frances (1818–95)
  Animals 8
  Class 8
Alexander, William
(c.1567–1640)
  Women 7
Alfonso 'the Wise'
(1221–84)
  Universe 1
Ali, Muhammad
(1942–)
  Sport 28, 29
Allen, Fred
(1894–1956)
  America 19
  Management 6
Allen, Woody (1935–)
  Death 60, 61
  Self 12
  Sex 26, 28, 30, 31
Allingham, William
(1824–89)
  Supernatural 7
Ambrose, St
(AD c.339–97)
  Behaviour 3
Amery, Leo
(1873–1955)
  Politicians 16

Ames, Fisher
(1758–1808)
Government 15
Amis, Kingsley
(1922–)
Alcohol 20
Death 62
Education 29
Men and Women 24
Old Age 37
Anacharsis
(6th century BC)
Law 1
**Andersen, Hans
Christian** (1805–75)
Truth 18
**Andrewes, Bishop
Lancelot** (1555–1626)
Church 4
Seasons 5
Anka, Paul (1941–)
Living 13
Anouilh, Jean
(1910–87)
Fate 11
God 20
Life 53
Love 65
**Apollinaire,
Guillaume** (1880–1918)
Custom 10
Inventions 12
Memory 12
**Appleton, Thomas
Gold** (1812–84)
America 5, 7
Arabin, William
(1773–1841)
Crime 10, 11
Law 21
Arbuthnot, Dr
(1667–1735)
Law 11

Archilochus
(7th century BC)
Knowledge 1
Archimedes
(c.287–212 BC)
Inventions 2
Technology 1
Arendt, Hannah
(1906–75)
Good 26
Revolution 18
Aristotle (384–322 BC)
Acting 1
Certainty 2
Friendship 2
Good 2
Nature 1
Politics 1
Solitude 2
Truth 2
War 1
Armstrong, Louis
(1901–71)
Music 29, 30
Armstrong, Neil
(1930–)
Achievement 17
Armstrong, Robert
(1927–)
Truth 35
Arnold, Matthew
(1822–88)
Behaviour 14
Belief 11
Cats 3
Change 16
France 8
Leadership 2
Life 25
Memory 8
Middle Age 1
People 11
Perfection 11
Places 14, 15

Arnold, Matthew
(*cont.*)
Poetry 15
Poets 12, 13
Seasons 16
Shakespeare 6
Solitude 9
Style 13
Arnold, Thomas
(1795–1842)
Crime 9
Education 13
Ascham, Roger
(1515–68)
Education 3
Teaching 3
Ashford, Daisy
(1881–1972)
Middle Age 2
Prayer 1
Asquith, Herbert
(1852–1928)
Political Comment 11
Statistics 6
Youth 8
Asquith, Margot
(1864–1945)
Lies 20
Supernatural 9
Astell, Mary
(1668–1731)
Woman's Role 3
Astley, Jacob
(1579–1652)
Prayer 4
Astor, Nancy
(1879–1964)
Alcohol 21
Atkinson, Brooks
(1894–1984)
Democracy 11
Past 18

Atkinson, E. L.
(1882–1929) and
**Cherry-Garrard,
Apsley** (1882–1959)
   Epitaphs 15
Attlee, Clement
(1883–1967)
   Democracy 13
   Politicians 22
   Politics 19
Aubrey, John
(1626–97)
   Gossip 2
   Medicine 10
   Reading 3
Auctoritates
Aristotelis
   Argument 2
   Parents 4
   Time 7
Auden, W. H.
(1907–73)
   Art 20
   Body 15
   Books 28
   Generation Gap 10
   Good 22
   Heart 6
   Humour 22
   Intelligence 12, 14
   Letters 8
   Love 62
   People 19
   Poetry 28
   Poets 17
   Power 13
   Science 31
   Self 10, 11
   Self-Knowledge 14
   Society 10
   Sorrow 20
   Success 19
   Suffering 18
   Transport 9

**Augustine, St, of
Hippo** (AD 354–430)
   Good 4
   Justice 4
   Living 4
   Moderation 5
   Sex 3
Aurelius, Marcus
(AD 121–80)
   Suffering 2
   Thinking 1
   Time 5, 6
Austen, Jane
(1775–1817)
   Advice 2
   Conversation 3, 4
   Gifts 9
   Gossip 6
   Happiness 9
   Humour 10
   Ignorance 5
   Literature 2
   Marriage 25, 26
   Men 4
   Money 14
   Morality 3
   Perfection 5
   Places 3
   Pleasure 5
   Women 14
   Writing 15, 16
Ayer, A. J. (1910–89)
   Life 68
Ayres, Pam (1947–)
   Medicine 20

Babbage, Charles
(1792–1871)
   Statistics 3
Bacon, Francis
(1561–1626)
   Action 1
   Anger 4
   Beauty 7
   Belief 4
   Books 3, 4
   Careers 2
   Certainty 4
   Change 5
   Children 10
   Dance 2
   Death 22
   Diplomacy 3
   Education 7, 8
   Fame 4
   Family 3
   Friendship 4, 5
   Gardens 3
   Indifference 2
   Inventions 3
   Knowledge 7, 8
   Life 11
   Marriage 6, 7
   Medicine 6, 7
   Misfortune 6
   Money 7
   Old Age 9
   Parents 6
   Past 4, 7
   Power 2, 3
   Praise 2
   Revenge 3
   Royalty 6
   Science 2
   Silence 1
   Travel 1
   Truth 7
   Virtue 8
   Wealth 3
   Words 6

Bagehot, Walter
(1826–77)
  Government 24
  News 7
  Politicians 9
  Royalty 14, 15, 16
  Women 21
  Writers 4
Bairnsfather, Bruce
(1888–1959)
  Advice 4
Baldwin, James
(1924–87)
  Money 24
  Poverty 19
  Prejudice 18
Baldwin, Stanley
(1867–1947)
  Political Comment 12, 14
  Politicians 17
  Secrets 8
  Truth 27
  War 29, 30
Balfour, Arthur James (1848–1930)
  News 15
  Politicians 18
Balliett, Whitney
(1926–)
  Critics 17
Barnard, Frederick R.
  Language 14
Barnes, Julian (1946–)
  Books 31
  Britain 8
  History 19
Barnum, Phineas T.
(1810–91)
  Fools 17

Barrie, J. M.
(1860–1937)
  Belief 15
  Charm 1
  Death 48
  Life 32
  Memory 16
  Practicality 5
  Scotland 11
  Self-Knowledge 13
Barrymore, John
(1882–1942)
  Solitude 16
Barth, Karl
(1886–1968)
  Musicians 9
Barthes, Roland
(1915–80)
  Transport 12
Baruch, Bernard
(1870–1965)
  Old Age 28
  Voting 8
Barzun, Jacques
(1907–)
  Life 60
Bastard, Thomas
(1566–1618)
  Generation Gap 2
Bateman, Edgar and **Le Brunn, George**
  Environment 11
Bates, Katherine Lee (1859–1929)
  America 9
Baudelaire, Charles
(1821–67)
  Change 18
  Class 9
  Inventions 9
  Progress 7
Baum, Vicki
(1888–1960)
  Marriage 41

Baxter, Beverley
(1891–1964)
  People 20
Beaumarchais
(1732–99)
  Human Race 16
  Humour 8
  Singing 2
Beaverbrook, Lord
(1879–1964)
  Science 26
Beckett, Samuel
(1906–89)
  Bores 10
  Custom 11
  Life 57
  Money 21
  Time 38
Becon, Thomas
(1512–67)
  Alcohol 3
Bede, The Venerable
(AD 673–735)
  Life 6
Beecham, Thomas
(1879–1961)
  Music 21, 25, 26, 27
  Musicians 5, 6, 7
Beerbohm, Max
(1872–1956)
  Philosophy 9
  Writing 24
Beethoven, Ludwig van (1770–1827)
  Fate 7
Beeton, Mrs (1836–65)
  Management 4
Behan, Brendan
(1923–64)
  Absence 7
  Fame 20

Behn, Aphra (1640–89)
 Money 9
 Poverty 4
 Secrets 6
Belloc, Hilaire
(1870–1953)
 Animals 10
 Books 19
 Certainty 11
 Class 12
 Food 23
 Life Sciences 6
 Medicine 12
 Misfortune 12
 Parents 11
 Pleasure 12
 Power 8
 Temptation 7
 Time 36
 Violence 5
 Voting 5
 Writers 6
Belloy, De (1727–75)
 Patriotism 5
Benchley, Robert
(1889–1945)
 Places 22
 Quotations 10
Benét, Stephen
Vincent (1898–1943)
 America 13
Bennett, Alan (1934–)
 Family 13
 Memory 21
 Morality 14
 Society 13
Bennett, Arnold
(1867–1931)
 Idealism 3
 Justice 22
 Marriage 38
 News 13
Bennett, Jill (1931–90)
 Marriage 48

Bentham, Jeremy
(1748–1832)
 Crime 8
 Human Rights 7
 People 7
 Poetry 13
 Society 6
Bentley, Edmund
Clerihew (1875–1956)
 Biography 7
 Royalty 18
Bentley, Richard
(1662–1742)
 Alcohol 5
Beresford, Lord
Charles (1846–1919)
 Apology 5
Berkeley, Bishop
George (1685–1753)
 Food 9
 Knowledge 9
 Mathematics 5
 Truth 12
Berlin, Irving
(1888–1989)
 Acting 14
 America 16
 Christmas 4
 Dance 8
Berlin, Isaiah (1909–)
 Liberty 24
 People 22
Bernanos, Georges
(1888–1948)
 Heaven 9
 Prayer 15
Bernard of Chartres
(d. c.1130)
 Progress 2
Berners, Lord
(1883–1950)
 Fame 17

Berra, Yogi (1925–)
 Beginnings 14
 Future 12
Berryman, John
(1914–72)
 Bores 13
 Cinema 12
 Fear 10
 Misfortune 16
Betjeman, John
(1906–84)
 Christmas 5
 Education 28
 England 29
 Environment 16
 Manners 13
 Sport 24
Bevan, Aneurin
(1897–1960)
 Management 5
 Medicine 17
 Moderation 10
 News 23
 Political Comment 16
 Political Parties 8
 Politicians 23, 24, 26,
 28
Beveridge, William
Henry (1879–1963)
 Progress 9
Bevin, Ernest
(1881–1951)
 Enemies 8
 Europe 9
 Political Comment 13,
 15
Bible
 Absence 1
 Alcohol 1, 2
 Anger 1, 3
 Animals 1
 Argument 1
 Beauty 2
 Beginnings 1

Bible (*cont.*)
Belief 1
Birth 1
Body 1, 2
Books 1
Careers 1
Certainty 1
Chance 1, 2
Change 1
Children 1, 2, 3, 4
Christmas 1
Crime 1, 2, 3
Death 2, 3, 5, 6
Enemies 1, 2
Environment 1, 2
Envy 1
Epitaphs 2
Equality 1
Fame 3
Family 1
Fate 1
Food 1
Fools 1, 2, 4
Forgiveness 1
Friendship 1
Gardens 1
Gifts 2, 3, 4, 5
God 1, 2
Good 1, 3
Greatness 1
Hatred 1
Heaven 1
Hope 1
Hypocrisy 2, 3
Idleness 1
Inventions 1
Justice 1, 2
Knowledge 3, 4, 5
Language 1
Law 4
Leadership 1
Life 1, 2
Living 1, 2, 3
Love 1, 3, 4, 5, 6

Bible (*cont.*)
Manners 1
Marriage 1, 2, 3
Medicine 4
Misfortune 1
Moderation 4
Money 1, 4
Murder 1
News 1, 2, 3
Old Age 1, 2
Parents 1, 2, 3
Peace 1, 2
Pollution 1
Poverty 1
Prayer 1
Present 2, 3
Pride 1, 2
Progress 1
Religion 4, 5
Revenge 1
Sea 1, 2
Secrets 1
Self-Knowledge 3, 4
Sleep 1
Solitude 1
Sorrow 1, 2
Success 1, 6
Supernatural 1
Teaching 1
Temptation 1
Time 1, 2
Transience 2, 3
Trust 1
Truth 4
Virtue 1, 2
Wealth 2
Women 1
Work 1, 2, 3
Bible (Apocrypha)
Business 1
Epitaphs 3
Medicine 1, 2
Truth 3

Bidault, Georges
(1899–1983)
Mistakes 15
Bierce, Ambrose
(1842–?1914)
Bores 5
History 14
Peace 10
Political Parties 5
Pollution 6
Prejudice 9
Religion 39
War 18
Binyon, Laurence
(1869–1943)
Epitaphs 16
Birkett, Lord
(1883–1962)
Speech 22
Birrell, Augustine
(1850–1933)
History 11
Bishop, Elizabeth
(1911–79)
Sleep 15
Bismarck, Otto von
(1815–98)
Europe 4
Political Comment 8
Politicians 11
Politics 8
Wars 9
Blacker, Valentine
(1728–1823)
Practicality 4
Blackstone, William
(1723–80)
Justice 12
Blake, Eubie
(1883–1983)
Old Age 36

Blake, William
(1757–1827)
  Anger 7
  Animals 5
  Cruelty 4
  England 9
  Environment 8
  Fools 13, 14
  Good 17
  Human Race 17, 18
  Imagination 5
  Knowledge 14, 15
  Love 40, 41
  Men and Women 6
  Poets 7
  Power 6
  Race 1
  Self-Knowledge 10
  Sorrow 11
  Time 21
  Transience 8
  Truth 16
**Blücher, Gebhard
Lebrecht** (1742–1819)
  London 6
Blythe, Ronald
(1922–)
  Country 10
Boethius
(AD c.476–524)
  Misfortune 2
Bogan, Louise
(1897–1970)
  Women 27
Bogart, John B.
(1848–1921)
  News 14
Bohr, Niels
(1885–1962)
  Belief 16
  Truth 34
Bold, Alan (1943–)
  Scotland 12

**Bolingbroke, 1st
Viscount** (1678–1751)
  Mistakes 7
  Politicians 2
Bolt, Robert (1924–)
  Wales 5
Bonhoeffer, Dietrich
(1906–45)
  Character 14
**Book of Common
Prayer** (1662)
  Conscience 3
  Day 5
  Death 26, 27
  Environment 3
  Languages 2
  Marriage 10, 11, 12
  Peace 8
  Sea 5
  Temptation 2
Boorstin, Daniel J.
(1914–)
  Fame 19
Boren, James H.
(1925–)
  Bureaucracy 5
Borges, Jorge Luis
(1899–1986)
  Languages 7
  Universe 10
  Wars 30
Borgia, Cesare
(1476–1507)
  Ambition 2
Borrow, George
(1803–81)
  Literature 5
Bosquet, Pierre
(1810–61)
  Army 6
**Bossidy, John
Collins** (1860–1928)
  Places 17

Boswell, James
(1740–95)
  Diaries 2
  Manners 6
Bottomley, Gordon
(1874–1948)
  Technology 4
Bottomley, Horatio
(1860–1933)
  Education 21
Boucicault, Dion
(1820–90)
  Time 23
**Boulay de la
Meurthe, Antoine**
(1761–1840)
  Mistakes 9
Boulez, Pierre (1925–)
  Revolution 19
Boulton, Matthew
(1728–1809)
  Technology 2
Bowen, Elizabeth
(1899–1973)
  Absence 6
  Children 22
  Envy 6
  Experience 7
  Fate 10
  Seasons 26
Bowen, Lord (1835–94)
  Justice 18
  Weather 9
Brackett, Charles
(1892–1969) and
Wilder, Billy (1906–)
  Cinema 6
Bradford, John
(c.1510–55)
  Chance 3

Bradley, F. H.
(1846–1924)
  Optimism 5
  Philosophy 8
  Universe 4
Bradshaw, John
(1602–59)
  Revolution 2
Bramston, James
(c.1694–1744)
  Time 19
Braque, Georges
(1882–1963)
  Art 21
  Lies 22
Braun, Wernher von
(1912–77)
  Science 36
Brecht, Bertolt
(1898–1956)
  Dress 9
  Heroes 4
  Morality 10
  Science 24
  War 36
Brenan, Gerald
(1894–1987)
  Bores 15
Brenner, Sydney
(1927–)
  Technology 14
Brereton, Jane
(1685–1740)
  Fools 12
Breton, Nicholas
(c.1545–1626)
  Enemies 3
Bridges, Robert
(1844–1930)
  Weather 8
Bright, John (1811–89)
  Government 23
  Political Comment 4
  Wars 7

**Brillat-Savarin,
Anthelme** (1755–1826)
  Food 16
  Inventions 8
Bronowski, Jacob
(1908–74)
  Action 11
  Cruelty 6
  Science 37
Brontë, Charlotte
(1816–55)
  Action 7
  Style 11
  Teaching 7
Brontë, Emily
(1818–48)
  Courage 8
  Love 46
Brontë, Patrick
(1777–1861)
  Biography 5
Brooke, Rupert
(1887–1915)
  Death 42, 43
  England 21
  Flowers 11
  Past 14
  Places 19
  Sleep 14
Brookner, Anita
(1938–)
  Women 39
Brown, H. Rap (1943–)
  Violence 7
Brown, Lew
(1893–1958)
  Life 43
Brown, T. E. (1830–97)
  Gardens 9
Brown, Thomas
(1663–1704)
  Hatred 3
Browne, Cecil (1932–)
  Prejudice 12

Browne, Sir Thomas
(1605–82)
  Death 25
  Human Race 11
  Life 15
  Mathematics 4
  Medicine 8
  Nature 5
  Praise 3
  Religion 12, 13, 14
  Sex 9
  Sleep 6, 8
  Truth 9
**Browning, Elizabeth
Barrett** (1806–61)
  People 10
  Prayer 9
  Sorrow 14
Browning, Frederick
(1896–1965)
  Wars 24
Browning, Robert
(1812–89)
  Achievement 12
  Ambition 10
  Beauty 15
  Belief 10
  Bible 5
  Birds 6
  Children 18
  Choice 5
  Cynicism 3
  Determination 9
  England 12
  God 11
  Hatred 6
  Ignorance 6
  Love 50, 51, 54
  Music 11
  Optimism 3
  Perfection 7, 10
  Progress 6
  Time 25
  Trust 6

Brummell, Beau
(1778–1840)
  Dress 4
Bruno, Frank (1961–)
  Sport 33
Buchan, John
(1875–1940)
  Belief 18
Buchanan, Robert
(1841–1901)
  Dress 5
Buchman, Frank
(1878–1961)
  Economics 8
Buffon, Comte de
(1707–88)
  Genius 4
  Style 7
Buller, Arthur
(1874–1944)
  Science 14
**Bulwer-Lytton,
Edward** (1803–73)
  Friendship 12
  Opening Lines 7
  Poets 11
  Reading 10
  Speech 10
  Writing 19
Bunting, Basil
(1900–85)
  Environment 13
Bunyan, John
(1628–88)
  Pride 3
  Religion 15
Burgess, Anthony
(1917–93)
  Opening Lines 16
  Sex 21
Burgess, Gelett
(1866–1951)
  Imagination 11

Burke, Edmund
(1729–97)
  Ambition 8
  Business 9
  Cooperation 2
  Custom 4
  Europe 1
  Family 4
  Fear 5
  Future 4, 5
  Good 15
  Government 8, 13
  Human Rights 5
  Law 14, 15
  Liberty 6
  Lies 5
  Politicians 4, 5
  Politics 3
  Practicality 3
  Revolution 6
  Society 4
  Success 10
  Taxes 4
Burke, Johnny
(1908–64)
  Weather 14
Burney, Fanny
(1752–1840)
  Marriage 22
Burns, John
(1858–1943)
  England 31
Burns, Robert
(1759–96)
  Animals 4
  Chance 6
  Cruelty 3
  Equality 6
  Food 14
  Friendship 8
  Love 43
  Scotland 5, 6
  Self-Knowledge 9

Burns, Robert (cont.)
  Temptation 3, 4
  Titles 2
**Burroughs, William
S.** (1914–)
  Good 25
Burton, Robert
(1577–1640)
  Love 29
  Poets 2
  Religion 11
**Busenbaum,
Hermann** (1600–68)
  Morality 1
Bush, George (1924–)
  Taxes 11
**Bussy-Rabutin,
Comte de** (1618–93)
  War 6
**Butler, Nicholas
Murray** (1862–1947)
  Knowledge 26
Butler, Samuel
(1612–80)
  Cynicism 2
  Hypocrisy 7
  Opinion 4
Butler, Samuel
(1835–1902)
  Art 12
  Bible 8
  Conscience 5
  Dogs 3
  Language 11
  Lies 15
  Life 33, 34, 35
  Life Sciences 5
  Marriage 34
  Meeting 14
  Men 7
  Praise 8

Byron, Lord
(1788–1824)
Beauty 10
Behaviour 10
Bores 4
Children 16
Critics 6
Dance 4
Fame 11, 12
Food 15
Hatred 5
Hope 9
Liberty 10
Lies 7
Literature 3
Marriage 24, 28
Men and Women 5
Nature 8
Places 5, 7
Pleasure 7, 8
Poets 10
Reading 9
Religion 28
Revenge 5
Scotland 8
Sea 9
Seasons 12
Self-Knowledge 11
Solitude 6
Truth 17
Women 16

**Cabell, James
Branch** (1879–1958)
Optimism 8
Caesar, Julius
(100–44 BC)
Ambition 1
Behaviour 2
Choice 1
Success 2
Callimachus
(c.305–c.240 BC)
Books 2
**Calonne, Charles
Alexandre de**
(1734–1802)
Achievement 11
Camden, William
(1551–1623)
Epitaphs 5
**Campbell, Mrs
Patrick** (1865–1940)
Marriage 42
Sex 19
Campbell, Roy
(1901–57)
Animals 15
Human Race 26
Writing 27
Campbell, Thomas
(1777–1844)
Books 13
Country 2
Environment 7
Camus, Albert
(1913–60)
Charm 5
Intelligence 13
Revolution 16, 17
Canetti, Elias
(1905–94)
Sleep 16
Canning, George
(1770–1827)
Friendship 9
Patriotism 13

Capote, Truman
(1924–84)
Places 27
Capp, Al (1907–79)
Painting 16
**Caracciolo,
Francesco** (1752–99)
England 7
Carlyle, Thomas
(1795–1881)
Biography 3
Civilization 1
France 7
Genius 6
History 6, 7
Idleness 7
Indifference 5
Libraries 5
People 8, 9
Statistics 1
Universe 3
Carmichael, Stokely
(1941–)
Woman's Role 12
Carnegie, Andrew
(1835–1919)
Wealth 9
Carr, J. L. (1912–)
Teaching 12
Carroll, Lewis
(1832–98)
Achievement 13
Beginnings 5
Belief 12
Books 16
Conversation 7
Education 15
Justice 16
Language 8
Manners 9
Meaning 3
Philosophy 7
Present 8
Reality 2

Carroll, Lewis (*cont.*)
   Truth 19
   Words 12
Carson, Rachel
(1907–64)
   Environment 18
Carter, Henry
(d. 1806)
   Patriotism 9
Cartwright, John
(1740–1824)
   Democracy 2
Casals, Pablo
(1876–1973)
   Old Age 33
Catherine the Great
(1729–96)
   Forgiveness 4
Catullus (*c.*84–*c.*54 BC)
   Meeting 1
Cavell, Edith
(1865–1915)
   Patriotism 16
Cecil, Lord Hugh
(1869–1956)
   Church 14
Centlivre, Susannah
(*c.*1669–1723)
   Money 11
Cervantes (1547–1616)
   Food 4
   Painting 2
**Chamberlain,
Neville** (1869–1940)
   Peace 11
   War 35
**Chamfort,
Nicolas-Sébastien**
(1741–94)
   Poverty 10
Chandler, Raymond
(1888–1959)
   Beauty 25
   Cinema 5

Chandler, Raymond
(*cont.*)
   Language 15
   Places 25
Chanel, Coco
(1883–1971)
   Europe 12
   Youth 12
**Channon, Henry
'Chips'** (1897–1958)
   Diaries 5
Chaplin, Charlie
(1889–1977)
   Cinema 13, 16
Chapman, George
(*c.*1559–1634)
   Education 6
   England 4
   Human Race 7
   Law 8
Chapman, Graham
(1941–89)
   Death 58
Charles I (1600–49)
   Apology 1
Charles II (1630–85)
   Behaviour 6
   Last Words 10
Charles V, Emperor
(1500–58)
   Languages 1
**Charles, Prince of
Wales** (1948–)
   Architecture 10
Chaucer, Geoffrey
(*c.*1343–1400)
   Beauty 3
   Behaviour 4
   Birds 2
   Education 1, 2
   Flowers 1
   Hypocrisy 4
   Love 9
   Murder 2

Chekhov, Anton
(1860–1904)
   Beauty 20
   Friendship 13
   Literature 7
   Pollution 5
   Sickness 7
**Cherry-Garrard,
Apsley** (1882–1959)
   see **Atkinson,
   E. L.** and
   **Cherry-Garrard,
   Apsley**
Chesterfield, Lord
(1694–1773)
   Advice 1
   Britain 4
   Chance 5
   Conversation 1
   Enemies 6
   Idleness 6
   Knowledge 12
   Manners 3, 4
   Religion 21
   Sex 13
   Time 20
   Truth 13
   Women 11
Chesterton, G. K.
(1874–1936)
   Crime 21
   Custom 8
   England 20
   Food 24
   Government 27
   Hypocrisy 12
   Ideas 5
   Imagination 10
   Ireland 6
   Knowledge 22
   Literature 9
   Memory 19
   Prejudice 8
   Religion 38

Chesterton, G. K.
(*cont.*)
  Transport 5
  Women 25
Chevalier, Maurice
(1888–1972)
  Old Age 30
Chomsky, Noam
(1928–)
  Language 18
Chuang-tzu
(c.369–286 BC)
  Self-Knowledge 2
Churchill, Charles
(1731–64)
  Achievement 9
  Hypocrisy 10
  Old Age 12
  Patriotism 4
  Speech 5
**Churchill, Lord
Randolph** (1849–94)
  Environment 10
  Ireland 5
  Mathematics 9
Churchill, Winston
(1874–1965)
  Alcohol 22
  Animals 17
  Beginnings 10
  Britain 5
  Certainty 14
  Crises 3
  Democracy 10
  Diplomacy 10
  Europe 8
  Food 31
  Future 10
  Language 16
  People 21, 28
  Places 13
  Politicians 19, 30, 31
  Prejudice 13
  Quotations 9

Churchill, Winston
(*cont.*)
  Sea 13
  Speech 16, 21
  Success 21
  Wars 17, 18, 19, 20, 23
  Words 15
**Ciano, Count
Galeazzo** (1903–44)
  Success 23
Cibber, Colley
(1671–1757)
  Crime 7
  Marriage 16
  Style 3
Cicero (106–43 BC)
  Behaviour 1
  Law 2, 3
  Mistakes 1
  Money 2
  Philosophy 2
  War 2
Cioran, E.M. (1911–)
  Idleness 11
Clare, John
(1793–1864)
  Hope 12
  Present 6
  Solitude 8
Clarendon, Earl of
(1609–74)
  People 2
Clark, Alan (1928–)
  Politicians 41
Clarke, Arthur C.
(1917–)
  Environment 23
  Science 35
Clarke, John (d. 1658)
  Home 3
**Clausewitz, Karl
von** (1780–1831)
  War 12, 13

Cleaver, Eldridge
(1935–)
  Management 10
**Clemenceau,
Georges** (1841–1929)
  Old Age 18
  War 23, 27
  Wars 13
Clive, Lord (1725–74)
  Moderation 8
Clough, Arthur Hugh
(1819–61)
  Crime 15
  Determination 6
  Envy 5
  Fear 6
  God 13
  Knowledge 18
  Murder 7
  Religion 32
Cobbett, William
(1762–1835)
  London 7
Cockburn, Claud
(1904–81)
  News 22
Cocteau, Jean
(1889–1963)
  Behaviour 16
  Life 42
  People 18
Cohan, George M.
(1878–1942)
  Fame 16
Cohen, Leonard
(1934–)
  Optimism 13
Coke, Desmond
(1879–1931)
  Sport 13
Coke, Edward
(1552–1634)
  Business 3
  Home 2

Coleridge, Samuel Taylor (1772–1834)
Acting 6
Birth 5
Chance 8
Day 7
Hope 11
Humour 9
Men and Women 7
Poetry 7, 12
Poets 8
Politics 5
Pollution 3
Prayer 8
Pride 4
Religion 29
Sea 7
Seasons 13
Singing 3
Weather 4
Collingwood, R. G. (1889–1943)
Work 15
Colman, George, the Elder (1732–94) and
Garrick, David (1717–79)
Love 36
Colman, George, the Younger (1762–1836)
Writers 3
Colton, Charles Caleb (c.1780–1832)
Country 4
Education 12
Praise 6
Speech 9
Comden, Betty (1919–) and
Green, Adolph (1915–)
Beginnings 12

Compton-Burnett, Ivy (1884–1969)
Men and Women 23
Poverty 17
Condell, Henry (d. 1627)
see **Heming, John** and **Condell, Henry**
Congreve, William (1670–1729)
Gossip 3
Love 34
Marriage 14, 15
Music 6
Revenge 4
Secrets 7
Connolly, Cyril (1903–74)
Art 16
Character 13
Charm 2
Children 23
Fame 18
Memory 20
Men and Women 21
Self 9
Style 14
Connolly, James (1868–1916)
Woman's Role 10
Conrad, Joseph (1857–1924)
Action 8
Ambition 13
Equality 8
Memory 15
Conran, Shirley (1932–)
Home 15
Practicality 8
Constable, John (1776–1837)
Beauty 13
Painting 4

Constant, Benjamin (1767–1834)
Art 3
Cook, Dan
Beginnings 15
Cook, Eliza (1818–89)
Crime 14
Coolidge, Calvin (1872–1933)
Civilization 4
Cope, Wendy (1945–)
Men 14
Poets 20
Copland, Aaron (1900–90)
Music 20
Cornford, Frances (1886–1960)
Meeting 17
Cornford, Francis M. (1874–1943)
Custom 9
Lies 18
Cornuel, Mme (1605–94)
Heroes 1
Coubertin, Baron Pierre de (1863–1937)
Sport 14
Coué, Émile (1857–1926)
Medicine 14
Courteline, Georges (1858–1929)
Youth 9
Coward, Noël (1899–1973)
Acting 18
Class 14
England 23
Cowley, Abraham (1618–67)
Life 14

Cowper, William
(1731–1800)
  Change 10
  Country 1
  Environment 6
  God 10
  Pleasure 4
  Solitude 1
Crabbe, George
(1754–1832)
  Custom 5
  Gossip 5
  Poverty 9
Crane, Hart
(1899–1932)
  Skies 9
Crashaw, Richard
(c.1612–49)
  Christmas 2
  Love 31
  Marriage 8
**Creighton, Bishop
Mandell** (1843–1901)
  Good 19
Crick, Francis (1916–)
  Life Sciences 10
Crisp, Quentin (1908–)
  Biography 10
  Home 14
Critchley, Julian
(1930–)
  Politicians 39
  Speech 24
Cromwell, Oliver
(1599–1658)
  Last Words 8
  Meeting 8
  Mistakes 3
  Painting 3
Crossman, Richard
(1907–74)
  Bureaucracy 4

Crowley, Aleister
(1875–1947)
  Living 12
**Cumberland, Bishop
Richard** (1631–1718)
  Idleness 4
cummings, e. e.
(1894–1962)
  Body 11
  Politicians 21
  Progress 10
**Curran, John
Philpot** (1750–1817)
  Liberty 8
Curtis, Tony (1925–)
  Cinema 10
Curtiz, Michael
(1888–1962)
  Cinema 3
Cyprian, St
(AD c.200–258)
  Church 2

Dalton, Hugh
(1887–1962)
  Ambition 15
Daniel, Samuel
(1563–1619)
  Sleep 2
Dante Alighieri
(1265–1321)
  Achievement 3
  Heaven 2
  Love 8
  Misfortune 3
  Opening Lines 2
  Peace 5
**Danton, Georges
Jacques** (1759–94)
  Courage 6
Darrow, Clarence
(1857–1938)
  Belief 14
Darwin, Charles
(1809–82)
  Animals 6
  Life Sciences 2
  Nature 12
Darwin, Francis
(1848–1925)
  Science 13
Davies, Sir John
(1569–1626)
  Dance 1
Davies, Scrope
(c.1783–1852)
  Madness 8
Davies, W. H.
(1871–1940)
  Birds 10, 12
  Leisure 3
  Transience 9
Davis, Sammy, Jnr.
(1925–90)
  Prejudice 17

Dawkins, Richard
(1941–)
  Death 63
  Life Sciences 9

Day-Lewis, C.
(1904–72)
  Poetry 25

**de Beauvoir,
Simone** (1908–86)
  Woman's Role 11

**Debs, Eugene
Victor** (1855–1926)
  Revolution 12

Decatur, Stephen
(1779–1820)
  Patriotism 11

Defoe, Daniel
(1660–1731)
  Church 5
  Class 4
  Custom 2
  Poverty 6
  Power 5
  Religion 17
  Royalty 9
  Teaching 4
  Virtue 10

Degas, Edgar
(1834–1917)
  Art 15

de Gaulle, Charles
(1890–1970)
  Diplomacy 14
  France 11
  War 31

de la Mare, Walter
(1873–1956)
  Flowers 10
  Opening Lines 10
  Skies 8
  Transience 10

de Leon, Walter and
Jones, Paul M.
  Life 46

Dempsey, Jack
(1895–1983)
  Sport 17

Denham, John
(1615–69)
  Character 5

Dennis, John
(1657–1734)
  Acting 5
  Words 9

**De Quincey,
Thomas** (1785–1859)
  Murder 6

Derby, 14th Earl of
(1799–1869)
  Political Comment 5

Descartes, René
(1596–1650)
  Practicality 1
  Thinking 4

**Destouches,
Philippe Néricault**
(1680–1754)
  Absence 3

De Vries, Peter
(1910–)
  Parents 21

Dewar, James
(1842–1923)
  Prejudice 10

Dewar, Lord
(1864–1930)
  Transport 7

**Diana, Princess of
Wales** (1961–)
  Birth 13

Diaz, Porfirio
(1830–1915)
  Places 20

Dickens, Charles
(1812–70)
  Bureaucracy 1
  Business 13
  Chance 9

Dickens, Charles
(*cont.*)
  Children 17
  Christmas 3
  Class 5
  Education 14
  Food 17
  Knowledge 19
  Last Words 19
  Law 19, 20, 22
  Love 47
  Minorities 3
  Money 17
  Opening Lines 9
  Optimism 4
  Places 9
  Pride 5
  Supernatural 6
  Weather 7

Dickinson, Emily
(1830–86)
  Meeting 13
  Writing 22

Didion, Joan (1934–)
  Choice 10

Dillon, Wentworth
(*c.*1633–1685)
  Reading 2

Dimnet, Ernest
  Architecture 7

Dinesen, Isak
(1885–1962)
  Human Race 24

**Dionysius of
Halicarnassus**
(fl. 30–7 BC)
  History 1

Dirac, Paul (1902–84)
  Critics 20
  Science 32

Disraeli, Benjamin
(1804–81)
  Apology 2
  Biography 1

Disraeli, Benjamin
(*cont.*)
  Experience 3
  Government 19
  Human Race 19
  Ireland 4
  Justice 14
  Language 9
  Lies 11
  Life 24
  Peace 9
  Political Parties 2, 3, 4
  Politics 6
  Royalty 17
  Speech 14
  Statistics 4
  Success 13
**Dobson, Henry
Austin** (1840–1921)
  Art 8
  Fame 15
  Time 27
Dodd, Ken (1931–)
  Humour 23
Donleavy, J. P.
(1926–)
  Life 58
Donne, John
(1572–1631)
  Animals 2
  Death 15, 16, 21
  Fools 5
  Imagination 3
  Letters 1, 2
  Love 14, 26, 27
  Men and Women 3
  Prayer 3
  Self-Knowledge 7
  Sex 4
  Skies 2
  Society 1
Dors, Diana (1931–84)
  Letters 9

Dostoevsky, Fedor
(1821–81)
  Beauty 18
  God 17
**Douglas, Lord
Alfred** (1870–1945)
  Love 56
Douglas, Keith
(1920–44)
  Death 54
  Misfortune 15
Douglas, O.
(1877–1948)
  Letters 7
Dowson, Ernest
(1867–1900)
  Memory 11
Doyle, Arthur Conan
(1859–1930)
  Country 7
  Crime 20
  Genius 11
  Imagination 9
  Intelligence 5
  Inventions 11
  Libraries 6
  Thinking 9
  Truth 23
Drabble, Margaret
(1939–)
  England 35
Drake, Francis
(c.1540–96)
  Achievement 4
  Sport 2
Drayton, Michael
(1563–1631)
  Meeting 7
  News 4
Drinkwater, John
(1882–1937)
  Silence 5

Dryden, John
(1631–1700)
  Anger 6
  Character 6
  Fools 7
  Genius 1
  Government 6
  Happiness 3
  Humour 6
  Idleness 2
  Love 32
  Men 2
  Minorities 2
  Mistakes 4
  Patriotism 2
  Poetry 4
  Poets 3, 4
  Secrets 4
  Women 10
  Writing 6
Du Bellay, Joachim
(1522–60)
  France 1
Du Deffand, Mme
(1697–1780)
  Achievement 10
Dumas, Alexandre
(1802–70)
  Cooperation 4
Du Maurier, Daphne
(1907–89)
  Opening Lines 12
Dumouriez, General
(1739–1823)
  Behaviour 8
Duncan, Ronald
(1914–82)
  Animals 16
Dunning, John
(1731–83)
  Royalty 12
Duport, James
(1606–79)
  Madness 6

Duppa, Richard
(1770–1831)
  Language 6
Durocher, Leo
(1906–91)
  Sport 25
**Dürrenmatt,
Friedrich** (1921–)
  Thinking 12
Dworkin, Andrea
(1946–)
  Sex 29
Dyer, Edward
(d. 1607)
  Sorrow 4
Dyer, John (1700–58)
  Transience 6
Dylan, Bob (1941–)
  Generation Gap 8
  Money 28
  Success 26

Eddington, Arthur
(1882–1944)
  Science 17, 18
  Time 32
Edgeworth, Maria
(1768–1849)
  Men 3
**Edison, Thomas
Alva** (1847–1931)
  Genius 9
**Edmonds, John
Maxwell** (1875–1958)
  Epitaphs 18
Edward VIII
(1894–1972)
  Parents 23
Edwards, Jonathan
(1703–58)
  Death 32
Edwards, Oliver
(1711–91)
  Food 13
Egan, Raymond B.
(1890–1952)
  see **Kahn, Gus** and
  Egan, Raymond B.
Einstein, Albert
(1879–1955)
  Chance 10
  Future 8
  God 18
  Intelligence 9
  Mathematics 13
  Religion 45
  Science 25
  Success 24
  War 28
**Eisenhower, Dwight
D.** (1890–1969)
  Peace 12
  War 42

Elgar, Edward
(1857–1934)
  Art 11
  Music 14
Eliot, George
(1819–80)
  Gossip 7
  Humour 13
  Marriage 32
  Meeting 11
  Silence 4
  Sorrow 17
  Voting 3
  Women 19, 20
Eliot, T. S. (1888–1965)
  Beginnings 7, 8, 9
  Birth 7
  Crime 25
  Day 13, 14
  Death 45
  Experience 8
  Fear 7, 8
  Forgiveness 7
  Heaven 12
  Knowledge 25
  Life 44, 48
  Medicine 16
  Memory 14, 18
  Men and Women 19
  Morality 11
  Old Age 17
  Poets 14, 15, 18
  Pollution 8
  Reality 3, 4
  Seasons 23
  Speech 19
  Success 20, 22
  Time 29, 34
  Travel 11
  Weather 11
  Words 17, 18
Elizabeth I (1533–1603)
  Ambition 4
  Birth 3

Elizabeth I (*cont.*)
Forgiveness 2
Government 4
Last Words 6
Royalty 1
Secrets 2
Trust 4
Elizabeth II (1926–)
Misfortune 17
**Elizabeth, the
Queen Mother** (1900–)
Family 11
Wars 21
Elliott, Ebenezer
(1781–1849)
Politics 7
Ellis, George
(1753–1815)
Seasons 9
Ellis, Havelock
(1859–1939)
Pollution 7
Revolution 14
Elstow, Friar
Death 9
**Emerson, Ralph
Waldo** (1803–82)
Achievement 14
Ambition 11
Architecture 4
Art 6
Friendship 11
Gardens 8
Greatness 5
Heroes 2
History 8
Honour 7
Justice 15
Language 7
Quotations 4, 5

Engels, Friedrich
(1820–95)
see **Marx, Karl** and
Engels, Friedrich
Ertz, Susan
(1894–1985)
Bores 8
Essex, 2nd Earl of
(1566–1601)
Thinking 2
Estienne, Henri
(1531–98)
Generation Gap 1
Euclid (fl. *c*.300 BC)
Mathematics 2
Euripides
(*c*.485–*c*.406 BC)
Hypocrisy 1
Evans, Abel
(1679–1737)
Epitaphs 11
**Ewer, William
Norman** (1885–1976)
Prejudice 11

Fadiman, Clifton
(1904–)
Food 28
People 23
Falkland, Viscount
(1610–43)
Change 7
Faraday, Michael
(1791–1867)
Inventions 10
Farouk, King
(1920–65)
Royalty 19
Farquhar, George
(1678–1707)
Money 10
Poverty 5
Faulkner, William
(1897–1962)
Writers 10
Fawkes, Guy
(1570–1606)
Revolution 1
Fenton, James
(1949–)
Environment 22
**Ferdinand I,
Emperor** (1503–64)
Justice 5
Field, Eugene
(1850–95)
Acting 7
Field, Frank (1942–)
Certainty 17
Fielding, Henry
(1707–54)
Education 10
Envy 4
Gossip 4
Marriage 19
Sex 10
Fields, Dorothy
(1905–74)
Determination 12

Fields, W. C.
(1880–1946)
  Epitaphs 19
  Fools 20
  Humour 19
  Voting 7
Firbank, Ronald
(1886–1926)
  Universe 5
Fisher, H. A. L.
(1856–1940)
  Europe 7
Fisher, John
Arbuthnot (1841–1920)
  War 16
Fitzgerald, Edward
(1809–83)
  Flowers 9
  Past 10
  Present 7
  Satisfaction 4
Fitzgerald, F. Scott
(1896–1940)
  America 17
  Hope 18
  Intelligence 10
  Middle Age 3
  Wealth 11
Fitzsimmons,
Robert (1862–1917)
  Sport 11
Flanders, Michael
(1922–75) and
Swann, Donald
(1923–94)
  Transport 11
Flaubert, Gustave
(1821–80)
  Art 5, 7
  Books 15
  Enemies 7
  Poetry 14
  Speech 11
  Style 12

Flecker, James
Elroy (1884–1915)
  Knowledge 23
  Sea 12
Fleming, Marjory
(1803–11)
  Mathematics 6
Fleming, Peter
(1907–71)
  Food 26
Fletcher, Andrew
(1655–1716)
  Singing 1
Fletcher, Phineas
(1582–1650)
  Love 24
Florian, Jean-Pierre
Claris de (1755–94)
  Love 39
Florio, John
(c.1553–1625)
  England 1
Foch, Ferdinand
(1851–1929)
  Wars 10, 15
Foot, Michael (1913–)
  Political Comment 24
  Politicians 35
  Speech 23
Foote, Samuel
(1720–77)
  Bores 3
Forbes, Miss C. F.
(1817–1911)
  Dress 6
Ford, Gerald (1909–)
  Government 30
Ford, Henry
(1863–1947)
  Choice 9
  Good 20
  History 15

Forgy, Howell
(1908–83)
  Practicality 7
Forster, E. M.
(1879–1970)
  Bureaucracy 2
  Critics 14
  Cynicism 6
  Democracy 12
  England 25
  Gossip 11
  Literature 11
  Manners 10
  Mind 6
  Music 15
  Patriotism 20
  Transport 4
  Writers 7
  Writing 25, 26
Fox, Charles James
(1749–1806)
  Revolution 5
Fox, Robin Lane
(1946–)
  Gardens 12
Fox, Theodore
(1899–1989)
  Medicine 18
France, Anatole
(1844–1924)
  Critics 12
  Lies 17
  Poverty 13
  Wealth 10
Franklin, Benjamin
(1706–90)
  Business 7, 8
  Cooperation 3
  Hope 8
  Human Race 14
  Inventions 6
  Taxes 6
  War 9

Frederick the Great
(1712–86)
  Government 12
  Prejudice 2
Freeman, E. A.
(1823–92)
  History 12
French, Marilyn
(1929–)
  Men 13
Freud, Sigmund
(1856–1939)
  Body 10
  Life 51
  Sleep 13
  Women 31
Frisch, Max (1911–)
  Technology 9
Frohman, Charles
(1860–1915)
  Last Words 24
Frost, Robert
(1874–1963)
  Beginnings 6
  Change 20
  Choice 7
  Cooperation 6
  Determination 11
  Happiness 15
  Home 11
  Humour 21
  Poetry 24, 26
  Politics 15
  Secrets 9
  Solitude 12
Fry, Christopher
(1907–)
  Home 12
  Language 17
  Virtue 17
Fry, Roger (1866–1934)
  Art 17

**Fuller, R.
Buckminster**
(1895–1983)
  Environment 19
Fuller, Thomas
(1608–61)
  Anger 5
  Architecture 2
Fuller, Thomas
(1654–1734)
  Wealth 6

Gabor, Zsa Zsa
(1919–)
  Hatred 8
  Violence 10
**Gainsborough,
Thomas** (1727–88)
  Last Words 12
Gaitskell, Hugh
(1906–63)
  Europe 11
  Political Parties 10
Galbraith, J. K.
(1908–)
  Advertising 6
  Economics 9, 16
  Politics 20
  Satisfaction 8
  Wealth 15
Galileo Galilei
(1564–1642)
  Skies 3
Galsworthy, John
(1867–1933)
  Action 10
  Beauty 23
Galt, John (1779–1839)
  Scotland 9
Gamow, George
(1904–68)
  Science 30
Gandhi, Mahatma
(1869–1948)
  Civilization 6
Garbo, Greta
(1905–90)
  Solitude 14
Gardiner, Richard
(b. c.1533)
  Gardens 2
Gardner, Ed (1901–63)
  Singing 7

Garrick, David
(1717–79)
  Food 12
  see also **Colman,**
  George, the Elder
  and **Garrick, David**
Garrison, William
Lloyd (1805–79)
  Political Comment 3
Gaskell, Elizabeth
(1810–65)
  Men 5
  Patriotism 14
  Thinking 6
Gay, John (1685–1732)
  Choice 3
  Enemies 4
  Epitaphs 9
  Marriage 17, 18
Geddes, Eric
(1875–1937)
  Revenge 6
George II (1683–1760)
  Madness 7
George III (1738–1820)
  Royalty 11
  Shakespeare 5
George V (1365–1936)
  Last Words 26, 27
George VI (1895–1952)
  Diplomacy 9
Gershwin, Ira
(1896–1983)
  see **Heyward,**
  Du Bose and
  Gershwin, Ira
Gibbon, Edward
(1737–94)
  History 3
  Languages 6
  London 4
  Religion 23

Gibran, Kahlil
(1883–1931)
  Parents 15
  Truth 28
  Work 14
Gilbert, W. S.
(1836–1911)
  Beauty 19
  Behaviour 15
  Crime 16, 17, 18
  England 14
  Equality 7
  Language 10
  Law 24
  Meaning 4
  Men 6
  Old Age 15
  Politicians 10
  Pride 7
  Sleep 12
  Transport 1
  Voting 4
  Words 14
Gill, Eric (1882–1940)
  Work 16
Giraudoux, Jean
(1882–1944)
  Law 26
  Poetry 22
Gladstone, W. E.
(1809–98)
  Biography 6
  Democracy 4
  Economics 3
  Future 6
  Government 21
  Speech 15
Glasse, Hannah
(fl. 1747)
  Food 10
Glendinning,
Victoria (1937–)
  Pleasure 14

Gloucester, Duke of
(1743–1805)
  Writers 2
Godard, Jean-Luc
(1930–)
  Cinema 11, 17
Goebbels, Joseph
(1897–1945)
  War 32
Goering, Hermann
(1893–1946)
  Race 3
  War 33
Goethe, Johann
Wolfgang von
(1749–1832)
  Art 2
  Character 9
  Fame 13
  Last Words 17
  Love 42
  Reality 1
  Self-Knowledge 12
  Women 17
Goldsmith, Oliver
(1730–74)
  Argument 4
  Knowledge 11
  Law 13
  Life 18
  Love 37
  Marriage 21
  Old Age 13
Goldwater, Barry
(1909–)
  Moderation 11
Goldwyn, Sam
(1882–1974)
  Certainty 16
  Cinema 8, 14
  Law 27
Gordon, Adam
Lindsay (1833–70)
  Life 29

Goya (1746–1828)
Sleep 10
Grahame, Kenneth
(1859–1932)
Transport 2, 3
Grant, Ulysses S.
(1822–85)
Law 23
Graves, Robert
(1895–1985)
Language 13
Weather 13
Gray, John Chipman
(1839–1915)
Home 8
Gray, Thomas
(1716–71)
Children 13
Day 6
Death 31
Fame 8, 9
Ignorance 3
Suffering 9
Youth 5
Greaves, Jimmy
(1940–)
Sport 32
Greeley, Horace
(1811–72)
America 3
Green, Adolph
(1915–)
see **Comden, Betty**
and **Green, Adolph**
Greene, Graham
(1904–91)
Children 25
Good 24
Heart 8
Indifference 12
News 26
Sorrow 21
Success 27

Greene, Robert
(c.1560–92)
Time 8
Greer, Germaine
(1939–)
Men and Women 27
Woman's Role 14
Grellet, Stephen
(1773–1855)
Good 18
Grenfell, Joyce
(1910–79)
Dance 10
Grenfell, Julian
(1888–1915)
Life 37
Grey, Lord (1862–1933)
Civilization 3
Griffith-Jones,
Mervyn (1909–79)
Censorship 10
Grocott, Bruce
(1940–)
Work 23
Gromyko, Andrei
(1909–89)
Politicians 40
Grossmith, George
(1847–1912) and
Grossmith, Weedon
(1854–1919)
Home 7
Misfortune 11
Guedalla, Philip
(1889–1944)
Writers 5
Guibert, Hervé
(1955–91)
Sickness 15
Gurney, Dorothy
Frances (1858–1932)
Gardens 11

Guthrie, Woody
(1912–67)
America 22

Haig, Earl (1861–1928)
  Character 12
Hailsham, Lord
(1907–)
  Political Parties 12
Haldane, J. B. S.
(1892–1964)
  Statistics 7
  Universe 7
Haldeman, H. R.
(1929–93)
  Secrets 10
**Hale, Edward
Everett** (1822–1909)
  Politicians 13
Hale, Nathan
(1755–76)
  Patriotism 7
**Halifax, Marquess
of** (1633–95)
  Crime 6
  Liberty 3
  Power 4
Hall, Bishop Joseph
(1574–1656)
  Perfection 2
Hamilton, Alex
(1936–)
  Character 18
Hamilton, William
(1788–1856)
  Mind 4
**Hammerstein,
Oscar, II** (1895–1960)
  Places 24
  Seasons 27
Hanrahan, Brian
(1949–)
  Wars 29
Harbach, Otto
(1873–1963)
  Sorrow 19

Harcourt, William
(1827–1904)
  Political Comment 9
**Hardy, Godfrey
Harold** (1877–1947)
  Mathematics 12
Hardy, Thomas
(1840–1928)
  Birds 9
  Body 9
  History 13
  Hope 16
  Love 53
  Speech 13
  War 19
  Weather 12
  Words 13
Hare, Maurice Evan
(1886–1967)
  Fate 9
Harington, John
(1561–1612)
  Trust 5
Harlech, Lord
(1918–85)
  Britain 6
**Harman, Lord
Justice** (1894–1970)
  Business 22
Hart, Lorenz
(1895–1943)
  Behaviour 17
Harte, Bret
(1836–1902)
  Justice 17
Hartley, L. P.
(1895–1972)
  Past 19
Harvey, F. W. (b. 1888)
  Birds 13
**Haskins, Minnie
Louise** (1875–1957)
  Trust 8

Hawking, Stephen
(1942–)
  Mathematics 14
  Universe 12
Hay, Ian (1876–1952)
  Humour 18
  War 20
Hazlitt, William
(1778–1830)
  Conversation 5
  Country 3
  Genius 5
  Hatred 4
  Last Words 16
  Prejudice 4, 5
Healey, Denis (1917–)
  Politicians 36
Heaney, Seamus
(1939–)
  Ireland 10
Heath, Edward
(1916–)
  Political Comment 25
Heath-Stubbs, John
(1918–)
  Sickness 12
**Heber, Bishop
Reginald** (1783–1826)
  Religion 27
Hegel, G. W. F.
(1770–1831)
  History 5
  Philosophy 6
  Society 5
Heine, Heinrich
(1797–1856)
  Censorship 4
  Last Words 18
  Revolution 9
Heisenberg, Werner
(1901–76)
  Mistakes 17

Heller, Joseph
(1923–)
  Madness 9
Hellman, Lillian
(1905–84)
  Conscience 8
  Cynicism 7
Helmsley, Leona
(c.1920–)
  Taxes 10
Hemans, Felicia
(1793–1835)
  Opening Lines 8
Heming, John
(1556–1630) and
Condell, Henry
(d. 1627)
  Shakespeare 3
Hemingway, Ernest
(1899–1961)
  Courage 10, 11
  Places 28
  Sex 18
Henley, W. E.
(1849–1903)
  Determination 7, 8
Henri IV (1553–1610)
  Cynicism 1
  Poverty 3
Henry VIII (1491–1547)
  Painting 1
Henry, Matthew
(1662–1714)
  Death 30
Henry, Patrick
(1736–99)
  Liberty 5
  Political Comment 1
Heraclitus
(c.540–c.480 BC)
  Change 2
  Character 1

Herbert, A. P.
(1890–1971)
  Country 8
  Humour 17
  Marriage 43
Herbert, George
(1593–1633)
  Hope 3
  Religion 9, 10
  Seasons 6
  Secrets 3
  Truth 8
Herman, Henry
(1832–94)
  see **Jones, Henry
  Arthur** and
  Herman, Henry
Herrick, Robert
(1591–1674)
  Body 6
  Dress 2, 3
  Marriage 9
  Present 5
  Seasons 7
  Transience 5
Hervey, Lord
(1696–1743)
  Lies 4
Hesse, Hermann
(1877–1962)
  Class 11
  Hatred 7
Hewart, Lord
(1870–1943)
  Justice 21
Heyward, Du Bose
(1885–1940) and
Gershwin, Ira
(1896–1983)
  Seasons 25
Hicks, J. R. (1904–)
  Business 18

Hicks, Seymour
(1871–1949)
  Old Age 25
Hill, Aaron (1685–1750)
  Courage 5
Hill, Joe (1879–1915)
  Revolution 11
Hill, Rowland
(1744–1833)
  Music 10
Hillary, Edmund
(1919–)
  Achievement 16
Hillingdon, Lady
(1857–1940)
  Sex 15
Hilton, James
(1900–54)
  Old Age 22
Hippocrates
(c.460–357 BC)
  Art 1
  Medicine 3
Hislop, Ian (1940–)
  Justice 25
Hitchcock, Alfred
(1899–1980)
  Acting 11
  Broadcasting 7
Hitler, Adolf
(1889–1945)
  Lies 19
Hobbes, Thomas
(1588–1679)
  Last Words 9
  Life 13
  Opinion 3
  Society 3
  Truth 10
  War 5
Hodgson, Ralph
(1871–1962)
  Animals 11
  Time 28

Hoffmann, Max
(1869–1927)
  Army 17
Hogben, Lancelot
(1895–1975)
  Technology 8
Holbach, Baron d'
(1723–89)
  Science 6
**Holland, Henry
Scott** (1847–1918)
  Death 41
Holmes, John H.
(1879–1964)
  Universe 9
Homer
(8th century BC)
  Death 1
  Transience 1
Hood, Thomas
(1799–1845)
  Poverty 11
  Seasons 14
**Hooper, Ellen
Sturgis** (1816–41)
  Life 22
Hope, Anthony
(1863–1933)
  Children 19
  Economics 4
  Epitaphs 17
Hope, Bob (1903–)
  Money 22
**Hopkins, Gerard
Manley** (1844–89)
  Beauty 17
  Birds 8
  Environment 9
  Hope 13, 14
  Mind 5
  Places 16
  Pollution 4
  Prayer 13
  Seasons 19

**Hopkins, Gerard
Manley** (*cont.*)
  Silence 3
  Skies 7
Horace (65–8 BC)
  Achievement 2
  Anger 2
  Crises 1
  Death 4
  Economics 1
  Fame 2
  Fools 3
  Happiness 2
  Hope 2
  Literature 1
  Mistakes 2
  Moderation 2
  Money 5
  Nature 2
  Patriotism 1
  Poetry 1
  Present 1
  Style 1
  Words 1
**Horsley, Bishop
Samuel** (1733–1806)
  Law 17
Housman, A. E.
(1859–1936)
  Alcohol 9
  Nature 17
  Past 11
  Prejudice 15
  Seasons 21
  Travel 8
Howell, James
(c.1593–1666)
  Languages 4
Hubbard, Elbert
(1859–1915)
  Apology 3
  Genius 10
  Life 36

Hubbard, Elbert
(*cont.*)
  News 12
  Technology 3
Hughes, Langston
(1902–67)
  Race 2
Hughes, Ted (1930–)
  Birds 15
Hughes, Thomas
(1822–96)
  Sport 8
Hugo, Victor (1802–85)
  God 12
  Ideas 3
  Suffering 12
Hull, Josephine
(?1886–1957)
  Shakespeare 9
Hume, David
(1711–76)
  Beauty 9
  Books 7
  Custom 3
  Happiness 6
  Money 13
  Religion 20
  Self 4
Hutcheson, Francis
(1694–1746)
  Society 3
Huxley, Aldous
(1894–1963)
  Apology 6
  Change 23
  Education 22
  Experience 6
  Happiness 13
  Manners 11
  Sex 16
Huxley, Julian
(1887–1975)
  God 21

Huxley, T. H.
(1825–95)
Certainty 9
Knowledge 21
Science 9, 10
Thinking 8
Truth 20, 21

Ibarruri, Dolores
(1895–1989)
Liberty 18
Wars 16
Ibsen, Henrik
(1828–1906)
Dress 7
Lies 12
Minorities 5
Illich, Ivan (1926–)
Society 14
Inge, Dean (1860–1954)
Argument 7
Bores 9
Human Race 23
Liberty 20
Power 9
Ingersoll, Robert G.
(1833–99)
God 16
Nature 15
Ingham, Bernard
(1932–)
News 30
Ingres, J. A. D.
(1780–1867)
Painting 5
Irving, Washington
(1783–1859)
Change 12
Speech 8
Issigonis, Alec
(1906–88)
Management 15

Jackson, Holbrook
(1874–1948)
Knowledge 24
Jacobs, Joe
(1896–1940)
Sport 19, 20
Jago, Richard
(1715–81)
Absence 4
James I (1566–1625)
Poets 1
James V (1512–42)
Scotland 1
James, Henry
(1843–1916)
Art 10
Character 10
Conversation 9
Critics 11
Day 12
Life 30
Literature 6
Living 11
James, William
(1842–1910)
Alcohol 12
Certainty 10
Lies 14
Men and Women 14
Success 17
Jarrell, Randall
(1914–65)
Children 29
Ideas 8
Manners 14
Jeans, James
(1877–1946)
Life Sciences 7
Universe 8
Jefferson, Thomas
(1743–1826)
Liberty 7
Politicians 6, 7
Revolution 4

**Jeffrey, Francis,
Lord** (1773–1850)
Critics 7
Jenkins, David
(1925–)
God 24
Jerome, Jerome K.
(1859–1927)
Idleness 9
Work 12
Jerrold, Douglas
(1803–57)
France 9
Love 49
Places 13
Jewel, Bishop John
(1522–71)
Church 3
Joad, C. E. M.
(1891–1953)
Environment 14
Meaning 7
**Johnson, Lyndon
Baines** (1908–73)
Enemies 9
Intelligence 15
**Johnson, Philander
Chase** (1866–1939)
Optimism 7
Johnson, Philip
(1906–)
Architecture 9
Johnson, Samuel
(1709–84)
Achievement 8
Advertising 1
Alcohol 6
Behaviour 7
Belief 6
Books 9
Careers 4
Change 8
Conversation 2
Cooperation 1

Johnson, Samuel
(cont.)
Critics 4, 5
Death 33
Education 11
Equality 4, 5
Fame 10
Food 11
Friendship 6
Genius 3
Ignorance 4
Imagination 4
Intelligence 2
Justice 13
Knowledge 13
Language 5
Languages 5
Libraries 2, 3
Life 17
Living 8
London 2, 3
Love 35, 38
Marriage 20, 23
Moderation 9
Music 7, 8
Opinion 7
Patriotism 6
Philosophy 4
Poetry 5
Poets 6
Politics 2
Poverty 7, 8
Praise 5
Quotations 2, 3
Reading 6
Scotland 3, 4
Sea 6
Sex 12
Solitude 4
Sorrow 10
Sport 7
Suffering 10
Taxes 2
Travel 3, 4

Johnson, Samuel
(cont.)
Truth 14
Virtue 12
War 8
Wealth 8
Weather 2
Woman's Role 4
Words 10, 11
Writers 1
Writing 9, 11, 13
Johst, Hanns
(1890–1978)
Civilization 8
Jolson, Al (1886–1950)
Singing 4
Jones, Henry Arthur
(1851–1929) **and
Herman, Henry**
(1832–94)
Past 13
Jones, Paul M.
see **de Leon, Walter**
and **Jones, Paul M.**
Jonson, Ben
(c.1573–1637)
Education 5
Epitaphs 6
Law 7
Lies 2
Men and Women 2
Religion 7
Shakespeare 1, 2, 4
Jowett, Benjamin
(1817–93)
Lies 9
Joyce, James
(1882–1941)
Art 14
Ireland 8
Julian of Norwich
(1343–after 1416)
Optimism 1

Jung, Carl Gustav
(1875–1961)
  Heart 9
  Life 62
Juvenal
(AD c.60–c.130)
  Children 5
  Crime 4
  Poverty 2
  Sickness 2
  Sport 1
  Trust 3
  Truth 5
  Virtue 3

Kafka, Franz
(1883–1924)
  Law 25
  Liberty 17
  Opening Lines 11
Kahn, Gus
(1886–1941) and
Egan, Raymond B.
(1890–1952)
  Poverty 15
Kalmar, Bert
(1884–1947)
  Honour 8
  Meeting 15
Kant, Immanuel
(1724–1804)
  Happiness 8
  Human Race 15
  Morality 2
Karr, Alphonse
(1808–90)
  Change 15
  Crime 13
Keating, Paul (1944–)
  Titles 10
Keats, John
(1795–1821)
  Alcohol 7
  Beauty 11, 12
  Change 11
  Day 8
  Death 35
  Epitaphs 13
  Imagination 7
  Inventions 7
  Knowledge 17
  Love 45
  Music 9
  Nature 9
  Opening Lines 6
  Philosophy 5
  Pleasure 6
  Poetry 9
  Reading 8

Keats, John (cont.)
  Seasons 11
  Silence 2
  Sorrow 12
  Weather 5, 6
  Women 15
  Writing 17
Keller, Helen
(1880–1968)
  Indifference 8
Kennedy, John F.
(1917–63)
  Beginnings 13
  Diplomacy 13
  Liberty 25
  Political Comment 20
  Race 6
Kennedy, Joseph P.
(1888–1969)
  Determination 14
Kerr, Jean (1923–)
  Beauty 26
**Keynes, John
Maynard** (1883–1946)
  Government 25, 26
  Money 19
  Politics 14
  Time 31
Khrushchev, Nikita
(1894–1971)
  Satisfaction 7
Kierkegaard, Sören
(1813–1855)
  Life 23
Kilmuir, Lord
(1900–67)
  Political Parties 11
Kilvert, Francis
(1840–79)
  Travel 5
**King, Benjamin
Franklin** (1857–94)
  Optimism 6

King, Martin Luther
(1929–68)
  Cooperation 7
  Equality 10
  Idealism 4
  Justice 23
  Race 4, 5
  Violence 6
Kingsley, Charles
(1819–75)
  Bible 6
  Virtue 14
Kinnock, Neil (1942–)
  Patriotism 21
Kipling, Rudyard
(1865–1936)
  Army 9, 10
  Art 9
  Cats 4
  Character 11
  Crises 2
  Dogs 4
  England 15
  Gardens 10
  Men and Women 11,
    15
  News 19
  Opinion 9
  Parents 9
  Pride 8
  Sea 10
  Sex 14
  Sickness 9
  Solitude 11
  Sport 12
  Success 18
  Words 16
Kissinger, Henry
(1923–)
  Management 13
  Power 17
Klee, Paul (1879–1940)
  Painting 10, 11

**Klopstock,
Friedrich** (1724–1803)
  Meaning 2
Knox, John
(c.1505–72)
  Woman's Role 1
Knox, Ronald
(1888–1957)
  Belief 13
  Children 27
  God 19
Knox, Vicesimus
(1752–1821)
  Woman's Role 6
Koestler, Arthur
(1905–83)
  God 23
  Writing 31
Kray, Charlie (c.1930–)
  Crime 26
Krishnamurti, Jiddu
(d. 1986)
  Religion 42
  Truth 29
Kristofferson, Kris
(1936–)
  Liberty 26
Kronecker, Leopold
(1823–91)
  Mathematics 8
**Krutch, Joseph
Wood** (1893–1970)
  America 20
  Cats 7
Kubrick, Stanley
(1928–)
  Politics 21
Kyd, Thomas
(1558–94)
  Children 7

Labouchere, Henry
(1831–1912)
  Politicians 14
la Bruyère, Jean de
(1645–96)
  Life 16
Lacroix, Christian
(1951–)
  Dress 12
**la Fontaine, Jean
de** (1621–95)
  Death 29
Laforgue, Jules
(1860–87)
  Life 31
**Lamb, Lady
Caroline** (1785–1828)
  People 5
Lamb, Charles
(1775–1834)
  Absence 5
  Children 5
  Family 5
  Gardens 6
  Humour 12
  Libraries 4
  Manners 7
  People 6
  Pleasure 9
  Time 22
**Lambton, John
George** (1792–1840)
  Money 15
Lamont, Norman
(1942–)
  Business 25
  Economics 15
  Government 32
**Lampedusa,
Giuseppe di**
(1896–1957)
  Change 26
Lance, Bert (1931–)
  Management 14

Lang, Andrew
(1844–1912)
Statistics 5
Lang, Julia (1921–)
Beginnings 11
Langer, Suzanne K.
(1895–1985)
Art 22
Larkin, Philip
(1922–85)
Books 30
Bores 11
Day 16
Environment 21
Life 63
London 8
Old Age 35
Optimism 11
Parents 26
Sex 27
Work 20
**la Rochefoucauld,
Duc de** (1613–80)
Absence 2
Home 4
Hypocrisy 9
Misfortune 7, 9
Latimer, Hugh
(c.1485–1555)
Determination 2
Lawrence, D. H.
(1885–1930)
Death 46
Literature 10
Seasons 24
Sex 17
Shakespeare 8
Sorrow 18
Writing 28, 29
Lawrence, T. E.
(1888–1935)
Life 47

Lazarus, Emma
(1849–87)
America 6
Leach, Edmund
(1910–)
Family 12
Leacock, Stephen
(1869–1944)
Advertising 2
Parents 13
Sport 16, 22
Leavis, F. R.
(1895–1978)
Poets 19
Lebowitz, Fran
(1946–)
Fame 23
Peace 14
Women 37
Le Brunn, George
see **Bateman,
Edgar** and **Le
Brunn, George**
Lec, Stanislaw
(1909–66)
Censorship 11
Progress 11
Le Corbusier
(1887–1965)
Architecture 6
**Ledru-Rollin,
Alexandre Auguste**
(1807–74)
Leadership 3
Lee, Henry
(1756–1818)
America 2
Lee, Robert E.
(1807–70)
War 14
Lehrer, Tom (1928–)
Achievement 18
Life 55

Leigh, Vivien
(1913–67)
Acting 15
LeMay, Curtis E.
(1906–90)
Wars 26
Lenin (1870–1924)
Liberty 16
People 15
Politics 13
Technology 5
Lennon, John
(1940–80)
Fame 21
Wealth 16
Lennon, John
(1940–80) and
McCartney, Paul
(1942–)
Friendship 15
Money 27
Old Age 32
Peace 13
Solitude 17
Leonardo da Vinci
(1452–1519)
Life 7
Nature 3
Lermontov, Mikhail
(1814–41)
Friendship 10
Lerner, Alan Jay
(1918–86)
Charm 4
Men 12
Lessing, Doris (1919–)
Charm 6
Seasons 28
Lessing, G. E.
(1729–81)
Prayer 7
**Leverhulme,
Viscount** (1851–1925)
Advertising 3

Leverson, Ada
(1865–1936)
  People 17
Levin, Bernard
(1928–)
  Past 21
  Politicians 32
Lévis, Duc de
(1764–1830)
  Government 16
Lewis, C. S.
(1898–1963)
  Courage 12
  Future 9
  Women 32
Lewis, Sinclair
(1885–1951)
  Literature 12
  Transport 6
Liberace (1919–87)
  Critics 16
**Lichtenberg, Georg
Christoph** (1742–99)
  News 6
**Ligne,
Charles-Joseph,
Prince de** (1735–1814)
  Diplomacy 5
Lincoln, Abraham
(1809–65)
  Beauty 16
  Change 17
  Critics 9
  Democracy 3
  Fools 15
  Political Comment 7
  Voting 2
Linklater, Eric
(1899–1974)
  Revolution 15
Lippmann, Walter
(1889–1974)
  Leadership 5

Lively, Penelope
(1933–)
  Language 20
  Languages 9
Livy (59 BC–AD 17)
  Success 5
Lloyd George, David
(1863–1945)
  Britain 3
  Diplomacy 8
  Political Comment 10
  Politics 12
  Titles 5
  Wars 14
Locke, John
(1632–1704)
  Experience 2
  Law 10
  Mistakes 5
  Opinion 5
  Truth 11
Lodge, David (1935–)
  Children 28
  Sex 23
Long, H. Kingsley
see **McArthur,
Alexander** and
Long, H. Kingsley
Long, Huey
(1893–1935)
  Politicians 20
**Longfellow, Henry
Wadsworth** (1807–82)
  Ambition 12
  Biography 2
  Day 9
  God 15
  Life 21
  Solitude 10
  Youth 7
Longford, Lord
(1905–)
  Pride 11

Loos, Anita
(1893–1981)
  Practicality 6
  Women 28
Lorenz, Edward N.
  Chance 11
Lorenz, Konrad
(1903–89)
  Science 34
Louis XIV (1638–1715)
  Management 1
  Royalty 7
Louis XVIII
(1755–1824)
  Army 4
  Manners 8
Lovelace, Richard
(1618–58)
  Honour 5
  Liberty 1
Lovell, Bernard
(1913–)
  Youth 13
Lover, Samuel
(1797–1868)
  Writing 20
Low, David
(1891–1963)
  War 40
Lowe, Robert
(1811–92)
  Taxes 7
**Lowell, James
Russell** (1819–91)
  Seasons 17
  Work 9
Lowell, Robert
(1917–77)
  Middle Age 7
  Optimism 12
Lowndes, William
(1652–1724)
  Money 12

Lowry, Malcolm
(1909–57)
  Love 63
Luce, Clare Booth
(1903–)
  Woman's Role 13
Lucilius (*c.*180–102 BC)
  Birth 2
Lucretius (*c.*94–55 BC)
  Life 5
  Religion 2
Luther, Martin
(1483–1546)
  Good 5
  Pleasure 2
Luxemburg, Rosa
(1871–1919)
  Liberty 15
Lydgate, John
(*c.*1370–*c.*1451)
  Words 2
Lyte, Henry Francis
(1793–1847)
  Change 14

**McArthur,
Alexander and
Long, H. Kingsley**
  Poverty 16
Macaulay, Lord
(1800–59)
  Bible 4
  Church 9
  Government 18
  History 4
  Imagination 8
  Liberty 11
  Morality 4
  Places 10
  Pleasure 10
  Suffering 11
Macaulay, Rose
(1881–1958)
  Opening Lines 15
McCarthy, Mary
(1912–89)
  America 24
  Europe 10
  People 30
McCartney, Paul
(1942–)
  Musicians 10
  see also **Lennon,
  John** and
  McCartney, Paul
**McClellan, General
George B.** (1826–85)
  Wars 8
McCrae, John
(1872–1918)
  Wars 11
McGough, Roger
(1937–)
  Death 57
McGregor, Jimmy
  Sport 27
McGregor, Lord
(1921–)
  News 31

Machiavelli, Niccolò
(1469–1527)
  Government 2
  Revenge 2
Mackintosh, James
(1765–1832)
  Political Comment 2
**Maclaren,
Alexander** (1826–1910)
  Church 12
**MacLeish,
Archibald** (1892–1982)
  Poetry 20
McLuhan, Marshall
(1911–80)
  Technology 10, 12
  Transport 13
Macmillan, Harold
(1894–1986)
  Morality 13
  Political Comment 17,
  18, 19, 22, 27, 28
  Politicians 25
MacNeice, Louis
(1907–63)
  Birth 10, 11
  Marriage 44
  Music 19
  Religion 44
  Time 37
McWilliam, Candia
(1955–)
  Children 31
Madan, Geoffrey
(1895–1947)
  Belief 17
**Mahaffy, John
Pentland** (1839–1919)
  Ireland 9
Mahler, Gustav
(1860–1911)
  Music 16

Major, John (1943–)
  Crime 27
  Economics 14
  Politicians 42
**Mallory, George
Leigh** (1886–1924)
  Achievement 15
Malraux, André
(1901–76)
  Art 19
Mancroft, Lord
(1914–87)
  Sport 30
Mann, Thomas
(1875–1955)
  Death 47
**Mansfield,
Katherine** (1888–1923)
  Travel 10
Mao Tse-tung
(1893–1976)
  Politics 16
  Power 12
Marie-Antoinette
(1755–93)
  Indifference 3
**Marlborough, Sarah,
Duchess of**
(1660–1744)
  Sex 11
**Marlowe,
Christopher** (1564–93)
  Beauty 4
  Love 18
  Religion 6
Marquis, Don
(1878–1937)
  Idleness 10
  Misfortune 13, 14
  News 20
  Optimism 9
  Poetry 23

Marshall, Arthur
(1910–89)
  Life 50
Martial (AD c.40–c.104)
  Hatred 2
  Love 7
  Sickness 1
Martin, Dean (1917–)
  Alcohol 23
Marvell, Andrew
(1621–78)
  Gardens 4
  Hope 4
  Love 33
  Time 17
Marvell, Holt
(1901–69)
  Memory 17
Marx, Groucho
(1895–1977)
  Books 22
  Memory 22
  Pride 9
Marx, Karl (1818–83)
  Custom 6
  History 9
  Religion 30
  Society 8
Marx, Karl (1818–83)
and
Engels, Friedrich
(1820–95)
  Class 6, 7
**Mary, Queen
Consort** (1867–1953)
  Country 9
**Mary, Queen of
Scots** (1542–87)
  Beginnings 2
Masefield, John
(1878–1967)
  Sea 11

Massinger, Philip
(1583–1640)
  Action 4
  America 1
Mathew, James
(1830–1908)
  Justice 19
**Maugham, W.
Somerset** (1874–1965)
  Books 25
  Certainty 13
  Men and Women 16
  Money 18
  Morality 9
  Old Age 20
  Parents 12
  Suffering 15
  Women 26
**Mayakovsky,
Vladimir** (1893–1930)
  Poets 16
Mead, Margaret
(1901–78)
  Men and Women 25
Medawar, Peter
(1915–87)
  Science 33
Melba, Nellie
(1861–1931)
  Singing 6
Melbourne, Lord
(1779–1848)
  Art 4
  Certainty 5
  Government 20
  Politicians 8
  Religion 31
Menander
(342–c.292 BC)
  Life 4
  Youth 1

Mencken, H. L.
(1880–1956)
  Conscience 6
  Intelligence 6
  Love 64
  Men and Women 22
Meredith, George
(1828–1909)
  Certainty 6
  Cynicism 4
  Food 20
  Nature 14
  Speech 12
  Women 18
Meredith, Owen
(1831–91)
  Genius 7
**Merritt, Dixon
Lanier** (1879–1972)
  Birds 11
Metternich, Prince
(1773–1859)
  Mistakes 10
  Places 11
Meyer, Anthony
(1920–)
  War 48
Mikes, George (1912–)
  England 32
  Sex 20
Mill, John Stuart
(1806–73)
  Happiness 10
  Liberty 12
**Millay, Edna St
Vincent** (1892–1950)
  Children 21
Miller, Alice Duer
(1874–1942)
  England 28
Miller, Arthur (1915–)
  Business 19
  Death 56
  News 24

Milligan, Spike
(1918–)
  Money 26
Milne, A. A.
(1882–1956)
  Education 24
  Food 25
  Ideas 4
Milton, John (1608–74)
  Action 5
  Books 5, 6
  Censorship 1
  Change 6
  Dance 3
  England 6
  Fame 5
  Good 11, 12
  Heart 3
  Heaven 3, 4
  Hypocrisy 8
  Liberty 2
  Men and Women 4
  Mind 1
  Misfortune 8
  Music 4, 5
  Opening Lines 4, 5
  Opinion 2
  Peace 7
  Philosophy 3
  Poetry 3
  Skies 5
  Sleep 5
  Speech 4
  Sport 5
  Time 15
  Violence 1
  Virtue 9
  Wealth 4
  Writing 4, 5
Mitchell, Adrian
(1932–)
  Poetry 27
Mitchell, Joni (1945–)
  Life 65

Mitchell, Margaret
(1900–49)
  Birth 9
  Hope 17
  Indifference 9
  Taxes 9
Mitford, Nancy
(1904–73)
  Titles 7
  Travel 12
Mizner, Wilson
(1876–1933)
  Places 26
  Success 25
  Writing 30
Molière (1622–73)
  Death 24
  Food 7
  Fools 6
  Justice 11
  Language 3, 4
  Medicine 9
  Secrets 5
**Montagu, Lady Mary
Wortley** (1689–1762)
  Enemies 5
Montague, C. E.
(1867–1928)
  War 25
Montaigne (1533–92)
  Belief 3
  Cats 1
  Children 6
  Home 1
  Ideas 1
  Life 8
  Living 7
  Love 10
  Self-Knowledge 5
  Solitude 3

Montesquieu
(1689–1755)
  Birth 4
  God 7
  History 2
Montgomery, Lord
(1887–1976)
  Sex 22
  War 45
Moore, George
(1852–1933)
  Travel 9
Moore, Thomas
(1779–1852)
  Books 11
  Love 44
  Memory 4
More, Hannah
(1745–1833)
  Woman's Role 5
More, Sir Thomas
(1478–1535)
  Last Words 3, 4
  Meeting 2
Morley, Christopher
(1890–1957)
  Life 38
Morris, Charles
(1745–1838)
  Country 6
Morris, Desmond
(1928–)
  Society 12
Morris, William
(1834–96)
  Home 6
Mortimer, John
(1923–)
  Law 29
**Muggeridge,
Malcolm** (1903–90)
  Minorities 7
  Sex 24
  Virtue 18

Muller, Herbert J.
(1905–)
  Business 21
Mumford, Lewis
(1895–1982)
  America 25
  Generation Gap 7
Murdoch, Iris (1919–)
  Hope 20
  Marriage 47
Murrow, Ed (1908–65)
  Speech 20
  Wars 27

Nabokov, Vladimir
(1899–1977)
  Life 54
  Opening Lines 14
  Writers 11
Napoléon I
(1769–1821)
  Army 3
  Courage 7
  England 10
  Past 9
  Success 12
Nash, Ogden
(1902–71)
  Alcohol 16
  Animals 13, 14
  Careers 7
  Cats 6
  Dogs 7
  Environment 15
  Family 8
  Life 52
  Middle Age 5
  Parents 17, 18
  Transport 10
Nashe, Thomas
(1567–1601)
  Death 12
Nelson, Lord
(1758–1805)
  England 8
  Last Words 13, 14
  Wars 2
Newbolt, Henry
(1862–1938)
  Sport 9, 10
Newman, Cardinal
(1801–90)
  Behaviour 11
  Belief 8
  Certainty 7
  Religion 33

Newton, Isaac
(1642–1727)
 Inventions 5
 Progress 3
 Science 4
Nicholas I, Emperor
(1796–1855)
 Places 12
Nicholson, Vivian
(1936–)
 Money 25
Nicolson, Harold
(1886–1968)
 Royalty 20
 Society 11
Niebuhr, Reinhold
(1892–1971)
 Change 25
 Democracy 9
Niemöller, Martin
(1892–1984)
 Cooperation 8
Nietzsche, Friedrich
(1844–1900)
 Human Race 20
 Humour 14
 Living 10
 Morality 6
 Women 22
North, Christopher
(1785–1854)
 Law 18
Northcliffe, Lord
(1865–1922)
 Censorship 6
 Titles 6
Norton, Caroline
(1808–77)
 Death 39
Nye, Bill (1850–96)
 Musicians 2

**Oates, Captain
Lawrence** (1880–1912)
 Last Words 22
O'Brien, Edna (1936–)
 Seasons 29
O'Casey, Sean
(1880–1964)
 Change 22
 Old Age 29
 Writers 9
Ochs, Adolph S.
(1858–1935)
 News 8
O'Donoghue, Denise
 Broadcasting 9
Ogilvy, David (1911–)
 Advertising 7
Ogilvy, James
(1664–1730)
 Scotland 2
O'Kelly, Dennis
(c.1720–87)
 Sport 6
Olivier, Laurence
(1907–89)
 Acting 19
O'Neill, Eugene
(1888–1953)
 Crime 23
Ono, Yoko (1933–)
 Women 36
**Oppenheimer, J.
Robert** (1904–67)
 Science 27
**Ortega y Gasset,
José** (1883–1955)
 Environment 12
Orton, Joe (1933–67)
 Birth 12
 Body 14
 Sex 25

Orwell, George
(1903–50)
 Advertising 5
 Argument 9
 Body 12, 13
 Class 13
 England 27, 30
 Equality 9
 Future 11
 Government 28
 Liberty 21
 Opening Lines 13
 Politics 18
 Power 14
 Prejudice 16
 Thinking 11
 War 38, 41
Osborne, Dorothy
(1627–95)
 Letters 3
Osborne, John
(1929–)
 Acting 16
 Royalty 21
 Women 33
Osler, William
(1849–1919)
 Medicine 15
 Men 8
O'Sullivan, John L.
(1813–95)
 Alcohol 10
 Government 17
Otis, James (1725–83)
 Taxes 3
Otway, Thomas
(1652–85)
 Prayer 5
Ovid (43 BC–AD c.17)
 Character 2
 Moderation 3
 Religion 3
 Time 4

Owen, Wilfred
(1893–1918)
  Army 14
  Death 44
  Poetry 18
  War 21
Oxenstierna, Count
(1583–1654)
  Government 5

Paine, Thomas
(1737–1809)
  Belief 7
  Government 9, 14
  Patriotism 8
  People 4
  Religion 24, 25
  Revolution 8
  Success 11
Palafox, José de
(1780–1847)
  Wars 3
Paley, William
(1743–1805)
  Argument 5
Palmerston, Lord
(1784–1865)
  Cooperation 5
  Last Words 20
  Political Comment 6
Pankhurst,
Emmeline (1858–1928)
  Argument 8
Parker, Charlie
(1920–55)
  Music 24
Parker, Dorothy
(1893–1967)
  Acting 10
  Birth 8
  Cinema 9
  Death 52
  Dress 10, 11
  Gifts 11
  Heaven 10
  Life 49
  Love 60
Parkinson, C.
Northcote (1909–93)
  Management 7, 8
  Money 23
  Work 21

Partridge, Frances
(1900–)
  Solitude 18
Pascal, Blaise
(1623–62)
  Body 7
  Death 28
  Heart 2
  Human Race 12
  Letters 4
  Self 2
  Skies 4
  Style 2
Pasternak, Boris
(1890–1960)
  Life 59
Pasteur, Louis
(1822–95)
  Science 8
Pater, Walter
(1839–94)
  Painting 6
  Success 14
Patmore, Coventry
(1823–96)
  Home 9
Payn, James
(1830–98)
  Misfortune 10
Payne, J. H.
(1791–1852)
  Home 5
Peacock, Thomas
Love (1785–1866)
  Humour 11
  Marriage 27
Pearson, Hesketh
(1887–1964)
  Titles 8
Péguy, Charles
(1873–1914)
  Liberty 14

Pembroke, 2nd Earl of (c.1534–1601)
  Government 3
Pembroke, 10th Earl of (1734–94)
  Style 9
Penn, William (1644–1718)
  Children 11
Penrose, Roger (1931–)
  Mind 10
Pepys, Samuel (1633–1703)
  Crime 5
  Diaries 1
  Marriage 13
  Money 8
  Royalty 8
  Sleep 7
Pericles (c.495–429 BC)
  Fame 1
  Women 2
Persons, Ted
  Past 17
Pétain, Marshal (1856–1951)
  Biography 9
Peter, Laurence (1919–)
  Management 11, 12
Petronius (d. AD 65)
  Death 7
  Sex 2
Phelps, Edward John (1822–1900)
  Mistakes 12
Philby, Kim (1912–88)
  Trust 9
Philip, Duke of Edinburgh (1921–)
  Food 29

Philips, Ambrose (c.1675–1749)
  Beauty 8
Picasso, Pablo (1881–1973)
  Genius 12
  God 22
  Painting 15
Pinter, Harold (1930–)
  Acting 17
Pirsig, Robert M. (1928–)
  Mind 9
Pitt, William, the Elder (1708–78)
  Environment 5
  Youth 4
Pitt, William, the Younger (1759–1806)
  Europe 2
  Last Words 15
Pius VII, Pope (1742–1823)
  Diplomacy 4
Planck, Max (1858–1947)
  Science 28
Plath, Sylvia (1932–63)
  Women 34
Plato (429–347 BC)
  Justice 3
  Religion 1
Pliny the Elder (AD 23–79)
  Inventions 3
  Places 1
Poincaré, Henri (1854–1912)
  Science 11
Pompadour, Madame de (1721–64)
  Revolution 3

Pompidou, Georges (1911–74)
  Politicians 33
Pope, Alexander (1688–1744)
  Achievement 7
  Bores 2
  Children 12
  Dogs 1
  Education 9
  Environment 4
  Food 8
  Fools 9, 11
  Forgiveness 3
  Good 14
  Government 7
  Happiness 5
  Heart 4, 5
  Hope 6, 7
  Human Race 13
  Ignorance 2
  Intelligence 1
  Knowledge 10
  Law 12
  Meeting 9
  Mistakes 6, 8
  Old Age 11
  Opinion 6
  Perfection 3
  Poets 5
  Political Parties 1
  Practicality 2
  Praise 4
  Reading 5
  Royalty 10
  Science 5
  Self 3
  Self-Knowledge 8
  Style 5
  Teaching 5
  Titles 1
  Virtue 11
  Writing 7, 8

Porter, Cole
(1891–1964)
  Change 24
  Love 66
Potter, Stephen
(1900–69)
  Alcohol 19
  Argument 10
Pound, Ezra
(1885–1972)
  Literature 13
  Middle Age 4
  Music 18
  Poetry 17
  Seasons 22
Powell, Anthony
(1905–)
  Books 29
  Character 15
  Old Age 34
  Parents 20
Powell, Enoch (1912–)
  War 46
**Power, John
O'Connor** (b. 1846)
  Political Parties 7
Preston, Keith
(1884–1927)
  Poetry 21
Priestley, J. B.
(1894–1984)
  Class 17
  Sport 18
Prior, Matthew
(1664–1721)
  Sickness 6
  Woman's Role 2
Pritchett, V. S.
(1900–)
  Books 26
Protagoras
(b. c.485 BC)
  Human Race 1

**Proudhon,
Pierre-Joseph**
(1809–65)
  Society 7
Proust, Marcel
(1871–1922)
  Day 15
  Heaven 8
  Memory 13
Publilius, Syrus
(1st century BC)
  Beauty 1
  Gifts 1
Punch
  Behaviour 13
  Choice 4
  Diplomacy 6
  Marriage 29
  Mind 3
  Prejudice 6
Puzo, Mario (1920–)
  Law 28
  Power 16

Quarles, Francis
(1592–1644)
  Human Race 10
  Work 6
Quennell, Peter
(1905–93)
  People 24
**Quiller-Couch,
Arthur** (1863–1944)
  Perfection 12

Rabelais, François
(c.1494–c.1553)
  Food 2
  Last Words 5
  Living 6
Racine, Jean
(1639–99)
  Women 8
**Rainborowe,
Thomas** (d. 1648)
  Human Rights 2
Ralegh, Walter
(c.1552–1618)
  Ambition 3
  Death 18, 19
  Last Words 7
  Time 14
Raleigh, Walter
(1861–1922)
  Education 23
  Human Race 22
  Quotations 8
Ramey, Estelle
  Men and Women 29
Ratner, Gerald
(1949–)
  Business 24
Rattigan, Terence
(1911–77)
  Class 15
Rayner, Claire (1931–)
  Happiness 17
Reade, Charles
(1814–84)
  Custom 7
Reagan, Ronald
(1911–)
  Character 19
  Work 22
Reed, Henry (1914–86)
  Army 19
  Books 27
  War 39

Reger, Max
(1873–1916)
  Critics 13
**Rendall, Montague
John** (1862–1950)
  Broadcasting 1
Reynolds, Joshua
(1723–92)
  Work 7
Reynolds, Malvina
(1900–78)
  Environment 17
Rhodes, Cecil
(1853–1902)
  England 17
  Last Words 21
Rhys, Jean
(c.1890–1979)
  People 29
  Suffering 17
  Women 29
Rice, Grantland
(1880–1954)
  Sport 21
Rice-Davies, Mandy
(1944–)
  Lies 23
Richards, I. A.
(1893–1979)
  Science 16
Richardson, Ralph
(1902–83)
  Acting 13
Rimbaud, Arthur
(1854–91)
  Europe 5
Ritz, César
(1850–1918)
  Business 17
Rivarol, Antoine de
(1753–1801)
  France 5

**Robespierre,
Maximilien** (1758–94)
  Human Rights 6
Robin, Leo (1900–)
  Wealth 14
Roche, Boyle
(1743–1807)
  Speech 7
Rochester, Earl of
(1647–80)
  Courage 4
  Epitaphs 8
Rockefeller, John D.
(1839–1937)
  Business 16
Rogers, Samuel
(1763–1855)
  Action 6
  Marriage 31
  Solitude 7
Rogers, Will
(1879–1935)
  Cinema 2
  Civilization 5
  Heroes 3
  Humour 5
  Ignorance 7
  News 17
  Political Parties 6
  Taxes 8
  Time 33
Roland, Mme
(1754–93)
  Liberty 9
Rolle, Richard
(c.1290–1349)
  Class 1
Roosevelt, Eleanor
(1884–1962)
  Pride 10
**Roosevelt, Franklin
D.** (1882–1945)
  America 14
  Censorship 9

**Roosevelt, Franklin
D.** (*cont.*)
  Fear 9
  Human Rights 9
  Wars 22
**Roosevelt,
Theodore** (1858–1919)
  America 12
  Diplomacy 7
  News 11
  War 17
Rossetti, Christina
(1830–94)
  Memory 9
  Seasons 18
Rossini, Gioacchino
(1792–1868)
  Musicians 1
Rostand, Jean
(1894–1977)
  Death 53
  Murder 8
Rosten, Leo (1908–)
  Children 24
  Dogs 6
Roth, Philip (1933–)
  Parents 24
Roupell, Charles
  Sport 15
**Rousseau,
Jean-Jacques**
(1712–78)
  Liberty 4
**Routh, Martin
Joseph** (1755–1854)
  Knowledge 20
Rowland, Helen
(1875–1950)
  Fools 19
  Men 9, 10
Rowland, Richard
(c.1881–1947)
  Cinema 1

Royden, Maude
(1876–1956)
  Church 13
Rumbold, Richard
(c.1622–85)
  Democracy 1
Runyon, Damon
(1884–1946)
  Life 45
  Money 20
Rusk, Dean
(1909–94)
  Crises 5
Ruskin, John
(1819–1900)
  Beauty 14
  Books 17
  Human Rights 8
  Painting 7
  Work 10, 11
Russell, Bertrand
(1872–1970)
  Belief 19
  Bores 7
  Censorship 7
  Cruelty 5
  Leisure 4
  Mathematics 10, 11
  Minorities 6
  Parents 16
  Science 29
  Technology 6
  Work 17, 18
**Russell, William
Howard** (1820–1907)
  Army 8
Rutherford, Ernest
(1871–1937)
  Science 21, 22, 23

Sagan, Françoise
(1935–)
  Envy 7
**Saint-Exupéry,
Antoine de** (1900–44)
  Children 26
  Love 61
Saki (H. H. Munro)
(1870–1916)
  Beauty 22
  Children 20
  Dress 8
  Food 22
  Lies 16
  Politicians 15
Salisbury, Lord
(1830–1903)
  Europe 6
  News 10
Salisbury, Lord
(1893–1972)
  Politicians 29
Samuel, Lord
(1870–1963)
  Libraries 7
  Marriage 46
Sandburg, Carl
(1878–1967)
  Language 19
  Nature 16
  Past 16
  Places 21
  War 34
  Weather 10
**Sanders, Henry
'Red'**
  Sport 26
Santayana, George
(1863–1952)
  Determination 10
  England 22
  Past 12

Sargent, John Singer (1856–1925)
Painting 12

Sarraute, Nathalie (1902–)
Broadcasting 5

Sartre, Jean-Paul (1905–1980)
Belief 21, 20
Heaven 11
Hope 19
Liberty 19
Time 35

Sassoon, Siegfried (1886–1967)
Army 15, 16
Sickness 8

Sayers, Dorothy L. (1893–1957)
Advertising 4
Men and Women 20

Scalpone, Al
Prayer 16

Scanlon, Hugh (1913–)
Liberty 27

Schelling, Friedrich von (1775–1854)
Architecture 3

Schiller, Friedrich von (1759–1805)
Happiness 7
Intelligence 3

Schnabel, Artur (1882–1951)
Music 22, 23
Musicians 3

Schumacher, E. F. (1911–77)
Economics 12
Environment 20

Schumpeter, J. A. (1883–1950)
Economics 6

Schurz, Carl (1829–1906)
Patriotism 15

Schweitzer, Albert (1875–1965)
Intelligence 7

Schwitters, Kurt (1887–1948)
Painting 13

Scott, C. P. (1846–1932)
News 16

Scott, Robert Falcon (1868–1912)
Last Words 23
Places 18

Scott, Sir Walter (1771–1832)
Chance 7
Indifference 4
Lies 6
Patriotism 10
Scotland 7
Style 10
Women 13
Writing 18

Scott-Maxwell, Florida
Parents 25

Searle, Ronald (1920–)
see **Willans, Geoffrey** and **Searle, Ronald**

Segal, Erich (1937–)
Love 67

Selden, John (1584–1654)
Bible 2
Law 9
Past 8
Pleasure 3
Words 8

Seldon, Arthur (1916–)
Government 31

Sellar, W. C. (1898–1951) and **Yeatman, R. J.** (1898–1968)
Economics 5
Education 25
History 17
Teaching 10

Seneca ('the Younger') (c.4 BC–AD 65)
Death 8
Ignorance 1
Teaching 2

Service, Robert W. (1874–1958)
Time 30
War 24

Sexby, Edward (d. 1658)
Murder 5

Sexton, Anne (1928–74)
Old Age 31

Shaftesbury, 1st Earl of (1621–83)
Religion 16

Shaftesbury, 3rd Earl of (1671–1713)
Thinking 5

Shakespeare, William (1564–1616)
Achievement 5, 6
Acting 2, 3, 4
Action 2, 3
Alcohol 4
Ambition 5, 6, 7
Argument 3
Army 1
Beauty 5, 6
Behaviour 5
Bible 1

Shakespeare, William (*cont.*)

Body 3, 4, 5
Business 2
Careers 3
Certainty 3
Chance 4
Change 4
Character 3, 4
Children 8, 9
Choice 2
Class 2, 3
Conscience 1, 2
Courage 2, 3
Cruelty 1, 2
Custom 1
Day 1, 2, 3
Death 10, 11, 13, 14, 17
Determination 3
Diplomacy 1
Dress 1
Education 4
England 2, 3
Envy 2, 3
Epitaphs 7
Equality 2, 3
Family 2
Fate 2, 3, 4
Fear 1, 2, 3
Flowers 2, 3, 4, 5, 6
Food 3, 5
Friendship 3
Future 1, 2
Generation Gap 3
Gifts 7, 8
Good 6, 7, 8, 9, 10
Gossip 1
Greatness 2, 3, 4
Heart 1
Honour 1, 2, 3, 4
Human Race 4, 5, 6, 8, 9
Humour 2, 3, 4, 5
Hypocrisy 5, 6

Shakespeare, William (*cont.*)

Imagination 1, 2
Indifference 1
Justice 6, 7, 8, 9
Language 2
Law 5, 6
Leisure 1
Libraries 1
Lies 1
Life 9, 10, 12
Love 11, 12, 13, 15, 16, 17, 19, 20, 21, 22, 23
Madness 2, 3, 4, 5
Manners 2
Marriage 4, 5
Meaning 1
Medicine 5
Meeting 3, 4, 5, 6
Memory 1, 2, 3
Men 1
Men and Women 1
Misfortune 4, 5
Moderation 6, 7
Money 6
Murder 3, 4
Music 1, 2, 3
Nature 4
News 5
Old Age 3, 4, 5, 6, 7, 8
Opening Lines 3
Parents 5
Past 3, 5, 6
Peace 6
Perfection 1
Politicians 1
Pollution 2
Power 1
Praise 1
Prayer 2
Prejudice 1
Present 4
Reading 1
Religion 8

Shakespeare, William (*cont.*)

Royalty 2, 3, 4, 5
Satisfaction 1
Sea 3, 4
Seasons 2, 3, 4
Self 1
Self-Knowledge 6
Sex 5, 6, 7, 8
Sickness 3, 4
Skies 1
Sleep 3, 4
Sorrow 5, 6, 7, 8
Speech 1, 2, 3
Sport 3
Success 8
Suffering 3, 4, 5, 6, 7, 8
Supernatural 2, 3, 4
Thinking 3
Time 9, 10, 11, 12, 13
Truth 6
Universe 2
Virtue 5, 6, 7
Wales 1
War 3
Weather 1
Women 4, 5, 6
Words 3, 4, 5, 7
Work 4, 5
Writing 2, 3
Youth 2, 3

Shankly, Bill (1914–81)
Sport 31

Shaw, George Bernard (1856–1950)
Action 9
Alcohol 11, 14
Army 11, 12, 13
Art 13
Beauty 21
Careers 5
Censorship 5
Choice 6
Cinema 4

**Shaw, George
Bernard** (cont.)
  Crime 22
  Dance 9
  Democracy 5
  England 18, 19
  Fame 14
  Forgiveness 6
  Generation Gap 6
  Happiness 11, 12
  Heaven 7
  Home 10
  Hope 15
  Imagination 13
  Indifference 6
  Languages 8
  Liberty 13
  Love 58
  Marriage 37
  Medicine 13
  Men and Women 13
  Music 13
  Parents 14, 19
  Patriotism 18
  Politicians 12
  Poverty 14
  Progress 8
  Religion 35, 36
  Self 7
  Speech 17
  Teaching 8
  Titles 4
  Violence 2, 3
  Virtue 16
  Woman's Role 9
  Women 24
**Shelley, Percy
Bysshe** (1792–1822)
  Birds 4
  Death 36, 37
  Flowers 8
  Heaven 5
  Hope 10
  Life 20

**Shelley, Percy
Bysshe** (cont.)
  Memory 6
  Places 4, 6
  Poetry 8, 10, 11
  Poets 9
  Religion 26
  Seasons 10
  Skies 4
  Sleep 11
  Sorrow 13
**Sheridan, Philip
Henry** (1831–88)
  Prejudice 7
**Sheridan, Richard
Brinsley** (1751–1816)
  Books 8
  Character 7
  Friendship 7
  Manners 5
  Speech 6
  Women 12
  Writing 10
Sherman, General
(1820–91)
  War 15
Shirley, James
(1596–1666)
  Death 23
Sibelius, Jean
(1865–1957)
  Critics 15
Sidney, Philip
(1554–86)
  France 2
  Gifts 6
  Humour 1
  Poetry 2
  Writing 1
**Sieyès, Abbé
Emmanuel Joseph**
(1748–1836)
  Revolution 10

Simenon, Georges
(1903–89)
  Writing 32
Simon, Paul (1942–)
  Music 32
  Silence 6
Simonides
(c.556–468 BC)
  Epitaphs 1
Simpson, N. F. (1919–)
  Management 9
Sisson, C. H. (1914–)
  Bureaucracy 3
Skinner, B. F.
(1904–90)
  Education 30
  Thinking 13
Smart, Christopher
(1722–71)
  Cats 2
Smiles, Samuel
(1812–1904)
  Food 21
  Management 3
Smith, Adam
(1723–90)
  Business 11, 12
  Taxes 5
  Wealth 7
**Smith, Alfred
Emanuel** (1873–1944)
  Democracy 7
Smith, Dodie
(1896–1990)
  Family 10
Smith, F. E.
(1872–1930)
  Ambition 14
  Manners 12
**Smith, Logan
Pearsall** (1865–1946)
  Books 24
  Careers 6
  Conscience 7

Smith, Logan
Pearsall (*cont.*)
   Happiness 14
   Hypocrisy 13
   Old Age 21
   Reading 11
   Wealth 12
   Youth 10
Smith, Stevie
(1902–71)
   Death 59
   England 26
   Indifference 11
   Past 20
Smith, Sydney
(1771–1845)
   Books 14
   Church 8, 10
   Conversation 6
   Country 5
   Crime 12
   Critics 8
   Death 38
   England 13
   Food 18, 19
   Heaven 6
   Intelligence 4
   Ireland 3
   Living 9
   Marriage 30
   Mathematics 7
   Minorities 4
   Poverty 12
   Prayer 10
   Scotland 10
Smith, Walter
Chalmers (1824–1908)
   God 14
Socrates (469–399 BC)
   Knowledge 2
   Last Words 1
   Philosophy 1
   Truth 1
   Wealth 1

Solon
(*c.*640–after 556 BC)
   Happiness 1
Solzhenitsyn,
Alexander (1918–)
   Power 15
Somoza, Anastasio
(1925–80)
   Voting 10
Sondheim, Stephen
(1930–)
   America 23
Sontag, Susan (1933–)
   Critics 18
   Reality 5
   Sickness 14
Soper, Lord (1903–)
   Politicians 37
Sophocles
(*c.*496–406 BC)
   Human Race 2
   Life 3
   Sex 1
Southey, Robert
(1774–1843)
   Letters 6
Spark, Muriel (1918–)
   Life 61
   Parents 22
   Teaching 11
Sparrow, John
(1906–92)
   Dogs 8
Spencer, Herbert
(1820–1903)
   Life Sciences 4
   Morality 5
   Perfection 6
   Progress 5
   Thinking 7
Spencer, Stanley
(1891–1959)
   Painting 14.

Spender, Stephen
(1909–)
   Transport 8
Spenser, Edmund
(*c.*1552–99)
   Languages 3
Spring-Rice, Cecil
(1859–1918)
   Patriotism 17
Spurgeon, C. H.
(1834–92)
   Lies 8
Squire, J. C.
(1884–1958)
   Alcohol 17
   Science 15
Staël, Mme de
(1766–1817)
   Behaviour 9
   Opinion 8
Stalin, Joseph
(1879–1953)
   Class 10
   Power 10
Stanley, Henry
Morton (1841–1904)
   Meeting 12
Stark, Freya
(1893–1993)
   Women 30
Stead, Christina
(1902–83)
   Wealth 13
Steele, Richard
(1672–1729)
   Letters 5
   Reading 4
   Wealth 5
Steffens, Lincoln
(1866–1936)
   Revolution 13

Stein, Gertrude
(1874–1946)
  America 15
  Last Words 28
  Self 8
Steinbeck, John
(1902–68)
  Human Race 25
Steinem, Gloria
(1934–)
  Men and Women 30
  Women 38
Stendhal (1783–1842)
  Literature 4
Stephens, James
(1882–1950)
  Perfection 13
Sterne, Laurence
(1713–68)
  Determination 4
  France 4
  Ideas 2
  Reading 7
Stevens, Anthony
  Men and Women 28
Stevens, Wallace
(1879–1955)
  Beauty 24
  Birds 14
  Music 17
Stevenson, Adlai
(1900–65)
  America 21
  Good 23
  Liberty 22
  People 27
  Political Parties 9
  Praise 9
Stevenson, Anne
(1933–)
  Birds 16

**Stevenson, Robert
Louis** (1850–94)
  Crime 19
  Epitaphs 14
  Lies 10
  Marriage 33
  Politics 9
  Seasons 20
  Travel 6, 7
Stinnett, Caskie
(1911–)
  Diplomacy 12
Stone, Oliver
  see **Weiser,
  Stanley** and
  Stone, Oliver
Stoppard, Tom
(1937–)
  Life 64
  Literature 14
  News 27
  Voting 9
  War 47
Stowell, Lord
(1745–1836)
  Law 16
Strachey, Lytton
(1880–1932)
  Biography 8
  Last Words 25
  People 14, 16
Stravinsky, Igor
(1882–1971)
  Music 28, 31
  Musicians 8
Strunsky, Simeon
(1879–1948)
  Quotations 11
**Studdert Kennedy,
G. A.** (1883–1929)
  Indifference 7
  War 22

Suckling, John
(1609–42)
  Love 28, 30
Sullivan, J. W. N.
(1886–1937)
  Science 19
**Sullivan, Louis
Henri** (1856–1924)
  Architecture 5
Sully, Duc de
(1559–1641)
  England 5
  France 3
Summerskill, Edith
(1901–80)
  Truth 33
Surtees, R. S.
(1805–64)
  Animals 7
  Behaviour 12
  Courage 9
  Dance 5
  Pleasure 11
Swaffer, Hannen
(1879–1962)
  News 25
Swann, Donald
(1923–)
  see **Flanders,
  Michael** and
  Swann, Donald
Swift, Jonathan
(1667–1745)
  Business 6
  Church 7
  Critics 3
  Epitaphs 12
  Genius 2
  Lies 3
  Life Sciences 1
  Old Age 10
  Progress 4
  Religion 18

Swift, Jonathan
(*cont.*)
  Science 3
  Style 6
  Travel 2
Swinburne,
Algernon Charles
(1837–1909)
  Memory 10
  Seasons 15
  Virtue 15
Szasz, Thomas
(1920–)
  Children 30
  Forgiveness 8
  Happiness 16
  Justice 24
  Medicine 19
Szent-Györgyi,
Albert von (1893–1986)
  Inventions 13
  Life Sciences 8

Tacitus
(AD *c.*56–after 117)
  Peace 3
  Success 7
Tagore,
Rabindranath
(1861–1941)
  Prejudice 14
Talleyrand,
Charles-Maurice de
(1754–1838)
  Beginnings 3
Tawney, R. H.
(1880–1962)
  Titles 9
Taylor, A. J. P.
(1906–90)
  History 18
  Mistakes 16
  Wars 25
Tebbit, Norman
(1931–)
  Patriotism 22
Temple, Archbishop
William (1881–1944)
  Religion 43
  Sport 23
Tennyson, Alfred,
Lord (1809–92)
  Army 7
  Beginnings 4
  Belief 9
  Birds 5, 7
  Change 13, 19
  Church 11
  Day 10 .
  Death 40
  Determination 5
  Europe 3
  Fate 8
  Forgiveness 5
  Gardens 7
  Honour 6
  Idleness 8

Tennyson, Alfred,
Lord (*cont.*)
  Love 48
  Meeting 10
  Memory 7
  Men and Women 8, 10
  Mistakes 11
  Nature 10, 11
  Perfection 8, 9
  Prayer 11
  Science 7
  Sorrow 15
  Statistics 2
  Time 26
  Titles 3
  Trust 7
Terence
(*c.*190–159 BC)
  Human Race 3
  Opinion 1
Teresa, St, of Ávila
(1512–82)
  God 5
Tertullian
(AD *c.*160–*c.*225)
  Belief 2
  Church 1
Tessimond, A. S. J.
(1902–62)
  Cats 5
Thackeray, William
Makepeace (1811–63)
  Family 6
  Men and Women 9
Thatcher, Margaret
(1925–)
  Gifts 12
  Leadership 6
  News 29
  Political Comment 26
  Society 15

Thomas à Kempis
(c.1380–1471)
  God 4
  Virtue 4
Thomas, Dylan
(1914–53)
  Death 51
  Home 13
  Life 56
  Old Age 26
  Power 11
  Wales 2
  Youth 11
Thomas, Edward
(1878–1917)
  Past 15
Thomas, Gwyn
(1913–)
  Wales 4
Thomas, R. S. (1913–)
  Wales 3
Thompson, Francis
(1859–1907)
  Future 7
  Religion 40
  Suffering 14
Thomson, James
(1700–48)
  Britain 1
  Teaching 6
Thomson, Roy
(1894–1976)
  Broadcasting 6
**Thoreau, Henry
David** (1817–62)
  Life 27, 28
  Self 5
  Time 24
  Writing 21
Thorpe, Jeremy
(1929–)
  Political Comment 21

Thurber, James
(1894–1961)
  Alcohol 18
  Humour 20
  Mistakes 14
  Sickness 10
  Technology 7
**Thurlow, Edward,
1st Baron** (1731–1806)
  Conscience 4
**Tocqueville, Alexis
de** (1805–59)
  England 11
  France 6
  History 10
  Places 8
Tolstoy, Leo
(1828–1910)
  Body 8
  Family 7
  Hypocrisy 11
Toussenel, A.
(1803–85)
  Dogs 2
Townshend, Pete
(1945–)
  Generation Gap 9
Toynbee, Polly
(1946–)
  Woman's Role 15
Travis, Merle
(1917–83)
  Poverty 18
**Tree, Herbert
Beerbohm** (1852–1917)
  Acting 9
  Bores 6
Trevelyan, G. M.
(1876–1962)
  Civilization 9
  Education 26
  France 10
Trillin, Calvin (1935–)
  Writers 12

Trinder, Tommy
(1909–89)
  America 18
Trollope, Anthony
(1815–82)
  Business 14
  Love 52
  Pride 6
  Suffering 13
Trotsky, Leon
(1879–1940)
  Civilization 7
  Old Age 23
  Violence 4
Truman, Harry S.
(1884–1972)
  Economics 10
  Government 29
  Leadership 4
  Politicians 27
**Tuchman, Barbara
W.** (1912–89)
  War 44
Tucker, Sophie
(c.1884–1966)
  Wealth 17
  Women 35
Tupper, Martin
(1810–89)
  Books 12
Turgenev, Ivan
(1818–83)
  Nature 13
  Prayer 12
Turgot, A. R. J.
(1727–81)
  People 3
**Turner, Walter
James Redfern**
(1889–1946)
  Imagination 12
Tusa, John (1936–)
  Management 16

Twain, Mark
(1835–1910)
  America 10
  Anger 8
  Books 20
  Certainty 8
  Education 16, 17
  Fools 16, 18
  Generation Gap 4
  Gossip 9
  Human Race 21
  Lies 13
  News 9
  Quotations 7
  Success 15
  Temptation 6
  Truth 22, 25
  Writing 23
Tynan, Kenneth
(1927–80)
  Critics 19
  People 25, 26

**Unamuno, Miguel
de** (1864–1937)
  Certainty 12
Updike, John (1932–)
  America 26
  Bores 14
  England 34
Ustinov, Peter (1921–)
  Army 20
  Diplomacy 11
  Friendship 16

Valéry, Paul
(1871–1945)
  Politics 17
  Science 20
  Solitude 15
Vanbrugh, John
(1664–1726)
  Good 13
  Women 9
van Damm, Vivian
(c.1889–1960)
  Acting 12
Vaughan, Harry
  Character 16
Vaughan, Henry
(1622–95)
  Day 4
  Time 16
**Vaughan Williams,
Ralph** (1872–1958)
  Musicians 4
Veblen, Thorstein
(1857–1929)
  Leisure 2
  Science 12
Vegetius
(fourth century AD)
  Peace 4
Vespasian, Emperor
(AD 9–79)
  Taxes 1
Victoria, Queen
(1819–1901)
  Conversation 8
  Humour 15
  Royalty 13
  Success 16
  Woman's Role 8
Vidal, Gore (1925–)
  Business 23
  Lies 24
  Politicians 38
  Success 28, 29

Vidor, King
(1895–1982)
Marriage 40
**Viera Gallo, José
Antonio** (1943–)
Politics 22
Villon, François
(1431)
Past 2
Virgil (70–19 BC)
Achievement 1
Courage 1
Experience 1
Love 2
Money 3
Opening Lines 1
Pleasure 1
Science 1
Sorrow 3
Success 3, 4
Suffering 1
Time 3
Trust 2
Women 3
Voltaire (1694–1778)
Bores 1
Censorship 2, 3
Change 9
God 8, 9
Last Words 11
Management 2
Optimism 2
Perfection 4
Supernatural 5
Writing 12

Walker, Alice (1944–)
Life 66
Violence 9
**Wallace, William
Ross** (d. 1881)
Parents 8
Wallas, Graham
(1858–1932)
Meaning 6
Walpole, Horace
(1717–97)
Fear 4
Life 19
Seasons 8
Style 8
Virtue 13
Weather 3
Walpole, Robert
(1676–1745)
Politicians 3
Wars 1
Walsh, William
(1663–1708)
Hope 5
Walton, Izaak
(1593–1683)
Animals 3
Food 6
Sickness 5
Sport 4
**Warburton, Bishop
William** (1698–1779)
Religion 22
Warhol, Andy
(1927–87)
Fame 22
Washington, George
(1732–99)
Truth 15
Watson, William
(1858–1936)
Dogs 5

Watts, Isaac
(1674–1748)
God 6
Idleness 3
Time 18
Waugh, Evelyn
(1903–66)
Bores 12
Britain 4
Charm 3
Class 16
Crime 24
England 33
Manners 15
News 21
Present 9
Webb, Sidney
(1859–1947) and
Webb, Beatrice
(1858–1943)
Marriage 45
Webster, Daniel
(1782–1852)
Ambition 9
Webster, John
(c.1580–c.1625)
Death 20
Fate 5
Satisfaction 2
Wedgwood, Josiah
(1730–95)
Prejudice 3
Weil, Simone
(1909–43)
Economics 7
Weiser, Stanley
(1946–) and
Stone, Oliver
Economics 13
Weisskopf, Victor
(1908–)
Ignorance 8

**Weissmuller,
Johnny** (1904-84)
  Men and Women 18
Welles, Orson
(1915-85)
  Cinema 7
  Civilization 10
Wellington, Duke of
(1769-1852)
  Army 2, 5
  Books 10
  Life 26
  War 10, 11
  Wars 4, 5, 6
Wells, H. G.
(1866-1946)
  England 24
  History 16
  Morality 8
  Shakespeare 7
  Society 9
Wells, John (1936-)
  Self-Knowledge 15
Wesley, John
(1703-91)
  Church 6
  Old Age 14
  Religion 19
Wesley, Samuel
(1662-1735)
  Style 4
West, Mae (1892-1980)
  Choice 8
  Diaries 6
  Good 21
  Meeting 16
  Men 11
West, Rebecca
(1892-1983)
  Trust 10
Wetherell, Charles
(1770-1846)
  Biography 4

Wharton, Edith
(1862-1937)
  Singing 5
Whately, Richard
(1787-1863)
  Economics 2
**Whistler, James
McNeill** (1834-1903)
  Argument 6
  Critics 10
  Painting 8, 9
  Quotations 6
White, E. B.
(1899-1985)
  Democracy 8
  Transport 14
White, Patrick
(1912-90)
  Old Age 27
**Whitehead, Alfred
North** (1861-1947)
  Art 18
  Civilization 2
  Intelligence 11
  Morality 12
  Philosophy 10
  Truth 32
**Whitehorn,
Katharine** (1926-)
  Cinema 15
Whitman, Walt
(1819-92)
  America 4
  Animals 9
  Gifts 10
  Self 6
**Whittier, John
Greenleaf** (1807-92)
  Sorrow 16
Whittington, Robert
  People 1
Whitton, Charlotte
(1896-1975)
  Men and Women 26

**Wilberforce, Bishop
Samuel** (1805-73)
  Life Sciences 3
Wilbur, Richard
(1921-)
  Mind 8
  Universe 11
  War 43
**Wilcox, Ella
Wheeler** (1855-1919)
  Religion 41
  Solitude 1
Wilde, Oscar
(1854-1900)
  Advice 3
  America 8
  Bible 7
  Books 18
  Cynicism 5
  Diaries 1
  England 16
  Experience 4
  Genius 8
  Gossip 8
  Idealism 1
  Literature 8
  Love 57
  Marriage 35
  Medicine 11
  Men and Women 12
  Mistakes 13
  Parents 10
  People 13
  Temptation 5
  Truth 24, 26
  Women 23
  Work 13
Wilder, Billy (1906-)
  see **Brackett,
  Charles** and
  Wilder, Billy

Willans, Geoffrey
(1911-58) and
Searle, Ronald
(1920-)
  Christmas 6
William III (1650-1702)
  Fate 6
Williams, Kenneth
(1926-88)
  Quotations 12
**Williams,
Tennessee** (1911-83)
  Human Race 27
**Williams, William
Carlos** (1883-1963)
  Mind 7
Wilson, Charles E.
(1890-1961)
  Business 20
Wilson, Harold
(1916-)
  Food 30
  Money 29
  Political Comment 23
  Technology 11
**Wilson,
McLandburgh** (1892-)
  Optimism 10
Wilson, Woodrow
(1856-1924)
  Democracy 6
**Wittgenstein,
Ludwig** (1889-1951)
  Language 12
  Philosophy 11, 12
  Speech 18
  Universe 6
Wodehouse, P. G.
(1881-1975)
  Apology 4
  Books 21
  Family 9
  Marriage 39
  Satisfaction 6

Wogan, Terry (1938-)
  Broadcasting 8
Wolfe, Humbert
(1886-1940)
  News 18
**Wollstonecraft,
Mary** (1759-97)
  Mind 2
  Parents 7
  Woman's Role 7
Wolsey, Cardinal
(c.1475-1530)
  Last Words 2
Woodroofe, Thomas
(1899-1978)
  Broadcasting 2
Woolf, Virginia
(1882-1941)
  Books 23
  Diaries 4
  Food 27
  Friendship 14
  Life 39, 40
  Men and Women 17
  Satisfaction 5
  Writers 8
**Woollcott,
Alexander** (1887-1943)
  Pleasure 13
**Wordsworth,
William** (1770-1850)
  Birds 3
  Birth 6
  Children 14
  Death 34
  Flowers 7
  Good 16
  Imagination 6
  Knowledge 16
  London 5
  Memory 5
  Nature 6, 7
  People 12
  Places 2

**Wordsworth,
William** (cont.)
  Poetry 6
  Revolution 7
  Satisfaction 3
  Transience 7
  Work 8
  Writing 14
  Youth 6
Worrall, Terry
  Weather 15
Wotton, Henry
(1568-1639)
  Architecture 1
  Critics 1
  Diplomacy 2
  Sorrow 9
Wright, Frank Lloyd
(1867-1959)
  Architecture 8
Wroth, Lady Mary
(c.1586-c.1652)
  Love 25

Yates, Bishop John
(1925–)
  Belief 22
**Ybarra, Thomas
Russell** (b. 1880)
  Religion 37
Yeatman, R. J.
(1898–1968)
  see **Sellar, W. C.**
  and **Yeatman, R. J.**
Yeats, W. B.
(1865–1939)
  Change 21
  Dance 6
  Day 11
  Death 49, 50
  Generation Gap 5
  Heart 7
  Idealism 2
  Indifference 10
  Ireland 7
  Life 41
  Love 55, 59
  Old Age 16, 19, 24
  Perfection 14
  Poetry 16, 19
  Suffering 16
Yin, Xiao-Huang
  Democracy 14
Young, Edward
(1683–1765)
  Belief 5
  Critics 2
  Fools 10
  Idleness 5
  Quotations 1
  Sleep 9
  War 7
Young, George W.
(1846–1919)
  Alcohol 8

Zamyatin, Yevgeny
(1884–1937)
  Thinking 10
Zangwill, Israel
(1864–1926)
  America 11
  Religion 34
Zappa, Frank
(1940–93)
  News 28